MICROCONTROLLERS AND MICROCOMPUTERS

MICROCONTROLLERS AND MICROCOMPUTERS

PRINCIPLES OF SOFTWARE AND HARDWARE ENGINEERING

Fredrick M. Cady

Department of Electrical Engineering
Montana State University

New York   Oxford
OXFORD UNIVERSITY PRESS
1997

Oxford University Press

Oxford   New York
Athens   Auckland   Bangkok   Bogota   Bombay   Buenos Aires
Calcutta   Cape Town   Dar es Salaam   Delhi   Florence   Hong Kong
Istanbul   Karachi   Kuala Lumpur   Madras   Madrid   Melbourne
Mexico City   Nairobi   Paris   Singapore   Taipei   Tokyo   Toronto
and associated companies in
Berlin   Ibadan

Published by Oxford University Press, Inc.,
198 Madison Avenue, New York, New York, 10016
http://www.oup-usa.org

Library of Congress Cataloging-in-Publication Data
Cady, Fredrick M., 1942–
Microcontrollers and microcomputers : principles of software and
hardware engineering / Fredrick M. Cady.
p.   cm.
Includes bibliographical references and index.
ISBN-13 978-0-19-511008-1
ISBN 0-19-511008-0
1. Programmable controllers.   2. Microcomputers.   3. Software
engineering.   I. Title.
TJ223.P76C33   1997   004.16—dc20   96-23410

8 9
Printed in the United States of America
on acid-free paper

To my wife, Katie,
for her encouragement, support, and proofreading,
and to Al Gray,
who taught me that "Computers are dumb and they don't care."

CONTENTS

Chapter 3   **Introduction to the CPU: Registers and Condition Codes   25**

Chapter 4   **Addressing Modes   34**

Chapter 5   **Assembly Language Programming and Debugging**   48

Chapter 9   **Computer Memories**   152

Chapter *10*　**Serial Input/Output**　179

PREFACE

There are a number of ways to write an introductory textbook about microcomputers and micro-controllers and to teach an associated course. Some adopt a particular processor unit and instruct the student how to use it and give programming examples. Textbooks taking this approach are available for many of the more popular microcomputers and microcontrollers. Sometimes, when textbooks aren't available, course are taught directly from the manufacturer's reference data books. Usually, very few general principles of design are given, but the student can learn to be proficient with the particular processor. The hope of the instructor is that the student will be able to transfer this particular information to more general application and to other processors in the future. Perhaps a better approach combines general design information, including hardware and software design, with examples from a particular processor showing how the general principles are implemented in practice. All too often, however, the author with wonderful explanations of general principles illustrates them with a different processor than the one we are using in the laboratory. Or a book with good hardware information skimps on dealing with software issues, or vice versa. Thus the idea of a two-part textbook was born to separate excellent coverage of software and hardware design from the specifics of a particular microcontroller. *Microcontrollers and Microcomputers: Principles of Software and Hardware Engineering* has been designed to be used with *Software and Hardware Engineering: Motorola M68HC11* for courses based on this popular microcontroller. However, you may use it with any other processor by providing students with supplemental information or requiring them to learn from the manufacturers' reference data books. The material in this book is aimed at the sophomore, junior, or senior Electrical Engineering, Electrical Engineering Technology, or Computer Science student taking a first course in microcomputers. A prerequisite is a digital logic course. The student must understand the principles of numbers systems, coding, and combinatorial and sequential logic design. A first course in a programming language is also a normal prerequisite.

I teach my courses because I think we learn best by first teaching something about the hardware and then some software and then by practicing in the laboratory. We then repeat the process by learning more hardware and more software details. At each step of the way, general principles are illustrated by using specific examples from a specific processor. For example, one of the first things we might learn about a processor is what the registers are used for and how the bits in the condition code register are used. After learning the principles and the specifics of these hardware elements, and the part of the instruction set dealing with them, we can go to the laboratory and practice what we have learned.

The organization of *Microcontrollers and Microcomputers: Principles of Software and Hardware Engineering* (and *Software and Hardware Engineering: Motorola M68HC11*) generally follows my own course organization. I like to start by explaining the mystery of a stored-program computer by creating a plausible design. We then explore the resources of the processor used in the laboratory. Our initial goal is to be able to begin laboratory exercises while teaching other concepts. To do this, we introduce the basic hardware registers, the arithmetic and logic unit (ALU), and the condition codes. The explanation of the condition code register allows us to discuss binary codes and coding. Special attention is paid to codes used for arithmetic and how the various codes affect the operation of the condition code register.

By this time the student is starting the concurrent laboratory and needs to know how to program the computer. We point out that learning the instruction set of a processor involves knowing what registers are available, what addressing modes have been implemented, and what general categories of instructions are available.

The mechanics of using an assembler are presented so that the student can assemble and run small programs in the laboratory. The complete instruction set for the processor used is covered, at least in instruction categories. It is sufficient at this stage to lead the student through examples using various instructions, particularly those with different addressing modes. Later, as the student matures and gains confidence, more difficult programming assignments can be given.

By now the student is able to write, assemble, download, and run simple programs in the laboratory. His or her experience will show the need for debugging tools, and we discuss here debugging tools in general. Now the instructor must help the student learn about the specific debugging software used in the laboratory. *Software and Hardware Engineering: Motorola M68HC11* discusses the debugging monitor supplied by Motorola with their EVB system. In courses where other debugging software or hardware is used, instructors can provide their own information.

A large portion of the cost of developing any microcomputer system is the software. A key chapter is dedicated to software design. The basic elements of software design are presented, and the differences between design methodologies and design tools are discussed. Top-down design is presented, and pseudocode, probably the most widely used design tool, is promoted. This should reinforce software design concepts the student has learned in a previous course. The student is shown how to use structured programming principles in assembly language. The design of software modules, with attention paid to reducing interaction between modules, is also presented.

While the student is tackling more complex programming assignments, bus architectures, interfaces between external devices and a CPU, and programmed input and output can be covered. It is here we learn the need for interrupts and real-time operations.

By now the student understands that memory stores programs and data. We can discuss the different types of memory, ROM and RAM, and why a system has both. This is a good time to discuss the details of memory interfaces and especially timing signals.

Many engineers have a terrible time with serial interfaces, especially the RS-232-C "standard," because they don't understand why all the signals in the standard interface are there. Chapter 10 presents a complete description of the handshaking signals developed for communication channels. Interface cables for various RS-232-C devices are shown, and other common interface standards such as RS-422, RS-423, and RS-485 are defined.

The text concludes with a discussion of the concepts of A/D conversion and its companion, D/A conversion.

I would like to thank my wife Katie for her encouragement and assistance with early versions of the text and Heather Burnham, graduate student in Electrical Engineering, for proofreading help. Thanks also go to several generations of EE361 students at Montana State University who helped make the text better.

Bozeman, Montana
October, 1996

F.M.C.

MICROCONTROLLERS AND MICROCOMPUTERS

Chapter 1

Introduction

1.1 Computers, Microprocessors, Microcomputers, Microcontrollers

A computer system is shown in Figure 1.1. We see a *CPU* or *Central Processor Unit, memory*, containing the program and data, an *I/O interface* with associated *input and output devices*, and three *buses* connecting the elements of the system together. The organization of the program and data into a single memory block is called a *von Neumann* architecture, after John von Neumann, who described this general-purpose, stored-program computer in 1945. This is a classical computer system block diagram, and all computers discussed in this text have this basic architecture.

Until the Intel Corporation introduced the first microprocessor, the 4004, in 1971, the CPU was constructed of many components. Indeed, in 1958 the Air Force SAGE computer required 40,000 square feet, 3 megawatts of power, and had 30,000 tubes with a 4Kx32 bit word magnetic core memory.[1] The Digital Equipment Company's PDP-8 was the first mass-produced minicomputer and appeared in 1964. This was the start of a trend toward less expensive, smaller computers suitable for use in nontraditional, non-data processing applications. Intel's great contribution was to integrate the functions of the many-element CPU one (or at most a few) integrated circuits. The term *microprocessor* first came into use at Intel in 1972[2] and, generally, refers to the implementation of the central processor unit functions of a computer in a single, large-scale integrated (LSI) circuit. A *microcomputer*, then, is a computer built using a microprocessor and a few other components for the memory and I/O. The Intel 4004 allowed a four-chip microcomputer consisting of a CPU, a read-only memory (ROM) for program, read/write memory (RAM) for data, and a shift register chip for output expansion.

> A *microcomputer* is a microprocessor with added memory and I/O.

The Intel 4004 was a four-bit microprocessor and led the way to the development of the 8008, the first eight-bit microprocessor, introduced in 1972. This processor had 45 instructions, a 30-microsecond average instruction time, and could address 16K bytes of memory. Today, of course, we have advanced far beyond these first microcomputers.

This course is primarily about using computers in applications where the system is dedicated to performing a single task or a single group of tasks. Examples of dedicated applications are found almost everywhere in products such as microwave ovens, toasters, and automobiles. These are often *control* ap-

---

[1] *The History of Electronic Computing,* Association for Computing Machinery.
[2] Noyce, R. N., and M. E. Hoff, Jr., *A History of Microprocessor Development at Intel,* IEEE MICRO, Feb. 1981.

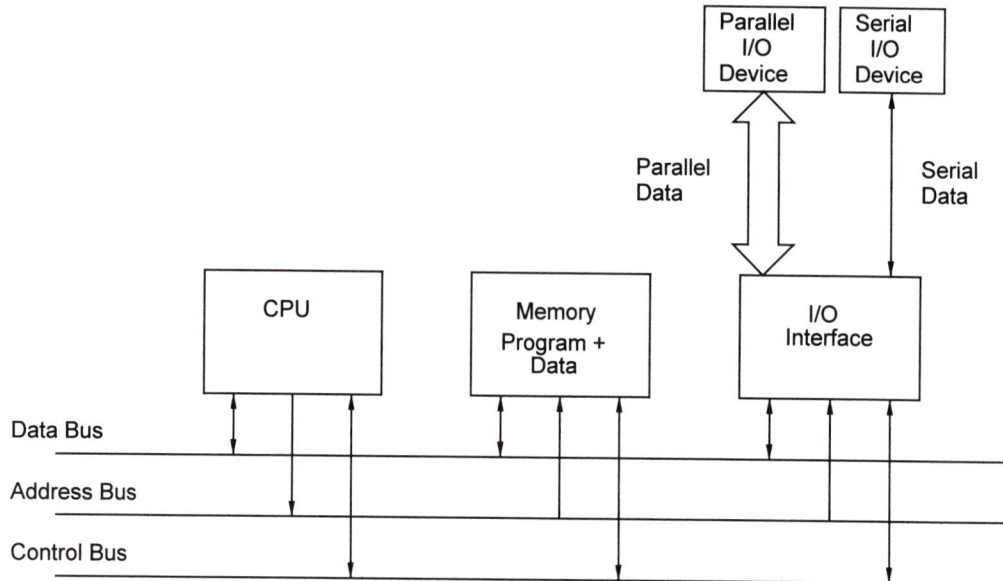

Figure 1-1   Basic computer system.

> A *microcontroller* is a computer with *CPU*, *memory*, and *I/O* in one integrated circuit chip.

plications and make use of microcontrollers. A *microcontroller* is a microcomputer with its memory and I/O integrated into a single chip. The number of microcontrollers used in products is mind-boggling. In 1991, over 750 million 8-bit microcontrollers were delivered by the chip manufacturers.[3]

1.2 Some Basic Definitions

Throughout this text we use the following digital logic terminology:

Logic high: The higher of the two voltages defining logic true and logic false. The value of a logic high depends on the logic family. For example, in the TTL family, logic high (at the input of a gate) is signified by a voltage greater than 2.0 volts. This voltage is known as V_{IHMIN}.

Logic low: The lower of the two voltages defining logic true and false. In TTL, a logic low (at the input of a gate, V_{ILMAX}) is signified by a voltage less than 0.8 volts.

Assert: Logic signals, particularly signals that control a part of the system, are *asserted* when the control, or action named by the signal, is being done. A signal may be low or high when it is asserted. For example, the signal **WRITE** means that it is asserted when the signal is logic high.

Active low: This term defines a signal whose assertion level is logic low. For example, the signal $\overline{\text{READ}}$ is asserted low and is stated "read-bar."

Active high: Used to define a signal whose assertion level is logic high.

---

[3]   *EDN,* January 21, 1993.

Mixed polarity notation: The notation used by most manufacturers of microcomputer components defines a signal by using a name, such as **WRITE**, to indicate an *action*, and a polarity indicator to show the *assertion level* for the signal. It is common practice to use the complement "bar" for active low signals and the lack of the complement for active high. Thus the signal **WRITE** indicates that the CPU is doing a write operation when the signal is high. $\overline{\textbf{READ}}$ denotes a read operation is going on when the signal is low.

1.3 Notation

The symbols used to denote numbers in hexadecimal (base 16) differ from manufacturer to manufacturer. This text will use the Motorola designation, where a $ is a prefix for the number. For example, $FFFF is the hexadecimal number whose decimal equivalent is 65,535. The supplement for any specific processor will use the manufacturer's designation. For example, in the Intel notation, the letter H is used after the hexadecimal symbols (0–F), and all hexadecimal numbers must start with a digit (0–9). So in the Intel notation, $FFFF is written 0FFFFH.

1.4 Study Plan

The designs of dedicated application systems and other more general-purpose computers are very similar. Our goal for this course is not to make you an expert in using a specific processor, but to give you the knowledge and tools to be able effectively to apply any processor in any application. We will do that by first studying the general principles necessary to understand each part of the system. Then examples for a specific microprocessor may be covered using a manufacturer's reference manual or a text designed to support a microcontroller like the Motorola M68HC11.[4]

The basic operation of a stored-program, general-purpose computer is to be studied first. You'll learn about registers, the arithmetic and logic unit, and how a computer works. You next will see how these principles are applied in a specific microprocessor. You must learn the microprocessor's instruction set, how to operate an assembler, and how to write good assembly language programs. After the beginning assembly language programming exercises, it is time to learn how to design more complex software properly. As your laboratory assignments become more complex, you will start to apply the software design techniques and tools covered in Chapter 6. During this time you will also start to learn about the rest of the hardware in a computer system. This includes parallel and serial I/O, interrupts and real-time events, computer memory, and analog signal input and output.

---

[4]   Cady, F. M., *Software and Hardware Engineering: Motorola M68HC11*, Oxford University Press, NY, 1997.

Chapter *2*

The Picoprocessor: An Introduction to Computer Architecture

OBJECTIVES

This chapter introduces the ideas of a stored-program computer by designing one to satisfy a few, simple specifications. When finished, you should understand the principles underlying computer hardware. You will see the importance of the instruction fetch, how the sequence controller works, and how to determine system timing. You will understand how memory, I/O, and branch instructions operate and how they affect the design of the computer.

2.1 Introduction

In this chapter we will go through a step-by-step process to design a simple computer. Although the computer won't be practical, it will show how a general-purpose computer works. Our goal is to have you see that a computer is *not* a mysterious box. It is a collection of basic digital logic components that you could design. By the end of this chapter you will appreciate that a computer works in a predictable way and that you have absolute control over what it does at all times.

2.2 Computer Operation Codes

The first step in the design of a computer is to define the set of operations that it is to do. Our simple computer is to be capable only of inputting and outputting eight-bit binary numbers and

> A computer operation is encoded with a binary code called the *op code*.

adding or subtracting them. The input, output, adding, and subtracting capabilities are called *operations*, and we encode them by using *operation*, or *op*, *codes*. Because computers are digital devices, all information is encoded as binary signals—1s and 0s. If there are four operations, two bits are needed to provide a unique code for each. Table 2–1 shows the codes that are selected.

TABLE 2-1 Computer operations and op codes	
Operation	**Operation code**
ADD	00
SUB	01
IN	10
OUT	11

2.3 Basic Computer Hardware

Hardware for Addition and Subtraction

Let us look at the hardware required to add or subtract two eight-bit binary numbers. These operations require two *operands*—the two binary numbers that are added or subtracted. In order for the adder or the subtracter to work, these binary numbers are held in registers while the addition or subtraction is being carried out. Registers are arrays of memory elements, usually flip-flops, which may be loaded with binary values. There are two registers—called the A and B registers—that hold the operands. In your logic class you probably learned how to design a ripple-carry full-adder to add eight-bit numbers and produce an eight-bit result plus a carry. Similar hardware could be designed to subtract two numbers. As the design of this computer progresses, we will probably want to add more capabilities, perhaps logic operations like AND and OR. The hardware for these arithmetic and logic operations can be placed into a black box called the *arithmetic and logic unit (ALU)*, and we will not concern ourselves with the specific hardware within the ALU. It is sufficient to know that hardware can be designed to do addition and subtraction. The design at this stage is shown in Figure 2–1. The arrows in the figure show that the numbers we want to add or subtract flow from the registers to the ALU. Our answer flows from the ALU back into the A register, which is called an *accumulator* because it accumulates answers. The B register is a general-purpose register that holds numbers while the addition is being done.

> An *operand* is data to be operated on.

> An *accumulator* is a register that may hold one operand for an ALU operation and also be used for the answer.

At this stage of the design we will ignore some details of using registers. For example, a register needs a clock signal. We will develop that later. We'll also ignore the carry signal that is produced by the adder circuit in the ALU until later.

Input and Output Hardware

At this point, we have registers to hold numbers and an ALU to add or subtract them. We need a *source* for the numbers and a *destination* for the answer. Let's use a set of eight switches to enter

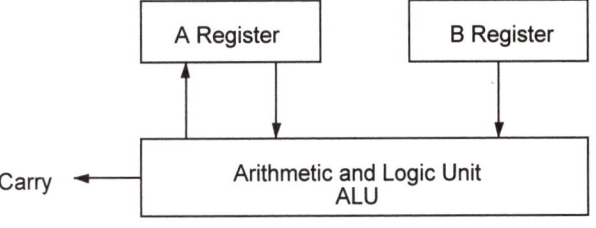

Figure 2-1 Accumulator register (A), general-purpose register (B), and arithmetic and logic unit (ALU).

EXAMPLE 2–1   **Show how to use eight D-type latches to construct an 8-bit register.**

Solution:

D7   D6   D1   D0

| D   Q | | D   Q | • • • | D   Q | | D   Q |
| Clock | | Clock | | | Clock | | Clock |

Clock

EXAMPLE 2–2   **Show how to make an 8-bit ripple-carry adder using seven full adders and one half-adder.**

Solution:

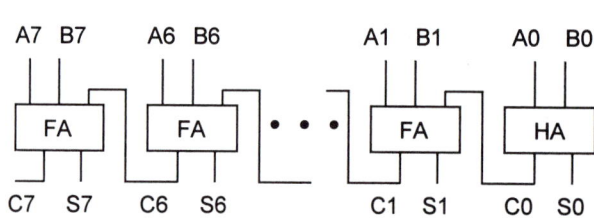

---

the numbers and eight light-emitting diodes (LEDs) to display the result. Figure 2–2 shows an input device, the switches, and an output device, the LEDs, added to the registers and ALU.

The hardware to input numbers and display the results is adequate for now, but let's look ahead and design in some additional capabilities. Most computers have many sources of information. For example, a binary number may be input from an analog-to-digital converter, or we may put the result of the addition out to a digital-to-analog converter instead of the display LEDs. To do that, we must specify which of several devices the computer must input from or output to. A design decision must be made. How do we make the computer input information from more than one source? There are two choices. There could be separate operation codes to do the separate operations. For example, two new input operations, IN1 and IN2, where IN1 inputs information from the switches and IN2 from an analog-to-digital converter, could be defined. Our other choice is to include an *operand* with the *operation*. The combination of an operation and an operand is called a *computer instruction*. The instruction defines what is to be done—the operation—and what is to be operated upon—the operand. Let us allow up to four of each of the input and output devices. A code is needed to specify which of the four devices is to

> A computer *instruction* is an *operation* plus an *operand*.

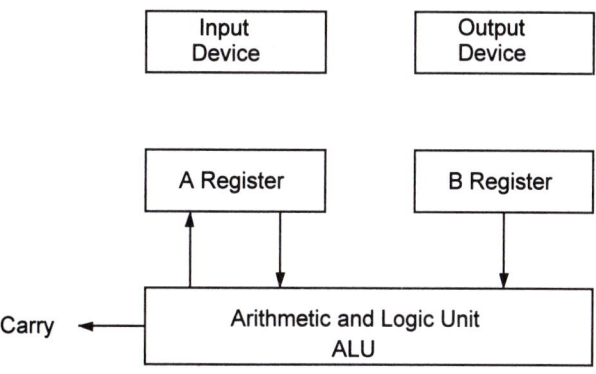

Figure 2-2 Adding input and output devices to the registers and ALU.

be used for the input or output instruction. We add this code, called the *operand code,* to the operations previously defined. This is shown in Table 2–2, where the two-bit code for the operand is arbitrarily placed in the last two bits of an eight-bit instruction code byte. The input device number is to be encoded with the two bits *ii* and the output device number by the bits *oo*. Dashes are bits that haven't been assigned yet. Almost all computer instructions consist of an operation plus one or more operands.

When the computer does an input instruction, we know the information comes from the set of switches, which we will be calling input device #1. Where does the information go? It is common practice for the destination of an input operation to be the accumulator (A) register. It is also common to design the output hardware always to transfer information from the A register to the output device. Figure 2–3 gives an updated diagram showing up to four potential input and output devices.

The Move Operation

We have created a problem by making the decision to transfer data from the input device to the A register only. Think about what must be done to add two numbers. You put the first number in the switches and then the computer will input it into the A register. What is done with the second number? Somehow the first number must be moved into the B register before the second number can be input. Computer designers invented the *MOV* (some manufacturers call it *LD*[1]) oper-

TABLE 2-2 Adding operands to the IN and OUT operations

Operation	Operand	Instruction code = op code + operand code
ADD	None	00 – – – – – –
SUB	None	01 – – – – – –
IN	Device #	10 – – – – i i
OUT	Device #	11 – – – – o o

---

[1] MOV is the mnemonic, or short-hand code, for a move operation. LD is the mnemonic used for a load operation.

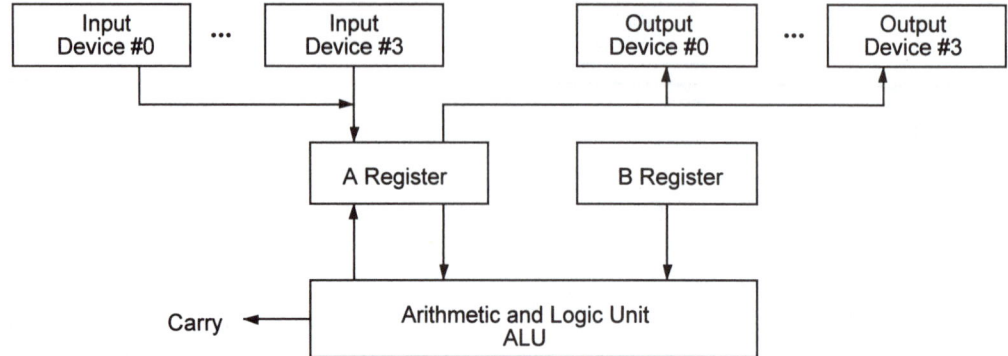

Figure 2-3   Adding multiple input and output devices.

ation to be able to transfer information between the registers. Let's define a MOV operation to move information from the A to the B register. The MOV operation *copies* the data from the source to the destination; the information in the source register is not destroyed. This additional operation requires us to add a bit to the operation code in our instruction because now there are five operations. The operations and their codes (the complete computer instruction set) are shown in Table 2–3 and an updated hardware diagram in Figure 2–4.

TABLE 2-3 The MOV operation is added to the instruction set

Operation	Operand	Op code + operand code
ADD	None	001 – – – – – –
SUB	None	011 – – – – – –
IN	Device #	101 – – – – i i
OUT	Device #	111 – – – – o o
MOV	None	010 – – – – – –

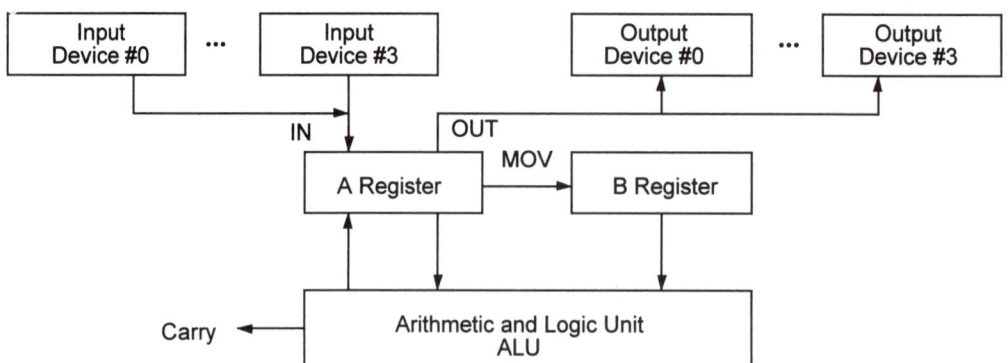

Figure 2-4   Information flow after the MOV operation is added.

TABLE 2-4 A program to input two numbers, add them together, and display the result

Line	Operation field	Operand field	Comment field
1	IN	1	(A) ← (Switches). The contents of the A register are replaced by the contents of the switch.
2	MOV		(B) ← (A). The contents of the B register are replaced by the contents of the A register.
3	IN	1	(A) ← (Switches)
4	ADD		(A) ← (A) + (B). The contents of A are replaced by the contents of A plus the contents of B.
5	OUT	2	(LED) ← (A). The contents of the LEDs are replaced by the contents of A.

Adding Two Numbers

An *assembly language program* instructs the computer what to do by specifying each operation and operand.

Although the design is far from complete, there are enough hardware components and computer instructions to see how a program could be written to add two numbers together. We write the program in *Assembly Language*. This is a computer programming language that has a statement for each of the operation codes the computer can execute. To add two numbers with this hardware, we (and the computer) must do the following:

1. Set the switches (by hand) to the first number to be input.
2. Let the computer input the number into the A register.
3. Let the computer move the number into the B register.
4. Set the switches to the second number.
5. Let the computer input the number into the A register.
6. Let the computer add the two numbers.
7. Let the computer output the result to the LEDs.

This sequence of steps defines what the assembly language program, and therefore what the computer, is to do. For each step above that starts with "Let the computer . . . ," we write an assembly language statement. The assembly language program is shown in Table 2–4.

The format shown in Table 2–4 is typical of an assembly language program, and there are several fields on each line. First is the *operation field,* where the *mnemonic,* an English-like code for the computer operation, is written. Following that is the *operand field,* where the operand, if there is one, is written. A *comment field* may follow the operand field.[2] Usually comments explain the design or the purpose of the program. Here we have chosen to show a shorthand notation that many manufacturers use to define exactly what the instruction is to do. For example, in line 1, the operation mnemonic is IN, the operand is device #1, and the comment shows that the contents of the A register are to be replaced by the contents of the switches.

A *mnemonic* is the English-like shorthand for the operation.

---

[2] There is another field to the left of the operation field not shown in this example. This is the label field, and we will see how to use this later in Chapter 5 and when you learn how to use an assembler.

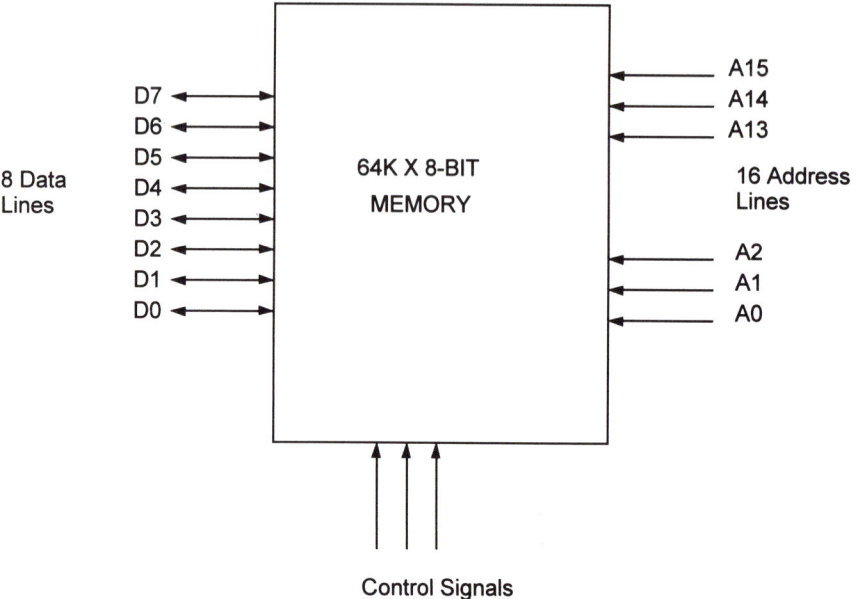

Figure 2-5   A memory device.

The Computer Memory

As you know from your own experience with computers, programs go into memory. A memory block to be added to the hardware is shown in Figure 2–5.

We can envision the memory as an array of flip-flops that store data. In this memory there are eight bits (a byte), D7 . . . D0, in each memory location, and there are 65,536 (64 kilobytes)[3] locations. To access one specific location in these 64K locations, a 16-bit address, A15 . . . A0, must be supplied. When this is done and when certain control signals about which we will learn in Chapter 9 are activated, information can be read from or written to the memory.

The Contents of the Computer Memory

The computer memory contains binary information or data. Therefore, the program shown in Table 2–4 must be *encoded* using the codes defined in Table 2–3. This is called *assembling* a program, a process that turns the instructions into the 1s and 0s that go into the computer memory. *All* computer programs, no matter the language in which they are written, must be assembled, or converted, into binary words called *machine code*. The result of this is shown in Table 2–5.

The first location in the memory is *address zero*. For each memory location you can look at the binary codes and, referring to Table 2–3, decode them to find out what the computer is going to do. We now design hardware to do just this.

> A program is *assembled* when its operation mnemonics and operands are converted to the binary codes placed into memory.

---

[3]   A kilobyte (Kbyte) is $2^{10} = 1024$ bytes.

TABLE 2-5 How the program looks in memory

Memory location address	Contents (machine code)
0:	1010 0001
1:	0100 0000
2:	1010 0001
3:	0010 0000
4:	1110 0010

EXAMPLE 2-3   **Assemble the memory contents for the following program:**

```
IN   1
MOV
ADD
ADD
OUT  2
```

Solution:

Address	Contents
0:	1010 0001
1:	0100 0000
2:	0010 0000
3:	0010 0000
4:	1110 0010

What would you expect to be displayed on the LEDs?

Solution:

Three times the number that was input from the switches.

Instruction Register and Decoder

The information in the memory of the computer is the assembled program, and each memory location has one computer instruction. (Later, we will see that an instruction may be more than one byte.) When an instruction is fetched from the computer memory, it is transferred to an instruction register and decoder as shown in Figure 2–6.

The instruction register is like the A or B register except that it holds the binary instruction code for the "brain" of the computer—the instruction decoder. The decoder is a multiple-input/multiple-output, combinational logic circuit like the ones designed in your introductory logic course. It takes the operation code bits from the instruction and generates logic signals that are *asserted*, or made *logic true*, for each operation designed into the computer. These logic signals go to appropriate places in the computer. For example, Figure 2–7 shows how hardware for the IN and OUT operations might be designed. When the IN line is asserted by the instruction decoder, it provides a clock signal to latch

> The *instruction decoder* decodes the operation code and *asserts* a control signal appropriate for each operation.

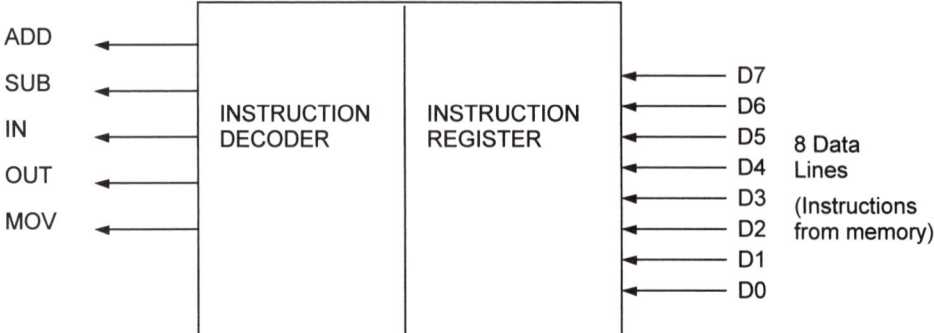

Figure 2-6   Program instructions transfer from memory into an instruction register and decoder.

the data from the switches into the A register. When an OUT operation is decoded, the data in the A register are transferred to the LEDs. We will need other control signals as well, such as decoded operand bits to select the devices.

Program Counter and Memory Address Register

The program listed in Table 2–4 is encoded as shown in Table 2–5. Visualize these bits being transferred from memory to the instruction decoder. To execute the program, the memory must be provided with a sequence of addresses, starting at zero, and stepping up to four. There are two pieces of hardware needed to accomplish this.

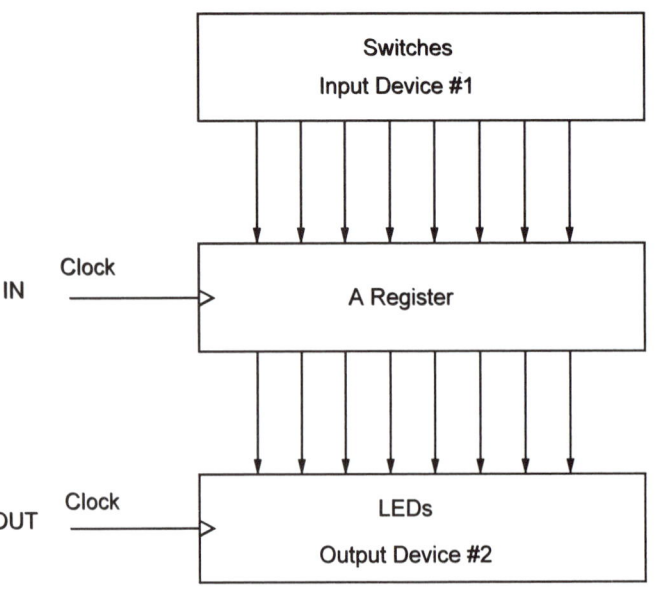

Figure 2-7   Signals from the instruction decoder allow the different operations to occur.

The *program counter* and *memory address register* supply the memory with the addresses of the instruction codes.

Figure 2–8 shows a *Program Counter* and a *Memory Address Register* to step through the program. A reset signal ensures that the program counter starts at zero. The memory address register is like all other registers in the computer except that instead of holding data for an operation it holds an address while it is being used by the memory.

2.4 Computer Timing

When we add the program counter to the design, we must start to think about the time it takes to execute each instruction. Let us define the idea of an instruction execution cycle and design hardware to minimize the time taken for each instruction.

The Instruction Execution Cycle

Let's walk through the execution of a computer instruction. Assume that the program is in memory and that the program counter is reset to zero.

1. The contents of the program counter are transferred to the memory address register to be held for the memory.

2. The contents of that memory location are transferred to the instruction register and decoder.

3. The instruction decoder asserts the IN signal line and the data in the switches are transferred into the A register.

4. The program counter is incremented to 0001 and the process repeats for the next instruction.

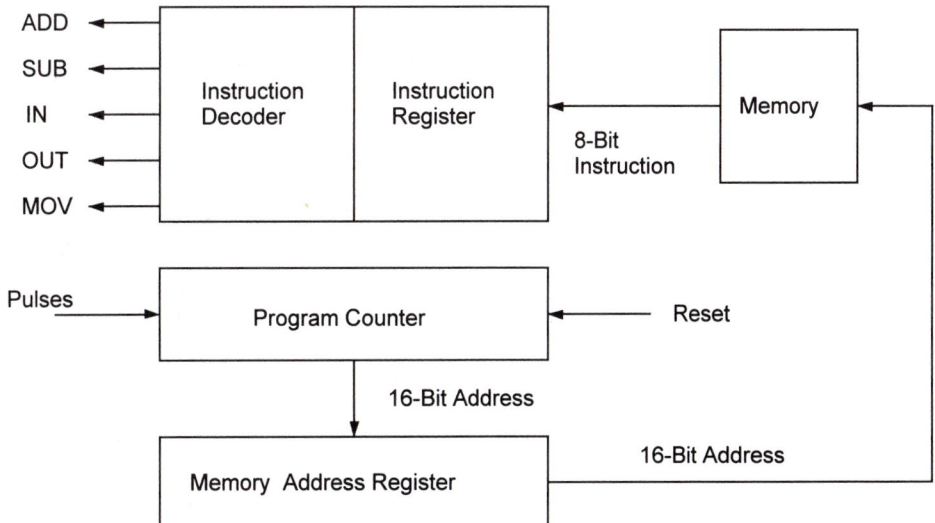

Figure 2-8   The program counter steps through the addresses of the program.

The next instruction is MOV, and after it is decoded the MOV control line is asserted. This activates gates between the A and B registers and causes the data transfer. After this is done, the program counter is incremented. The process continues for the next instruction, and the next, and the next . . . until the program is over.

> The *instruction execution cycle* is the sequence of steps that the processor goes through to do the complete instruction and to get ready for the next.

We have just described the *instruction execution cycle.* The instruction is fetched from memory and decoded, control signals are activated, the information transfer is effected, and the program counter is incremented to the next instruction's memory location for *each* instruction in our program. Forever. Or until something is done to make it stop.

System Timing and the Sequential State Machine

We see in Figure 2–8 that there are pulses going into the program counter. Where do these pulses come from, and, even more important, how fast do they come? The name of the game in computer design is speed, and the computer should be designed to run as fast as possible. The time it takes for a change in the input to a logic circuit to appear at the output is called the *propagation time.* The total time depends on the integrated circuit technology and the number of gates contributing to the delay. We might think that the best way to specify the clock frequency would be to analyze the instructions and see which takes the longest. For this instruction set, add and subtract instructions take the longest time. If we could find out how much time this is, we would make sure that the program counter's clock runs no faster than this. Is there a better way?

We can break the instruction execution cycle described in the previous section into smaller elements of time. To see the partition, consider the sequential state machine diagram shown in Figure 2–9 and the timing diagram shown in Figure 2–10.

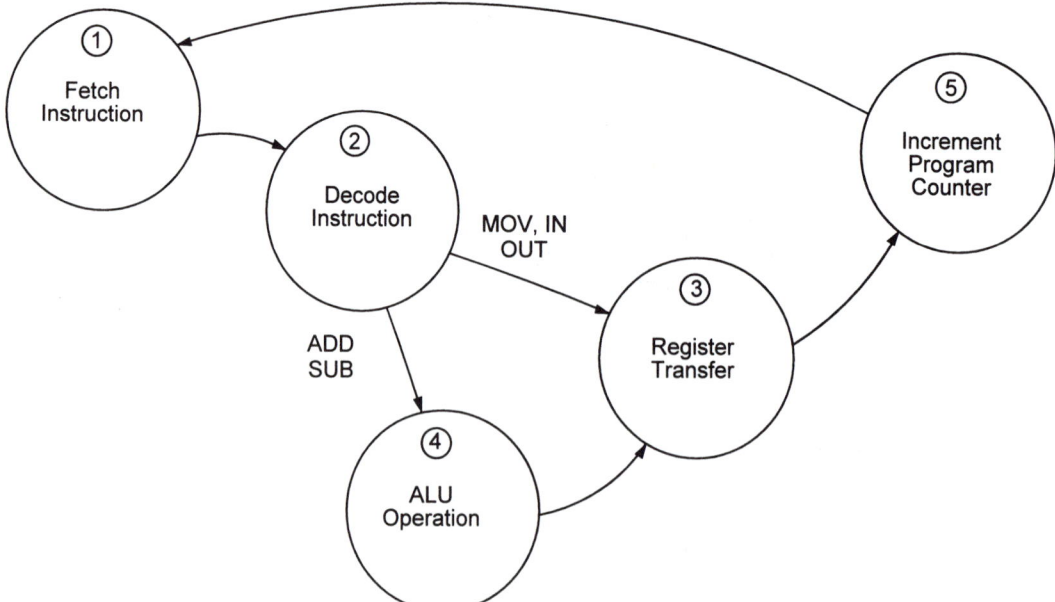

Figure 2-9   A sequential state transition diagram for the operation of the picoprocessor.

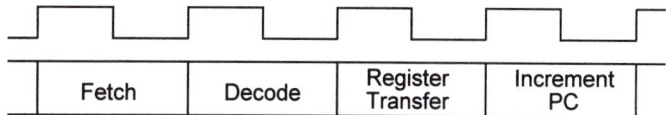

(a) Timing for the IN instruction.

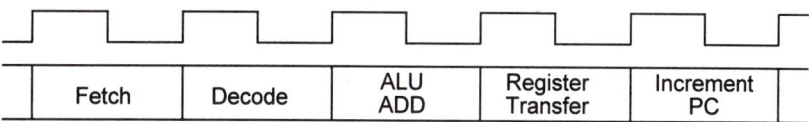

(b) Timing for the ADD instruction.

Figure 2-10   Instruction timing diagrams.

The instruction execution cycle is partitioned into five different states. Each state is an element of time long enough to allow an event to occur. In State 1, the instruction is fetched from memory; in State 2 it is decoded by the instruction decoder. Then, either State 3 or State 4 is entered depending on the instruction. State 3 is chosen if a register transfer operation, such as IN, OUT, or MOV, has been decoded. State 4 is chosen if an ADD or SUB ALU operation is the current instruction. After State 4, State 3 is entered to transfer the ALU result back into the A register. In State 5, the program counter is incremented and the memory address register updated. The state machine should be designed so the time required to do a task in each state is the same.

The combination of the sequential state machine and the instruction decoder is called a *sequence controller*, and it generates control signals at the *correct time* for a particular function. For example, we saw in Figure 2–7 that a clock signal is needed at the A register to latch the data being input from the switches. The sequence controller generates that signal in State 3 when it is doing the IN instruction.

> The *sequence controller* allows different instructions to be executed in different amounts of time.

All computers have some kind of sequence controller. There are several ways to design one, but the basic function and purpose remain the same. The sequence controller generates control signals required by the currently executing instruction, at the correct time, to accomplish the information transfer or other operation. These timed control signals are shown in Figure 2–11.

Program Execution Time

The sequential state machine is operated by a clock, and different instructions may now take different amounts of time. Normally, this time is given as the number of states the sequential state machine uses to complete the instruction. The actual time is calculated by multiplying the number of states by the time per state. Let's say that the basic clock frequency is 1 MHz, giving 1 microsecond for each state, and let's analyze the time it takes to execute the program to add two numbers together. The timing analysis is shown in Table 2–6.

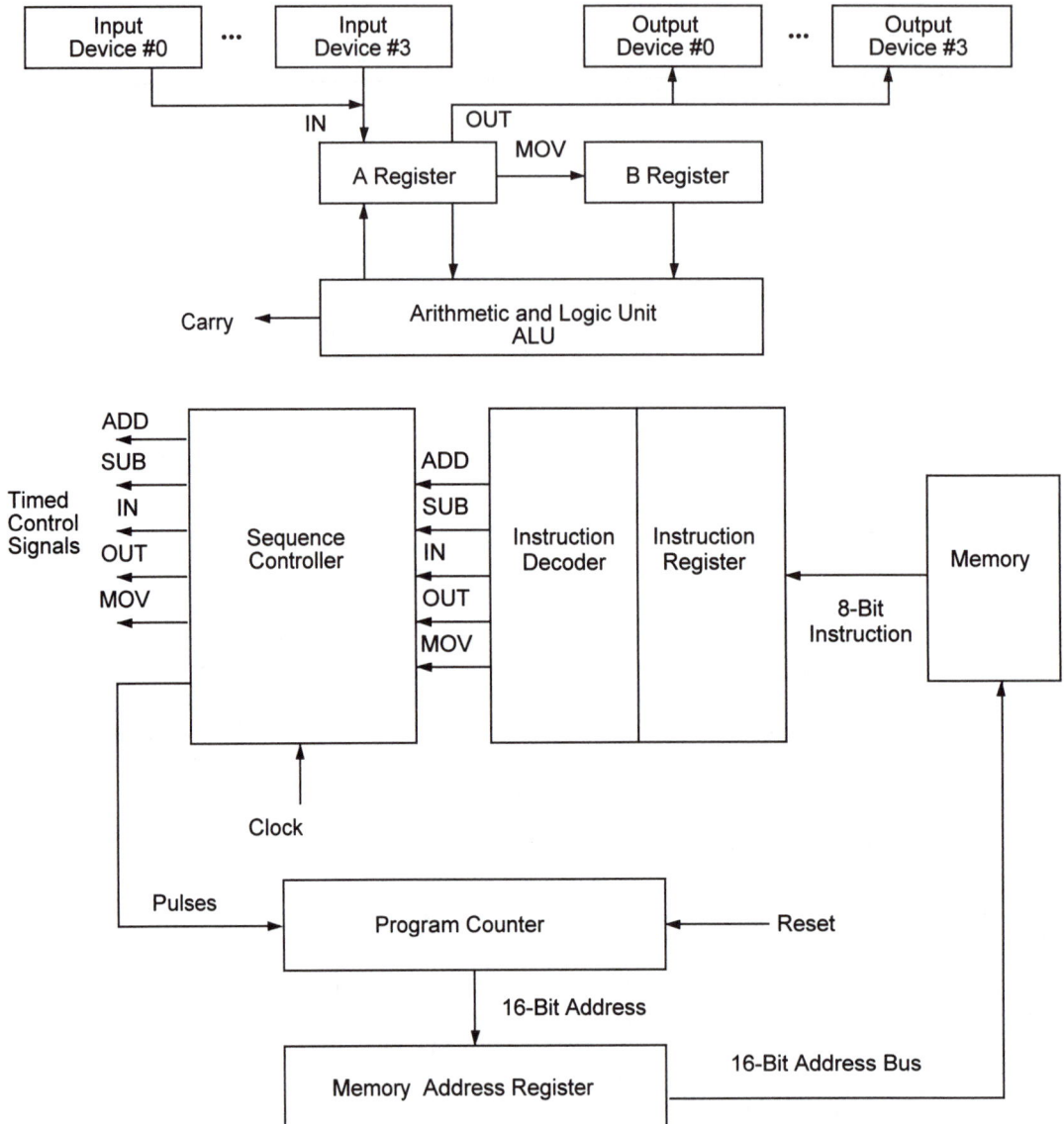

Figure 2-11   A sequence controller allows high-speed operation of the computer.

I/O Synchronization

It is important to understand that the computer's sequential operation and the time it takes to execute an instruction are controlled by the sequence controller, so let us review the operation of the computer. First, the switches are set for the first number to be added. Then the program is started by pressing the reset button. The program counter starts at zero and the first instruction is fetched and executed in 4 microseconds. This places the first number into the A register. The program counter is incremented and the second instruction (the MOV) is fetched and executed in the next

TABLE 2-6 Program execution time

Instruction	Number of states
IN 1	4
MOV	4
IN 1	4
ADD	5
OUT 2	4
	21 states = 21 μs

4 microseconds. The program counter is incremented and the next instruction, the second IN, is executed in the next 4 microseconds. Is it possible that between the time the program is started and when the computer takes the second number from the switches you can change the data from the first number to the second? Hardly. We have found a problem with the design. We must somehow synchronize the speedy microprocessor with the slow human operator of the switches.

Wait States

Here is a solution to the problem. We add an additional state, called a *wait state*, to the sequential state machine. This is shown in Figure 2–12.

When the instruction decoder detects an IN instruction, the sequential state machine goes into the WAIT state, where it stays until an external control signal, called READY, is asserted by the

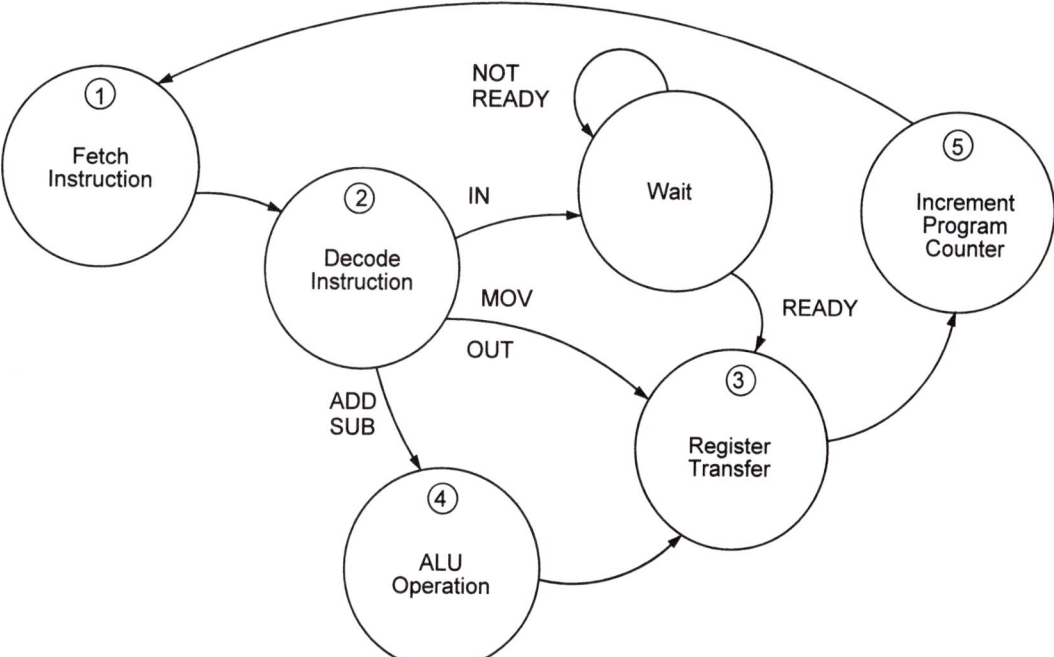

Figure 2-12   A wait state is added to the sequential state transition diagram to allow synchronization with slow input devices.

A *wait state* is a state where the processor "spins its wheels" until a *ready* signal is asserted.

user of the computer. This signal is like the ENTER button on your calculator. After entering the first number into the switches, you must assert the READY signal and allow the computer to progress to State 3, where it does the register transfer. The MOV instruction is executed at full speed and the program counter is incremented. When the second IN instruction is fetched and decoded, the sequence controller enters the WAIT state again to wait for you to assert the READY line after entering the second number. Although we haven't shown it in this diagram, the output instruction could be designed to enter the wait state also. Then the output device would have to assert the READY line when it had received the data. We will learn more about this I/O synchronization method, called *handshaking*, in Chapter 7.

2.5 More Instructions

A More Versatile Move Instruction

Before going on with another programming example, let's introduce two more instructions. Adding more instructions is straightforward once the instruction decoder and sequence controller are in hand. A more versatile move instruction is needed. Now, information can be moved only from the A register into the B register. It would be useful to be able to move from the B into the A. We also might like two more registers, say C and D, to be added to hold information temporarily. We will define the move operation as one that moves data from a source register to a destination register. The resultant move instruction is shown in Table 2–7.

A Memory Reference Instruction

This computer's hardware allows the user to get data from the input device only. The memory of this computer serves only to store the instructions of the program. This is a severe restriction and we must add an instruction to be able to retrieve data from the memory. There are a number of these instructions, called *memory reference instructions*, in a real instruction set. Memory reference

TABLE 2–7 A more versatile move instruction allows movement from a source register to a destination register

Operation	Dest. operand	Source operand	
MOV	dd,	ss	(dd) ← (ss)

where dd and ss are the two-bit binary codes for the destination and source registers.

Register codes
    A = 00
    B = 01
    C = 10
    D = 11
Example
    MOV B,A = 010-0100

TABLE 2–8 A two-byte instruction—the move immediate

Operation	Dest. operand	Data	Comments
MVI dd,			8-bit data; (dd) ← (memory location following the op code)
Example			
MVI A,65			
First byte:	110 – – –00		Operation plus operand code
Second byte:	010 0 0 001		Data

instructions *read* data from or *write* data to memory. We learned in Section 2.3 that a particular location is accessed by providing the memory with an address. The various ways of generating this address are called *addressing modes*. One of these is immediate addressing. A move-immediate instruction is shown in Table 2–8. This is a two-byte instruction where the first byte contains the operation and operand codes. The second byte *immediately* follows the instruction byte and contains the data. Of course we must modify the instruction decoder and sequence controller to be able to decode the instruction and generate the control signals.

There are other types of memory reference instructions that can read data from or write data into any memory location. You will learn more about these instructions and other addressing modes in Chapter 4 and when you study a real processor.

Adding a Constant to the Sum of Two Variables

Let's make use of the move-immediate instruction to modify the addition program to add a constant to the previous addition.

Table 2–9 shows a program to add two numbers that are input from the switches, add a constant (decimal 65), and then output the result to the LEDs. Now analyze how the computer executes this program. The program counter will be reset to zero and the first instruction fetched from memory location zero. The instruction decoder decodes the IN operation, and the sequence controller goes into the WAIT state to wait for the READY signal to be asserted when we have finished entering the first number into the switches. The data are then transferred from the switches

TABLE 2–9 A program to input two numbers from the switches, add them together, and add a constant.

Location	Contents	Operation	Operand	Comments
0:	1010 0001	IN	1	(A) ← (Switches)
1:	0100 0100	MOV	B,A	(B) ← (A)
2:	1010 0001	IN	1	Get the 2nd number
3:	0010 0001	ADD	A,B	(A) ← (A) + (B)
4:	1100 0010	MVI	C,65	(C) ← (Memory Location 5)
5:	0100 0001			The data = 65_{10}
6:	0010 0010	ADD	A,C	(A) ← (A) + (C)
7:	1110 0010	OUT	2	(LEDs) ← (A)

into the A register, the program counter is incremented to a value of one, and the instruction execution cycle is repeated for the second instruction.

What happens when the computer gets to the instruction at line 4? The MVI C instruction code is fetched and decoded as usual. But what happens then? The sequence decoder must be designed with more states to increment the program counter to "point" to the data and to generate control signals to fetch the data, *not* into the instruction register, but into the C register. The sequence controller then increments the program counter again to point to the next instruction to be executed.

Notice that at line 6 operands have been added to the ADD instruction. This instruction now allows us to ADD the contents of the C register to the contents of the A register. This may be done with more changes to the sequence controller.

What happens after our computer fetches and executes the instruction at line 7? The program counter is incremented and *the next byte in the computer memory is fetched and executed!* The instruction execution cycle is going to continue as it has been designed to do until we instruct the computer to do something else.

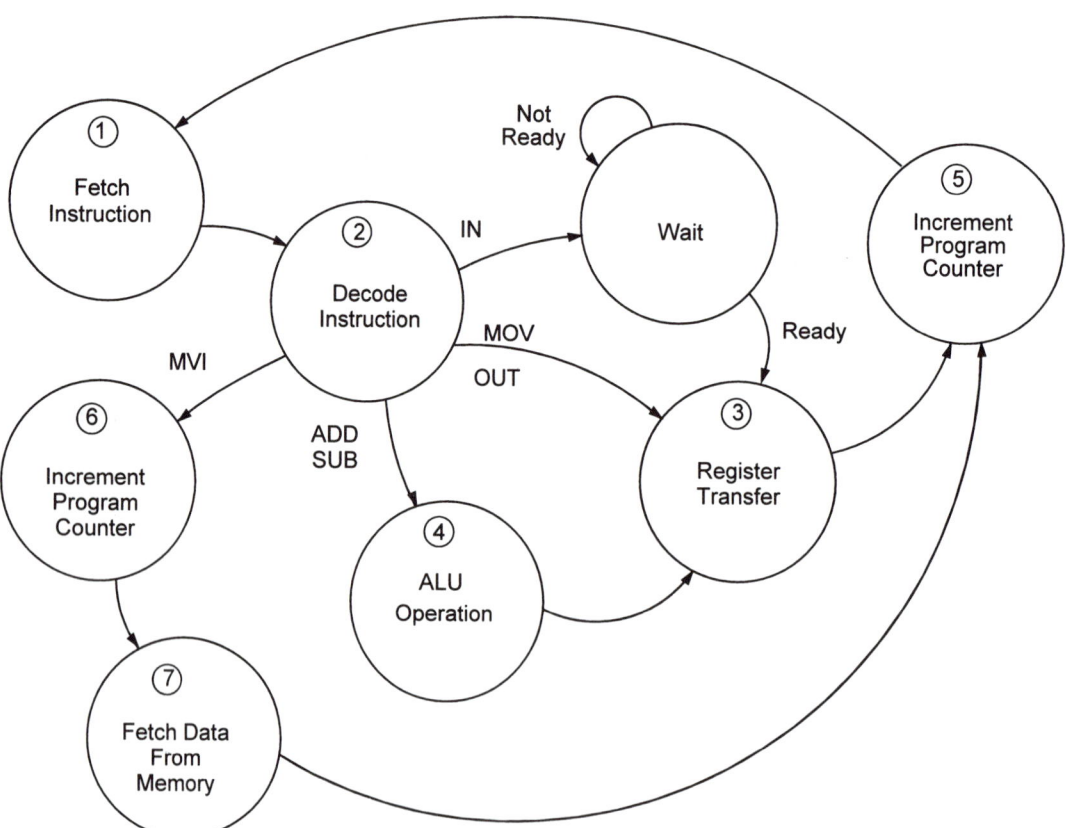

Figure 2-13   State transition diagram for the MVI instruction.

EXAMPLE 2–4   Draw a state transition similar to figure 2.12 for a move-immediate instruction.

Solution:

See Figure 2–13.

2.6 Control Instructions

The Halt Instruction

A problem was discovered in the preceding section. There is no way to stop the computer after the program is finished. After the OUT instruction, it continues fetching bytes from memory and executing them. We must discuss a new class of computer instructions. Up to now, all the instructions have to do with manipulating the data and the computer is little more than a calculator. Control instructions to control the computer's operation are needed. A simple control instruction to solve our problem is HALT. HALT simply stops the clock pulses going to the sequence controller. A flip-flop will be needed and we could use the reset signal to start the clocks again at the start of the program.

The Branch Instruction

Another example of a control instruction seen in other programming languages is a GOTO. A GOTO in assembly language is called a *jump* or *branch instruction*. These instruct the computer to branch to another place in memory and start executing the program at that point. For example, after the program outputs the sum of the three numbers to the LEDs in line 7, we might want to branch back to the beginning of the program to do it again. The operand for a branch instruction is the location in memory from which the computer must fetch its next instruction, that is, the location to which the computer "jumps." Table 2–10 shows an instruction known as *branch always*. Its mnemonic is *BRA* and it is a three-byte instruction; the first byte is the operation code and the next two bytes specify the 16-bit branch address. The sequence controller must be modified to transfer these address bytes from the memory to the memory address register.

Jump or *branch* instructions transfer the program counter from one part of the program to another.

TABLE 2–10 A branch instruction has as its operand the address of the next instruction to be executed

Operation	Operand
BRA	Memory branch address

Conditional Branch Instructions

The branch-always instruction is an *unconditional branch* because the processor always does the branch. Another type of branch instruction is a *conditional branch*, where the computer takes the branch if some condition, or set of conditions, is true. If the condition is false, the next instruction in the memory is fetched and executed. For example, in the addition program we might want to show some error if the addition of the two eight-bit numbers results in a number too large for the eight-bit accumulator. This can be done by attaching a flip-flop to the arithmetic and logic unit. It is called the *carry flag* and is set when the adder circuit generates a carry and is reset when it does not. Other flip-flops can store other information such as a zero result, negative result, two's complement overflow, and odd or even parity. These flip-flops are contained in a register called the *status*, or *condition code*, register. The status register bits are connected to the sequence controller. We may then design branch-if-carry, branch-if-no-carry, and other conditional branch instructions.

> The *status* or *condition code register* contains bits which are set or reset when an ALU operation is performed.

2.7 The Final Design

Figure 2–14 shows the final design. There has been some reorganization of the information flow and a new address register added; so let's briefly discuss these changes.

We see that the registers and the ALU are connected by an internal 8-bit data bus. Data can now flow between any of the registers and ALU. A special interface device, called a three-state driver, is used to allow multiple sources of information to coexist on the same bus. We will study three-state devices in more detail in Chapter 7. The data path to the external memory and I/O devices is over an external 8-bit data bus. You can see that information from memory can be transferred into the instruction register for instructions, or any of the registers or ALU for data.

The status bits, which are set or reset by ALU operations, are connected to the sequence controller. They are used to determine if the branch in a conditional branch instruction is to be taken.

A temporary address register has been added. This is used for branch addresses that are retrieved from memory. For example, when a JMP address is fetched from memory, it must be done one byte at a time. The temporary address register holds the address as it is being fetched before it is placed into the program counter.

The final change is in how the I/O devices are selected. In this design, two bits encode which device data are input from or output to. These two bits are placed onto the address bus where they can be decoded at the I/O devices. In a more realistic processor, more bits are used to address I/O devices.

2.8 Chapter Summary Points

- All computer programs become 1s and 0s in the memory of the computer.

- During an instruction execution cycle, the instruction code is fetched from the memory and decoded by the instruction decoder. A sequence controller progresses through the states to generate the control signals necessary to execute the instruction. Finally, the program counter is incremented (or modified by the instruction) to point to the next instruction to be executed.

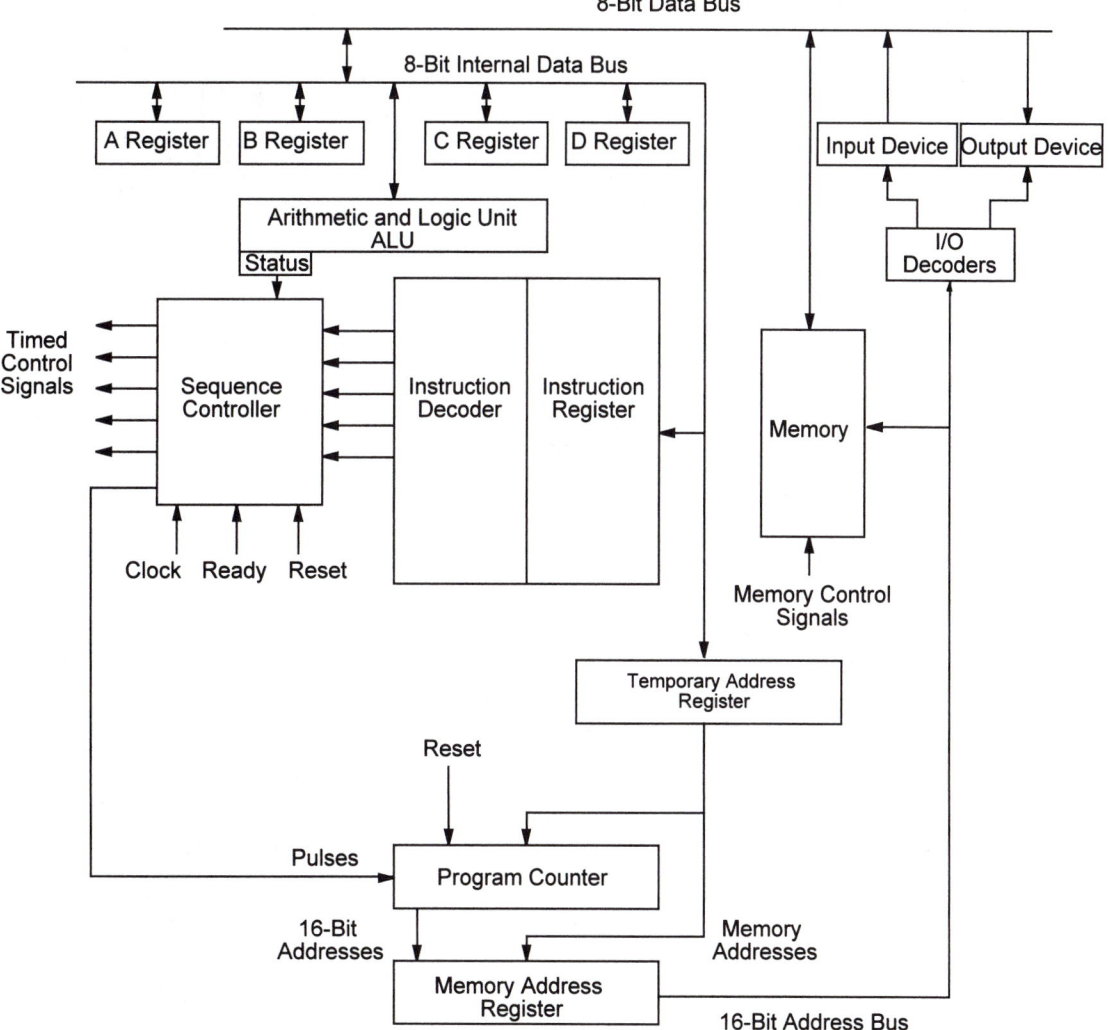

Figure 2-14   A microcomputer is a microprocessor plus memory plus input/output.

- Branch instructions control the sequence of instructions to be executed.

- After the instruction execution cycle is completed, the program counter is pointing at the next instruction to be fetched and executed.

- The computer executes instructions forever, or until it fetches an instruction that causes it to halt.

- You have absolute control over the computer because you specify the instruction codes that go into the memory.

2.9 Problems

2.1   If all move instructions are coded in one byte with source and destination operands as shown in Table 2–7, how many move instructions can be defined?

2.2   Design the instruction decoder shown in Figure 2–6 using AND, OR, and inverter gates to decode the 3-bit op codes and produce the ADD, SUB, IN, OUT, and MOV control signals.

2.3   What is the purpose of the instruction decoder?

2.4   What is the purpose of the program counter?

2.5   Explain why computers have *ready* or *wait* control lines.

2.6   Discuss the changes that must be made to the sequence controller to add the move-immediate instruction discussed in Section 2.5.

2.7   The hardware designers propose adding four more general-purpose registers. What impact does this have on the design of the move instruction and the sequence controller?

2.8   What changes would you suggest to allow the IN instruction to input data from up to 256 different devices?

2.9   Design the hardware required to implement the HALT instruction described in Section 2.6.

2.10   Describe the operation of the sequence controller.

2.11   Describe the instruction execution cycle for the MOV instruction.

2.12   Describe the instruction execution cycle for the MVI instruction.

2.13   Discuss the changes that must be made to the sequence controller of Figure 2–14 to add a direct address memory reference instruction. This is a three-byte instruction with the first byte the op code, and the next two bytes the address of the data location in memory.

2.14   Draw a state transition diagram, similar to Figure 2–12, that describes the states needed for a direct memory reference instruction as described in Problem 2–13.

Chapter 3

Introduction to the CPU: Registers and Condition Codes

O B J E C T I V E S

In this chapter we begin to learn about real processors. The steps you take here will be the same ones taken for processors you will meet later in your career. To start, we will learn about the registers, particularly the condition code register, which make up what is known as the *programmer's model*.

3.1 Introduction

In this chapter we start to evaluate a processor by looking at the hardware resources. At the basic level, these include the registers in the CPU such as accumulators, memory addressing registers, and the condition code register. For some processors, such as microcontrollers like the Motorola M68HC11 or the Intel 8051, the CPU may contain other hardware resources such as timers, parallel and serial I/O, and analog I/O.

3.2 CPU Registers

The central processor unit (CPU) contains the registers used in your programs. Depending on the design of the processor, the registers may have 8, 16, 32, or more bits; in any CPU there are several different types of registers.

Accumulators: Accumulators are registers that accumulate answers, such as the A register in the picoprocessor of Chapter 2. An accumulator can serve simultaneously as the source register for one operand and the destination for an ALU operation.

General-purpose registers: These registers hold data, serve as source and destination operands for data transfer instructions, and serve as sources for ALU operations.

Doubled registers: The number of bits in a register depends on the general architecture of the CPU. An eight-bit CPU generally has eight-bit data registers. Sometimes two of the data registers may be used together to double the number of bits.

Pointer registers: Pointer registers address memory. The register is said to "point" to a memory location. In most processors, pointer registers can be incremented or decremented, either by a program step or automatically after their use.

Stack pointer register: This is a pointer register dedicated to addressing memory used for variable data and subroutine return address storage.

Index registers: Index registers are also used to address memory. Unlike pointer registers, the memory address is found by adding a constant value, often called an offset, to the contents of the index register. This sum is called the *effective address* and is the address generated by the CPU to retrieve or store data. For a pointer register, the effective address is just the contents of the register.

Segment registers: In some machines, depending on how memory addressing is organized, the physical address consists of two parts. These are a segment part, which defines a certain area or page in the memory, and an offset part, which specifies a particular place in the page.

Condition code register: The condition code register is also called the flags or status register. It holds condition code bits generated by the processor when instructions are executed.

3.3 Register Transfers

Many instructions in any computer involve the transfer of information. Sometimes the information is just transferred from one place to another, such as in a MOV A,B instruction. Here the B register is the *source* of the information and the A register is the *destination.* Other instructions may modify the information along the way. For example, ADD A,B will add the contents of the A and B registers and place the result in the A register. In all register transfer instructions, the source operand is not destroyed or changed by the transfer unless a source register is also used as the destination, as in the ADD instruction.

Manufacturers provide a symbolic notation that precisely and succinctly describes the operation of each instruction. This is sometimes called a *register transfer language.* Typically, a register name in parentheses means that the operation involves the contents of the register. A left arrow (←) denotes a replacement operation. For example, an instruction that replaces the contents of the A register with the contents of the B register has the symbolic notation (A) ← (B). Table 3–1 shows examples of register transfer language statements, all indicating that the contents of the A register are replaced by the contents of the B register.

> A *register transfer language* succinctly describes what the instruction accomplishes.

3.4 Your Real Processor's Registers

Turn now to the material that describes what CPU registers are available in your laboratory processor. Be sure to note which registers are accumulators, which are general-purpose registers, and which address memory; then return here to learn more about the condition code register.

TABLE 3–1 Examples of register transfer language

(A) ← (B)
A ← B
(B) → (A)
B → A

3.5 The Condition Code Register

The condition code register, also called the flags register, has bits that are modified (set or reset) when the computer does an instruction involving data. Usually arithmetic and logic (ALU) operations modify one or more of the flags. Sometimes a data transfer, like a load or move operation, modifies the flags, too, and most processors have instructions that can directly set or reset the bits. Let's look at the bits found in a condition code register and understand how to interpret them.

The Carry Bit

The carry bit is set if there is a carry, or borrow, out of the most significant bit during an addition or subtraction. Consequently, it is sometimes called the carry/borrow bit. For example, if we add or subtract the numbers shown in Example 3–1, the carry/borrow bit is set (=1) by each operation.

What does the carry bit being set (or reset) mean? How do we use this information? *It depends on the code.* The meaning of *any* information *always* depends on the code. If the code is unsigned-binary, as in Example 3–1, the presence of the carry bit = 1 means that an *overflow* has occurred. Let's define overflow:

> An *overflow* indication means there is an error in the result.

An *overflow* occurs when the result of an arithmetic operation cannot be represented by the number of bits available. This could mean the result is too large or too small, although the latter is sometimes called *underflow*.

In Example 3–1 the addition $179 + 147 = 326$ yields a result too large for an eight-bit, unsigned-binary number (whose maximum is 255). Further, $147 - 179 = -32$, a number that *cannot* be represented with an unsigned-binary code. Thus, if we are using the unsigned-binary code to represent numbers, the carry bit is set for errors such as overflow or a negative result.

The carry bit can be used when doing multiple-byte addition or subtraction. Consider adding two 16-bit, unsigned-binary (or two's-complement) numbers, but add them one byte at a time. In Example 3–2 we see that the carry out from the addition of the least significant bytes is added into the addition of the most significant bytes. The microprocessor has special instructions for this.

EXAMPLE 3–1   Addition or subtraction of unsigned-binary numbers.

Addition		Subtraction	
147	1 0 0 1 0 0 1 1	147	1 0 0 1 0 0 1 1
+179	+ 1 0 1 1 0 0 1 1	−179	− 1 0 1 1 0 0 1 1
326	1 0 1 0 0 0 1 1 0	− 32	1 1 1 1 1 0 0 0 0 0
	↑		↑
	Carry		Borrow

EXAMPLE 3–2 Use of the carry bit in multiple-byte arithmetic.

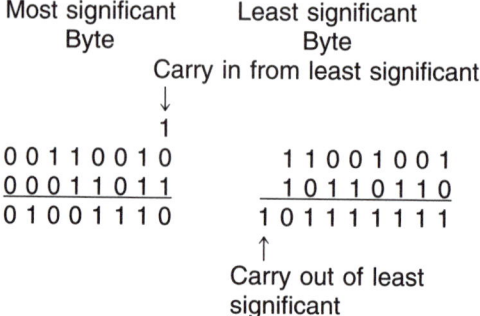

```
        Most significant      Least significant
              Byte                  Byte
                          Carry in from least significant
                                       ↓
                                       1
        0 0 1 1 0 0 1 0       1 1 0 0 1 0 0 1
        0 0 0 1 1 0 1 1       1 0 1 1 0 1 1 0
        0 1 0 0 1 1 1 0       1 0 1 1 1 1 1 1
                                 ↑
                          Carry out of least
                          significant
```

Two's-Complement Overflow Bit

What does the carry bit mean if the numbers to be added or subtracted are encoded with an eight-bit, two's-complement code? Look at Example 3–3.

The binary operands and the binary result are the same as Example 3–1. In the addition, the sum of -109 and -77 is more negative (larger) than the most negative number we can represent with this code (the most negative is -128). Therefore, it appears that the carry bit will allow us to detect an overflow. However, when -77 is subtracted from -109, the answer, -32, is OK. No overflow has occurred even though the carry bit is set. In one case the carry bit indicates an overflow and in the other it does not! We conclude that when using two's-complement codes in addition or subtraction, the carry bit cannot be used to indicate an overflow. Fortunately, microcomputer manufacturers include a bit to be set if a *two's-complement overflow* has occurred (or reset if it has not). There are several algorithms for overflow, and probably the easiest to understand (but not the easiest to do in hardware) is the following:

When two's-complement numbers are being added:

Two's-complement overflow occurs if the two operands are the same sign AND the sign of the result is different.

Two's-complement overflow cannot occur if the two operands are opposite sign.

EXAMPLE 3–3 Addition or subtraction of two's-complement numbers.

```
Addition          Subtraction
 − 109     1 0 0 1 0 0 1 1        − 109     1 0 0 1 0 0 1 1
+(−77)     1 0 1 1 0 0 1 1       −(−77)     1 0 1 1 0 0 1 1
 − 186   1 0 1 0 0 0 1 1 0        − 32    1 1 1 1 0 0 0 0 0
               ↑                             ↑
             Carry                         Borrow
```

EXAMPLE 3–4 **Show by example that two's-complement overflow cannot occur when the numbers are of opposite sign.**

Solution:

The test for positive overflow (result $> +127$) is to add $+127$ and -1

$+\ 127$	0111 1111	
$+\ -1$	1111 1111	
$+\ 126$	0111 1110	No overflow

A test can be made for negative overflow (result < -128)

$-\ 128$	1000 0000	
$+\quad 0$	0000 0000	
$-\ 128$	1000 0000	No overflow

When two's-complement numbers are being subtracted, take the two's-complement of the subtrahend and proceed as in addition.

As you can see in Examples 3–1 and 3–3, the binary numbers and the results are identical for each addition and subtraction. The hardware to do addition and subtraction is the same in each case. This is the beauty of the two's-complement code. The binary result can be interpreted correctly by the program because the hardware provides the two's-complement overflow bit to be tested when two's-complement codes are being used.

Sign Bit

The *sign bit* is equal to the most significant bit of the result and gives the sign *only* if signed number codes are being used.

The sign bit shows that an ALU (or other) operation gave a result in which the most significant bit is a 1 (or a 0). Notice we didn't say resulted in a negative (1) or positive (0) number because the meaning of the bit depends on the code. In an unsigned-binary number computation, there can be no negative result because there are no codes for negative numbers. The sign bit *means* negative *only* if one's-complement or two's-complement codes are being used to represent signed information.

Zero Bit

The zero bit is true, or set, if the result of an operation is equal to zero. Otherwise it is false, or reset.

Parity Bit

Some processors have a bit that shows if a result has even or odd parity. An even-parity bit is set if the result has even parity, that is, an even number of 1's. An odd-parity bit is set for a result with an odd number of 1's. The parity bit, along with conditional branching instructions for parity-even

---

EXAMPLE 3–5   **Show by example that two's-complement overflow can occur when numbers of the same sign are added.**

Solution:

An example of positive overflow is:

+ 127	0111 1111
+ 1	0000 0001
− 128	1000 0000 Overflow

An example of negative overflow is:

− 128	1000 0000
+ −1	1111 1111
+ 127	0111 1111 Overflow

---

and parity-odd, is useful for checking to see if errors have occurred in data transmitted over long distances. We will learn more about parity when we discuss serial I/O in Chapter 10.

Other Condition Code Register Bits

There may be other bits in the condition code register that are not directly related to conditional branching. These typically include bits to control the interrupt capabilities. We will study these later when we discuss interrupts.

EXAMPLE 3–6   **Give an example showing the addition of two binary numbers which result in:**

(a) Overflow if the numbers are unsigned binary but no overflow if they are two's-complement binary.
(b) No overflow if the numbers are unsigned binary but overflow if they are two's-complement binary.

Solution:

(a)

	Unsigned Value	Signed Value
1 1 1 1 1 1 1 1	255	−1
0 0 0 0 0 0 0 1	+ 1	+1
0 0 0 0 0 0 0 0	0	0
C=1, V=0	Overflow	No overflow

(b)

	Unsigned Value	Signed Value
0 1 1 1 1 1 1 1	127	+127
0 0 0 0 0 0 0 1	1	+ 1
1 0 0 0 0 0 0 0	128	−128
C=0, V=1	No overflow	Overflow

EXAMPLE 3–7 Do the following binary additions and show what the carry (C), two's-complement overflow (V), sign (S), and zero (Z) bits are after the addition.

```
10101101        10101101        10101101
10110010        01001101        01010011
```

Solution:

```
01011111        11111010        00000000
C=1 V=1         C=0 V=0         C=1 V=0
S=0 Z=0         S=1 Z=0         S=0 Z=1
```

How Do the Bits Get Set or Reset?

The condition code register bits are modified by hardware during the execution of some instructions. The bits are set or reset according to the hardware regardless of the code you are using in the computation.

Using the Condition Code Register

The condition code register (or flags register) is attached to the sequence controller for use by the conditional branch instructions. With these we can answer questions like the following:

"Is bit zero on the I/O port equal to one?"
"Are the contents of the A register greater than the B register?"
"Is the sign of the result minus?"
"Has an overflow error occurred?"

Notice that the answer to these questions must be yes or no. When we write programs we would like to do one thing if the answer is yes and another if the answer is no. For example, let's add two eight-bit, unsigned-binary numbers together and detect (and perhaps ring a bell) if the resultant addition is too large for the eight-bit data word. The program could be as shown in Example 3–10.

EXAMPLE 3–8 For each of the 8-bit, binary additions shown in Example 3.7, assume the data are unsigned-binary numbers. Give the decimal equivalents of each operand and the answer, and state whether overflow has occurred.

Solution:

```
10101101  173    10101101  173    10101101  173
10110010  178    01001101   77    01010011   83
01011111   95    11111010  250    00000000    0
Overflow         No overflow      Overflow
```

EXAMPLE 3–9   For each of the 8-bit, binary additions shown in Example 3.7, assume the data are two's-complement binary numbers. Give the decimal equivalents of each operand and the answer, and state whether overflow has occurred.

Solution:

10101101 −83	10101101 −83	10101101 −83
10110010 −78	01001101 77	01010011 83
01011111 95	11111010 −6	00000000 0
Overflow	No overflow	No overflow

3.6 The Programmer's Model

The *programmer's model* is the set of registers that the programmer can manipulate and must manage during the programming of the processor. It includes the accumulators and data registers, memory addressing registers, the stack pointer register, and the condition code register. As we will see when we learn more about assembly language programming, the programmer's responsibilities also include memory locations used for data storage.

3.7 Chapter Summary Points

- The CPU contains a variety of registers. Some are data registers and accumulators, and some are used for addressing memory.

- A register transfer language is used by manufacturers to describe each operation in the instruction set.

- The condition code register contains bits that are modified when various instructions, generally arithmetic and logic unit instructions, are executed.

- Among the bits found in the condition code register are bits that indicate a carry, a two's-complement overflow, sign, a zero, and parity.

EXAMPLE 3–10   Programs use conditional branch instructions to test the condition code register bits.

LOAD the A register with the first byte.
LOAD the B register with the second byte.
ADD the B register to the A register with the result
    ending up in the A register and the condition
    code register modified by the ADD operation.
BRANCH IF THE CARRY BIT IS SET to the part of the
    program that rings the bell.
Otherwise continue with whatever we want to do.

• The condition code register bits are used by conditional branch instructions to allow yes/no decisions to be made.

• The programmer's model includes the registers the programmer is responsible for managing during the program.

3.8 Problems

3.1   Do the following 8-bit binary additions and for each case give the expected result in the carry, zero, sign and overflow flags.

(a)   10100011   (b)   11111111   (c)   01110001
    + 00111011   + 00000001   + 01000000

(d)   10100010   (e)   01111111   (f)   10101010
    + 10000000   + 10000000   + 01010101

3.2   For problem 3.1, assume the binary numbers are in unsigned binary code. Show the equivalent decimal arithmetic operations and indicate if overflow has occurred.

3.3   For problem 3.1, assume the binary numbers are in two's-complement binary code. Show the equivalent decimal arithmetic operations and indicate if overflow has occurred.

3.4   What is overflow?

3.5   What is the meaning of the sign bit = 1 when unsigned-binary coded numbers are added?

3.6   What is the meaning of the sign bit = 1 when two's-complement binary coded numbers are added?

3.7   What is the meaning of the carry bit = 1 when unsigned-binary coded numbers are added?

3.8   What is the meaning of the carry bit = 1 when two's-complement binary coded numbers are added?

3.9   What is the meaning of the zero bit = 1 when unsigned-binary coded numbers are added?

3.10   What is the meaning of the zero bit = 0 when two's-complement binary coded numbers are added?

3.11   What is the meaning of the overflow bit = 1 when unsigned-binary coded numbers are added?

3.12   What is the meaning of the overflow bit = 1 when two's-complement binary coded numbers are added?

Chapter 4

Addressing Modes

OBJECTIVES

This chapter describes the addressing modes available in most processors. Most instructions have a variety of ways to address operands, and after these are learned, learning the instruction set is not a daunting task.

4.1 Introduction

The instruction set of a real processor has only a few categories of instructions such as data transfers, arithmetic and logic operations, and branch and control instructions. Many instructions use one or more operands in registers or memory and often have several ways to address them. The different ways an instruction can specify operands are called *addressing modes*, and if you learn these, along with the few categories of instructions, you will soon be writing assembly language programs.

In this chapter we describe a variety of addressing modes that improve the efficiency of a CPU's operation by either allowing fewer bits to encode the instruction, or by letting the CPU execute instructions faster, or both. In addition, some modes may allow instructions that can calculate an address at the time the program is running. For example, if you want to step through a table of data and know the start of the table, the next address can be calculated by adding the number of bytes for each data element to the current address. In some computers, an address can be specified relative to the program counter. This is useful for branch instructions that don't branch very far from the current instruction.

4.2 Addressing Terminology

Physical address: The physical address is the actual address that must be supplied to the memory. The number of bits in the physical address fixes the maximum number of memory locations that can be addressed.

Segment address: A segment address gives the location of a block or segment of memory that is smaller than the full physical memory.

Offset address: An offset address is one that is calculated from the start of a segment of memory.

Logical address: Sometimes the complete, or physical address, is not needed or provided by an instruction. For example, in segmented memory architectures as discussed below, only the offset from the start of a segment is needed to specify the address of an operand. This offset is the logical address. The physical address is computed or generated from the logical address and other segment information, depending on the memory architecture used.

Effective address: This term refers to an address that is calculated by the processor. The effective address may be a physical or logical address and is the actual address of the operand.

Auto-increment and auto-decrement: In some systems, registers that address memory can be incremented or decremented automatically during use. This provides very efficient addressing for stepping through tables of data.

RAM: Random access memory can be read from and written to.

ROM: Read only memory can only be read from.

Memory and I/O maps: A memory or I/O map shows what addresses are used for what purposes. A memory map may show which addresses contain ROM, which RAM, and which may have no memory installed at all.

4.3 Memory Architectures

There are two types of memory architectures. These are linear addressing, favored by Motorola processors, and segmented addressing, as used by Intel in their 80xxx CPUs. The type of memory architecture directly affects how an instruction generates the physical memory address.

Linear Addressing

In a *linear addressing* scheme, the instructions specify the full physical address. The Motorola microprocessors, such as the MC68000 family, use linear addressing. A memory map for a linear addressing scheme is shown in Figure 4–1.

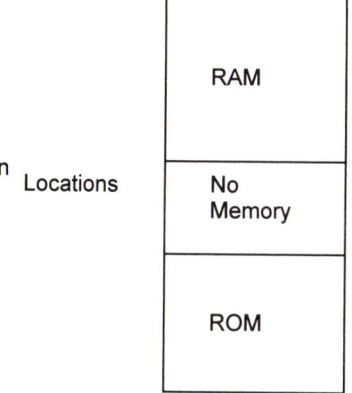

Figure 4–1 Linear addressing memory map for an n-bit address.

Linear addressing is the easiest to understand, but in large systems, instructions that directly address memory must have many bits. The Motorola MC68000 microprocessor's 24-bit address can access 16,777,216 locations. An MC68020 has a full 32-bit address, giving a four-gigabyte address space.

Segmented Addressing

As the amount of memory that the processor can address increases, so does the number of bits needed to form the physical address. This means that each instruction must contain more bits and more memory is needed for the program. A way around this dilemma is the segmented memory architecture.

> *Segmented memories reduce the number of bits an instruction needs to specify an address.*

The Intel 80xxx microprocessors use a *movable segment architecture.* For example, in the 8086, the total memory space is one megabyte organized into segments, or blocks of memory. These segments may range in size from 16 bytes to 64 Kbytes, and the full 20-bit physical address consists of a *segment address* and an *offset address.* Segment addresses are maintained in separate *segment registers,* allowing the program counter and other memory addressing registers to be only 16 bits. Each memory reference instruction generates a 16-bit offset that is added to a 16-bit, segment register. The physical address is constructed by shifting the segment register contents left 4 bits and then adding the offset. In this way the 64-Kbyte segment can be located on any 16-byte boundary. Four 16-bit segment registers are available to the programmer, and all memory reference addresses are generated as shown in Figure 4–2.

In this segmented architecture, segments may be any length from 16 bytes to 64 Kbytes and may even overlap. This allows an efficient allocation of memory to various parts of the program, such as for code and data. Figure 4–3 shows an example.

Segmented architectures use fewer bits in each instruction because only the offset within a page must be specified. A disadvantage is that special programming techniques or special instructions are needed to cross over a page boundary or to allow data elements that are larger than the 64-Kbyte segments.

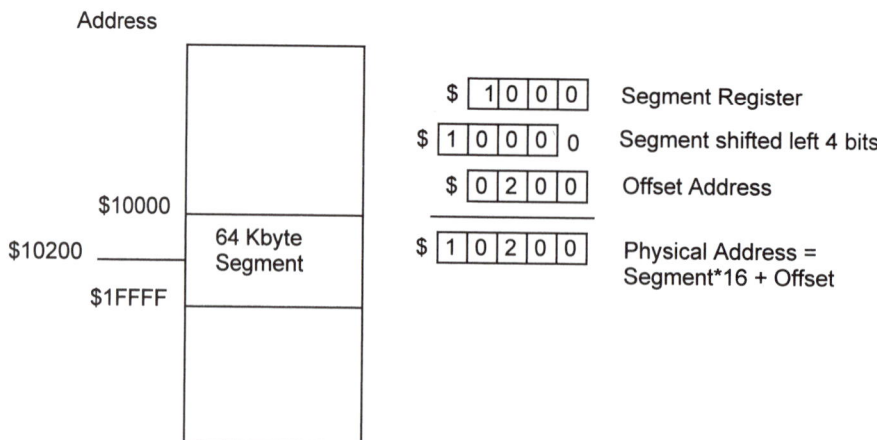

Figure 4–2 Intel 8086 segmented memory addressing.

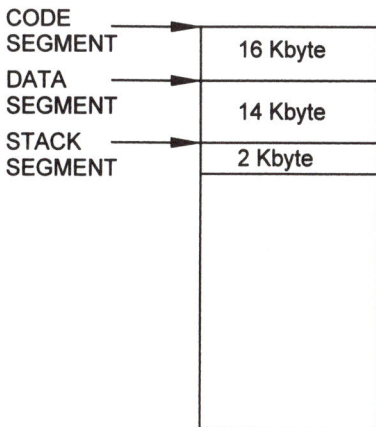

Figure 4-3 Variable sized segments used in a segmented memory architecture.

4.4 Addressing Modes

There are not many addressing modes to be learned. Large mainframes and minicomputers may have many addressing modes, but some microcomputers and microcontrollers have only a few.

Register Addressing

Register addressing needs only a few bits to define which register(s) are used for the data.

When operands are contained within registers in the CPU, such as in a MOV A,B instruction, the *register addressing* mode is used. Memory is not addressed, and only a few bits are required to specify the limited number of registers. Thus register addressing instructions are among the fastest to execute and use the fewest bits of any of the instructions. Some manufacturers call register addressing by other names. For example, Motorola uses the term *inherent addressing*.

Immediate Addressing

Immediate addressing is used for constants known when the program is written.

Immediate addressing is used when an operand is a constant known at the time the program is written. If this is the case, the data can *immediately* follow the instruction in the memory. A memory map of the immediate addressing mode is shown in Figure 4–4 where the data may be eight bits, sixteen bits, or more, depending on the size of the destination register.

Figure 4-4 Immediate addressing.

The data immediately follow the op code.

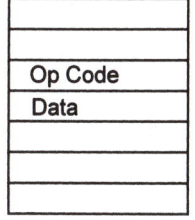

Direct Memory Addressing

In *direct memory addressing,* the instruction contains the address of the data. It may be the full physical address in linear addressing architectures or an offset for segmented architectures. In any event, the location of the data for this instruction is constant. There are two variants of this mode called (1) *direct addressing* and (2) *base page,* or *reduced direct addressing.* Different manufacturers use different terminology such as absolute addressing (Intel, Zilog), extended direct addressing, or long and short absolute addressing (Motorola).

> *Direct addressing* is a one-level address; the instruction contains the address of the data.

Direct addressing means that the address of the data, either the full address or an offset, is in the instruction. Absolute addressing is another term commonly used. Direct addressing is shown in Figure 4–5 for a processor with a 16-bit address space (64 Kbytes). It is a *single-level* addressing mode because the instruction contains the address of the data. The 16-bit address follows the operation code in the memory.

Direct addressing is the most simple mode to understand, and many beginning students try to use it exclusively. However, it often needs more bits than other addressing modes and the location of the data addressed by the instruction is fixed. It is especially unsuitable for addressing elements in a table of data.

In a CPU with *base page addressing,* the computer designers provide instructions that specify only the least significant bits of the full address. The processor then generates the complete address by filling the most significant bits with 0s. For example, in a machine with 16 address bits and a 256-byte base page, the base page addressing instructions specify only the eight least significant bits. The CPU provides the eight most significant bits, as shown in Figure 4–6.

Base page addressing offers the advantage that the instruction has to specify only eight bits of the full 16-bit address. This saves program bytes and makes the instructions execute faster. The disadvantage is that usually only a few memory locations are available for data storage.

Indirect Addresssing

Indirect addressing is a *two-level* addressing mechanism. The first level address is provided by the instruction and specifies where the *address* of the data is. This second level then specifies where the *data* are located. There are two types of indirect addressing—register indirect and memory indirect.

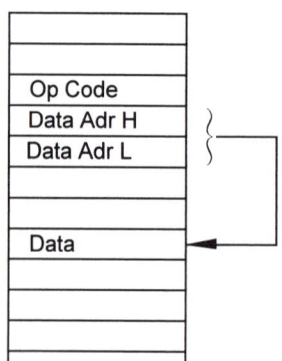

Figure 4–5   Direct memory addressing.

The data address is in the two bytes following the op code.

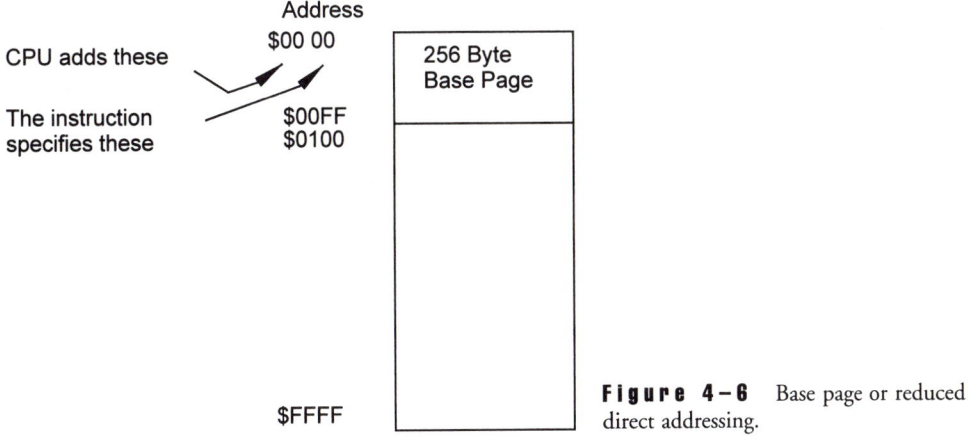

Figure 4–6   Base page or reduced direct addressing.

Register Indirect Addressing: This is also called *pointer register addressing* because the register (actually the contents of the register) "points" to the data. It is a two-level address because the instruction contains the address of which register has the address of the data. This addressing mode is shown in Figure 4–7.

> A register points to the data in *register indirect addressing*.

Register indirect addressing is efficient because it uses register addressing, and thus only a few bits, for the first-level address. Another advantage is that the address of the data can be calculated at run time as you might do when stepping through a table of data. Remember, though, to initialize the register with an address before using it.

Register Indirect Addressing with Auto-Increment and Auto-Decrement: When stepping through a table of data, the register pointing to the data must be incremented or decremented. Some processors have an addressing mode that automatically increments or decrements the register. You may have a choice of preincrementing or predecrementing, where the register is incremented or decremented before it is used. Postincrementing/decrementing, where the register is incremented/decremented after it is used, is also available.

Memory Indirect Addressing: In memory indirect addressing, the instruction contains the memory address of the address of the data. This addressing mode is shown in Figure 4–8. Memory indirect addressing is less efficient than direct memory or register indirect addressing because the CPU first reads the address of the address, then the address, and

> A memory address contains the address of the data in *memory indirect addressing*.

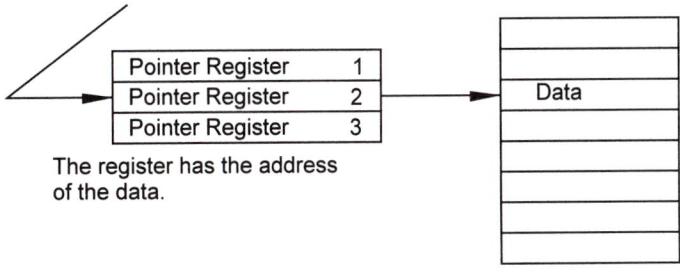

Figure 4–7   Register indirect addressing.

The instruction has the address of the address.

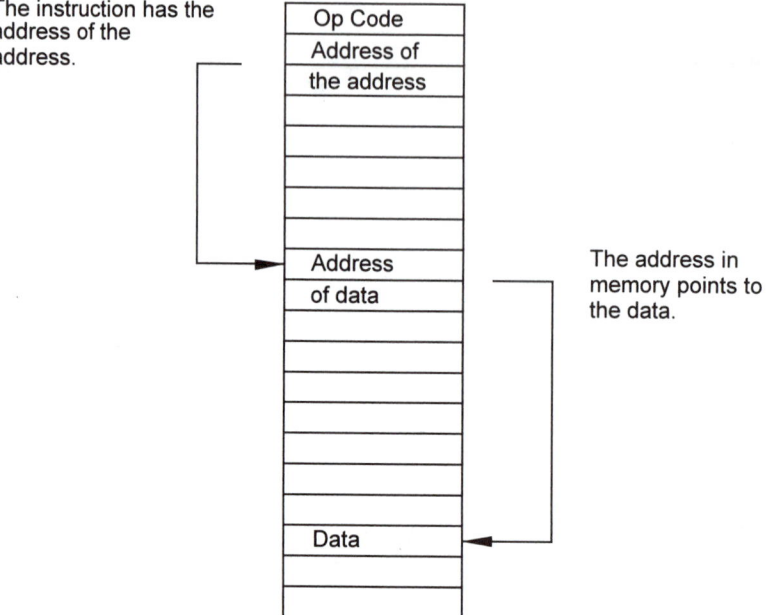

The address in memory points to the data.

Figure 4–8   Memory indirect addressing.

finally the data. The advantage of this mode is that the address of the data can be calculated and stored in memory before using it, and it can be changed while your program is running.

Indexed and Based Addressing

When the effective address is the sum of a register and a constant value, the mode is *indexed* or *based* addressing.

Indexed addressing finds a memory location based on an index. For example, if you have an array of bytes of data, you might refer to the individual elements as DATA[0], DATA[1], . . . , DATA[n]. The [n] is called the index of the array. The address of any element in the array consists of two parts—the starting address of the array and an offset from the starting address equal to n.[1] This sum is called the *effective address,* and there are two ways to form it. Both are a type of indexed addressing, although the second is called *based addressing* by some manufacturers.

Indexed Addressing: Figure 4–9 shows indexed addressing. The instruction contains the starting address of the array and the index register contains the offset to the element being addressed. To step through the array, the index register is incremented or decremented, either explicitly with a program instruction or automatically in processors that have the auto-increment/decrement addressing mode. Some processors can also scale the increment by the size of the data element. For example, if your data array is four bytes per element, incrementing the index register would add four to point to the next element in the array.

---

[1]   If the data elements are larger than one byte, the offset is n times the size of the element in bytes.

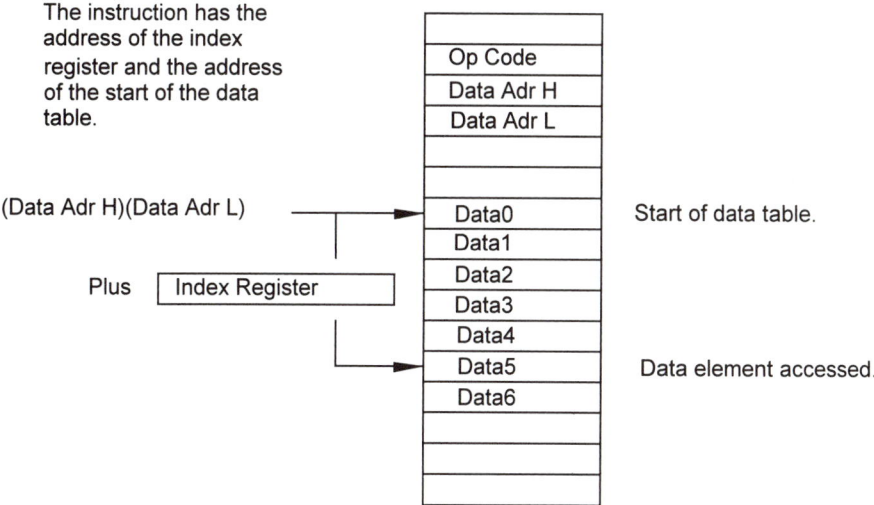

Figure 4–9 Indexed addressing.

This form of indexed addressing must have the direct address of the start of the array in the instruction; it uses more bytes than register indirect addressing. Consequently, manufacturers have included based addressing to reduce the number of bits carried by the instruction.

Based Addressing: Figure 4–10 shows how based addressing works. Here the "index" or "base" register has the starting, or base, address of the array. The instruction provides the offset into the array. The effective address is calculated by adding the base register and the offset. This is different from indexed addressing because the instruction contains the offset rather than the direct ad-

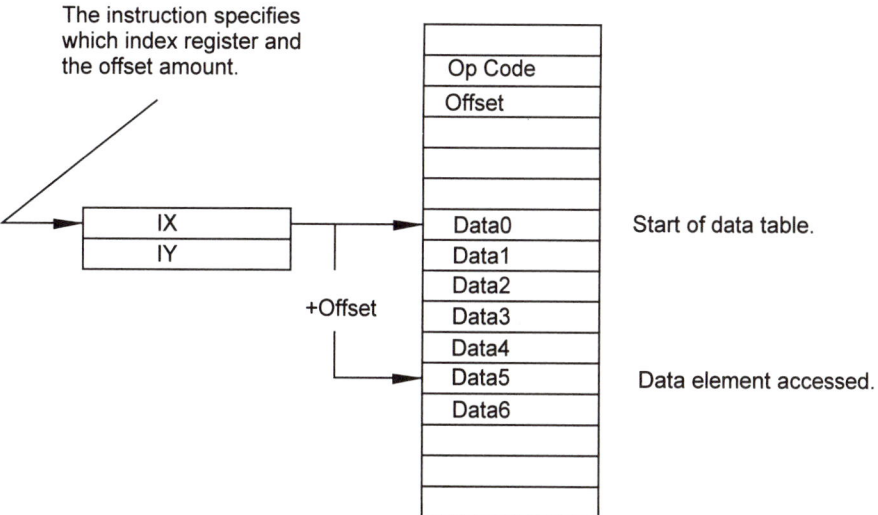

Figure 4–10 Based addressing.

dress of the start of the data. This scheme can reduce the number of bytes in the instruction when the offset is smaller than the full address range, say, eight bits instead of sixteen.

Based addressing is useful for transferring data from one place to another when there is a fixed offset between the data storage locations. In Figure 4–11, data are to be moved from one location to another. If the index register is initialized to the start of the source data, the processor can read the data with an offset of zero and store the data with a fixed offset to put it into the destination table. This allows one index register to address both the source and the destination.

Based addressing is almost as efficient as register indirect addressing. There is an additional byte (or two) to be fetched from memory for the offset and time is taken to add the offset to the contents of the index register to create the effective address. Unfortunately, to add to the confusion of the beginning student, based addressing is also called indexed addressing in some processors.

Relative Addressing

Relative addressing modes calculate the effective address by adding an offset to the current value of the program counter. This addressing mode is used mostly for branch instructions because, in well-written programs, branches jump over only a few bytes of code. Thus a programmer can save memory by using relative branch instructions. Figure 4–12 shows relative addressing.

> *Relative addressing* is used for branching short distances in the program.

The actual value of the offset is calculated from the memory location labeled *Next Op Code* in Figure 4–12 and is usually a two's-complement number to be able to branch forward and backward.

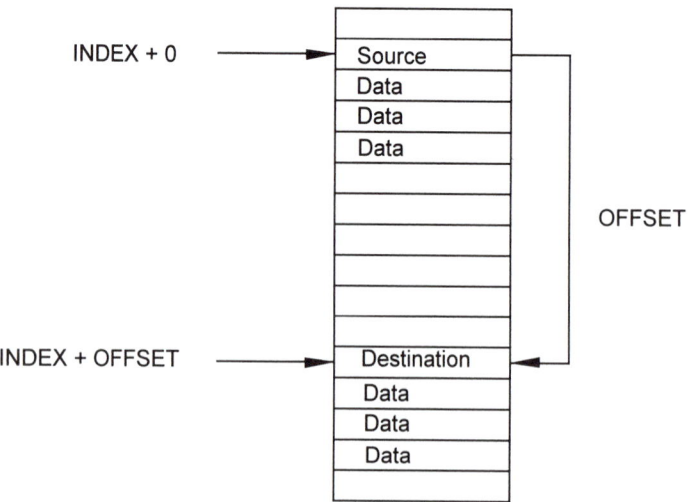

Figure 4–11   Based addressing is useful for transferring data from one buffer to another.

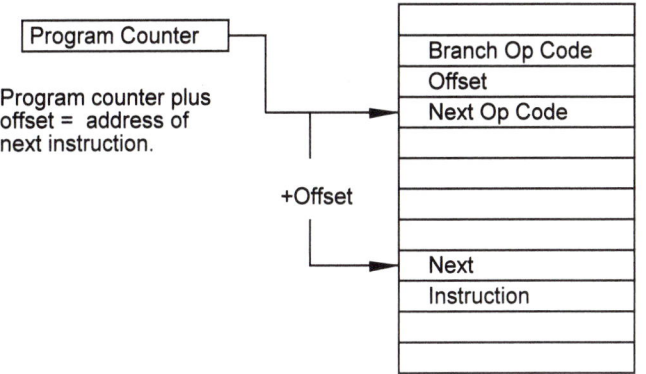

Figure 4–12 Relative addressing.

Bit Addressing

Many microprocessors and microcontrollers input and output individual bits. For example, you might want to read one or more switches and act depending upon whether the switch is open or closed. Designers provide *bit addressing* to read or write one bit at a time. Usually the bit is within a byte location, either in memory or I/O; so the instruction must supply the address of the byte plus a mask to specify which bit within this byte is to be addressed. Figure 4–13 shows bit addressing.

> *Bit addressing* can save memory by allowing eight binary variables to be saved in one byte.

Other Addressing Combinations

In some more powerful microprocessors, and in minicomputers, you may find addressing modes that are combinations of the basic modes described in the previous sections.

Based Indexed Addressing: The Intel 80xxx CPUs have an addressing mode where the effective address is the sum of a base register, index register, and a displacement.

Relative Addressing with Index Plus Displacement: The effective address is the program counter plus an index register plus a displacement.

4.5 Stack Addressing

The stack is an area of RAM that is reserved for temporary data storage. It operates on a last-in, first-out (LIFO) basis. That is, the last information stored on the stack is the first to be retrieved.

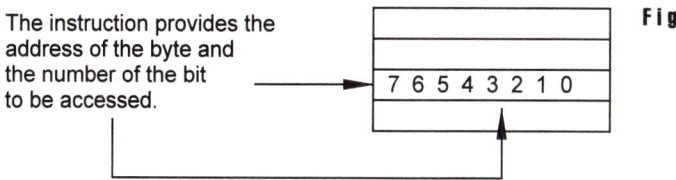

Figure 4–13 Bit addressing.

> The *stack* contains data and return addresses for subroutines.

The stack operates like the pile of plates in a dining hall. You always take the plate on the top of the stack, that is, the last one put there. Disaster awaits those who try to remove plates from the middle of the stack! Information is stored to and retrieved from the stack with a CPU register called the *stack pointer (SP)*. The stack pointer points to either the last information pushed onto the stack or to the next available location,[2] and must be initialized to point to the memory used for the stack.

A stack memory map is shown in Figure 4–14. Memory maps are usually drawn as shown with higher memory addresses at the bottom and lower at the top. Figure 4.14(a) shows the stack pointer pointing at the next location to be used when new information is placed onto the stack.

Push and Pull Operations

Placing data onto the stack is called a *push*. The stack pointer points to the memory location where the data is to go and is automatically decremented by the push instruction. The result of pushing two bytes is shown in Figure 4–14(b) and (c). *New Data1* and *New Data2* are now in memory, and the stack pointer has been decremented twice. The result of a *pull* (called a *pop* in some processors) is shown in Figure 4–14(d) and a subsequent push operation in Figure 4–14(e).

Subroutine Call and Return Operations

The stack saves the return address when the program branches to a subroutine. After the op code and the subroutine address are fetched from the program memory, the program counter is pointing to the instruction to be executed after the return from the subroutine. This is the return address that is pushed onto the stack before branching to the subroutine. Figure 4–15(a) and (b) show how the stack is used to save the return address.[3] At the end of the subroutine, a return instruction is executed. The return instruction pulls the return address from the stack, and the stack pointer is automatically incremented.

4.6 Chapter Summary Points

- Addressing modes are the different ways a processor specifies where an operand is located.
- Different addressing modes give the programmer flexibility in accessing data elements.
- The effective address is the physical or logical address of the data.
- Register addressing specifies data located in registers.
- Immediate addressing is used for constant data known when you write the program.

---

[2]   The stack pointer in Intel processors usually points to the last used location. In some Motorola processors, the M68HC11, for example, the stack pointer points to the next available location to be used. Which of these design strategies is used is immaterial because the processor automatically handles the stack pointer properly.

[3]   This assumes two memory locations are needed to store the full address.

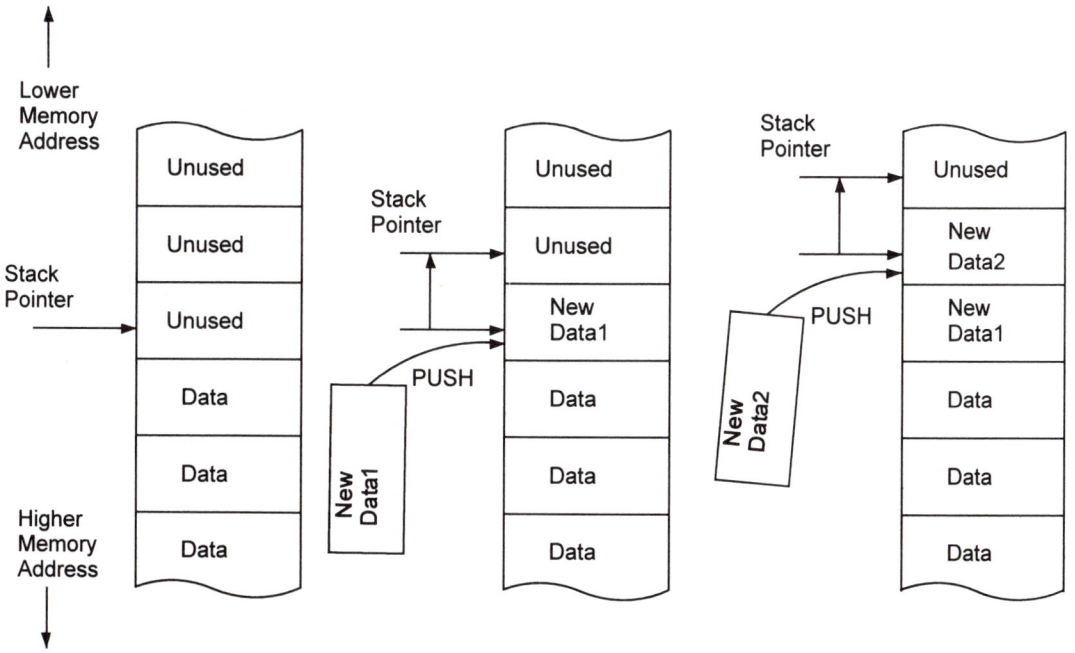

(a) Stack pointer before stack operations.

(b) Stack pointer after a a push operation.

(c) Stack pointer after second push operation.

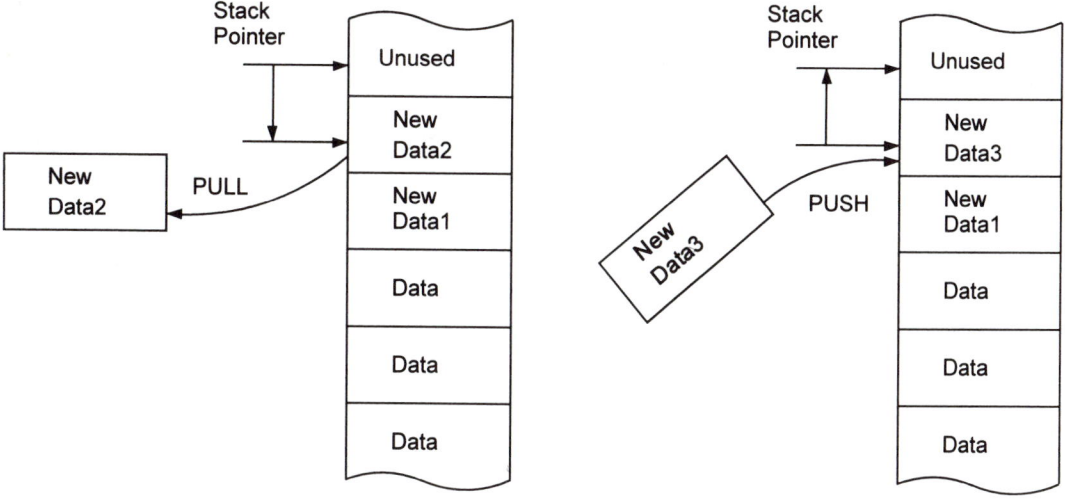

(d) Stack pointer after a pull operation.

(e) Stack pointer after third push operation.

Figure 4-14   Stack operations.

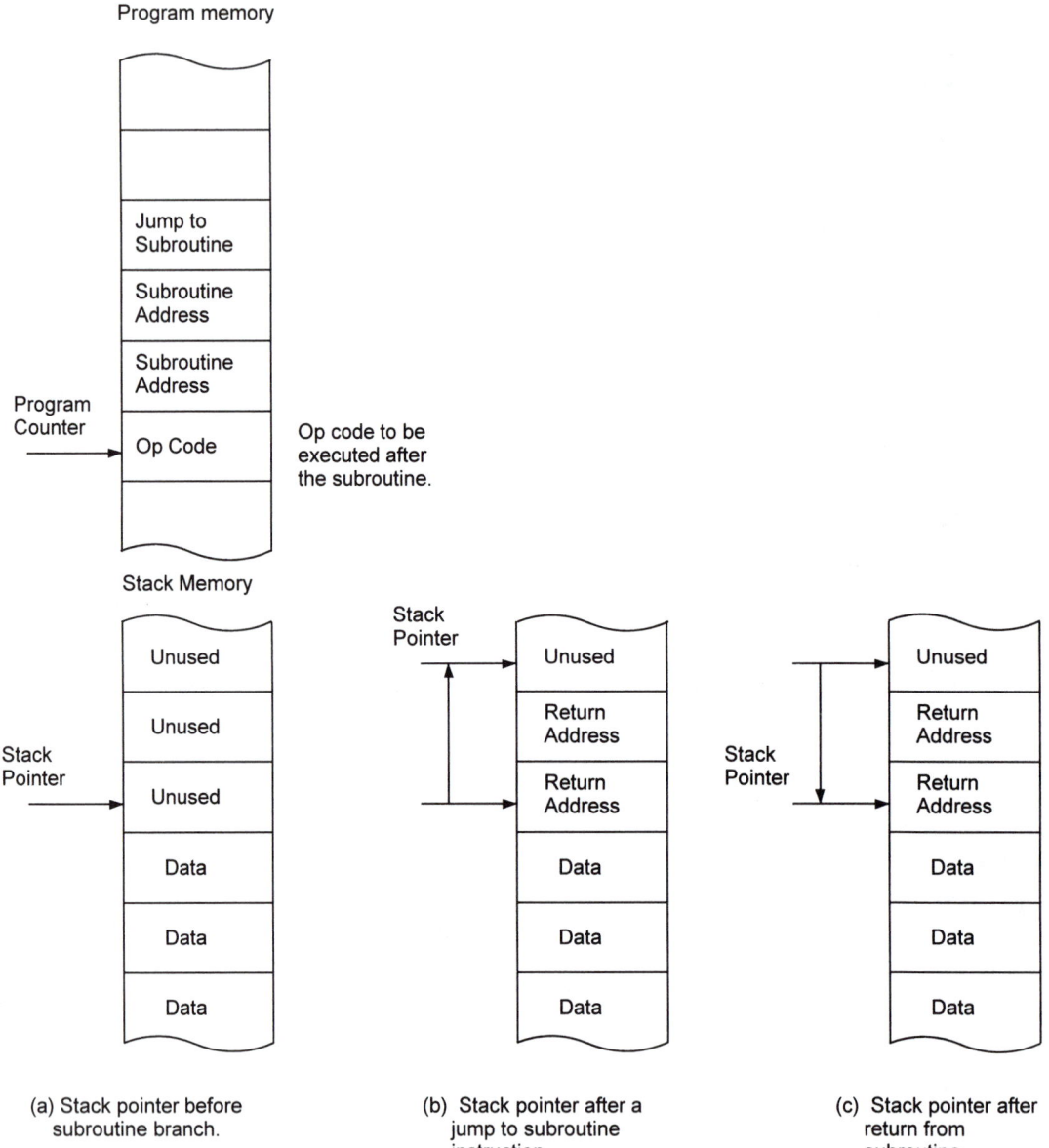

Figure 4-15   Stack operations during subroutine calls and returns.

- A direct addressing instruction contains the address of the data.

- Indirect addressing is a two-level addressing mode where the instruction specifies the address of the address of the data.

- In indexed addressing, the effective address is calculated by adding the contents of a register to a direct address contained in the instruction.

- In based addressing, the effective address is calculated by adding the contents of a register to an offset contained in the instruction.

- A relative addressing instruction contains an offset from the current value of the program counter. Relative addressing is used mostly for branch instructions.

- The stack is an area of RAM set aside for program use.

- The stack pointer register is used to store data and subroutine return addresses on the stack.

4.7 Your Own Processor's Addressing Modes

Turn now to your processor's material to study its specific addressing modes. You will find register, immediate, and direct addressing. Most likely indexed addressing and register indirect are offered also. If you are programming a processor such as the Intel 80xxx or Motorola 68xxx series, you will find that more complex addressing modes are available.

4.8 Problems

4.1   Name five ways to address an operand.

4.2   In the movable segment architecture described in Section 4.3, why is the segment located on a 16-byte boundary?

4.3   What kind of addressing mode is used to transfer data from one register to another?

4.4   What are the names of the addressing modes that form the effective address from a constant and the contents of a register?

4.5   What addressing mode is best to use to access several sequential elements in a data array—immediate, direct, indexed, or register?

4.6   What address mode is best to use when you want to compare what is in the A register with a constant—immediate, direct, extended, or indexed?

4.7   To increase the memory address space in a computer system, one must (a) increase the number of data lines; (b) increase the number of read and write control bits going to the memory; (c) increase the number of address lines.

4.8   A pointer is (a) an area in memory used for address storage; (b) a memory address held in a register; (c) a subroutine address held in the stack pointer.

4.9   A register indirect address instruction (a) has the address of the operand in the instruction; (b) has the address of the operand in a register; (c) uses the program counter to calculate the offset address of the operand.

4.10   Assume you are designing a CPU that is to have a 20-bit address bus with each memory location containing 16 bits. A base page is defined that has 1024 locations. Assume that memory indirect addressing using base page addresses is the ONLY kind of memory addressing this CPU has. How many bits in the instruction must be allocated for a memory reference instruction?

4.11   A colleague suggests adding a register to implement register indirect addressing in your CPU described in Problem 4.10. How many bits should the register have to be able to address the full range of addresses?

Chapter 5

Assembly Language Programming and Debugging

OBJECTIVES

This chapter describes how programs are assembled. Debugging tools are also discussed, and we will show you a selection of typical assembly language programming bugs. We conclude by listing a few of the tricks of the trade to help you write better programs.

5.1 Introduction

It is difficult for beginning assembly language programmers, particularly those with high-level language experience, to think at a low enough level. You must tell the computer, through the instructions in your program, *everything* that it must do. You must manage the resources—

> A good assembly language programmer must pay attention to many details.

the registers and the memory used for data storage—at every step of the way. You must keep track of the condition code register and know what instructions affect it before executing any conditional branches. This sounds tedious, if not difficult, and occasionally you will be frustrated with having to do everything in your program. However, the benefits of becoming a good assembly language programmer will pay off in the end. Learning assembly language programming will give you an appreciation of how the hardware works (including limitations) far better than programming in a high-level language. It will make you a better high-level language programmer, particularly for languages like C and C++. Finally, there are many applications that require assembly language programs for speed or optimal memory usage.

An assembly language program manipulates the resources given by the programmer's model. The model includes the registers and hardware resources in the CPU plus the memory used for data storage. At each instruction you must know what is in each register and all data areas. For example, an intermediate result may have been calculated that must be saved for later use. High-level language compilers, unless they are cleverly optimized, typically store intermediate results in memory, but it is faster and more efficient to keep an intermediate result in a register. The assembly language programmer, by keeping track of the registers, will know if one is available and can keep it available until needed at a later point. Thus the program can be faster and use less memory than one written in a high-level language. Knowing and keeping track of the resources given by the programmer's model is mandatory for assembly language programmers.

As you begin programming in assembly language, you will use the addressing modes learned in the preceding chapter. Your task is to look through the instructions in a category, find the correct mnemonic for the operation required, and then find the correct addressing mode. Often this requires preplanning, and some tricks of the trade to help plan your approach to assembly language programming are discussed in this chapter.

5.2 The Assembler

An *assembler program* converts a source file to the binary codes executed by the computer.

An assembler is a program that accepts the source code (as an input file) and produces the 1s and 0s that are to be placed into the memory of the computer. This is called the *machine code,* and there is a one-to-one correspondence between assembly language statements and the machine code in memory. Let us look at the source code format and how the assembler creates the machine code.

Assembly Source Code Fields

Each line in the source code has four fields—*label, operation (or op-code) mnemonic, operand,* and *comment* as shown in Table 5–1. The fields are separated by a white space (usually one or more tab characters, shown as ⟨tab⟩ so the fields line up), and there are specific rules for each field.

Label Field: The *label field* is optional but when used can provide a symbolic memory reference, such as a branch instruction address. A symbolic memory reference represents the address of the first byte in an instruction or data element. Labels are also used to define constants. Labels are merely symbols or identifiers and usually start with an alphabetic character but may contain digits and other characters. Most assemblers have a limit on the length of the label.

Labels supply symbolic memory references and constant definitions.

Operation Code Field: The *op_code* field contains either a *mnemonic* for the operation or an *assembler directive* or *pseudo-operation.* Operation mnemonics are assembled into code to be placed into the memory. Assembler directives or pseudo-operations are instructions to direct the assembler program how to do its job. Consider the following problem. Suppose you want to jump from one part of the program to another. You might pick the JMP (JuMP) mnemonic from the branch instruction category and supply a label for the jump address. The assembler source code would look like Table 5–2.

The assembler goes through the source file, reading a line at a time, and assembling each op_code and operand. When it reads the line with the JMP mnemonic, it generates the operation code and then must provide the address to which you want to jump. It reads the operand, the symbol TARGET, and when it finds the associated label, TARGET, it knows the address, at least relative

TABLE 5–1 Source code fields

Label field	Op_code field	Operand field	Comments field
EXAMPLE	mov	a,b	Restore A reg

TABLE 5-2 Branch instruction code example

Label field	Op_code field	Operand field
	ORG	$1000
	op_code	operand
	op_code	operand
	JMP	TARGET
	op_code	operand
	op_code	operand
	. . .	
TARGET	op_code	operand
	. . .	

to the location of the JMP op_code.[1] At this point, however, the *actual* address is unknown. We have to provide the assembler with information about where the code is going to be *located* in memory. One way to do this is with an *ORG* (for origination) directive, which specifies where the code is located.[2] The ORG is placed into the operation code field, *not* to generate code like an operation mnemonic, but to give the assembler information to do its job. Table 5–2 shows how to add the ORG directive to *locate* the code at memory address $1000. When the assembler encounters the ORG directive, it sets the value of an internal variable called the *current location counter* to the address given in the operand field. Each time a byte is assembled, the current location counter is incremented. Thus the assembler keeps track of all the bytes of code it generates, and when it encounters the label TARGET it can create the correct address for the operand TARGET.

> The *op code field* may have an operation mnemonic or an assembler directive.

Operand Field: The *operand field* contains information so the assembler can identify and produce the binary code for the operand. Operands can be the following:

1. Names of registers.

2. Numeric or symbolic constants.

3. Labels, as shown in Table 5–2.

4. Algebraic expressions that are evaluated by the assembler.

In some assemblers, the operand field specifies the addressing mode.

An *expression* is two or more operand symbols or constants combined by an arithmetic or logic operator. For example, if you wished to load the A register from memory location DATA1, a suitable instruction might be

    mov   a,DATA1

To get the data from the next location, the instruction

    mov   a,DATA1+1

---

[1] This is not *exactly* the process used by the assembler, but it is close enough for the current discussion. See Section 5.2 for a discussion of two-pass assemblers.

[2] Section 5.3 will discuss this code location problem and solutions in more detail.

TABLE 5–3 Assembler expressions

Expression	Assembler evaluation
COUNT+5	The assembler evaluates COUNT, probably from an *EQUATE*, and adds 5 to it.
BUFF_END-BUF_START	The assembler calculates the number of bytes between address BUF_START and BUF_END.
(END-START)*5	This evaluates as five times the number of bytes between START and END.
BYTE&0F	The result is the bitwise AND of the 8-bit value BYTE and 0F in hex.

would do the job. DATA1+1 is an expression that the assembler evaluates by adding 1 to the address represented by the label DATA1. Examples of other expressions are shown in Table 5–3.

> Include sufficient comments to be able to understand what the code is to do.

Comment Field: The *comment field* contains any other information you want to put into the program. The assembler ignores comments. In some assemblers, a special character, such as ";" or "*", denotes the start of the comment field. You may also have lines that are only comments or even blank lines. Use comments frequently to make the program more readable and understandable.

> *Assembler directives* instruct the assembler how to do its job.

Assembler Directives or Pseudo-Operations: The ORG directive to locate the code for the assembler was discussed in Section 5.2. There are other assembler directives used to define symbols, provide data in memory locations, reserve memory locations for data storage, define macros, and perform other assembler functions. We will discuss specific assembler directives in greater detail in the material dedicated to your laboratory processor.

Macro Assemblers

A macro assembler is one in which frequently used assembly instructions can be collected into a single statement. It makes the assembler more like a high-level language. For example, the problem might require the short code sequence

```
mov   a,c      ; Move contents of C into A

add   a,b      ; Add B to the A register

mov   c,a      ; Replace the contents of C with A+B
```

in many parts of your program. This code is too short to be written as a subroutine; so a macro is appropriate. Macros are often used for short segments of code, say, fewer than ten assembler statements. There are three stages of using a macro. The first is the *macro definition*, and a typical definition is shown in Table 5–4. The assembler directives DEF_MACRO and END_MACRO tell the assembler what code is to be substituted when the macro is invoked. The label Add_B_To_C

TABLE 5–4 Macro definition

```
Add_B_To_C      DEF_MACRO
                mov    a,c
                add    a,b
                mov    c,a
                END_MACRO
```

TABLE 5–5 Macro invocation

op_code	operand
op_code	operand
Add_B_To_C	
op_code	operand
op_code	operand

is used in the second stage—the *macro invocation*. It is written in the source program where the three lines of code would normally be placed. The third stage, *macro expansion*, occurs when the assembler encounters the macro name in the source code. The macro name is expanded into the full code that was defined in the definition stage. See Tables 5–5 and 5–6.

Macros and subroutines have similar properties.

- Both allow the programmer to reuse segments of code. However, each time a macro is invoked, the assembler expands the macro and the code appears "in line." A subroutine code is included only once. Thus macro expansions make the program larger.

- The subroutine requires a call or jump-to-subroutine and the macro does not. This means that the subroutine is a little slower to execute than the macro.

- Both macros and subroutines make the program easier to read and allow changes to be made in one place (the macro definition or the subroutine).

- Macros and subroutines also make the program easier to read by hiding details of the program. Usually, when reading a program, you do not need the details of how it is doing something, just an indication of what it is doing.

Two-Pass Assemblers

Most assemblers allow symbols to be used before they are defined. This is called a *forward reference*. Table 5–2 shows an example where the operand TARGET is not defined until later in the program. The assembler evaluates these symbols by making two passes through the source code. On the first pass, any symbol definitions it finds are recorded in a *symbol table*. This table contains values defined for symbols using the EQU (equate) directive and the memory locations for labels such as TARGET. On the second pass the assembler uses the symbol table to substitute the values for the symbols.

> A *two-pass assembler* allows symbols to be used before they are defined.

TABLE 5–6 Macro expansion

op_code	operand	
op_code	operand	
Add_B_To_C		
	mov a,c	(The assembler inserts
	add a,b	this code for the macro)
	mov c,a	
op_code	operand	
op_code	operand	

Cross Assemblers and Native Assemblers

Often, especially for microcontroller applications, a different computer, such as a personal computer, is used to edit and assemble the programs. This type of assembler is called a *cross assembler*. A *native assembler* is one that runs on the target processor.

Assembler Output Files

The assembler reads a source file and generates a file with the machine code that is to go into the memory of the computer. Depending on the type of assembler, this file may be the executable file or it may be an object file that must be processed further to create the executable file. Other files, such as the assembler listing, the symbol table, and a cross-reference listing, are useful for debugging and may be produced.

> The assembler list files are very useful in the program debugging stages.

The assembler listing contains your complete source code plus the assembled code. Use this listing instead of the source file listing when debugging the program. The symbol table shows how, and where, all symbols are defined. The cross reference lists all symbols and labels alphabetically and shows where they are referred to in the program.

5.3 The Code Location Problem

We have discussed how the ORG directive specifies (for the assembler) where the code is to be located in the memory of the computer. The ORG directive can also specify where data elements are located. In many systems, especially dedicated application microcontrollers, code, or the program, is in a different kind of memory than data. These different memory types will be discussed in more detail in Chapter 9, but for our discussion here it is necessary to know that there are two types, *RAM* and *ROM*. RAM, or *random-access memory*, can be both read from and written to. RAM, at least the semiconductor memory used in microcomputers, is also volatile. That is, when the power is turned off, the contents of RAM memory are lost. ROM, or *read-only memory*, is nonvolatile; removing the power does not destroy the contents of ROM. Any microcomputer system has both kinds of memory, and a typical memory map is shown in Figure 5–1. There may be addresses that are used for I/O instead of memory and some that are not used at all.

> In a dedicated application system, code is located in ROM and data in RAM.

The code location question is tied to the hardware's memory map. Various parts of the program must be allocated to the two different kinds of memory. Table 5–7 shows how to locate different parts of the program in a dedicated, ROM-based system where the program must exist in the computer after the power has been turned off and then on. Let us now consider two types of assemblers and how the code and data are located using each.

Absolute Assemblers

Table 5.2 is an example of source code that would be assembled with an *absolute assembler*. When writing programs, we must know where the code is to be located in memory. This information

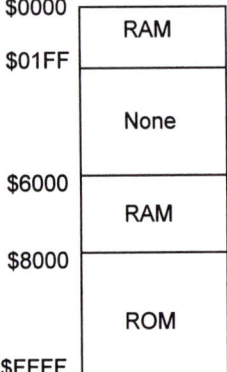

$0000
$01FF — RAM

None

$6000 — RAM

$8000

ROM

$FFFF

Figure 5-1 Memory map with both RAM and ROM.

is given to the assembler by the ORG directive. All code is located, *absolutely*, from this information.

This is the simplest form of assembler. It takes the source code file and produces an executable file that is either loaded and run on the computer that assembles it or is transferred (called *downloading*) to the target system. Figure 5–2 shows this process. A major disadvantage of the absolute assembler is that the source file must contain *all* the source code to be in the program. This means that when large programs are being written, all code must be assembled whenever any change is made. In addition, assembler listings, which are important for debugging, are soon out of date.

Downloading transfers an executable file from the computer that created it to the computer that executes it.

Relocatable Assemblers

The disadvantages of the absolute assembler are overcome by using a relocatable assembler. As shown in Figure 5–3, the assembler accepts a program, or a program segment, as a source file. The source file does not need to be the complete program, nor does it need to contain location information or ORG statements. The assembler produces an output file, called the *object* file, which contains the binary codes for the operations and as many operands as the assembler can evaluate. When an operand, such as a branch address, cannot be evaluated, the assembler adds this fact (that an address needs to be resolved) to the object file so a *linker* program can provide the final addresses. Notice that the program can be split into multiple source files and assembled at different times. Separately assembled object files are put together by the linker, and any addresses or operands that the assembler was not able to create are generated at this time. The programmer must supply the linker program with location information as shown in Figure 5–4.

Relocatable assemblers produce object files that are combined together with a *linker* program.

TABLE 5-7 RAM and ROM memory used in a microcontroller application

Memory type	Program use
ROM	1. All program code.
	2. Constants such as messages and lookup table data.
	3. Any other information that does not change.
RAM	1. Program variables and data.
	2. Stack data storage.

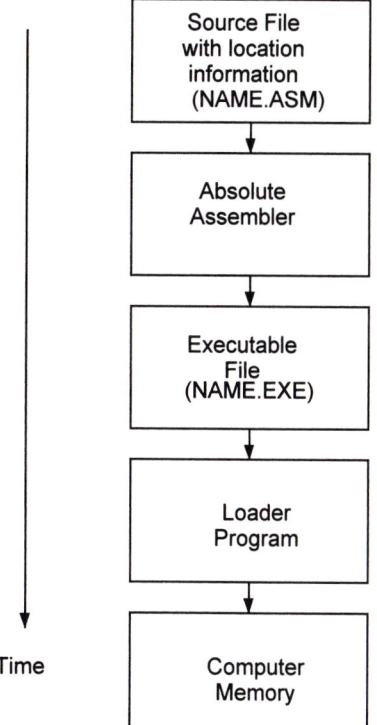

Figure 5-2   Absolute assembler operation.

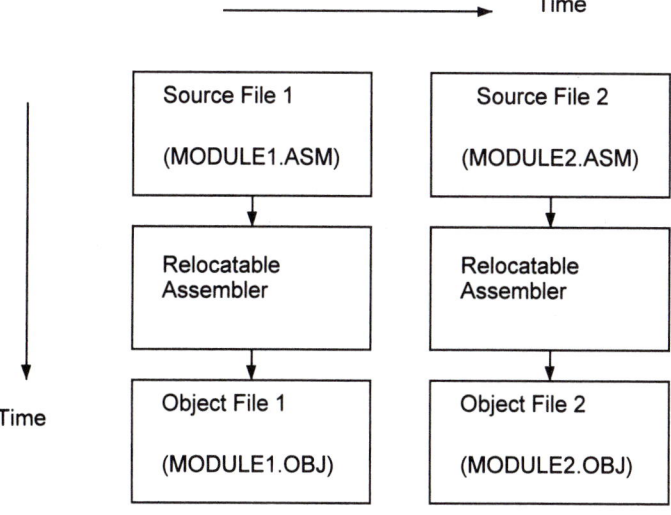

Figure 5-3   Relocatable assembler.

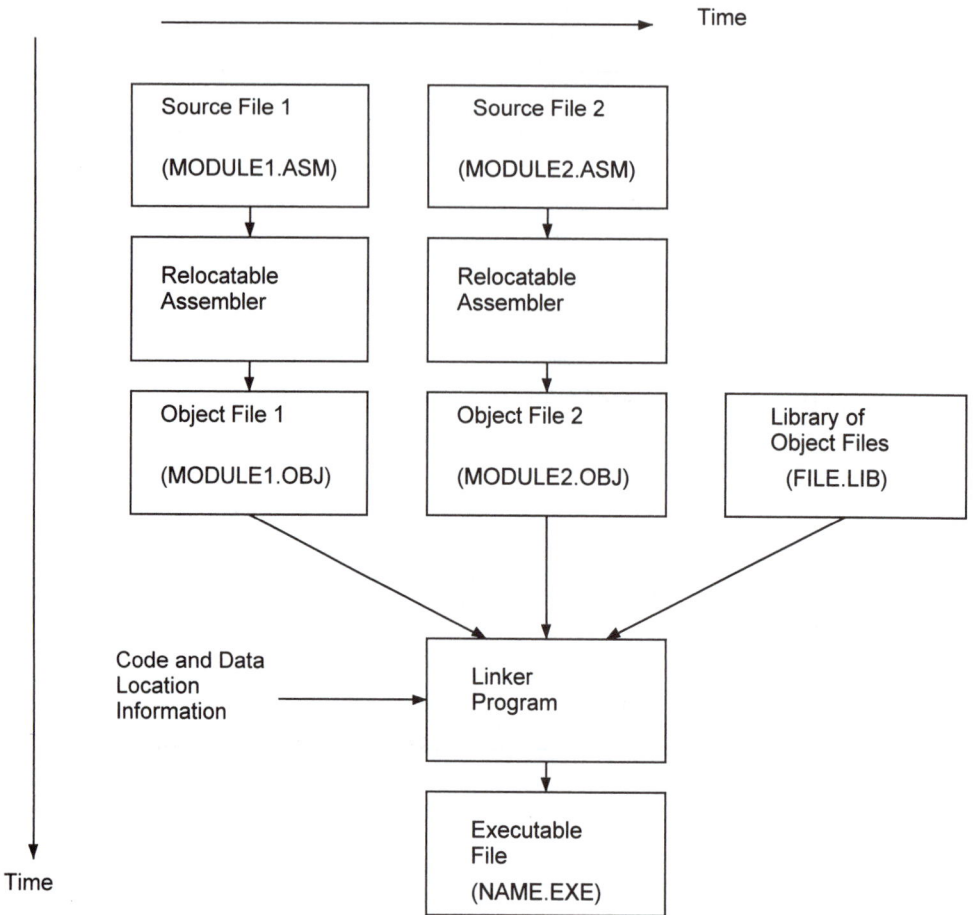

Figure 5-4   Linker/locater program.

5.4 The Linker

A *linker* program takes modules that have been assembled by a relocatable assembler, *links* them together, and *locates* all addresses. This is shown in Figure 5–4, where two source files, MODULE1.ASM and MODULE2.ASM, are separately assembled by a relocatable assembler. The object files are combined by the linker to produce the executable file. You can see in Figure 5–4 the location information for the code and data parts of the program may be given to the linker. This is an option at this stage because some systems may locate the program when it is loaded into the memory to be executed. Figure 5–4 also shows that object files can be linked from a library. Although the program is usually called a linker, it can also provide the locating function.[3]

> A *linker* puts assembled modules together.

---

[3]   In some computers, such as IBM PCs and compatibles, the programs are totally relocatable. That means they can be located anywhere in the memory of the computer. This is a consequence of the segmented memory architecture of the Intel CPU used in the PCs and compatibles. The locating function is done by the disk operating system (DOS) when the program is loaded into memory and executed.

5.5 The Librarian

As shown in Figure 5–4, the linker program may also receive object files from a library. *Libraries* are collections of object files that have been preassembled and bound together by a *librarian* program. The operation of the librarian program is shown in Figure 5–5. Separately assembled source files are packaged by the librarian in a library file to be used by a linker. The linker will pull from the library only those object files needed by the program.

5.6 The Loader

A loader program puts an executable file into the memory of the computer. The loader program can take many forms, including (1) the operating system as in MS-DOS programs, (2) a

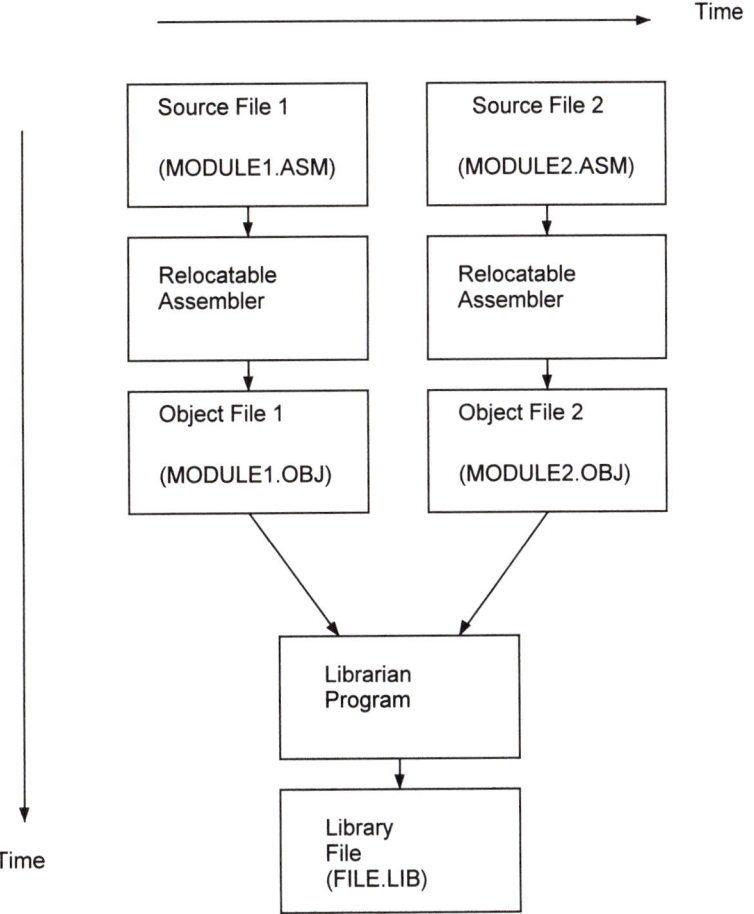

Figure 5–5 Librarian program.

modem/downloader program that takes files created on one computer and puts them into the memory of another, or (3) a system that burns a programmable read-only memory.

5.7 Assembly Time, Link Time, Load Time, and Run Time

The points at which data may be initialized and manipulated are important in assembly language programming. *Assembly time* refers to data values that are known at the time the program is assembled. These include constants such as loop counters and ASCII character codes. Operand expressions, as discussed in Section 5.2, are evaluated at assembly time. Certain addresses can be evaluated at this time, too, including absolute addresses in an absolute assembler and relative addresses in both absolute and relocatable assemblers. The assembler may not be able to evaluate all addresses at assembly time, particularly in relocatable assemblers. These are left for link time.

> Constant data may be initialized at *assembly time.*

The linking and loading processes that occur at *link time* are described in Sections 5.4 and 5.6. When the relocatable assembler cannot evaluate addresses or other constants, it places information to this effect in the object file. The addresses are then evaluated at link time during linking or loading.

Load time is when the executable file, produced by the linker at link time (or if it is an absolute assembler, at assembly time), is loaded into the memory of the computer. It is possible to initialize variables in RAM memory at load time by using assembler directives. This is not a good programming practice because if the power is turned off and then back on again, the data initialization is lost. Variables should be initialized at run time.

> Variable data elements are initialized at *run-time.*

Run time refers to the time during which the program is running. Usually data elements are initialized and manipulated, but addresses also can be calculated and manipulated at run time.

5.8 Your Assembler

It is now time to learn the specific details of how your assembler and associated software works. After you have had some practice with your assembler and have written some programs, you will want to return to the next sections to learn about program debugging.

5.9 The Debugger

By now you will have experienced writing and running simple assembly language programs on your laboratory equipment. You have also probably experienced the programmer's nightmare. Your program doesn't work. Sometimes it doesn't even appear to run. It's time for some program debugging.

Program Debugging

Program debugging is like solving a mystery. We start the program, fully expecting it to work perfectly, and it doesn't. Often, when beginning students are asked "What is your program doing?", they respond with "Nothing!" The computer *can't* be doing nothing. It has to be fetching op codes, executing them, incrementing the program counter, and fetching the next op code. Remember that *you* are responsible for the op codes the computer is executing. You must do some detective work to find the difference between what you expect the program to be doing and what it is actually doing. Debugging is the process of finding the clues and interpreting them to find the problem.

There are two approaches to fixing bugs in programs.[4] The first is a *synthesis* approach in which you try to fix the problem by changing the code somewhere. *This is wrong!* You must first find out what the program is doing before it can be fixed. This is the second approach—*analysis* of the problem. You first find out *what* it is doing, then *why* it is doing that, and then you will probably have enough clues to be able to *fix* it.

Programs have only two parts—the data and the logic. Data values are input to, stored and manipulated by, and output from the program. The logic determines the sequence in which program steps are executed and how the data are manipulated. Most program bugs are in the logic. We mean for the computer to do one thing, and we program it to do another. Normally the program's flow is affected by the data, and this helps us find the debugging clues. When using the analytical debugging technique, we try to match what we think the program should do for a particular input data set with what the program is doing.

> Programs that are not working properly should be *analyzed* to find out what they are doing before trying to fix them.

Figure 5–6 shows the idea of analytical debugging. An input data set is chosen. We predict what the program will do with these data at each step of the program and what the program will do next. This is a model of what the program should do. Now run the program and, using the tools described below, look for data values and program steps that differ from the model. Once we find out where the program deviates from the model, we are well on our way to finding out why it is going wrong and what will be needed to fix it.

Debugging Tools

All debugging programs offer a variety of tools. The features in a debugger depend on the computer on which the debugging program is run. Today, personal computer-based debuggers, particularly for the high-level languages, have many features. Debuggers that run on simple development boards, such as the Intel and Motorola single-board computers, are more limited in the features they offer. These debuggers are called *monitor* programs and contain rudimentary debugging tools and basic I/O functions.

Debugging Program Flow or Logic

> *Tracing* and *setting* *breakpoints* allow us to follow the program flow.

The first debugging task is to find out *where* the program is going wrong. You must follow the program flow until a deviation from the expected flow or expected output data is found. There are two ways to follow the program flow.

Program Trace: Tracing is stepping through the program a statement at a time. In the more powerful, high-level language debuggers, data elements may be displayed while tracing the code. In

---

[4]   The first program "bug" was found on September 9, 1945, by Grace Murray Hopper, when she found a moth between two contacts of a relay used in a computer logic circuit.

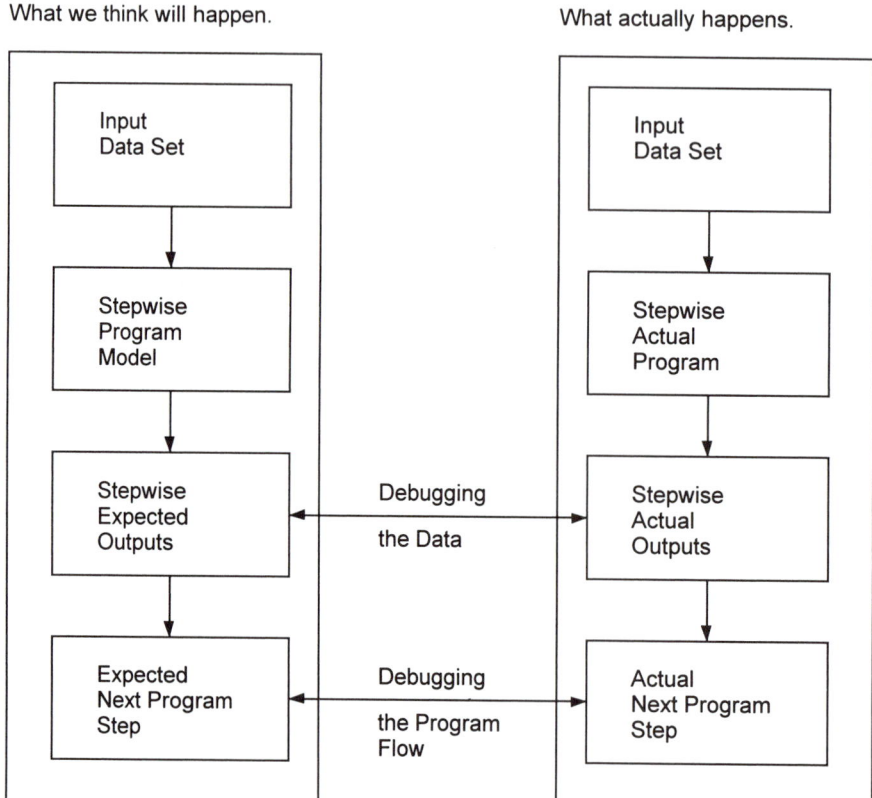

Figure 5-6 Analytical debugging model.

less powerful, assembly language debuggers, the register set is shown at each step but data elements in memory must be inspected manually.

Breakpoints: The program trace is a slow way to get through a program. A quicker way to find out where problems are occurring is to run the program at full speed to a breakpoint. A breakpoint is a set of conditions that cause the program flow to be interrupted and control to be returned to the debugging program. Normally breakpoints are set at program statements, but they also may be generated by a combination of other conditions. For example, in some debuggers, breakpoints can be generated when a particular data element becomes some specific value. In some systems, hardware breakpoint generators may be installed to create breakpoints when a condition or a set of bits on the computer's bus is detected.

Debugging Data Elements

As you are following the flow of the program, observe the data elements, both in the registers and in the memory.

Registers: The state of the registers at each step of an assembly language program must be known. Assembly language debuggers usually display the contents of all the registers, including the condition code register, in a register window. A hexadecimal display will usually have to be interpreted. While tracing the program, watch the contents of the registers change and watch for values that are different from those expected.

Memory: In high-level language debuggers, one can generally inspect any of the declared variables. Usually the display is formatted according to the type of declaration that has been made. In assembly language debugging monitors, the display of data elements is more crude, usually only in hexadecimal.

The Source Code Listing

An up-to-date listing of the program is necessary. The listing should be the assembler list file, not the source file. The list file shows the code the assembler has produced, and errors can frequently be spotted by using this listing instead of the source program.

The Debugging Plan

A debugging plan will help isolate where the problem is occurring and find out what is going wrong. Well-designed programs (program design will be covered in Chapter 6) consist of separate, independent sections of code written to do a particular function. For example, a program may simply input data, process it, and output it as shown by the flow chart in Figure 5–7. How do you know if the program is performing correctly? You must choose a test data set for which you know the correct output. Using these data, you can look for the problem. Let's assume that a problem exists in the program somewhere. Your first step is simply to analyze the program output. This can sometimes give clues about where the program is going wrong. If not, plan to set breakpoints after each section and inspect the data to see where it deviates from what is expected. In this way, the problem area is isolated. You can now move your debugging strategy into the offending block of code and continue the process.

Figure 5–7   A typical program flow chart.

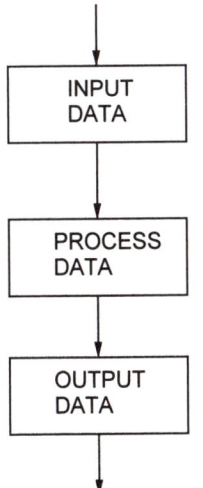

5.10 Typical Assembly Language Program Bugs

As you start your beginning programming assignments, you will commit many follies. Here are some common problems.

Improper transfer to subroutines: The return address from a subroutine must be on the stack. Use a branch-to-subroutine, jump-to- subroutine, or a call instruction. Never use a branch or jump that does not put the return address on the stack.

Forgetting to initialize the stack pointer: The stack pointer should be initialized pointing to an area of RAM. Do this in the very first few lines of code in an assembly language program. It *must* be done before calling any subroutine or using the stack for data storage.

Not allocating enough memory for the stack: A program grows from the bottom of memory to the top, while the stack grows from the top of memory to the bottom, as illustrated in Figure 5–8. If the stack and program overlap in a RAM-based system, stack operations will write data into the program area with unknown, and usually dire, consequences. In a system where the program is in ROM, there must still be enough RAM to hold the stack and all variable data.

Unbalanced stack operations: Make sure that there is the same number of pulls or pops as pushes. This is particularly true in subroutines where registers are temporarily saved on the stack. If the program does not return from a subroutine, it is likely there are unbalanced stack operations. Set a breakpoint at the beginning and the end of the subroutine and check the stack pointer at each place. Look for errors such as unbalanced stack operations when using a stack inside a program loop.

Using subroutines that wipe out registers: Well-designed subroutines should not modify registers that may be in use in the calling program. Push all registers used in the subroutine onto the stack when entering the subroutine and pull or pop them before returning to the calling program.

Transposed registers: A difficult problem to find is one in which the operands for an instruction have been transposed. For example, if data are to be moved from the B to the A register, the proper instruction is, say, MOV A,B. It is very easy to transpose the register operands and write MOV B,A. To find this error, trace the program, watch the registers, and compare them with what is expected.

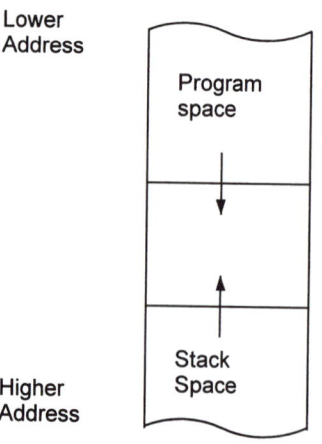

Lower Address

Program space

Stack Space

Higher Address

Figure 5–8   Program and stack segments grow toward each other.

Not initializing pointer registers: Register indirect and indexed addressing modes must have the register initialized with the address of the data.

Not initializing registers and data areas: Initialize registers and data areas before using them because the contents of registers and RAM memory are unknown when the computer's power is turned on. Do this at run time, not assembly time or load time.

Modifying condition code contents before conditional branch instructions: Be aware of all instructions that modify the contents of the condition code register. Make sure there are no instructions that change the condition code register between the time it is set and the time the conditional branch is executed.

Using the wrong conditional branch instruction: There are different instructions for signed and unsigned numbers. Conditional branches with the words "greater" or "less" are used for signed numbers and those with the words "higher" or "lower" for unsigned numbers.

Using the wrong memory addressing mode: Do not confuse immediate addressing with direct memory addressing. This is particularly easy to do in instruction sets where the addressing mode is specified by the operand. Remember that immediate addressing retrieves constant data from the memory immediately following the operation code. Direct memory addressing retrieves data, which may be constant or variable, from some other memory location.

Using a 16-bit counter in memory: Counters are used for many things in assembly language programming. The fastest and easiest-to-use counter is one that is kept in a CPU register; however, when one runs out of registers, counters must be kept in memory. A typical error occurs when changing a 16-bit memory counter with an 8-bit memory increment or decrement instruction. Instead of changing the full 16 bits, only 8 bits are changed. Load the 16-bit counter into a register, increment or decrement it, and store it back into memory. Make sure the store operation does not change the flags if a conditional branch based on the increment or decrement is to be done.

Not stopping the program properly: Depending on the type of program, you may be required to return to the debugging monitor or operating system. Use the proper instruction to exit the program.

5.11 Tricks of the Trade

Here are some tricks of the assembly language programming trade. Refer also to the supplemental material for more information and specific examples related to your processor.

Use register addressing when possible: Instructions that use internal registers execute faster and use less memory.

Use register indirect or indexed addressing: These modes are the next most efficient after register addressing. The address may be calculated at run time, allowing the location of the data to be a variable depending on the current state of the program. Often data must be stored in or retrieved from a buffer. An indirect addressing mode, such as register indirect or indexed addressing, is most efficient for this, especially if the register can be automatically incremented or decremented. Remember to load the register with the address before using it.

Use the stack for temporary data storage: When using the stack in subroutines, remember to pull or pop the registers before returning to the calling program.

Do not use magic numbers: Magic numbers are numbers that appear in your code. For example, if a counter is to be initialized, you might write the statement

```
        mov   b,54                Initialize loop counter
```

The 54 is a "magic" number. It is far better to define the number using an EQU directive, such as

```
    COUNT   EQU   54          Loop counter

            . . .

        mov   b,COUNT   Initialize loop counter
```

This makes the code more readable, and if the initialization code appears in several places in the program, and if it ever needs to be changed, the change is made only at the EQU statement.

Do not use the assembler to initialize variable data areas: Assemblers have directives or pseudo-operations to initialize the contents of memory locations. This works well in systems where the program is downloaded each time it is run. However, in a dedicated microcontroller application where the program resides in ROM, all data areas must be initialized at run time by the program. Use directives that merely allocate memory storage locations and then initialize them in the program.

Use assembler features and pseudo-operations: Study and use the assembler directives and pseudo-operations. It is mandatory to use labels for symbolic addresses. Never refer to a memory location by a direct address. Using the assembler to evaluate expressions can make programs more readable and more easily transferred to other applications. If a macro-assembler is available, use macros to make programs more readable.

Use but don't abuse comments: Make your comments mean something. The assembly statement and comment

```
        mov   b,c   Move c register into b register
```

is not an effective comment. Comments should relate to the problem solution. A better comment might be

```
        mov   b,c   Restore loop counter
```

A good commenting style uses a block of comments explaining what the following section of code is to do. Within the code block, comments can be placed on individual lines where it seems necessary. Table 5–8 gives an example.

TABLE 5–8 An effective commenting style

```
*   Comment block to describe what the
*   block of code to follow actually does.
        op_code     operand
        op_code     operand
        op_code     operand     Relevant comment
        op_code     operand
*   Next comment block for the next section of
*   code.
```

5.12 Chapter Summary Points

- An assembler creates the binary words to be loaded into the computer's memory from a source program.

- The source file has four fields—label, operation, operand, and comments.

- Assembler directives instruct the assembler how to do its job.

- Often, particularly for dedicated application systems, the code and the data must be located at their proper places in the memory map.

- Two kinds of assemblers are absolute and relocatable assemblers.

- Relocatable assemblers require a linker program to produce the executable program.

- Constant data values may be initialized at assembly time.

- Variable data elements must be initialized at run time.

- Debugging procedures should be analytical. You should find out what the program is doing before trying to fix it.

- Debuggers are programs that allow you to test the program flow and inspect data elements to find out what is going wrong.

5.13 Problems

5.1   Discuss the advantages of using a relocatable assembler versus an absolute assembler.

5.2   List the fields in an assembly language program source file.

5.3   Describe the operation of a two-pass assembler.

5.4   Discuss code location as it pertains to dedicated application systems.

5.5   What is a macro-assembler?

5.6   What is a cross-assembler?

5.7   What is a native assembler?

5.8   What function does a linker program provide?

5.9   Define what is meant by assembly time, link time, load time, and run time.

5.10 Describe the analytical debugging approach and compare it with the synthesis approach.

5.11 What is a breakpoint?

5.12 What is a trace?

5.13 What is the difference between a trace and a breakpoint?

5.14 The key to effective debugging is to: (a) Find an instruction to change to see if it fixes the problem; (b) Check the stack to find out what subroutines are being executed; (c)Find out what the program is actually doing; (d) Get the TA to look at the program.

5.15 Why must the stack pointer be initialized as one of the first things done in a program?

5.16 What instruction must never be used to transfer control to a subroutine? Why?

Chapter 6

Top-Down Software Design

OBJECTIVES

In this chapter we present a design procedure, called top-down design, suitable for both hardware and software projects. You will learn to use tools to design programs following the top-down design procedure and the principles of structured programming. We will show how to design effective software modules and show what is required to document your software projects.

6.1 The Need for Software Design

In the design and development of many systems, the cost of producing software is higher, often much higher, than the cost of the hardware. Frederick Brooks, in *The Mythical Man-Month,*[1] compares large-system programming that doesn't use good design techniques with the tar pits that swallowed sabertoothed tigers, dinosaurs, and mammoths. Few of these systems meet their goals in terms of schedules and costs. Designing the software before writing the code is vital to control costs and to meet requirements and schedules.

Software design means *designing* the software *before* writing the code. When beginning your studies of any processor, or any programming language, designing before writing is difficult. You are wrapped up in just learning the details of the processor and its instruction set or the syntax of the programming language. Trying to learn how to design programs simultaneously is foolish. Thus your first programs should be for simple problems that don't require much design. This is a good strategy for learning about the processor and language. Soon, however, the problems get more complicated, and, with your new-found mastery of the language, your efforts are spent in designing the solution to the problem instead of just programming the solution.

In this chapter we assume you have been learning the instruction set of a microprocessor and the operation of the assembler or high-level language compiler. Although there is more to learn, it

---

[1] Brooks, F.P. Jr., *The Mythical Man-Month,* Addison-Wesley, Reading, MA, 1982.

is time to start designing software properly instead of just writing it. We will look at various philosophies and at tools used to design software.

6.2 The Software Tree

The software we write becomes the 1s and 0s in the computer memory—codes for the instructions we wish the computer to execute. These binary words are like the leaves of the tree in Figure 6–1. We wouldn't want to have to remember the binary codes for all the computer's instructions, although early computer programmers did. Fortunately a programming tool, called an assembler, was developed to allow the programmer to write code in an "assembly language." As we know, this language uses mnemonics for the computer operations and various codes for the operands. The assembly language makes us more efficient because we only have to remember the mnemonics for the operations and how to encode the operands. Thus the assembly language appears as the branches in the software tree.

The trunks in the software forest are the high-level languages we use whenever possible. When we write in a high-level language, such as C, BASIC, or Pascal, we are efficiently producing the machine code that resides in the computer's memory. Each line of code in the high-level language is "compiled" (or converted) to several lines of assembly language code that is assembled into the machine code necessary to run the computer. In Table 6–1, one line of C code is compiled into four lines of assembly language code (and three bytes for variable data storage), which results in 10 memory locations for the machine code.

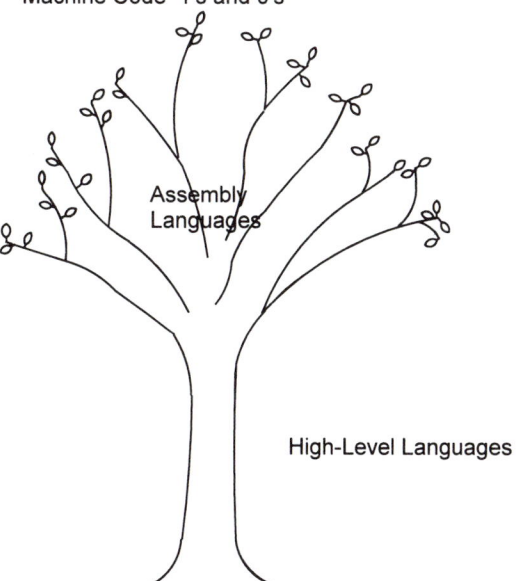

Figure 6–1 The software tree.

TABLE 6-1 C language–assembly language example

0001		*	Begin		
0002		*	i = a + b		
0003					
0004			* MC68HC11 Assembly code to do		
0005			* the C statement		
0006			* Create storage locations for		
			* i, a, and b		
0007 0000 00		i	RMB	1	Variable i
0008 0001 00		a	RMB	1	Variable a
0009 0002 00		b	RMB	1	Variable b
0010					
0011 0003 96 01			ldaa	a	Get variable a
0012 0005 d6 02			ldab	b	Get variable b
0013 0007 1b			aba		Add a to b
0014 0008 97 00			staa	i	Store in i

6.3 The Software Development Process

There are several steps to take when developing fully designed, coded, debugged, and documented software for any real system. These are (1) design, (2) coding of modules, (3) testing and debugging of modules, (4) system testing and verification, and (5) documentation.

Design: The design for any complex system might well take 50% or more of the total effort required for a project. In the sections below we will distinguish between design methodologies and design tools. A design methodology is a philosophy of how we do design. Design tools are the mechanics used to do the design. The goal of the design phase is to understand the problem completely and to propose a solution broken down into modules or functional elements that can be coded, tested, and documented.

> All software development starts with a *design* phase.

Coding: Coding means writing the program in the chosen programming language. We would hope to use a high-level language for most of the code, but often, especially in time-critical applications, assembly language must be used.

Module testing: If the design is done properly, we will have coded modules that can be tested and proven to work correctly. The testing and debugging tools used depend on how we have done the coding. Fortunately many high-level languages have very powerful debuggers that allow us to test and debug our software.

System testing: This step follows subsystem or module testing and is necessary to prove that the software works as a whole.

Documentation: Although mentioned last in the list of steps, *each step of software development is accompanied by documentation.* The design documentation specifies what the system is to do and how it is implemented; typically this work will form the basis of user manuals. Documentation effort is never wasted. Documentation begins in the design step, and various types of design documentation are discussed in later sections of this chapter. The documentation produced in the coding phase is the code itself. Code testing phases are documented with test plans and results. These become templates to show that the system meets the specifications and allow future modifications of the software to be tested to the same standard. Documentation efforts also include the installation and user manuals.

> *Documentation* is so important that it accompanies each step in the process.

6.4 Top-Down Design

A design methodology is a stepwise procedure for doing the design. We contrast this with design tools, which are the mechanical things we use (for example, pseudocode or flow charts) to produce the design. The top-down design (TDD) method is the design procedure of choice. If we follow the steps given below, we can almost assure ourselves that we will have a good design in the end.

Understand the Problem Completely

> Understand what is required of the system before starting to program.

This is the first principle of TDD. Unfortunately many programmers violate this right away because it is so much fun to program that they start before the problem is fully understood. For example, consider designing the hardware and software for a programmable read only memory (PROM) programmer. Questions that should be asked (and answered) before proceeding with the design might include the following:

"What kinds of PROMs are to be programmed?"
"Where do the data come from and what format are they in?"
"What user interaction must there be?"
"What programming algorithms are to be used?"

Understanding the problem means we must specify exactly what the software is required to do. It is not necessary to understand (at least in the initial stages of the design) how elements of the proposed solution work in detail. For example, when designing the PROM programmer, we do not need to know what format statement in the language produces the required output. We just have to know what the required output is.

A student recently suggested that this part of the design process be called "outside-in design" to emphasize that the specifications for the software often come from an outside customer. The specifications must be written so that both the end user and the engineer of the system know exactly what the system is to be.

A document that is produced during this phase of the design is called a *requirements specification*.

> The *requirements specifications* tell exactly what the program is supposed to do.

This bit of jargon simply means that you specify (write down) what the system is required to do. We are not specifying *how* something is to be done, just *what* is to be done.

The design process should consider potential error conditions and allow for them in the rest of the design. Often when customers supply specifications, they fail to consider all error conditions. You should make it your responsibility to think about errors and error handling requirements.

A statement that summarizes this first principle of top-down design is: "Think first, program later."

Design in Levels

After specifying the requirements, it is time to start designing a system to meet them. This is the "how" part of the design process. It is natural to feel overwhelmed by the complexity of the prob-

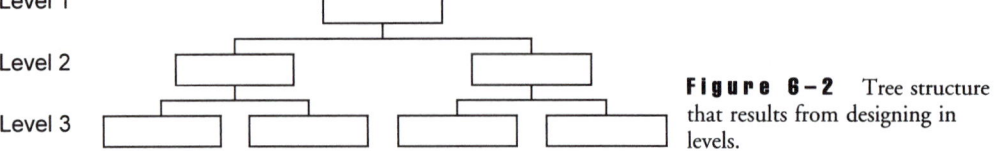

Level 1

Level 2

Level 3

Figure 6–2   Tree structure that results from designing in levels.

lem. Often one can't see a way to the end. Don't worry. The design procedures will help us through to the end.

Designing in levels means that we recognize that the whole solution to the problem cannot be seen at once. We start at an upper level and propose a solution to the problem. As we learn more about the problem and how to solve it, more detailed levels can be added to the design. When designing in levels, a tree structure as shown in Figure 6–2 is developed representing the design. The upper levels of the tree are more general statements of the problem solution, and, as one progresses down the tree, more detailed information is shown.

> Upper levels of the design are more general; lower levels are more detailed.

Let's look at an example. Consider designing the software for a PROM programmer. The requirements are:

Program Intel 27C256 PROMs.
Allow the user to input data and make corrections.
Program the PROM.
Check to see that it is programmed correctly.

We won't complete this design to the final level of details needed in a real-world project. Our goal is to show how to start a top-down design. The first two levels of the design are shown in Figure 6–3.

The top level is a simple statement of the problem, with the next level providing some details of how that top block is to be done. This level starts to focus our thoughts as we consider what should be done to program the 27C256. The design may not be correct or complete at this stage, but it is at least a start, and starting is often the hardest part of any project. Notice that the blocks in level two are algorithmic. That is, if we read them from left to right, they describe a sequence of things to be done to program the PROM.

Ensure Correctness at Each Level

The design started in Figure 6–3 isn't necessarily correct or complete after our first pass. Before going on to lower levels, we should make sure the algorithm is correct at this level. In going back

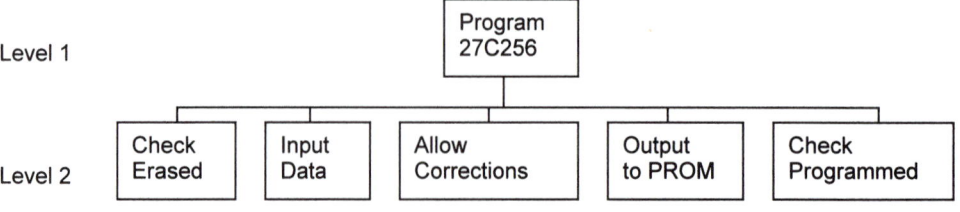

Level 1

Program 27C256

Level 2

Check Erased | Input Data | Allow Corrections | Output to PROM | Check Programmed

Figure 6–3   Two-level tree structure.

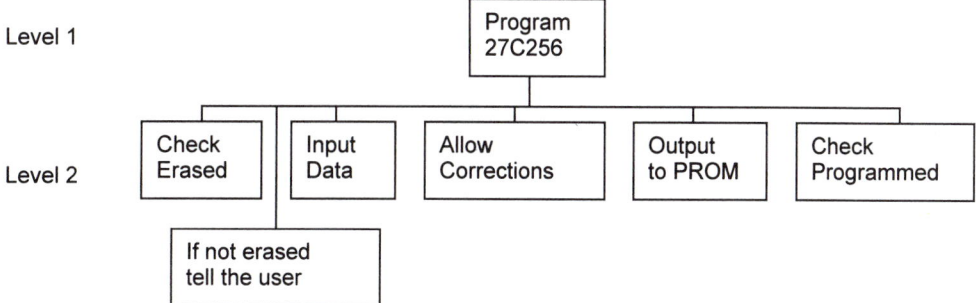

Figure 6-4 A more correct design for level two.

over the design, try to think if there is anything else that should be done. For example, something should be done if the PROM isn't erased. It is easy at this stage to add another block to the design as shown in Figure 6–4.

Postpone Details

There will be unknown and unresolved details at all upper levels of the design. Postpone thinking about the details until you reach the lower levels later in the design process. For example, when working at level two of the PROM programmer, we don't need to know the details of how to check if the PROM is erased. Nor do we need to know the details of the programming algorithm necessary to program the PROM. Thinking about and designing for these details can be postponed until later. It is only necessary at level two to know that the PROM will be checked to see if it is erased, not how that will be done.

Successively Refine Your Design

As we progress through the lower levels, we learn more about the details of what is required. Inevitably, as these lower-level details become apparent, we think of something that could be done at an upper level to make the lower-level design easier. That is OK. We have not invested any time in programming; so it is easy to change the design. Go back to the upper level, change it, make sure it is now correct at that level, and continue to work at the lower levels.

Design Without Using a Programming Language

The initial design should propose solutions to the problems that are independent of any programming language. It should make no difference to the design how the machine code in the memory of the computer is generated. We are now beginning to talk about design tools—the tools and techniques used to write down the design. One widely used design tool is pseudocode. This is a programminglike language used for design. For example, a pseudocode statement of the PROM programmer design at level two is shown in Table 6–2.

TABLE 6-2 Pseudocode design
Check if the PROM is erased
IF the PROM is not erased
THEN
Inform the user
ELSE
Input the data
Allow any corrections
Output the data to the PROM
Check to see if it is programmed correctly
ENDIF the PROM is not erased
Exit the program

6.5 Design Partitioning

The top-down design method allows us to partition the design into easily handled pieces. At the upper levels, we can concentrate on more general ideas, leaving the detailed design until later. Also, when working at the upper levels, it is usually easy to see where work can be divided among different people working on the project. In the PROM programmer design, it would be easy to split the design at level two into two parts. One engineer could work on checking to see if the PROM is erased, inputting the data, and allowing for corrections; another could work on the programming and checking algorithms. Partitioning of the design and allocating work to different people is part of managing a software development project.

> Most programming problems can be partitioned into elements that are divided among the programmers working on the job.

6.6 Bottom-Up Design

Bottom up is another design philosophy that some people use. They fool themselves into thinking they are doing top-down design, but they really are not. Here is how a designer could fall into a bottom-up design. We begin with a top-down design for the first levels. For example, the PROM programmer design could be started just as before. So far, so good, but the time comes when we start looking ahead to doing some coding. After all, we are programmers, aren't we? We can see that there will be some low-level drivers required, such as a routine that reads the PROM. This will be used in checking if the PROM is erased and if it is programmed correctly. Why not, we argue, take a break from this design stuff and do some programming for a change? Our design starts to look like Figure 6–5.

> In *bottom-up design*, low-level functions are designed, coded, and tested before the upper levels of the design are completed.

What is wrong with this? First, by writing programs before doing the complete design, we cast in code[2] how things are being done at lower levels before understanding the upper levels of the design. This violates the principle of postponing details. Ideally, we would like to *design* the lower levels based on a well-thought-out upper-level design. If we design and code the lower levels first, we may make decisions that could make the upper levels harder to implement. This also violates the principle of successive refinement of design. We do not want to invest time in writing code until all design levels have been completed. By coding the low levels first, we don't get a chance to

---

[2]   Sometimes very much like concrete!

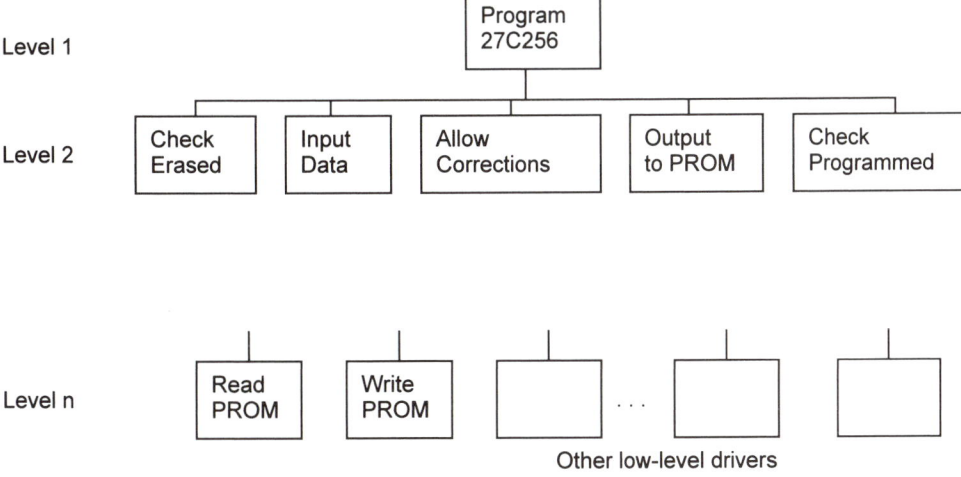

Figure 6-5   Bottom-up design.

optimize lower levels of the design based on decisions made for the higher levels. If later we do decide to change the low-level design, the work put into the coding is wasted.

Another problem with the bottom-up approach is that when code is written for the low-level drivers, extra code has to be written to test them. This means extra work for the programmer. The top-down approach, on the other hand, gives a testing structure that can test low-level programs. Top-down testing and debugging is discussed in Section 6.10.

Bottom-up design is not all bad, however. Bottom up can be a tool-building exercise. In any system one can see functional elements that need to be provided. If the tool-building phase is approached so that the new tools are not application specific, and they don't have a great impact on upper levels of the design, they can be used in several applications. This may save work in the end.

6.7 The Real-World Approach

Rarely in the real world do we have the opportunity to follow the ideals of the top-down philosophy and complete the design to all levels of detail before doing any coding. Often low-level functions are available that have been coded and tested; you can use them in your design. It makes sense to use these working functions and not have to redesign, code, and test them again. Most high-level languages come with libraries of functions, and your company or co-workers may have libraries that are useful. Using these functions

> Top-down design combined with judicious use of functions already programmed works best in the real world.

violates the principles of top-down design, but this is OK, providing you understand why the principles are being compromised and what the consequences may be. Using previously written low-level functions may impose constraints on the higher levels of the design. The disadvantages of these constraints are usually offset by the time saved from using already working functions. Note that this is different from the bottom-up philosophy. In bottom up, one sets out to write the low-level drivers, putting effort into their design, coding, and testing.

In summary, the real-world approach is one in which we recognize the power of the top-down method and attempt to do as much design as possible before coding, but we use previously developed and debugged functions where possible.

6.8 Types of Design Activity

> *Functional* design is the more general activity where the required functional elements are defined.

> *Detailed design* specifies the details necessary for each function called for in the functional design stage.

The top-down design philosophy supports two types of design activity found in any software development project. The first is oriented towards defining the *functionality* required in the software. We don't care *how* the software does its thing as much as *what* function has to be provided. The design is to be refined to a level where we have components that are manageable by one person. That function is then assigned to a person to program.

The second activity is the *detailed design* necessary to produce the functionality required in a module. The person who is assigned the job of producing a module takes the requirements specified by the first activity level and produces a detailed design to be programmed.

6.9 Design Tools

Design tools are used by the software engineer to help with the design. Here are some qualities of a good design tool.

1. It should be easy to use, and it should allow design modifications to be made easily.

2. It should support structured programming.

3. It should allow us easily to see the design at many levels.

4. It should have good documentation facilities.

Structured Programming

> Any program can be written with just *sequence, decision,* and *repetition* structures.

In the mid-1960s, people writing software for large systems were appalled at the cost of these systems and at the amount of time needed to develop them. A landmark paper by Bohm and Jacopini[3] in 1966 said that any proper program was equivalent to a program that contains only three structures. That is, *any program* can be constructed with only three basic structures, none of which is a GOTO statement. No one paid much attention until 2 years later, when Dijkstra wrote a provocative paper that said the GOTO statement in a program is harmful.[4] The three structures that Bohm and Jacopini suggested (and a few more that software designers couldn't resist adding) form the basis of structured programming and the structured languages we know today.

The three basic structures are (1) a *sequence,* (2) a *decision,* and (3) a *repetition.* Beyond these, several general principles of structured programming can be enumerated:

---

[3] Bohm, C., and G. Jacopini. "Flow diagrams, Turing machines and language with only two formation rules," CACM 9, 5, pp. 366–371, 1966.

[4] Dijkstra, E.W., "GOTO statement considered harmful," *CACM* 11, 3, pp. 147–48, 1968. Some programmers suggest that Dijkstra claimed that GOTO is a four-letter word.

1. Use these simple structures to aid in minimizing the number of interactions and interconnections between elements of the program.

2. Keep program segments small to keep them manageable.

3. Organize the problem solution hierarchically.

4. Organize each program segment so there is one input and one output (in terms of the program flow). This is not a data restriction but a restriction on the program flow. We would like to draw a box around a program segment and see that we enter that segment in only one place and leave it at only one place.

Structured programming really isn't a design tool. It is a way of writing programs. However, because the principles of structured programming fit so well with the top-down design procedure, the elements of structured programming have been adapted for use as a design tool. With that in mind, let's look at the sequence, decision, and repetition structures used in structured programming along with the pseudocode design tool. We will then see how pseudocode can be used in a top-down design exercise.

Pseudocode

The most frequently used design tool is the pseudocode technique. This is popular because it is easy to modify, doesn't require special graphical tools, and fits well with the documentation required for all design. Further, the design text can be included in the software code as comments.

There are many texts that give a complete treatment of the pseudocode design tool. Here is an abbreviated approach that shows how to pseudocode the three simple design structures: sequence, decision, and repetition.

Sequence: A sequence structure is a sequence of functions or operations that the program is to perform. A sequence usually doesn't show any logic. It should show the function provided by a process block and must have a beginning and end. These are explicitly stated to show the single input–single output form we would like to achieve in the design. Thus a sequence of A, B, C would be as shown in Table 6–3.

The ellipsis (. . .) represents the elements of the design provided in the A, B, and C blocks.

Decision: The decision structure is called an *IF-THEN-ELSE,* and Table 6–4 shows how to write the structure in pseudocode. The decision structure shows us that we do one of the two elements in the program. *If* X is true, *then* the process A is executed, otherwise (*else*) B is executed.

TABLE 6-3 SEQUENCE pseudocode

```
BEGIN A
   . . .
END A
BEGIN B
   . . .
BEGIN C
   . . .
END C
```

TABLE 6-4 DECISION pseudocode

```
IF X
THEN
        BEGIN A
          . . .
        END A
ELSE
        BEGIN B
          . . .
        END B
ENDIF X
```

Another view of the IF-THEN-ELSE structure is shown in Figure 6–6. This is a structured flow chart symbol, and while flow charts are not generally used as design tools these days, they are useful to help visualize the proper structure of a good design. It is easier to see that only one process block is executed in Figure 6–6 than in the corresponding pseudocode of Table 6–4.

Inspection of Table 6–4 and Figure 6–6 shows that a Boolean or logic decision is made and must be either true or false. It doesn't have to be a simple decision; you may use any of the Boolean logic learned in your logic design course. For example, the following is a Boolean function:

F is TRUE if (A is TRUE AND B is FALSE) OR C is TRUE OR D is FALSE.

The decision structure may be single-sided. That is, there might not be an ELSE part to the decision. Table 6–5 and Figure 6–7 show the pseudocode and the corresponding structure.

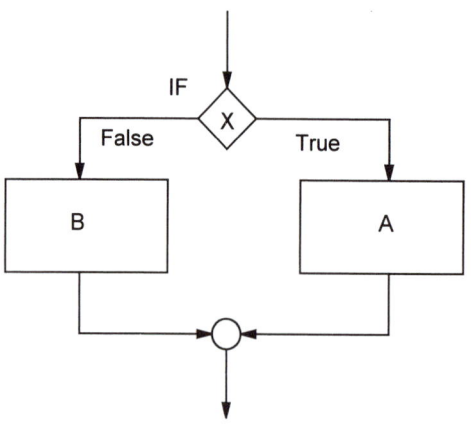

Figure 6-6 IF-THEN-ELSE decision element.

TABLE 6-5 Single-sided DECISION pseudocode

```
IF X
THEN
        BEGIN A
          . . .
        END A
ENDIF X
```

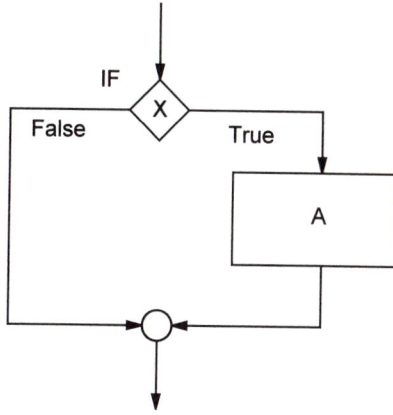

Figure 6-7   Single-sided DECISION structure.

Note that in the pseudocode the IF-THEN-ELSE block ends with an ENDIF X statement. The ENDIF, of course, signifies the end of the block. Repeating the conditional at this point is a good technique to help you remember what the decision was all about. This is especially useful when looking at the design later.

Repetition: The pseudocode for the repetition structure is shown in Table 6.6. This structure is called a *WHILE-DO*, and as you can see in Figure 6-8, *while* the Boolean X is true, the process elements S1, S2, and S3 are *done*.

There are some other variations of the repetition structure. One particularly useful in assembly language programming is the *DO-WHILE* shown in Table 6-7 and Figure 6-9. Here the processing blocks, S1, S2, and S3, are done before the Boolean decision block. Thus the code in the DO block is executed at least once.

Indentation: Indentation is often used in pseudocode. The code statements (or design requirements) for each block (bracketed by BEGIN and END) are indented to help show the structure of the design.

Single-input, single-output: A principle of structured programming is to keep things simple without many interconnections between different parts of the program. A way to do this is to write

TABLE 6-6 WHILE-DO pseudocode

```
WHILE X
DO
        BEGIN S1
          . . .
        END S1
        BEGIN S2
          . . .
        END S2
        BEGIN S3
          . . .
        END S3
ENDO WHILE X
```

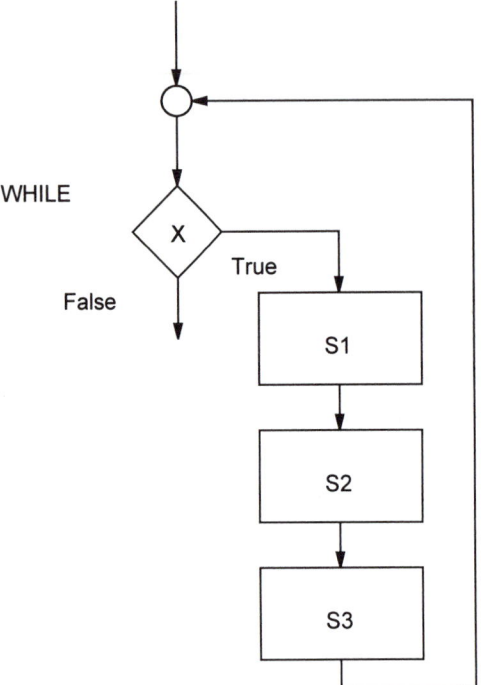

Figure 6–8 WHILE-DO structure.

the program so that elements of it (sequences, if-then-elses, and repetitions) have single entry and exit points. These ideas are best illustrated with an example.

Using Pseudocode Structured Elements as a Design Tool

A top down design can be done in several levels of pseudocode. For example, when you first start the design, you might know only that A and B have to be done. The level-one design is shown in Table 6–8.

TABLE 6–7 DO-WHILE pseudocode

```
DO
        BEGIN S1
            . . .
        END S1
        BEGIN S2
            . . .
        END S2
        BEGIN S3
            . . .
        END S3
    ENDO
    WHILE X
```

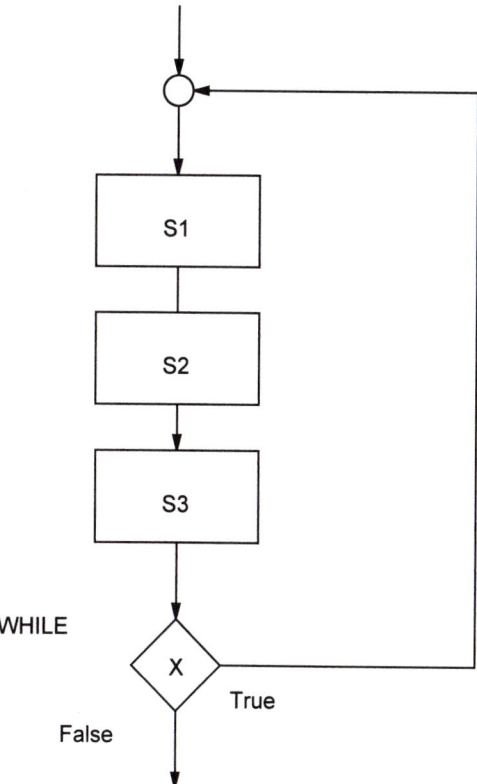

Figure 6-9 DO-WHILE structure.

As we start to know more about the sequence block A, we can begin to fill in its details. The level-two design becomes that shown in Table 6–9.

The design goes on to level-three (Table 6–10), where the C and D sequence blocks can be expanded.

In each of the design levels shown here, elements have been enclosed in boxes. This is to emphasize the single-input, single-output nature of the program flow. In Table 6–8 we can see that the A and B blocks are quite separate. By the time we get to Table 6–10, the separate blocks for A and B are still apparent even though A has been expanded.

TABLE 6-8 Level-one design

| BEGIN A |
| END A |

| BEGIN B |
| END B |

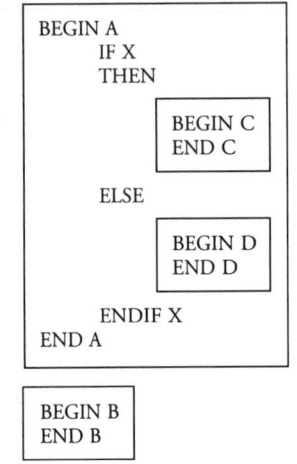

TABLE 6-9 Level-two design

```
BEGIN A
    IF X
    THEN
                BEGIN C
                END C

    ELSE
                BEGIN D
                END D

    ENDIF X
END A
```

```
BEGIN B
END B
```

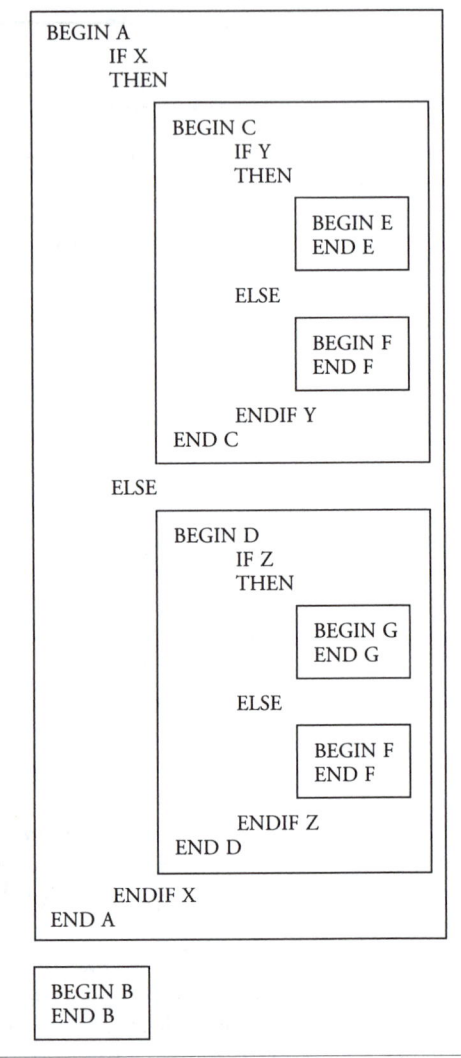

TABLE 6-10 Level-three design

```
BEGIN A
    IF X
    THEN
                BEGIN C
                    IF Y
                    THEN
                                BEGIN E
                                END E

                    ELSE
                                BEGIN F
                                END F

                    ENDIF Y
                END C

    ELSE
                BEGIN D
                    IF Z
                    THEN
                                BEGIN G
                                END G

                    ELSE
                                BEGIN F
                                END F

                    ENDIF Z
                END D

    ENDIF X
END A
```

```
BEGIN B
END B
```

6.10 Top-Down Debugging and Testing

Stubs are dummy programs for functions or subroutines that have not been written yet.

In the discussion of the bottom-up design technique in Section 6.6, we showed that extra code is required for testing the modules as they are being developed. However, if the code is developed in a top-down fashion by writing the higher-level modules first and postponing the details of lower-level modules, we have a program structure that tests itself. The program development might progress as illustrated in Tables 6–8–6–10. The upper level of the program is coded as calls to the modules that provide the functions A

TABLE 6-11 Level-two design using stubs for unfinished modules

```
BEGIN PROGRAM
     call subroutine_a
     call subroutine_b
END PROGRAM
BEGIN subroutine_a
     IF X
     THEN
          call subroutine_c
     ELSE
          call subroutine_d
     ENDIF X
     return
END subroutine_a
BEGIN subroutine_b
     return
END subroutine_b
BEGIN subroutine_c
     return
END subroutine_c
BEGIN subroutine_d
     return
END subroutine_d
```

and B. As we start to work on function A, delaying our work on the others, we must have something to substitute for function B so the top-level program will run. Thus any of the lower-level modules that haven't been coded yet are temporarily coded as a *stub*. A stub is just a return with no processing done. Table 6–11 shows how the program might look for the level-two design. Here, functions B, C, and D are coded as stubs. In the case where the function must process some data and return a value, a dummy or test value can be returned by the stub to be used by the calling program. In this way, you delay the actual programming of the lower-level functions but can still develop and test the upper levels. The whole design becomes the test jig for itself. It allows you to design and test program logic and to see how data are passed back and forth at higher levels before coding the lower levels.

6.11 Structured Programming in Assembly Language

Structured programming and structured languages were invented to increase our efficiency as programmers and to make it easier to produce software without bugs and problems. What if the program has to be written in assembly language? By now you know that assembly language programs have many jumps and branches that seem to violate the no GOTO policy of structured programming. Although this is true, it is still possible to write structured code in assembly language. You must remember the principles of structured programming, particularly the idea of a single-input, single-output for a process block. Make your process blocks small, with jumps that do not span over great chunks of code, and ensure that there are no jumps into the middle of a block of code. This is what a compiler does for programs written in a high-level language. Refer to your text supplement for the processor whose assembly language you are learning for specific examples showing how to code the sequence, decision, and repetition structures.

6.12 Modular Design

Top-down design naturally leads to programs that can be written in modules. A goal is to break the problem solution into easily understandable parts. Often, as this is being done, a

> *Modules* are functional elements of the design.

function may be found that is required in several places in the design. For example, looking back at Table 6–10, you can see that block F is needed in both C and D. If we jump out of block C into D to get to F, we violate the single-input, single-output criteria for design. The program element F should be programmed as a function or subroutine to be called at the right place in blocks C and D. This is called *modular design.* Another rationale for coding in modules is to make each section of the code small and easily understood. Naturally, there are good ways and poor ways to design modules.

There are several assumptions to be made about modular code. We assume that a module can be written by anyone and that we can then use it in our design. This means that the *module requirements* must be specified precisely. We don't care how a module does its job, just that we know what it does. If this is done, the module can be treated as a "black box." We also assume that when the call to the module is made, execution in the calling program stops and the called function starts. (This may not be true in parallel processors.) After the module finishes execution, control is then returned to the statement immediately following the function call.

As the software is designed, we keep in mind that beyond the other principles of structured programming and design, a major goal is to create modules that are independent of each other. Ideally there should be no interaction between modules. That way, if changes are made in how a module is coded, there is no effect on any other part of the program if it still provides the same function. One of the worst things that can happen to a programmer is that when code is changed to fix a bug in one part of the program, it causes another bug to appear somewhere else. We can avoid or reduce these problems by the proper design and coding of our modules.

A module has three attributes. These are the module's function, its coupling or linking to other modules in the system, and its logic.

Module Function

The function of a module is a description of what the module does. We should try to describe the module's function with a verb. For example, a module that turns a water pump on should be called "Turn Water Pump On" instead of "Water Pump Module." We know exactly what the module does in the first case but not in the second. There are three categories into which module functions can be classified. These are *coincidental modules, logical modules,* and *single-function modules.*

Coincidental modules: A coincidental module is one in which there are no meaningful relationships between elements in the module. A coincidental module may come about as we write the program and see that a sequence of code steps is repeated. We decide to lump together this code and call it a module or subroutine. Table 6–12 shows a coincidental module.

Although the coincidental module might hide some details of the program, it is difficult to treat this module as a black box. It does several things, none of which are related. In addition, if in the future we want to change one part of the program that uses this module, say to get data from another source, we must remember to check that any other parts of the program that use this mod-

TABLE 6-12 Coincidental module

A = B + C
GET A/D VALUE
IF A = A/D VALUE
THEN
        B = 4
ELSE
    C = 2

ule need that change, too. This is what is meant by interaction in the program. A change in one part of the program makes or requires a change in another part. To some extent, this is a problem with all modules that are used in several places. However, if the modules are properly designed to provide one function, and that function *never* changes, then the potential problems are greatly reduced.

Logical modules: A logical module is one in which there is some logical relationship between elements in the module. For example, let's write a program that has both analog and digital, input and output requirements. Because these functions are so closely related, it is tempting to write a single module that provides them all. We would then call the module with a control parameter that defines which of the four functions is to be provided. The structure of such a module looks like that shown in Figure 6–10.

> Logical modules need extra defensive code to decode the control parameter.

There are several potential drawbacks with grouping functions together like this. First, extra code must be written to decode the control parameter that determines what function is to be provided. This code must be defensive. That is, it must not only take care of the proper control parameters but also must handle improper parameters. Second, the analog and digital input programs may be very similar, and it is tempting to use parts of one in another. This leads to code that is interdependent. A change in one part may have unwanted ramifications in another. A third problem is that the module is now less of a black box. The user must know something about its operation, namely, which parameter to use to get which function. Proper and sufficient documentation must be provided to be able to use the module. A better design is to have four independent modules, one for each function required.

Although there are disadvantages to this logical module approach, there are many examples where

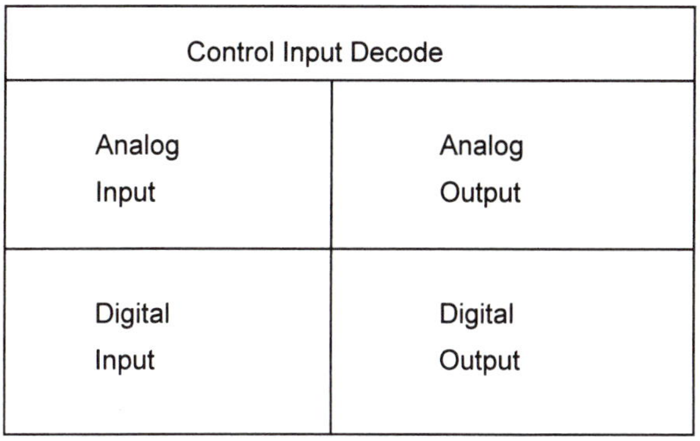

Control Input Decode	
Analog Input	Analog Output
Digital Input	Digital Output

Figure 6-10 Logical module.

it is used. Many functions provided in the operating system in personal computers are done with a single function call with a parameter to determine which function is to be provided.

Single-function modules: By far the best module design is one that provides a single function. All elements of the module are related to providing this function to the user. Single-function modules are easily described by a single action statement. For example, "Output D/A Value," "Get A/D Value," "Turn Water Pump On" are all single-function modules. One can look at the module title or name and tell what it does. You may not know how it does it, but you know when you call it that you will get that function.

> The best module provides a single function.

Single-function modules do not necessarily mean primitive or lowest level of detail modules. For example, a module might provide the function "Analyze 100 Data Points." This could be a high-level, single-function module and would probably contain many other lower-level modules.

Module Coupling

Module coupling describes how modules interact. This may be directly in how they execute or indirectly by transferring data between them. If the modules can be looked upon as black boxes providing some function, coupling between the different execution phases of the module is reduced. Most of the module coupling problems come from data that are acted upon by different modules. For example, in Figure 6–11, two modules modify a data element. These modules are coupled by that data element. If the execution of one module depends upon how the other module modifies the data element, then potential dangers lurk. Obviously, data coupling cannot be eliminated entirely because data do have to be operated upon by different modules. However, if we understand the dangers, we can take steps to reduce the coupling problems. Let us look at two different types of module coupling.

Control coupling: Control coupling refers to the situation that applies for logical function modules. The data that are passed into the module affect how the called module executes. Thus the calling module has some knowledge of the called module. We have already discussed the disadvantages of this approach.

Data coupling: Data coupling refers to those situations where modules interact through some data variable. This is frequently encountered, and our design goal must be to reduce the amount of coupling. The technique used is to restrict the knowledge of data variables to only those modules that must have access to them. Globally known variables are frowned upon. It is better to have local variables that are known only to the modules that use them. The best way to transfer infor-

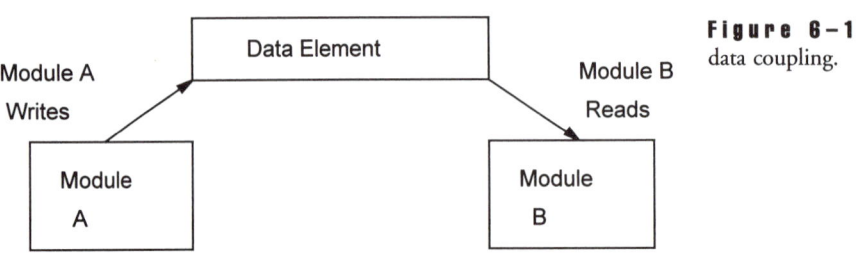

Figure 6–11 Module data coupling.

mation between modules is with a parameter list included in the function or module call. For example, in C, the following might be a program statement:

$$Return\_Value = put\_d\_to\_a\_value(\ Output\_Value\ );$$

Both Return_Value and Output_Value are local variables and are passed to and from the put_d_to_a_value function.

Module Logic

The module's logic is how a module does its job. In terms of the system design, the module's logic should be invisible and irrelevant to the user. Unfortunately, often the logic is dependent on data that may be operated on and returned to the user. Given our discussions above about module functions and coupling, we see that as we reduce the coupling, we can make the module's logic more transparent.

6.13 Interprocess Communication

Interprocess communication, also called parameter passing, refers to information that is transferred from one part of the program to another. Most information transfer in well-designed programs is between a subroutine or function and its calling function as shown in Figure 6–12.

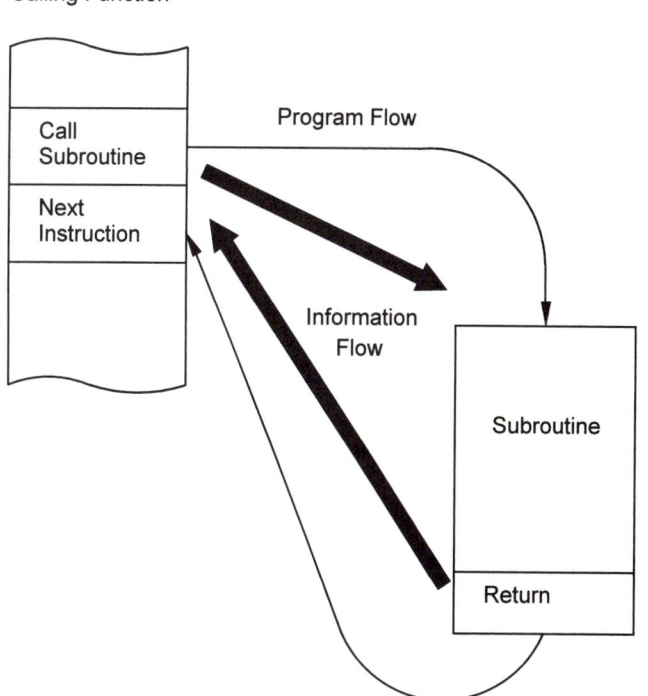

Figure 6–12   Information transfer between modules.

In choosing how information is transferred between modules, a goal is to reduce the chance of the subroutine accidentally changing other data. This also reduces the module coupling problems described in Section 6.12. There are several methods that can be used.

Information in Registers

The most efficient and fastest way to transfer information between parts of a program when writing in assembly language is to use the registers. This method also has the advantage that the subroutine does not access any other data areas and is thus more general. Documentation must be provided to show what registers are used for what purpose. A typical subroutine header describing the registers used is shown in Table 6.13.

Information in Global Data Areas

The main disadvantage of using registers is that most CPUs have only a few and some functions may need many bytes of data. Using global data areas is a solution with advantages and potential problems. Global data are data elements that can be reached from any part of the program. Figure 6–13 shows four modules using two global data elements.

The danger of maintaining global data is that a function may modify data that it shouldn't. For example, let's assume that Module_1 shares Data_Element_1 with Module_2 and Module_3 shares Data_Element_2 with Module_4. Now let's assume that you make a mistake (a bug) in the code that is supposed to write data into Data_Element_1 and write into Data_Element_2 instead. (This could be done by using a 16-bit store operation instead of an 8-bit one, or by having an incorrectly initialized pointer register, or simply by writing the wrong label in the operand field.) Now Module_4 is working with incorrect data. This is a difficult bug to find, particularly if the code in Module_1 is executed infrequently. Experienced assembly and high-level language programmers try to avoid using global data if other methods are available. Nevertheless, global data structures are widely used in assembly and high-level language programming.

TABLE 6–13 Subroutine header comments

Subroutine Name:	SQRT
Author:	F. M. Cady
Date:	July 19, 1993
Function:	Calculate the square root of a 16 bit integer number.
Input Registers:	BC = 16 bit integer number
Output Registers:	B = 8 bit integer square root
	Carry flag = 1 if input number is negative
	Carry flag = 0 if input number is positive
Registers modified:	B, condition code register
Global data modified:	none
Functions called:	none

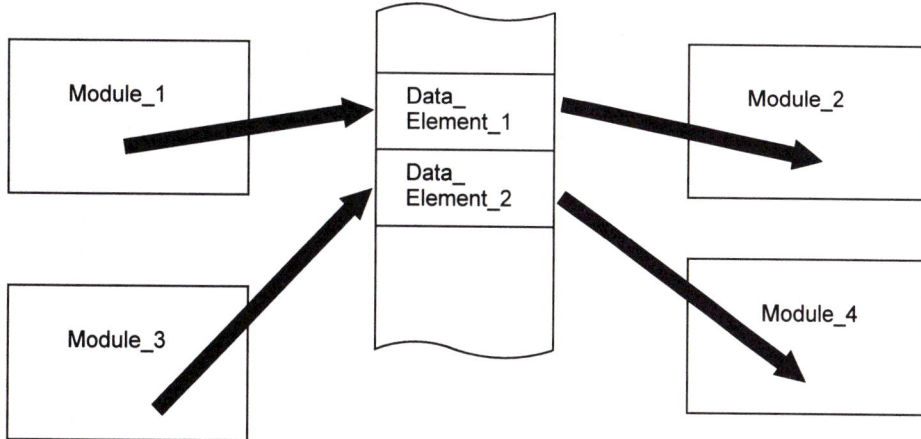

Figure 6-13 Information transfer using global data.

Information in Local Data Areas

Local data areas invoke the principle of "divide and conquer." Figure 6–14 shows modules and their common data elements that are separately assembled source files. When a relocatable assembler is used, as it must be here, any names or labels are local to that source file only, unless a special assembler directive called EXTERNAL is used. Thus the assembler will show an error if you assemble the file with Module_1, Module_2 and Data_Element_1, and accidentally refer to Data_Element_2. However, as you can see, the data elements are global within these localized structures.

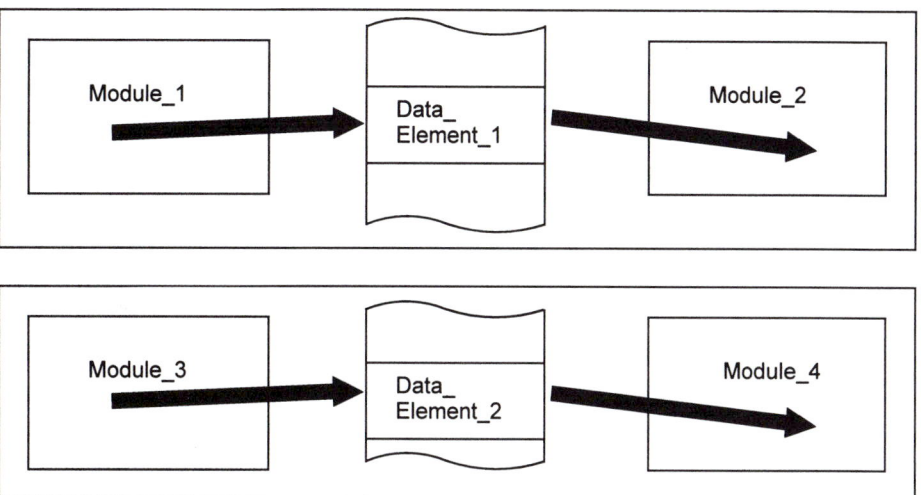

Figure 6-14 Information in local data areas.

Information on the Stack

Using the stack for temporary data storage, particularly for saving registers in subroutines, was discussed in Chapter 4. The stack can also be used to transfer data to and from a subroutine. When this is done, the data elements are localized on the stack and the subroutine is designed to operate with them alone. This reduces the chance of global data being accidentally corrupted. You must be careful when using the stack because, in addition to the data on the stack, the return address is there also. Figure 6–15(a) shows an example of four bytes of data pushed onto the stack for transfer to the subroutine. In Figure 6–15(b) the return address is placed there by the call or jump-to-subroutine instruction. Notice that in the subroutine the next pull or pop operation will retrieve, not data, but the return address. The stack pointer must be manipulated to retrieve the data first and then the proper return address. Figure 6–15(c) shows the stack just before the return at the end of the subroutine assuming one byte of data is to be returned to the calling program on the stack.

Using the stack to transfer information is very powerful and very general. Most compilers for high-level languages use this method. Programmers must be careful to make sure stack operations are balanced and good documentation must be provided.

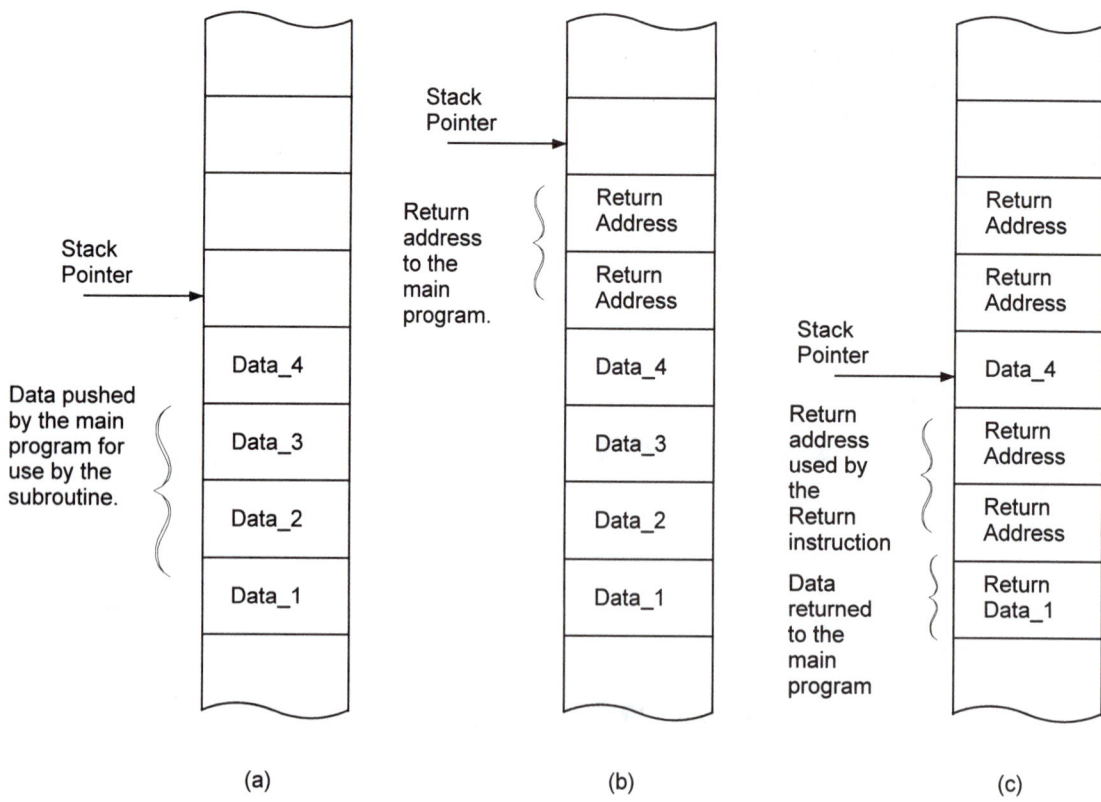

Figure 6–15   Using the stack for information transfer.

Using Addresses Instead of Values

Using global data areas, even with potential problems and disadvantages, is common, particularly where large amounts of data are to be shared between modules. One can avoid some problems by using a register to pass the address of the data. This is useful when accessing data buffers where, perhaps, one module fills the buffer and another processes the data. The two modules can be given the starting address of the buffer and the number of data elements (to avoid running over the end of the buffer).

Passing Boolean Information

At times a Boolean, or logic, value must be returned to the calling program. For example, you might want to indicate whether a procedure was successful and then act accordingly in the calling program. A register or a memory location could be allocated for this, but if you are programming in assembly language you may use a bit in the condition code register. All processors have the capability of setting or resetting the carry flag. This can be tested with a conditional branch instruction in the calling program.

6.14 Software Documentation

Each of the software development phases—design, coding, and testing—has associated documentation.

Software Requirements Specification

The software requirements specification (SRS) is a document or series of documents that define what is required of the software. At the upper levels of the best designed systems, the SRS should completely define what the user of the system is to see, that is, the user interface. This document can form the basis of the User Operator's Manual. It must be written first and agreed upon by the customer and the software developer. As you continue with the lower levels of the design, where one starts to think about how things are going to be done, the SRS documentation begins to define the functions required by modules in the system. You should be able to give an SRS document to a colleague and have him or her code the function and return a working module for inclusion into the system.

Software Design Document

The software design document (SDD) is the document produced for the detailed design of a module. It defines the logic required to produce a particular function. You start with the SRS for the module and use a design tool such as pseudocode described in Section 6.9.

Software Code

The coding phase has an element of software documentation. This means including comments in the software. We would like the code to be written clearly enough that extra comments are not necessary. High-level languages allow us to do some of this, but rarely should we write a program without any extra comments describing what is going on. In assembly language programs, comments are mandatory because the language is not as design oriented as high-level languages. It is particularly effective to use the pseudocode produced for the SDD for the comments in an assembly language program.

Software Verification Plan

The software verification plan (SVP) is a document that describes how we are going to test and verify that a particular module or system meets its specifications. The SVP should give the details of limiting values to be tested and what the expected results are. There may be levels of SVPs associated with the various levels of our design.

User Manuals

The four types of documents described above are often considered design documents to be used within the company and not delivered to the customer. Beyond these, there must be manuals for the customer's use. These include instructions on how to install the software (if appropriate) and instructions on using the software.

6.15 Chapter Summary Points

- The top-down design method is our choice of design approaches.

- The top-down design steps are as follows:

    Understand the problem completely before writing code.
    Design in levels.
    Ensure correctness at each level.
    Postpone details.
    Successively refine your design.
    Design without using a programming language.

- By doing bottom-up design and coding, decisions at lower levels may adversely affect the upper levels of the design.

- In the real world, we try to follow the principles of top-down design, but we pragmatically use functions that have been already designed, coded, and tested.

- The elements of structured programming can be listed:

  Use three simple structures—sequence, decision, and repetition—to write all programs.
  Keep program segments small to keep them manageable.
  Organize the problem solution hierarchically (use top-down design.)
  Use single-input, single-output program flow.

- The pseudocode technique is an effective design tool for all levels of top-down design.

- The top-down design method can lead to a top-down debugging and testing strategy where the structure of the design tests itself.

- The top-down design approach leads to software that is implemented in modules.

- A module that provides a single function and operates as a black box is the best.

- Module coupling refers to the interactions between modules. Module coupling should be reduced as far as possible.

- Information can be passed between modules in the following ways:

  By using registers.
  By using global data areas.
  By using local data areas.
  By using the stack.
  By using addresses instead of values.
  By using the condition code register bits for Boolean information.

- Software documentation is a vital part of all stages of software development and consists of the following:

  Software requirements specifications—SRS.
  Software design documentation—SDD.
  Software code with comments.
  Software verification plan—SVP.
  User manuals.

6.16 Problems

6.1 List five principles of top-down design.

6.2 What are the three basic elements of structured programming?

6.3 Write the pseudocode and draw the flow chart symbol to represent the decision IF A is TRUE, THEN B ELSE C.

6.4 Write the pseudocode and draw the flow chart symbol to represent the decision IF A is TRUE, THEN B.

6.5 Write the pseudocode and draw the flow chart symbol to represent the repetition WHILE A is TRUE, DO B.

6.6 Write the pseudocode and draw the flow chart symbol to represent the repetition DO B WHILE A is TRUE.

6.7   Write a design using structured flow charts or pseudocode to implement the following problem description:

> Prompt for and input a character from a user at the keyboard.
> If the character is alphabetic and is upper case, change it to lower case and output it to the screen.
> If the character is alphabetic and is lower case, change it to upper case and output it to the screen.
> If the character is numeric, output it with no change.
> If it is any other character, beep the bell.
> Repeat this process until an ESC character is typed by the user.

6.8   Write a design using structured pseudocode for an algorithm to retrieve data from the stack in a subroutine. Assume four bytes of data are to be transferred from the calling program to the subroutine and one byte is to be returned.

6.9   Show how to implement the following problem statement in software for a microprocessor controller using the pseudocode algorithmic method.

> In many cars the seat belt alarm buzzer is also used to warn against leaving the key in the ignition or leaving the lights on. The following statement describes how such a system might operate.
> The alarm is to sound if the key is in the ignition when the door is open and the motor is not running, or if the lights are on when the key is not in the ignition, or if the driver belt is not fastened when the motor is running, or if the passenger seat is occupied and the passenger belt is not fastened when the motor is running.

6.10   Design a program that initializes an 8-bit data storage accumulator to 0 and then inputs 10 successive 8-bit values from an input device located at address $70, adding each of them to the 8-bit data storage accumulator. If during this process a straight binary overflow occurs, halt the program. Otherwise, after the 10 values have been input and added, output the result to an output device at location $71. Run the process forever (or until the overflow occurs). Your design must be a structured design and must show REPETITION, DECISION, and SEQUENCE.

6.11   Give a design using structured pseudocode to accomplish the following:

> A user is to input a character to select one of three processes. Valid characters are A, B, C, and Q. A, B, and C select processes A, B, or C, respectively. Process A requires a byte of information to be input from an A/D converter, converted to a decimal value in the range of 0 to 5, and displayed on the screen. Processes B and C are not defined at this stage. Prompts and error messages are to be displayed. You do not have to give details of the decimal conversion required in process A.

6.12 Give a design using structured pseudocode to accomplish the following:

> A byte of data is to be input from an analog-to-digital converter and a critical value is to be input from a set of switches. If the A/D value is greater than the critical value, the CPU is to sound an alarm. Otherwise the alarm is to be turned off. This process is to continue forever.

Chapter 7

Computer Buses and Parallel Input/Output

OBJECTIVES

Computers doing real jobs must input and output (I/O) information. Two ways to do this are many bits at a time, in parallel, or one bit at a time, in serial. This chapter will explore parallel bus architectures and how to design the interfaces between external devices and the CPU. We will discuss the differences between memory-mapped and separate I/O and how to solve I/O synchronization problems between a fast processor and a slow I/O device. Some advanced bus ideas are covered, and both simple and programmable I/O devices are discussed.

7.1 Introduction

A computer system with CPU, memory, I/O, and the interconnecting computer buses is shown in Figure 7–1. Previous chapters have emphasized the CPU, its resources, and how to program it to do a particular task. We now look to the design of the rest of the system hardware.

> Parallel and serial I/O devices require an *interface* between the device and the bus.

Many computer applications involve the transfer of information, either in parallel or in serial, in or out of the CPU. Both parallel and serial I/O require a hardware interface between the source or destination of the information and the CPU. Let's approach this topic using the top-down design principles covered in Chapter 6. The preliminary problem specification is:

Design the hardware interface to transfer information from multiple sources to the CPU, and from the CPU to multiple destinations, using a computer bus.

This is a reasonable top-level statement of the problem, and our task is to go through the hardware design, adding details and refining it, until we have a workable system. At our level of expertise we need to know more about the computer bus and about information sources and destinations. We must also consider the timing of information transfer. The interface that is to be designed

93

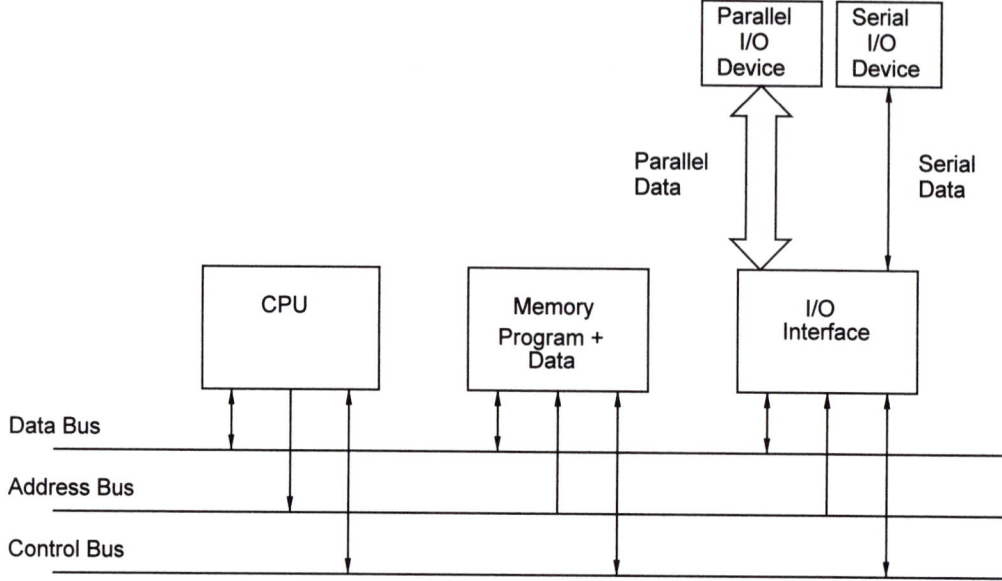

Figure 7–1 Bus-oriented computer architecture.

will be suitable for both parallel and serial I/O devices with the parallel case described in detail in this chapter. The details of serial I/O will be covered in Chapter 10.

7.2 The Computer Bus

What is the proper place to start the top-down design of the I/O interface? In solving any problem, begin work where you have some knowledge or expertise and progress toward those areas where you need to learn more, filling in the details as you come to them. This is the essence of top-down design for hardware. Let's start our design at the CPU and work out toward the I/O devices.

> A *bus* is a parallel, bidirectional, binary information pathway with multiple sources and destinations.

The CPU is interconnected to memory and I/O devices via the *data, address,* and *control* buses. In circuit diagrams, the parallel wires of the bus are generally reduced to a single line, as shown in Figure 7–2(a). The number of bits in each bus depends on the design of the system, and more data bits means the system can transfer data at a higher rate; more address bits allow more memory to be addressed. Bus lines are continuous, except some control signals are interrupted by the devices using them.

The data bus is bidirectional and transfers information (memory data and instructions, I/O data) to and from the CPU. The address bus may be bidirectional (with more than one source of information) but is most often unidirectional because the CPU is the only source of addresses. The control bus carries all other signals required to control the operation of the system.

There are several levels of bus design. The *component-level bus* is defined by the signals on the microprocessor chip, such as **READ/WRITE**. Component-level signals will be different for different manufacturers and are used when designing single-board computers or dedicated application systems. A *system-level* bus is one for which more generic signals, like **MEMRD** and **IORD**, are defined. A system-level bus is often designed for use as a *backplane* into which printed circuit boards are plugged. An example of a system-level bus is that defined for the IBM PC and compatible com-

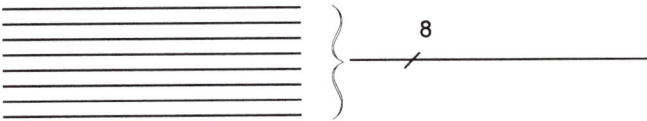

(a) Schematic notation for a computer bus.

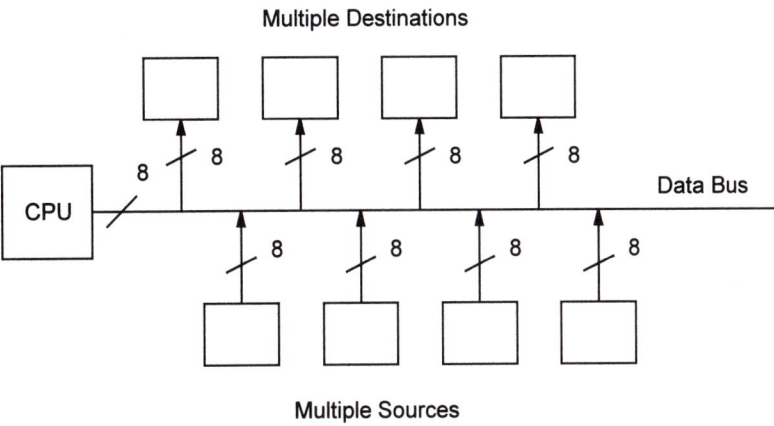

(b) Bus line with multiple sources and destinations.

Figure 7–2   The computer bus.

puters. A third type of bus is the *intersystem* bus that allows different systems to be connected. A good example is the IEEE 488 (GPIB) instrumentation bus. Our discussions in this chapter will be concerned with the system-level bus. More specific designs for component-level buses are given in the supplement for the processor you are studying.

Let us now consider the data bus in detail. Each line of the bus may have multiple sources and destinations for the information as shown in Figure 7–2(b). According to our design specification, we must design hardware to allow multiple sources to exist on the bus.

Information Sources—The Input Interface

Sources of binary information are usually the outputs of gates.[1] However, the output of two gates cannot be connected unless they are *three-state*[2] or open-collector gates. A typical three-state gate

---

[1]   It could also be some other circuit, such as a switch, that provides logic levels for binary 1s and 0s.

[2]   These gates are also know as Tristate™ gates. This term is a trademark of the National Semiconductor Company. This invention revolutionized the design of computer buses.

and its truth table are shown in Figure 7–3(a) and an open-collector gate in Figure 7–3(b). As the truth table for the three-state gate shows, **1G** must be asserted (set to 0) for the output to be active; otherwise the output is in the third state, known as high impedance. In this state the output cannot source or sink current to create a logic one or zero. The beauty of the three-state gate is that two or more gate outputs can be connected, providing only one is enabled at a time.

> An *input interface* provides three-state buffers between the source and the data bus.

A parallel, eight-bit input interface can be constructed with eight three- state gates whose enable lines are tied together. This eight-bit, three-state buffer provides the electrical interface between a binary source of data, such as a set of switches, and the data bus. A typical device is the 74LS244 octal buffer/line driver with three-state outputs.

> *Open-collector* gates require external pull-up resistors.

The *open-collector gate* is often used for control signals such as requests for interrupts. It is rarely used in place of a three-state buffer for data sources. Several open-collector gates tied to an external pull-up resistor is called a *wired-OR* (sometimes wired-AND) connection. The bus line is low if any of the wired-OR outputs is pulled low.

Information Destinations—The Output Interface

> The *output interface* must latch information from the data bus.

The interface between the data bus and a destination or output device is a latch, as shown in Figure 7–4. A data bus line is connected to the D input, and the Q output is used at the destination (to drive an LED display, for example). A control signal, generated by logic in the I/O interface, is needed to latch the data from the bus. The logic for this clock, and the enable on the input interface's three-state buffers, is generated in part by address decoding and in part by timing signals.

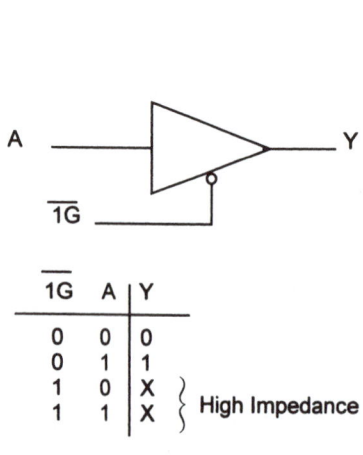

1G	A	Y
0	0	0
0	1	1
1	0	X
1	1	X

} High Impedance

(a) Three-state gate.

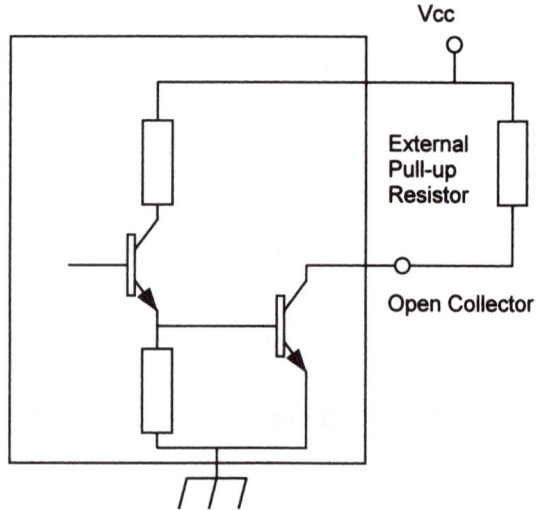

(b) Typical open-collector gate.

Figure 7–3   Typical bus interface gates.

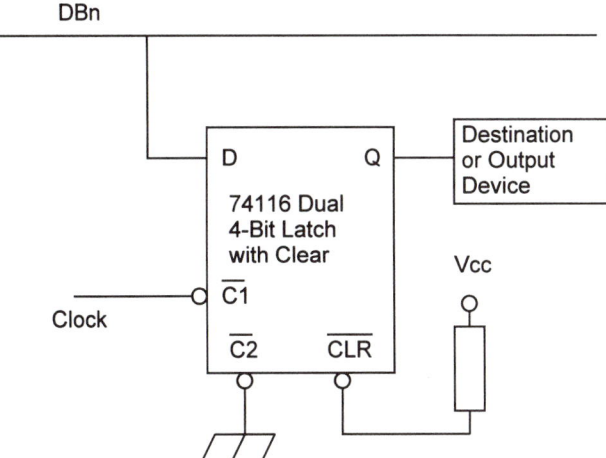

Figure 7-4 An output interface is a latch.

Multiple Sources and Destinations

Several basic input buffers and output latches can provide multiple input and output device interfaces. We must now consider how to select one source or destination for an information transfer. Let's refine the original problem specification to add the next requirement:

- Design the hardware interface to transfer information from multiple sources to the CPU, and from the CPU to multiple destinations, using a computer bus.

- *The interface must provide the ability for the CPU to select one of many sources and destinations.*

Address decoding allows us to select which is the destination or source.

Addressing and address decoding can select one out of many information sources and destinations. Figure 7–5 shows that two address bits, A1 and A0, may be decoded by a 74LS139 Dual 1-of-4 Decoder/Demultiplexer. One decoder provides the enable lines for the three-state buffers in the input interfaces, ensuring that only one is active at a time. For the output devices, the address decoder selects which of the latches is the destination. There is not an electrical[3] reason the information cannot be transferred to more than one destination at a time. Usually this is not done, and the address decoder selects only one.

In the I/O interface shown in Figure 7–5, address bits A1 and A0 select which of the four input or output devices are to be used. Two control signals, **WRITE_CONTROL** and **READ_CONTROL**, are also shown. These are generated by the CPU to provide timing information for the data transfer in and out of the CPU.

Timing Signals

A timing requirement must be added to the design specification:

- Design the hardware interface to transfer information from multiple sources to the CPU, and from the CPU to multiple destinations, using a computer bus.

---

[3] Except device loading and fan out.

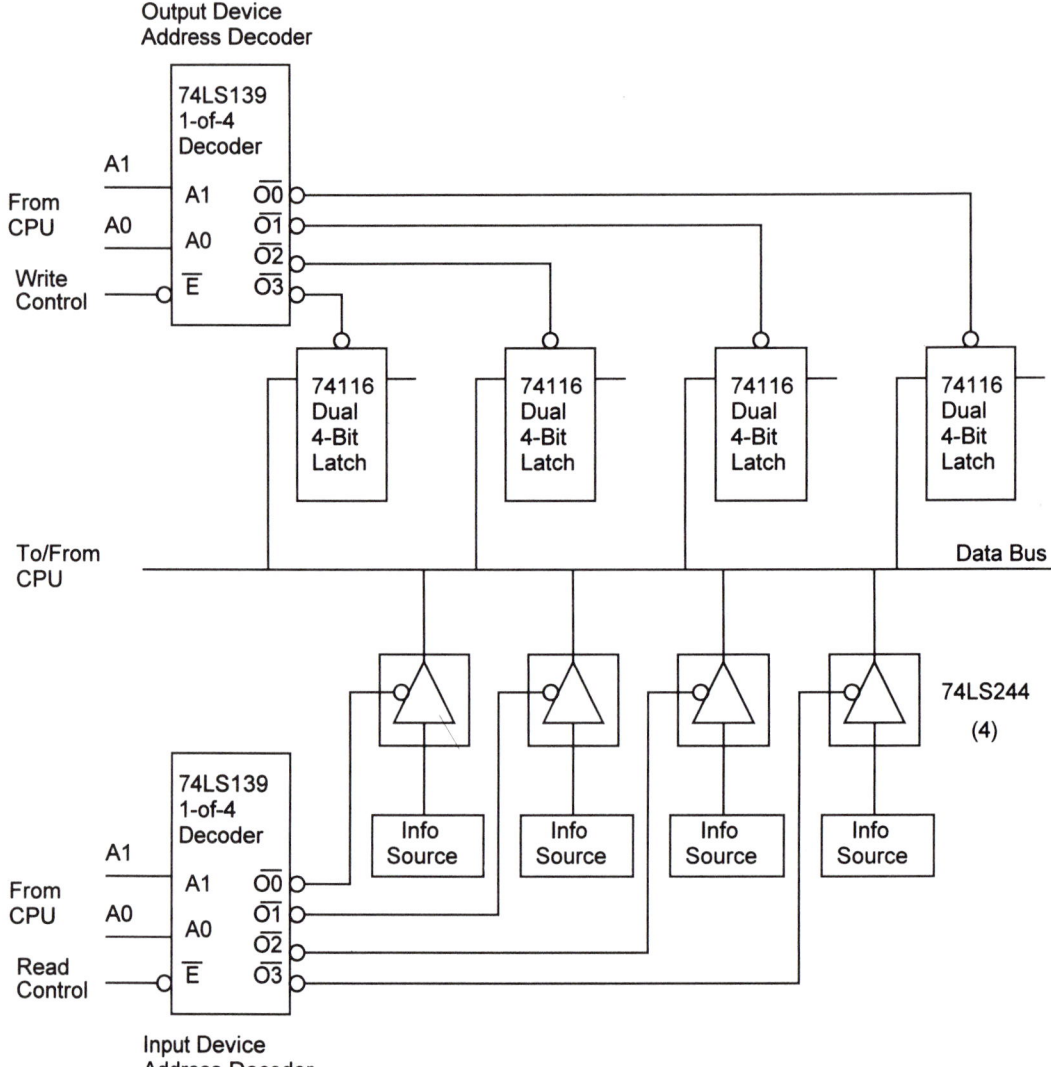

Figure 7–5   Address decoding for sources and destinations.

> Data must be taken from the bus or placed onto the bus at the correct time. The CPU controls this timing.

- The interface must provide the ability for the CPU to select one of many sources and destinations.

- *Provide timing and synchronization so the transfer of information occurs at the right time.*

The CPU, as the bus master, controls the timing of information transfer. Consider transferring data from a CPU register to an output data latch. The CPU's timing is controlled by its clock, and this output operation is called a *write cycle*. A typical CPU write cycle is shown in Figure 7–6(a).

The CPU places the address on the address bus at point A. In a real system there is likely to be a multiplexed address bus (discussed in Section 7.5), but in any event, there is a point A when all address bus lines are valid. The data bits are supplied at point B, and $\overline{\text{WRITE}}$ is asserted by the CPU a short time later at point C. This signal is used to create the clock to latch the data at the correct time. Depending on the type of latch and when $\overline{\text{WRITE}}$ is asserted, the data may be captured on the falling or rising edge.

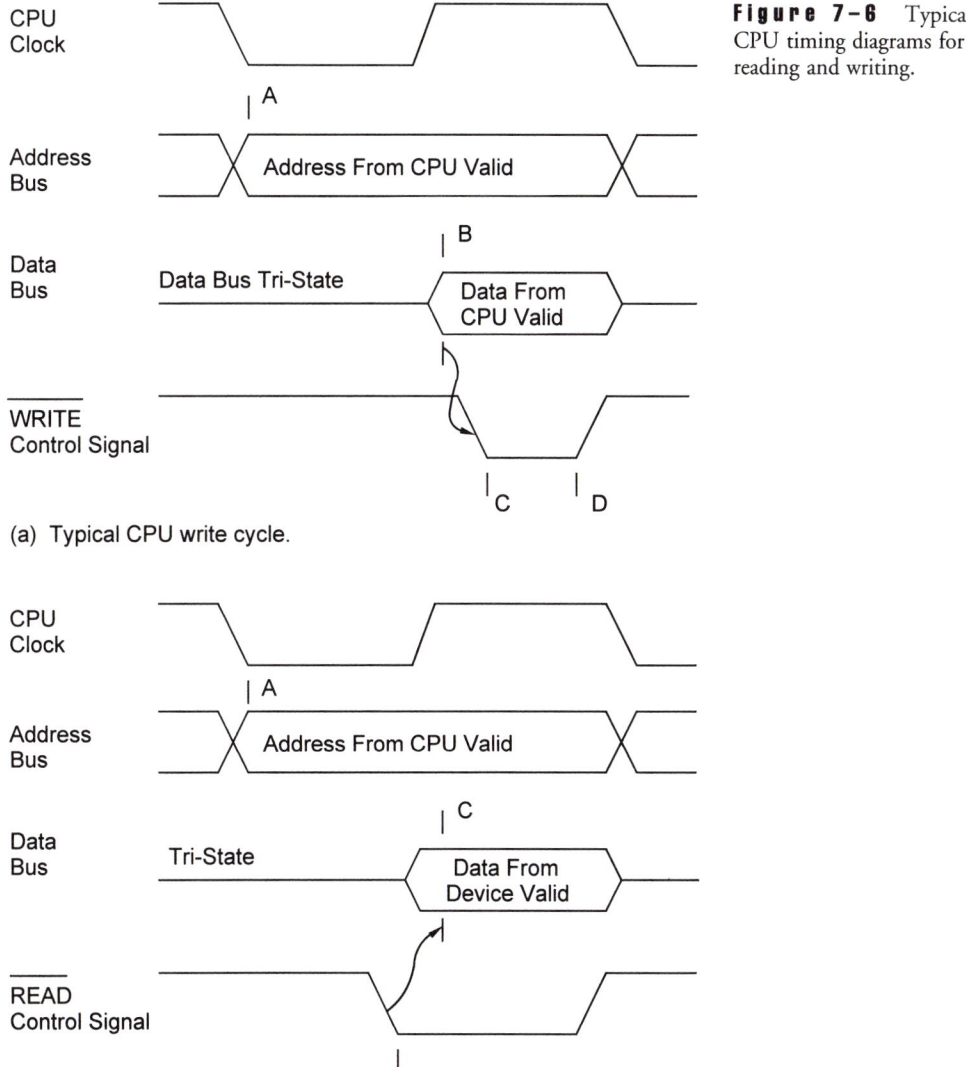

Figure 7–6 Typical CPU timing diagrams for reading and writing.

(a) Typical CPU write cycle.

(b) Typical CPU read cycle.

Transferring information from an external source to the CPU is called a *read cycle*. The CPU reads the data from the input device, and a typical CPU read cycle is shown in Figure 7–6(b). Again, addresses are supplied at point A. The control signal $\overline{\text{READ}}$ is asserted at point B to signal the external device that the CPU is ready to take the data from the data bus, which it does at point C. $\overline{\text{READ}}$ is used with the decoded address signal to enable the three-state buffers at the correct time for the correct device. An important point to mention at this time is that the CPU reads the data bus at point C whether or not the input device has it ready. If it is not, some form of I/O synchronization is needed. We will, for the moment, assume that the data are there and delay discussion this problem until Section 7.4.

> The CPU provides **READ** and **WRITE** control signals to define when these actions are taking place.

The addition of $\overline{\text{WRITE}}$ and $\overline{\text{READ}}$ control signals to the input and output interfaces is shown in Figure 7–7. In each case, $\overline{\text{WRITE}}$ and $\overline{\text{READ}}$ control the enable ($\overline{\text{E}}$) input on the address decoder. Thus the three-state enables and the latch clock signals are not asserted until the correct address is on the address bus AND the correct time in the write or read cycle has arrived. Notice that the address for both the input and output devices can be the same. This is possible because the CPU does not read and write simultaneously, and the $\overline{\text{WRITE}}$ and $\overline{\text{READ}}$ control signals ensure that only one device is active.

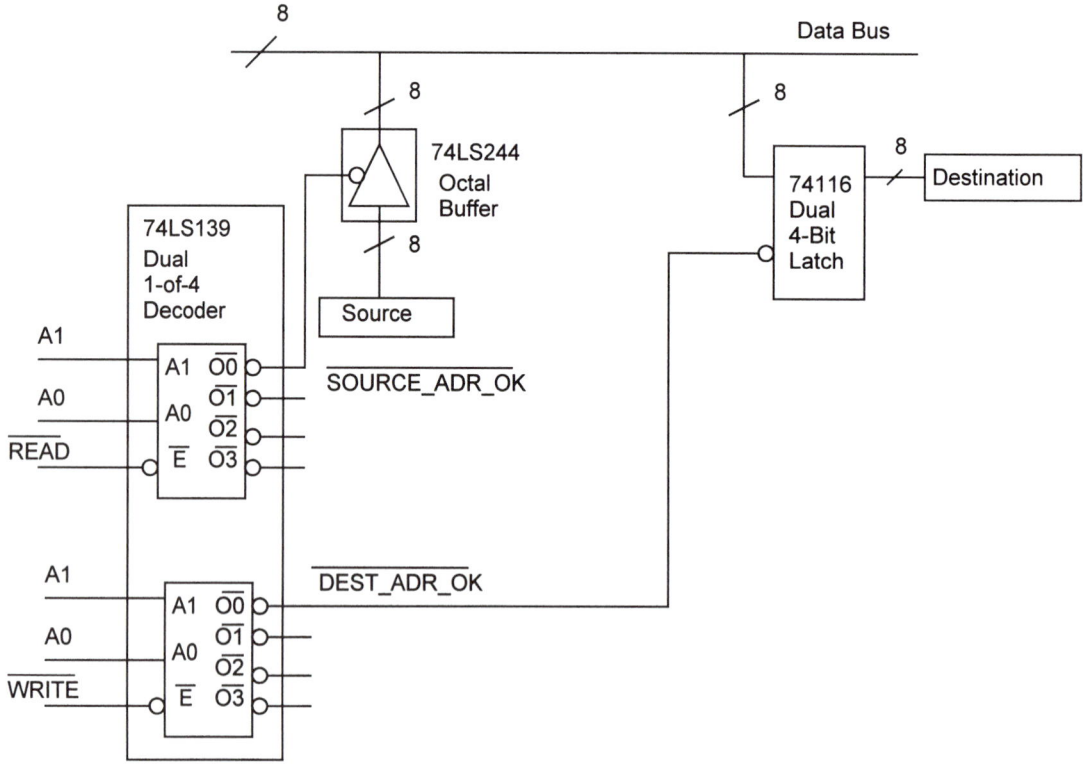

Figure 7–7   Complete I/O interface.

7.3 I/O Addressing

The address bus shown in Figure 7–1 is decoded by both memory and I/O to select a particular memory location or I/O device. When an instruction retrieves data from memory, the address from which the data is to come is placed on the address bus by the CPU. Although we have not yet discussed how the memory works, address decoders, much like those shown in Figure 7–7, are used in the memory circuits. The question that arises now is, "If the same address bus is used for both memory and I/O, how should the hardware be designed to differentiate between memory reads and writes and I/O reads and writes?" There are two solutions to this problem, *memory-mapped I/O* and *isolated* or *separate I/O*. These two choices affect how our programs access the I/O devices. In memory-mapped I/O, any instruction that reads or writes memory can also read or write I/O. For isolated I/O, the CPU designers must include separate input and output instructions.

> I/O addresses may be either *memory-mapped* or *separate* from the memory space.

Memory-Mapped I/O

> Memory-mapped I/O may require that the full address bus be decoded but allows any memory reference instruction to access I/O data.

The most simple I/O addressing scheme[4] is called *memory-mapped I/O*. Address decoders work equally well decoding memory or I/O addresses, and the control signals for timing the memory data transfers are available. Thus the CPU designer does not have to add any special capabilities to the CPU. The user of the CPU (the system designer) must divide the entire address space into memory and I/O space. This is shown in Figure 7–8(a).

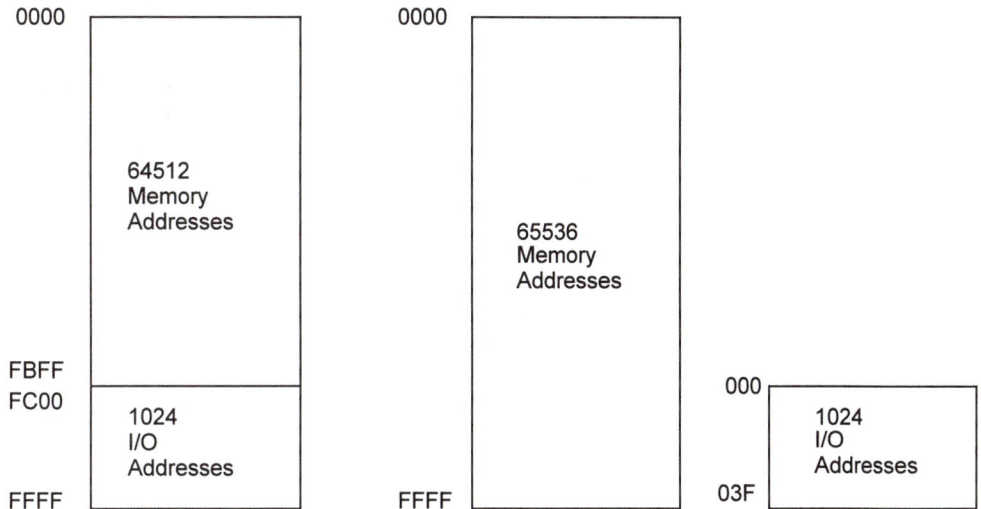

(a) Memory-mapped I/O. (b) Separate I/O.

Figure 7–8 Memory-mapped and separate I/O.

---

4 From the point of view of the CPU designer.

This design was popular in early minicomputers, such as the Digital Equipment Corporation PDP-8, and is used in many Motorola microcomputers. It offers the advantage of a simpler CPU hardware design and allows any memory reference instruction to access any I/O device. There are two disadvantages. First, as shown in Figure 7–8(a), I/O devices reduce the amount of memory available for application programs. Second, the address decoders may decode the full address bus to avoid conflict with memory addresses. This makes them more expensive than decoders operating on fewer bits.

Isolated or Separate I/O

The second method to resolve the dual use of the address bus is called *isolated* or *separate I/O*. Here, two maps, as shown in Figure 7–8(b), represent the memory and I/O spaces. Notice that the I/O map is smaller than the memory map because, in most systems, far fewer I/O devices are needed than memory. Fewer bits need to be decoded, resulting in less expensive address decoders than those needed for memory-mapped I/O.

Separate I/O requires that additional hardware features be added to the CPU. The address bus is used for both memory and I/O addresses, and because of this, the CPU must generate an additional control signal. This signal is called **IO/M** and prevents both memory and I/O trying to place data on the bus simultaneously. This signal is high for I/O use and low for memory.

> In a *separate I/O* design, cheaper address decoders may be used, but an additional control signal must be provided by the CPU.

The second change to the CPU hardware design is in the instruction decoder and sequence controller. Computers with separate I/O, and consequently the **IO/M** control signal, have I/O instructions that are separate from memory reference instructions. An easy way to decide if your computer has separate or memory-mapped I/O is to look for separate input and output instructions.

Figure 7–9(a) and (b) show I/O interfaces for memory-mapped I/O and separate I/O. Compare Figure 7–9(a) with Figure 7–7 and notice that they are logically the same except the **ADR_OK** signal is ANDed with the **WRITE** and **READ** signals external to the address decoder.

Figure 7–9(b) shows the additional logic required in a separate I/O interface. The **IO/M** control signal is ANDed with **READ** and **WRITE** to create **IO_READ** and **IO_WRITE**. In some processors, **IO_READ** and **IO_WRITE** are generated in the CPU itself. An alternative to the design shown in Figure 7–9(b) is to use **IO/M** as an enable input to the address decoder. The object is to *qualify* the three-state enable and the latch clock so that they are asserted only when I/O addresses are present.

Figure 7–9(a) and (b) show an address decoder with multiple ADR_OK outputs, one for each input and output device. This scheme could be used in a system where the logic circuits are together on one printed circuit board. On the other hand, in a system like a personal computer where I/O interfaces may be on separate printed circuit boards that plug into a motherboard, separate address decoders must be used for each device.

EXAMPLE 7–1   Show how to use $\overline{\text{READ}}$ and $\text{IO}/\overline{\text{M}}$ to enable the output of a 74LS139 Dual 1-of-4 decoder.

Solution:

See Figure 7.10.

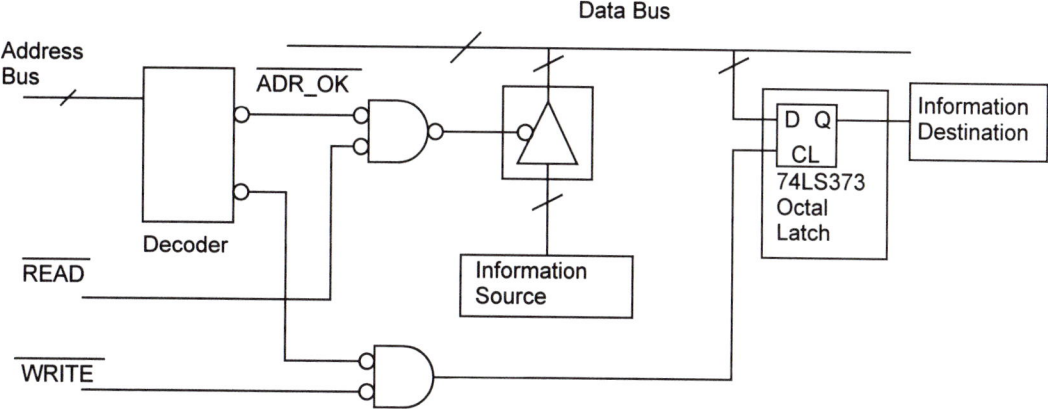

(a) I/O interface for memory-mapped I/O.

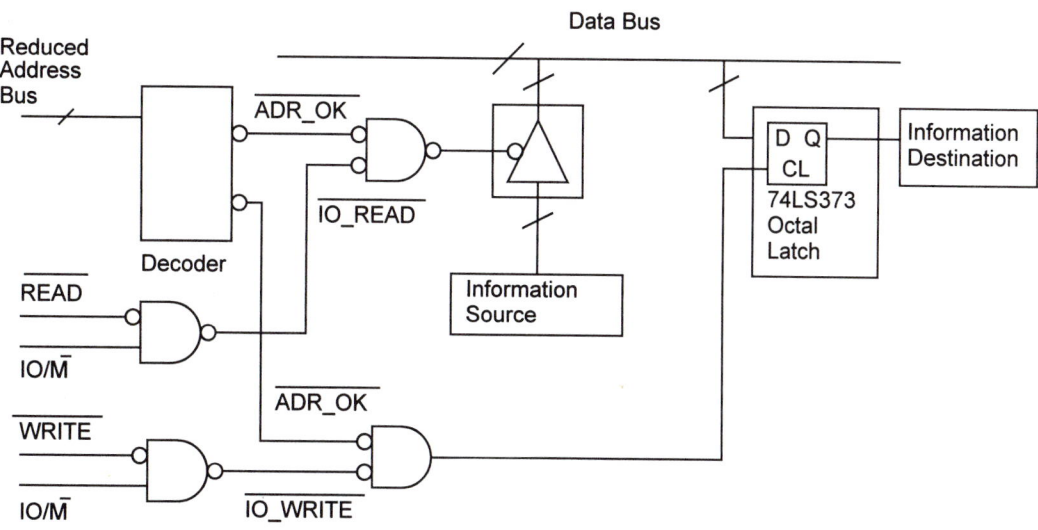

(b) I/O interface for separate I/O.

Figure 7-9   I/O interfaces for memory-mapped and separate I/O.

Address Decoding

We have seen how address decoding can select a particular device. The example of Figure 7–7 shows two address bits selecting one of four devices, but more bits are needed to decode addresses for real I/O devices. A disadvantage of the memory-mapped scheme is that more address bits must be de-

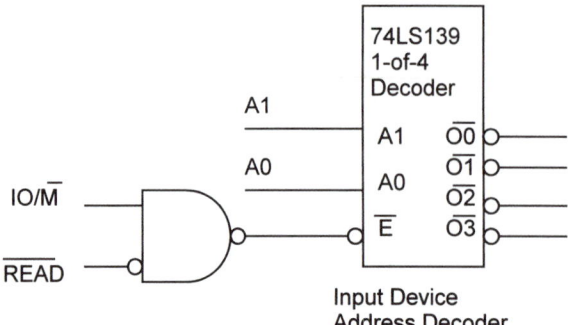

Figure 7-10   Using control signals to qualify the address decoder.

coded to select memory or I/O uniquely. This is, of course, a more expensive address decoder. In practical systems, the hardware designer chooses to decode only as many address bits as needed in the system.

Full Address Decoding

In a system with many I/O devices, the designer must decode enough bits to select each device uniquely. At the upper limit, allowing the maximum number of I/O devices, is *full address decoding*.

> Full address decoding requires that all address bits be decoded.

A typical address decoder is the 74LS138, 1-of-8 Decoder/Demultiplexer shown in Figure 7–11.[5] The truth table shows that the outputs are asserted low when the enable input **E3** is high and both **E1** and **E2** are low. Address bits can be used as enable inputs, and decoders can be cascaded as shown in Figure 7–12(a) to decode more address bits.

Discrete logic circuits can decode addresses. Figure 7–12(b) shows a 10- bit decoder for address $3E8 using a 74LS30 8-Input NAND, a 74LS27 Triple 3-Input NOR and one gate of a 74LS04 Hex Inverter. The inverter could be eliminated if an active high decoder output is allowed. Notice that the number of chips in (a) is less than (b) if the inverter is needed. Notice also that the discrete decoder provides decoding for only one address where the 74LS138 decoders provide other addresses. Your design can also use a combination of discrete logic and decoders.

EXAMPLE 7–2   Design a full address decoder to decode the 10-bit address $3E8.

Solution:

Starting with the most significant bit, assign address bits to decoder inputs. For the most significant decoder, select the appropriate output to serve as an enable input for the next decoder in the cascade. Apply the remaining address bits to decoder data and enable inputs and then choose the correct output for the address required. See Figure 7.12(a) for a possible solution.

---

[5]   A similar device is a 74154 4-to-16 Decoder/Demultiplexer.

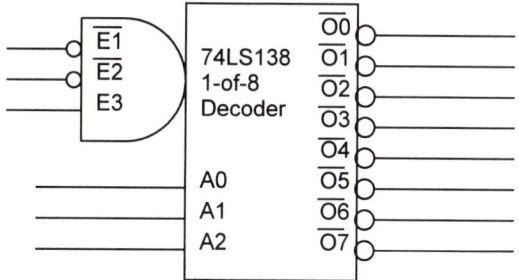

INPUTS						OUTPUTS							
$\overline{E1}$	$\overline{E2}$	E3	A2	A1	A0	$\overline{O0}$	$\overline{O1}$	$\overline{O2}$	$\overline{O3}$	$\overline{O4}$	$\overline{O5}$	$\overline{O6}$	$\overline{O7}$
H	X	X	X	X	X	H	H	H	H	H	H	H	H
X	H	X	X	X	X	H	H	H	H	H	H	H	H
X	X	L	X	X	X	H	H	H	H	H	H	H	H
L	L	H	L	L	L	L	H	H	H	H	H	H	H
L	L	H	L	L	H	H	L	H	H	H	H	H	H
L	L	H	L	H	L	H	H	L	H	H	H	H	H
L	L	H	L	H	H	H	H	H	L	H	H	H	H
L	L	H	H	L	L	H	H	H	H	L	H	H	H
L	L	H	H	L	H	H	H	H	H	H	L	H	H
L	L	H	H	H	L	H	H	H	H	H	H	L	H
L	L	H	H	H	H	H	H	H	H	H	H	H	L

Figure 7–11 74LS138 1-of-8 Decoder/Demultiplexer.

EXAMPLE 7–3 **Find the address decoded for each of the outputs of the second 74LS138 decoder in Figure 7–12(a).**

Solution:

The address bits to the decoder are:
Fixed Inputs = A9=1, A8=1, A7=1, A6=1, A4=0, A2=0, A0=0
Variable Inputs = A5, A3, A1

A9 A8	A7 A6 A5 A4	A3 A2 A1 A0	Address	Decoder Output
1 1	1 1 0 0	0 0 0 0	3C0	$\underline{O0}$
	0	0 1	3C2	$\underline{O1}$
	0	1 0	3C8	$\underline{O2}$
	0	1 1	3CA	$\underline{O3}$
	1	0 0	3E0	$\underline{O4}$
	1	0 1	3E2	$\underline{O5}$
	1	1 0	3E8	$\underline{O6}$
	1	1 1	3EA	$\underline{O7}$

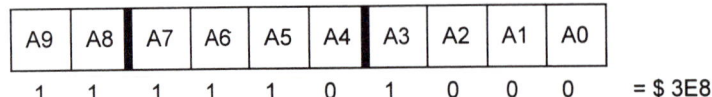

A9	A8	A7	A6	A5	A4	A3	A2	A1	A0
1	1	1	1	1	0	1	0	0	0

= $ 3E8

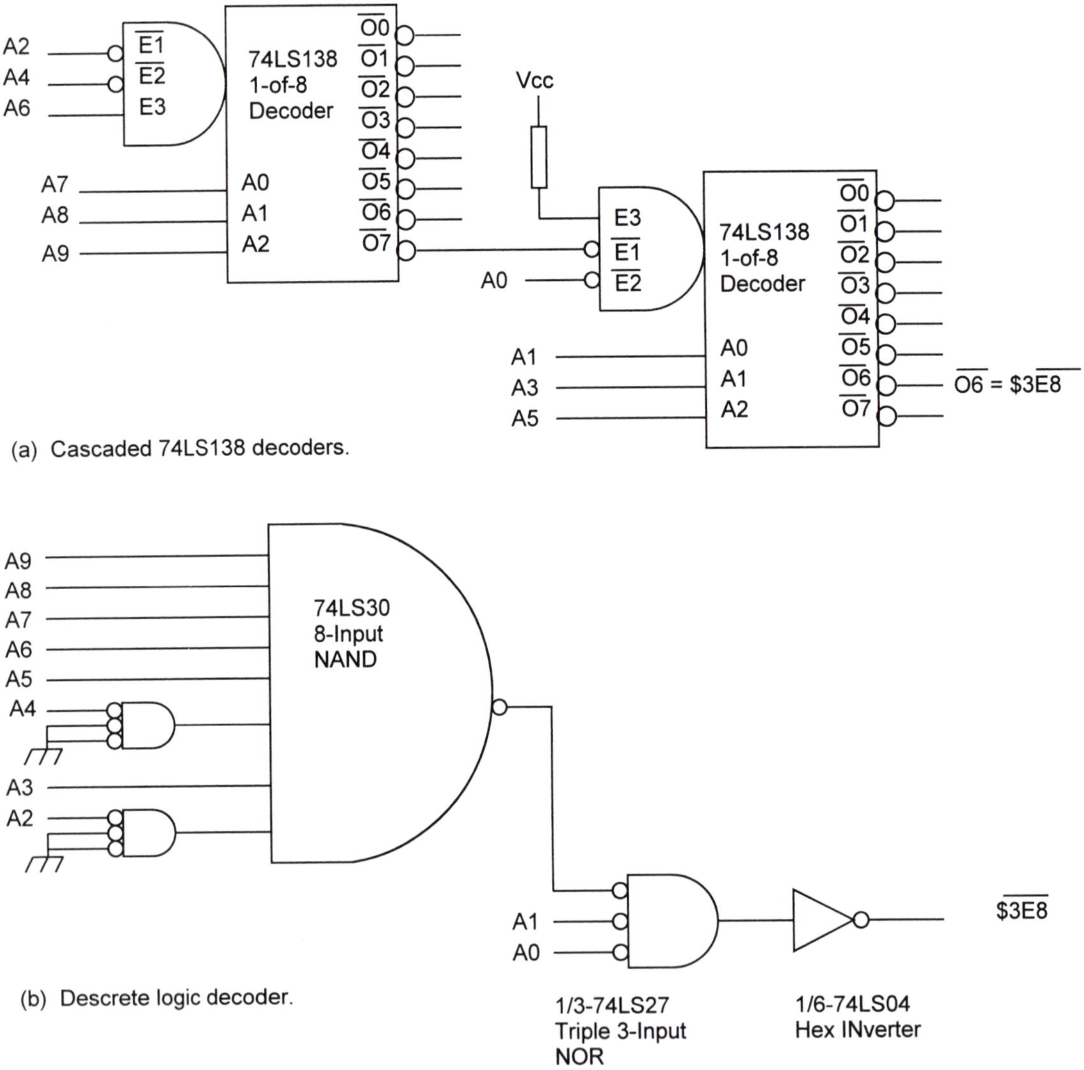

(a) Cascaded 74LS138 decoders.

(b) Descrete logic decoder.

1/3-74LS27
Triple 3-Input
NOR

1/6-74LS04
Hex INverter

Figure 7-12   Full 10-bit address decoders for address $3E8.

Incomplete Address Decoding

When a system does not need all the I/O address space, a designer can reduce hardware costs by *not* fully decoding the addresses. There are two methods used, *reduced* address decoding and *linear select* decoding.

EXAMPLE 7–4   For the address decoder in Figure 7–12(a), which output of the first and second decoders would you pick for address 142_{16}? Assume the address bits are input as shown.

Solution:

O2 for the first decoder and O1 for the second.

Reduced address decoding results in less complex decoders, but the decoded signal is asserted for more than one address.

Reduced address decoding: In reduced address decoding, the higher-order address bits are decoded and the lower-order bits are treated as don't cares. Figure 7–13 shows a 74LS138 decoding address bits A9–A4 and a 74LS30 8-Input NAND gate decoding bits A9–A2.

Each of the decoder output lines in Figure 7–13(a) responds to the addresses shown in Table 7–1. By not decoding the lower four bits of the address, each decoder output line is asserted for sixteen I/O addresses.

Linear select decoding: In very small systems with few I/O devices, each bit in the address bus can select a device. Consider a system where there are only six I/O devices and a ten-bit I/O address, as shown in Figure 7–14. If the I/O select signal is active-low, each of the six devices can be chosen by using the addresses given in Table 7–2. You must be careful *not* to generate addresses

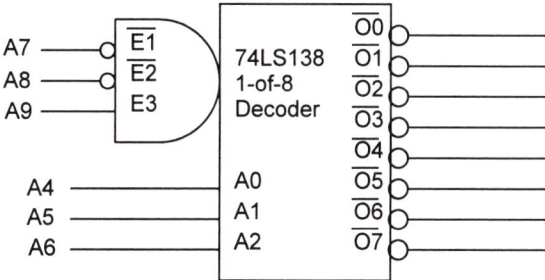

(a) 74LS138 decoder.

Figure 7–13   Reduced I/O address decoding.

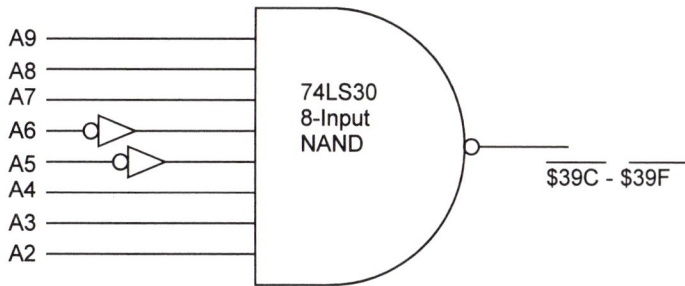

(b) 74LS30 NAND gate decoder.

TABLE 7–1 Reduced address decoding

Decoder output	Address bits								
	A9	A8	A7	A6	A5	A4	A3 A2 A1 A0		
	Decoder inputs								
	E3	$\overline{E2}$	$\overline{E1}$	A2	A1	A0	Not used	Valid HEX addresses	
$\overline{O0}$	1	0	0	0	0	0	0000 TO 1111	200 TO 20F	
$\overline{O1}$	1	0	0	0	0	1	0000 TO 1111	210 TO 21F	
$\overline{O2}$	1	0	0	0	1	0	0000 TO 1111	220 TO 22F	
$\overline{O3}$	1	0	0	0	1	1	0000 TO 1111	230 TO 23F	
$\overline{O4}$	1	0	0	1	0	0	0000 TO 1111	240 TO 24F	
$\overline{O5}$	1	0	0	1	0	1	0000 TO 1111	250 TO 25F	
$\overline{O6}$	1	0	0	1	1	0	0000 TO 1111	260 TO 26F	
$\overline{O7}$	1	0	0	1	1	1	0000 TO 1111	270 TO 27F	

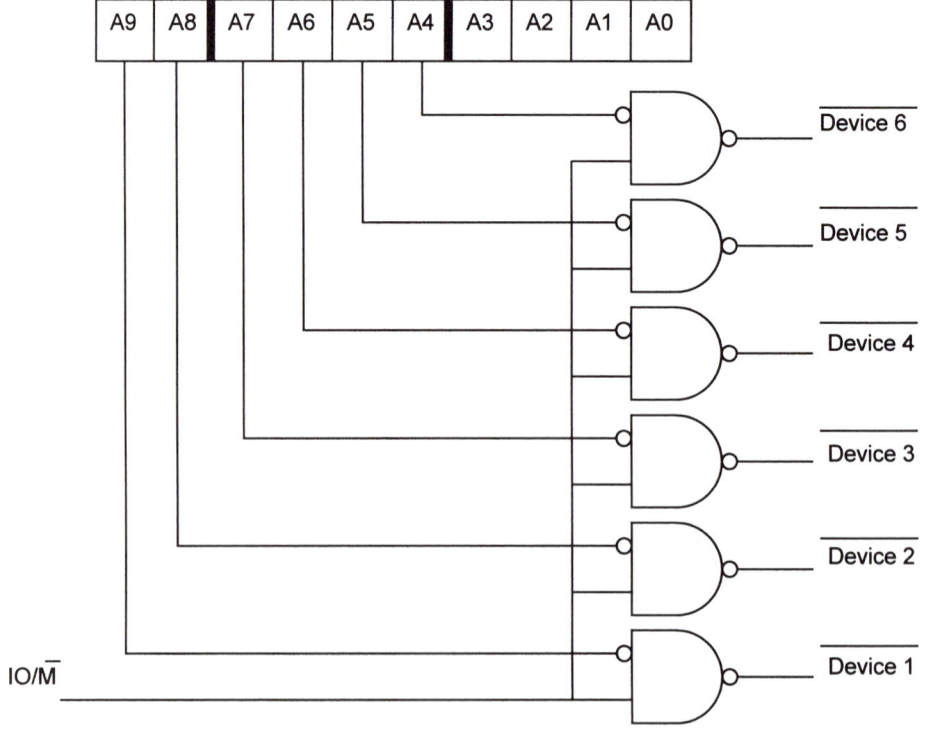

Figure 7–14   Linear select addressing.

TABLE 7-2 Linear select addressing

	Address Bits										
	A9	A8	A7	A6	A5	A4	A3	A2	A1	A0	I/O Address
Device 1	0	1	1	1	1	1	X	X	X	X	1F0–1FF
Device 2	1	0	1	1	1	1	X	X	X	X	2F0–2FF
Device 3	1	1	0	1	1	1	X	X	X	X	370–37F
Device 4	1	1	1	0	1	1	X	X	X	X	3B0–3BF
Device 5	1	1	1	1	0	1	X	X	X	X	3D0–3DF
Device 6	1	1	1	1	1	0	X	X	X	X	3E0–3EF

where more than one device is selected. For the example given in Table 7.2, an address such as 330 would select both devices three and four.

7.4 I/O Synchronization

There are three situations that can arise where the external I/O device and the CPU must be synchronized. First, and most common, the CPU may be faster than the I/O device. The design of the interface in Section 7.3 assumes that the output device (for a CPU write cycle) is ready to receive the data from the CPU by point D in Figure 7–6(a). For a read cycle, the input device must have placed the data on the bus by point C in Figure 7–6(b). When these timing requirements are not met, software or hardware must synchronize the fast CPU and the slow I/O. Another synchronization problem occurs when the I/O device needs to transfer data at unpredictable intervals. A third occurs when the I/O device is faster than the CPU. The software and hardware methods shown below can solve the first two problems, although unpredictable transfer times are better synchronized using interrupts, which we will cover in Chapter 8. The third problem is often solved with a technique called *direct memory access* (DMA), which avoids the CPU altogether. DMA techniques will be discussed in Section 7.5.

> I/O operations must be *synchronized* with the CPU.

Software I/O Synchronization

There are two software-based synchronization methods. The first is sometimes called *real-time* synchronization and uses a software delay to match the CPU to the timing requirements of the I/O device. Consider outputting data to a serial port that transmits at 9600 baud (960 characters/second). The time between characters is 1.04 milliseconds, but the program is likely to be able to read characters from memory and output to the serial device at a much higher rate. If the program does not have to do anything else during data output, a simple delay loop could synchronize the CPU with the serial port. One drawback of this approach is that the delay will change if the CPU clock frequency changes. Software timing loops are not very portable. Further, the CPU can't do anything else when it is wasting time in the delay loop.

> Real-time synchronization uses a software timing loop.

Another software synchronization method is *polled* I/O. A *status* register, with a **DATA_READY** bit, is added to the input device as shown in Figure 7–15. The software then reads the status register (it must have its own I/O address) and checks the **DATA_READY** bit. If the device is not ready, the program loops until it is and then reads the information. Figure 7–15(c) shows the software

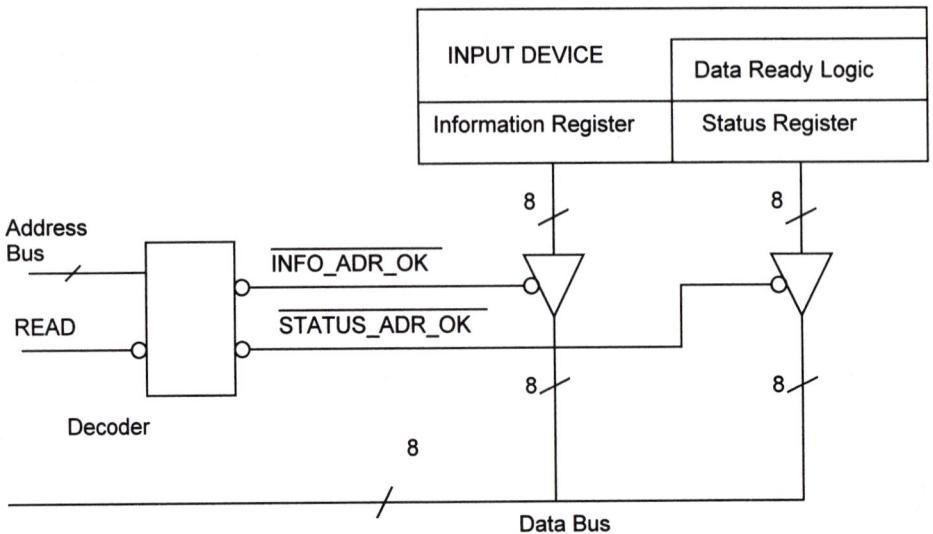

(a) Hardware needed for software I/O synchronization.

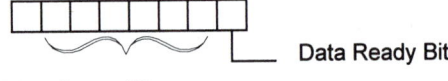

(b) Status register.

(c) Software design for polling I/O.

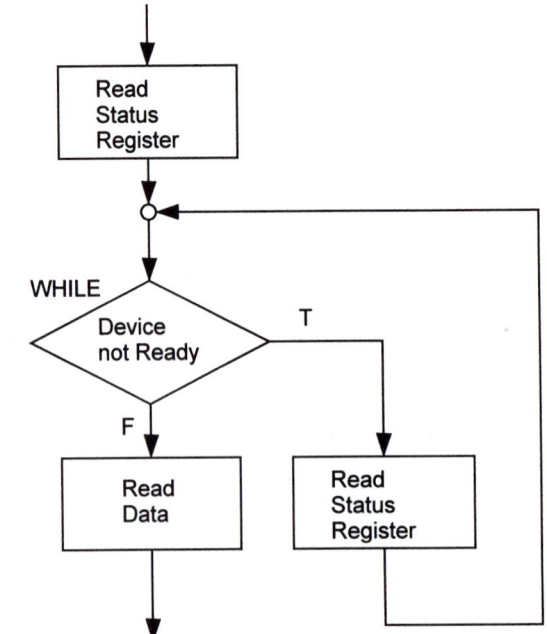

Figure 7-15 Software I/O synchronization using polling.

loop required. The input contains additional logic to set the **DATA_READY** bit and to reset it when the information register is read by the CPU.

Software synchronization for an output operation is accomplished with a **READY_TO_RECEIVE_DATA** bit in the status register and logic in the output device to set and reset this bit. The software polls the bit, waiting until it is asserted, before outputting the data to the output register.

Handshaking I/O

Although the software synchronization method is the most simple (in terms of the hardware required in the CPU), it adds additional software to the program. A hardware method is available in processors equipped with a control signal called **READY** or **WAIT**. When the **WAIT** signal is asserted by an external device, the sequence controller spins its wheels in a wait state until the control signal is deasserted, allowing the CPU to continue its operation. A timing diagram for a read operation with a waiting period (wait states or wait cycles) is shown in Figure 7–16(a).

The hardware required for input handshaking is shown in Figure 7–16(b). **INFO_ADR_OK**,, which activates the three-state gates, is also used by the input device as a **DATA_REQUEST** control signal. Logic in the input device then generates a **WAIT** signal that goes back to the CPU. If the CPU "sees" **WAIT** before it takes the data (at point C), it enters the waiting period. This time may be as long as the input device needs before it releases the **WAIT** control signal and allows the CPU to complete the input operation, taking the data at point F.

The handshaking scenario for the output operation is virtually identical to input handshaking. The **INFO_ADR_OK** signal takes on the meaning of a **DATA_AVAIL** signal to the output device. If the device is not ready to take the data, it asserts the **WAIT** signal, and the CPU enters the wait state until the output device releases it.

Software Versus Handshaking I/O

The method chosen to synchronize I/O devices depends on what hardware and control signals are available in the CPU. If it does not have a **WAIT** or **READY** input, the hardware handshaking method cannot be used unless other provisions have been made by the manufacturer. In processors with the **READY** or **WAIT** input, either method can be used.

Handshaking I/O is potentially faster than software polling and does not require additional program instructions to poll the status register. A disadvantage of handshaking I/O is that while the CPU is in a wait state, it cannot do anything else. You may not want to do this when other important processes need action. When polling is used, the CPU can be doing other things while it is waiting for the I/O device to become ready. The logic required in the I/O device is more complex for the software polling method because a register must be added to contain the status information. This is in addition to the logic required to know if the device is ready or not. However, from the point of view of the CPU design, software polling is more simple.

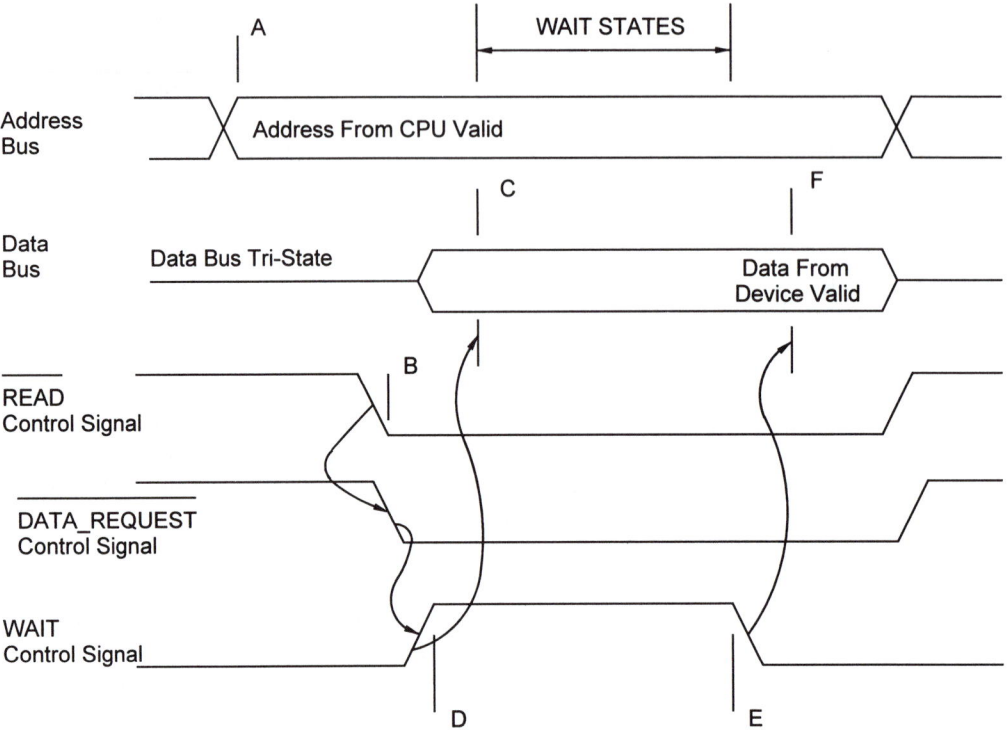

(a) Read cycle with wait states.

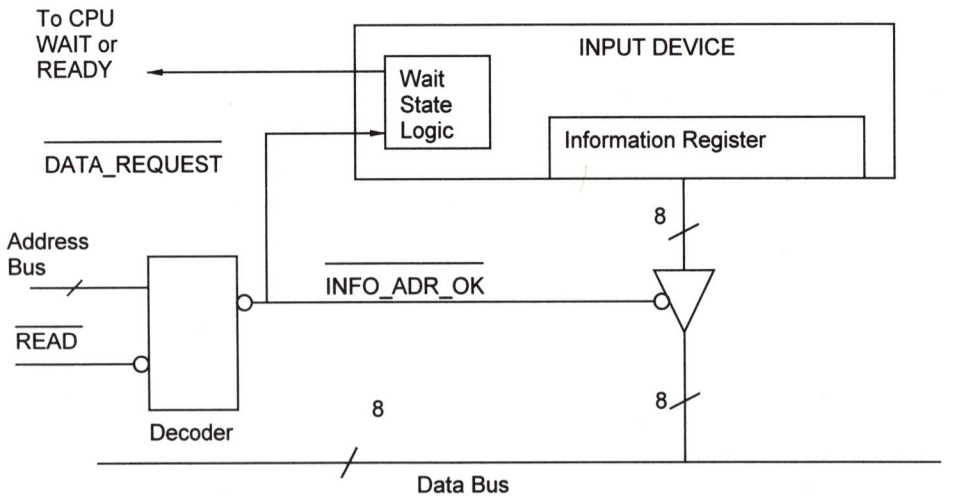

(b) Input handshaking hardware.

Figure 7-16   Hardware handshaking I/O synchronization.

I/O Synchronization with Interrupts

Another way to synchronize I/O and the CPU is to use interrupts. Interrupts allow an I/O device to signal the CPU that it is ready to be serviced. Interrupts will be covered in detail in Chapter 8.

7.5 More Bus Ideas

Multiplexed Bus

A problem with many processors is that there are not enough pins on the device to allow all the desired signals to be available, although the number of pins on the microprocessor chips has been steadily increasing (see Table 7–3). A solution to this problem is to time-multiplex bus and control signals. Time multiplexing means that the use of any pin may differ as a function of time. A common example is a multiplexed address bus. Consider a 16-bit address where the CPU is designed to provide only 8 bits at a time, a savings of eight pins that can be used for other functions. Figure 7–17(a) is a timing diagram showing how the CPU provides the address information. The higher eight bits, ADR15–ADR8, appear first (at A) and are followed by the lower eight bits (ADR7–ADR0) at B. A control signal, called **ADDRESS_STROBE(AS)** or **ADDRESS_LATCH_ENABLE (ALE)**, is provided by the CPU to latch the upper eight bits of the address as shown in Figure 7–17(b).

> Many CPUs have a *multiplexed bus* to reduce the number of pins needed on the chip.

Bidirectional Bus Transceiver

The data bus in Figure 7–1 is bidirectional because data must flow into and out of the CPU. In many systems, a bidirectional data bus buffer, or bus transceiver, such as that shown in Figure 7–18, is used between the CPU and the rest of the system. The $\overline{E}$ must be low to enable the three-state buffers and **DIR** controls the direction of data flow. The bus transceiver provides additional current to drive more devices on the data bus.

TABLE 7–3 CPU pinouts

CPU	Year	Adr	Data	Control	Power	Total	Multiplexing
8008	1972	14	8	8	2	18	None
6800	1974	16	8	11	3	40	None
8080	1974	16	8	12	4	40	None
8085	1976	16	8	22	2	40	Address/data
Z80	1976	16	8	14	2	40	None
8086	1978	20	16	17	3	40	Address/data/control
6809	1979	16	8	14	2	40	None
68000	1979	23	16	21	4	64	Control bits select lsb
8088	1979	20	8	21	3	40	Address/data/control
68020	1984	32	32	38	12	114	None
80386	1985	32	32	21	41	132	None

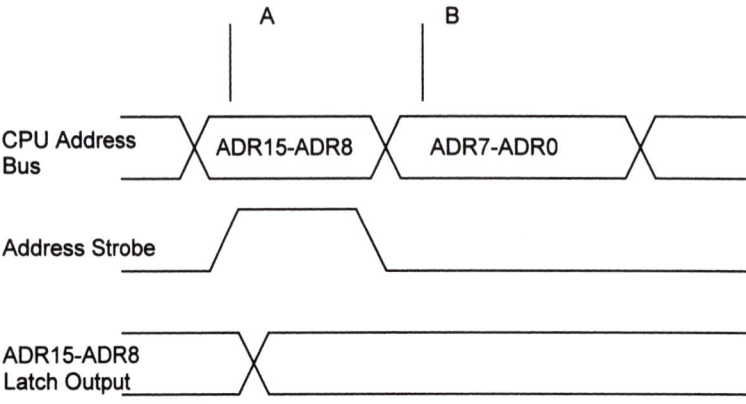

(a) Multiplexed address bus timing diagram.

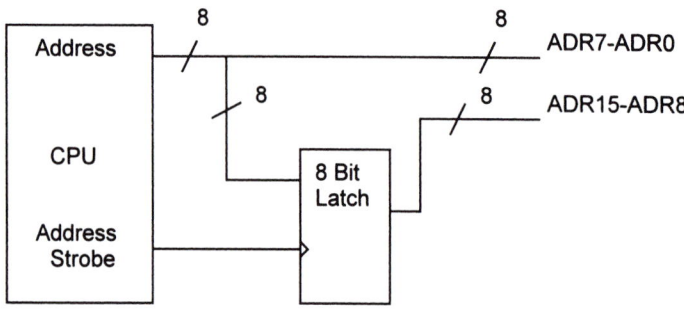

(b) Address bus demultiplexer.

Figure 7-17 Multiplexed address bus.

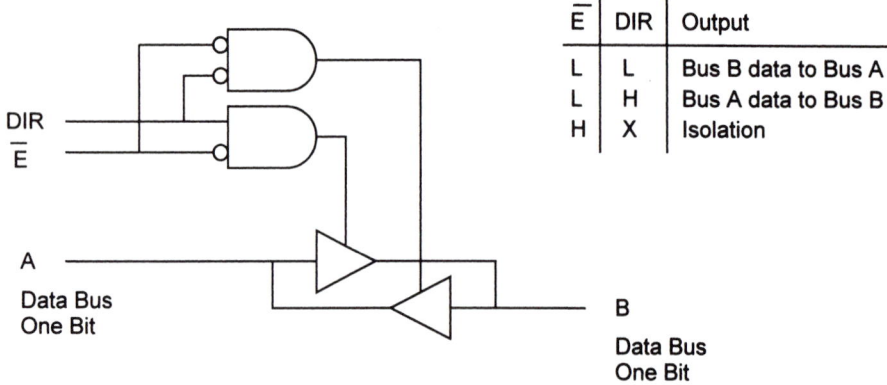

$\overline{E}$	DIR	Output
L	L	Bus B data to Bus A
L	H	Bus A data to Bus B
H	X	Isolation

Figure 7-18 One section of 74LS245 octal bus transceiver.

Synchronous, Semisynchronous, and Asynchronous Buses

These terms refer to bus timing protocols that define how and when devices are to respond to data transfers. In Section 7.2, the **READ** and **WRITE** control signals were introduced to show how the CPU informs external devices that data are either now available on the data bus, in an output operation, or are about to be taken, in an input operation. The bus transfer is completed in one cycle of the CPU clock, and all devices must respond within this time. This is an example of a *synchronous* bus protocol. The clock may or may not be part of the signals included in the control bus. The problem with the synchronous bus is that the clock frequency must be based on the slowest device in the system. In a system with a mixture of devices that respond in different times, we would like the design to respond to fast devices quickly and to slow the CPU down for the slower devices. A solution to this problem is the handshaking I/O shown in Figure 7–16(a). This is a *semisynchronous* bus protocol, and two additional control signals are required. These are DATA_REQUEST, which is generated within the slow device's I/O interface, and **WAIT**, which the slow device generates to signal the CPU. Most microcomputer systems using a CPU with a **WAIT** control signal use the semisynchronous bus. If the device can respond within one clock cycle, fine, but if more time is needed, **WAIT** causes the processor to generate wait states as shown in Figure 7–16(a). The timing of the arrival of **WAIT** is important because the CPU must "see" it before it starts to take the data. The required timing will be given by the CPU's data sheets.

There is little to distinguish the semisynchronous bus from *asynchronous* bus protocols. The DATA_REQUEST signal is included as part of the control bus, and all devices (even memory) must respond with a **WAIT** (or the absence of the **WAIT**) signal. Timing for a fully interlocked, asynchronous bus is the same as the semisynchronous bus shown in Figure 7–16(a).

Bus Masters and Slaves

Bus masters and slaves refer to how the buses are controlled. In the computer system shown in Figure 7–1, the CPU is the only bus master. All memory, I/O interfaces, and other devices on the buses are slaves. They take their orders from the CPU master. Figure 7–19 shows a scheme called *direct memory access (DMA)*. Suppose a block of data is to be retrieved from a fast I/O device. In the normal, programmed I/O sequence, the data must be input and then stored in memory, using several program steps and clock cycles. If the system includes a DMA controller, the block of data can be transferred directly to memory, bypassing the CPU altogether. Control signals, such as *Hold* and *Hold_Acknowledge* in Intel systems and *Bus_Request* and *Bus_Grant* in Motorola systems, allow the second bus master, the DMA controller, to suspend the operation of the CPU. The DMA controller generates addresses and control signals to transfer the data from the I/O device to the memory.

Bus Arbitration

Bus arbitration is needed if more than one bus master requests the bus at the same time.

Bus arbitration is required in systems with multiple (more than two) bus masters when more than one master wants to control the bus simultaneously. Consider Figure 7–20. A Motorola 68000 can be seen with several other bus masters that can be DMA devices or other microprocessors. When one of them wants to control the bus, it asserts

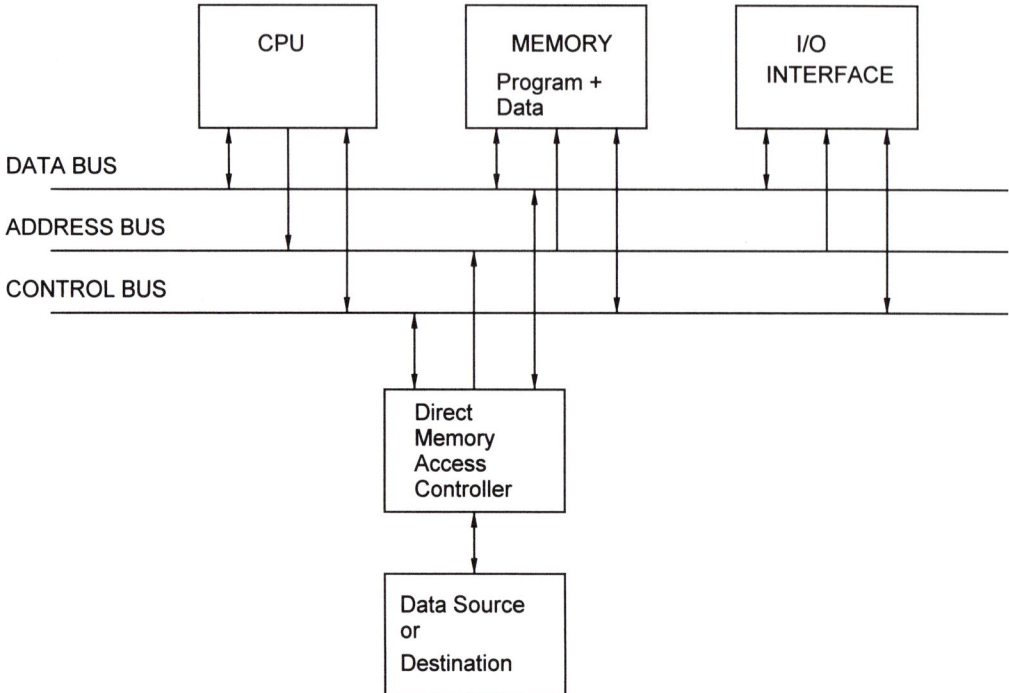

Figure 7-19   Direct memory access using multiple bus masters.

the $\overline{\textbf{BUS\_REQUEST}}$ ($\overline{\textbf{BR}}$) signal; this is answered by the CPU asserting the $\overline{\textbf{BUS\_GRANT}}$ ($\overline{\textbf{BG}}$) signal. Upon receipt of $\overline{\textbf{BG}}$,, the peripheral bus master asserts the $\overline{\textbf{BUS\_GRANT\_ACKNOWLEDGE}}$ ($\overline{\textbf{BGACK}}$) signal to tell the other bus masters it has control of the buses. A problem arises when there are simultaneous bus requests from two or more bus masters. Bus arbitration is needed to resolve this problem.

Figure 7–21(a) shows a daisy chain arbitration system designed for an Intel 8086 processor. Whenever any device wants to control the bus, it asserts **HOLD** and opens the switch in the **HOLD_**

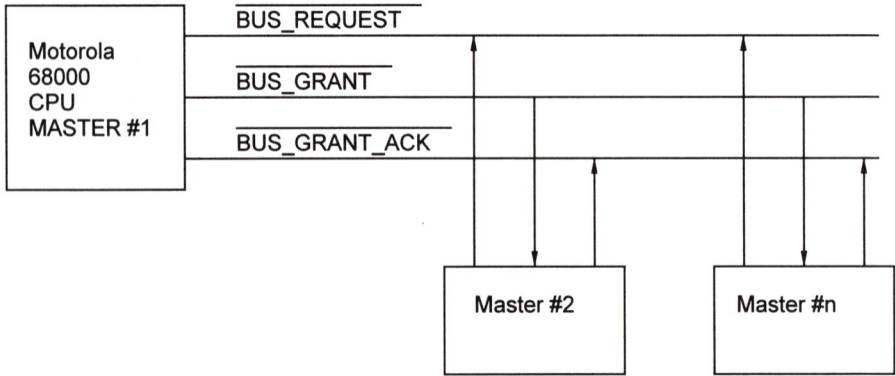

Figure 7-20   Multiple bus masters can cause bus conflicts.

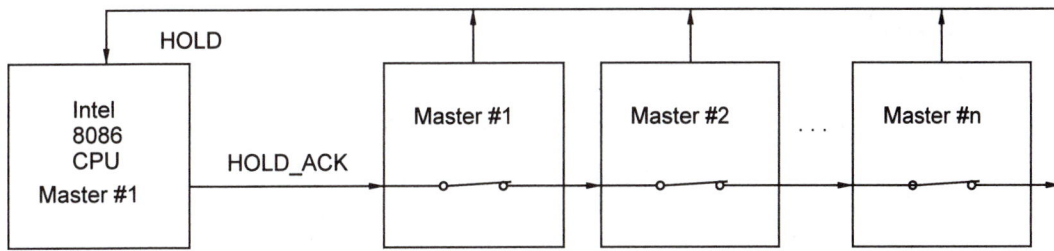

(a) Daisy chain bus arbitration.

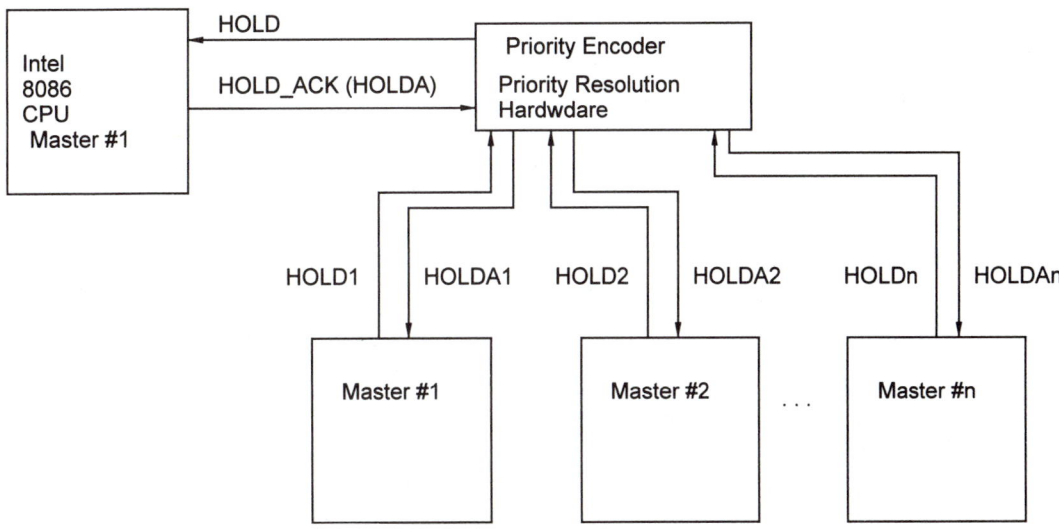

(b) Hardware priority bus arbitration.

Figure 7–21   Bus arbitration.

ACKNOWLEDGE (HOLDA) line. When **HOLD_ACKNOWLEDGE** is asserted by the CPU, it passes through each of the inactive bus masters until it reaches the active one. If a bus master farther right on the chain asserts **HOLD** before another master is finished, **HOLDA** is not passed along until the higher-priority device (closer to the CPU) is finished with its task and closes the switch. The daisy chain system also resolves simultaneous bus requests because the closest device (electrically) to the CPU will receive **HOLDA** first.

Figure 7–21(b) uses a priority encoder to resolve the conflict. Simultaneous **HOLD** signals are encoded so that only the highest priority device receives the hold acknowledge. See Problem 7.17.

Additional Bus Control Signals

We have discussed many of the control signals generated by the CPU to help with the timing of reading and writing data. You may find some of the following signals as well.

Interrupt_Request and Interrupt_Acknowledge: These signals activate the interrupt processing of the CPU. Interrupts will be discussed in detail in Chapter 8.

Clock: Some systems provide the CPU clock as part of the control bus. In Motorola systems, the E clock is required in the logic to generate `IO_READ` and `IO_WRITE` control signals.

Reset: The CPU `RESET` is sometimes provided as a bus signal to reset switching circuits in I/O devices.

7.6 Simple I/O Devices

The I/O interfaces shown in Figures 7–7 and 7–9 can interface parallel devices to the system buses. Let us look at some simple devices that use these interfaces.

Input Switches

The switch is the most basic of all binary input devices. Figure 7–22(a) shows a single-pole, single-throw (SPST) switch and a pull-up resistor. The switch output is high or low depending on the switch position. Figure 7–22(b) shows a multiple-pole, rotary switch. Pull-up resistors are necessary in each of these switches to provide a high logic level when the switch is open. If switches are to be interfaced to I/O ports on a microcontroller or a programmable I/O device, the pull-up resistors may already be in the chip. Check the specifications before adding external resistors.

A problem with all switches is *switch bounce.* When a switch makes contact, its mechanical springiness will cause the contact to bounce, or make and break, for a few milliseconds, as shown in Figure 7–22(c). If a program is counting switch closures and the software is fairly fast, it may count several bounces and return more counts than are real. Thus, depending on the application, switch debouncing may be necessary. There are several ways to debounce switches, including both software and hardware methods.

> The *switch bounce* problem must be solved when using mechanical switches.

Software Debouncing

There are two strategies for debouncing a switch in software. The first may be called "*wait and see.*" Switch bouncing usually lasts only 5–10 milliseconds. If the software detects a low logic level, indicating the switch has closed, it can simply wait for longer than 10 milliseconds, say 20–100 ms, and then test for the switch still being low. The other approach is an integrating debouncer. The idea is to initialize a counter with a value of 10 and, after the first logic low level is detected, to poll the switch every millisecond. If the switch output is low, decrement the counter. If the switch output is high, increment the counter. When the counter reaches zero, we know that the switch output has been low for at least 10 milliseconds. If, on the other hand, the counter reaches 20, we

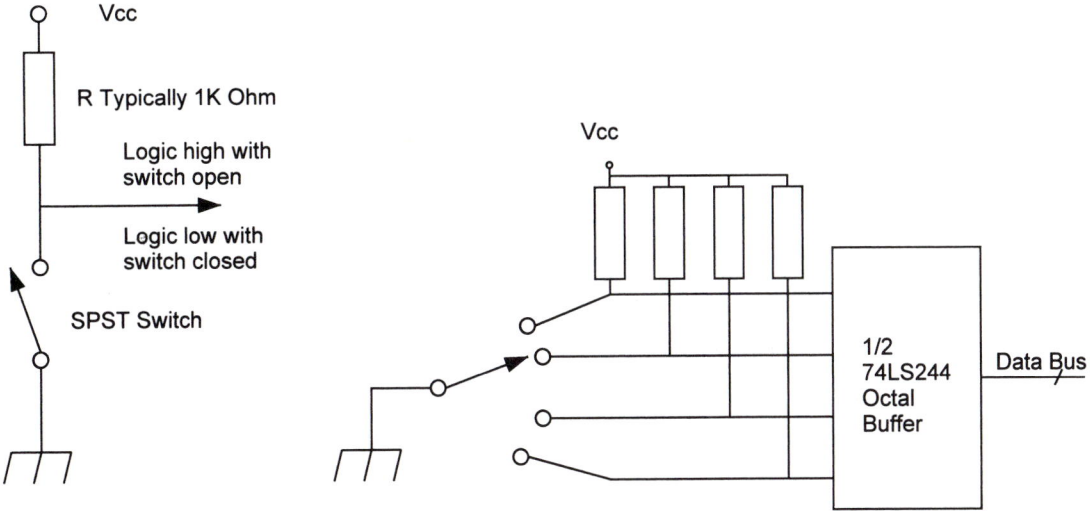

(a) Single-pole, single-throw (SPST) logic switch.

(b) Multiple pole switch.

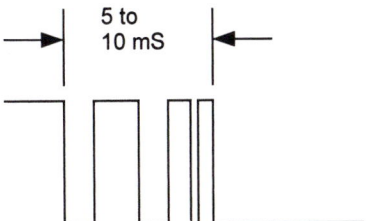

(c) Switch bounce.

Figure 7-22   Switch used for binary input.

know that the switch has been open for at least 10 milliseconds. Table 7–4 shows the pseudocode for this algorithm.

Hardware Debouncing

Figure 7–23 shows three hardware debouncing schemes. In (a) and (b), single-pole, double-throw (SPDT) switches are debounced with NAND and NOR latches. An integrating debouncer is shown

---

TABLE 7-4 Pseudocode design for integrating switch debouncer

```
INITIALIZE Count=10
WHILE Count > 0 and < 20
        DO
                     Delay 1 millisecond
                     Get Switch Input
                     IF Switch Closed
                                 THEN Decrement Count
                                 ELSE Increment Count
                     ENDIF Switch Closed
        ENDO
ENDWHILE Count > 0 and < 20
IF Count = 0
        THEN Switch is closed
        ELSE Switch is open
ENDIF Count = 0
```

---

in (c) with a Schmitt trigger gate. This gate has hysteresis and does not switch until the input voltage exceeds a threshold.

Arrays of Switches

Switches can be organized as linear or matrix arrays; a linear array is shown in Figure 7–24. The switch bounce problem must be solved and the array of switches must be scanned to find out which are closed or open. The output of the switch array could be interfaced directly to an eight-bit input port (at point A). To save some I/O lines, a 74LS151 8-Input Multiplexer can be used.

> Arrays of switches may have to be *scanned* to see which switch is activated.

Software is required to scan the array shown in Figure 7–24. As the software outputs a 3-bit sequence from 000 to 111, the multiplexer selects each of the switch inputs. The software scanner then reads one bit at an input port.

A keyboard is an array of switches arranged in a two-dimensional matrix as shown in Figure 7–25. A switch is connected at each intersection of the vertical and horizontal lines as shown by the blow-up view. Closing the switch connects the horizontal line to the vertical. An 8x8 keyboard can be interfaced directly to eight-bit output and input ports at points A and B. Some input and output lines can be saved by using a 74LS138 1-of-8 decoder and a 74LS151 8-Input Multiplexer. Software can scan the keyboard by outputting a three-bit code to the 74LS138 and then scanning the 74LS151 multiplexer to find the closed switch. The combination of the two 3-bit scan codes identifies which switch is closed. For example, the code 000000 scans switch 00 in the upper left-hand corner of Figure 7–25.

The diode shown in Figure 7–25 prevents a problem called ghosting. This occurs when a fat-fingered user pushes more than one key at once. Consider Figure 7–26 where switches 01, 10, and 11 are all closed, Column 0 is selected with a logic low, and assume the circuit does not contain the diodes. As the rows are scanned, a low is sensed on Row 1, which is acceptable because switch 10 is closed. In addition, Row 0 is seen to be low, indicating switch 00 is closed, which is not true. The diodes in the switches eliminate this problem by preventing current flow from R1 through switches 01 and 11. Thus Row 0 will not be low when it is scanned.

The problem with a typist hitting more than one key at once, or rapidly rolling the finger from

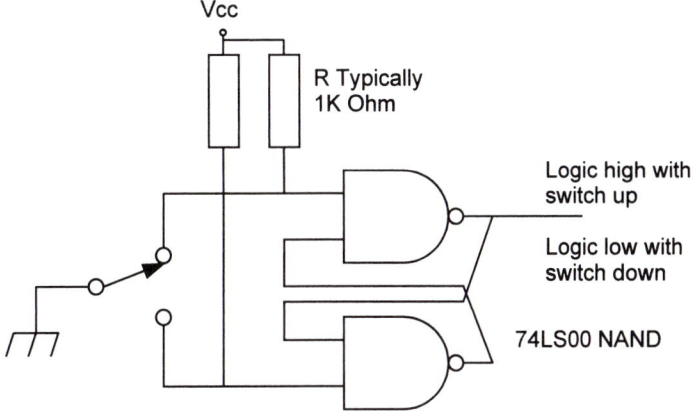

(a) NAND latch debouncer.

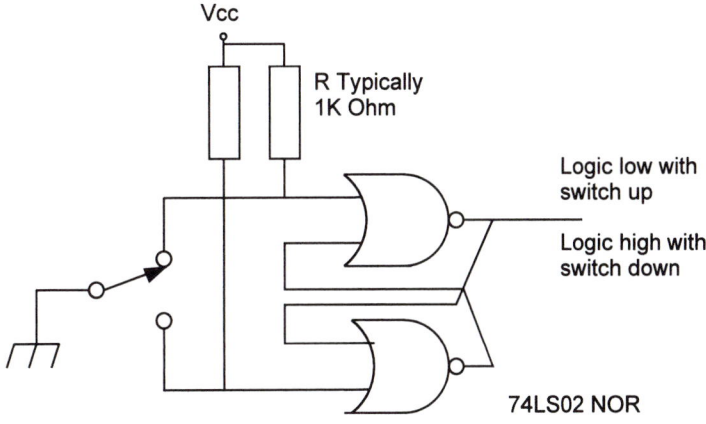

(b) NOR latch debouncer.

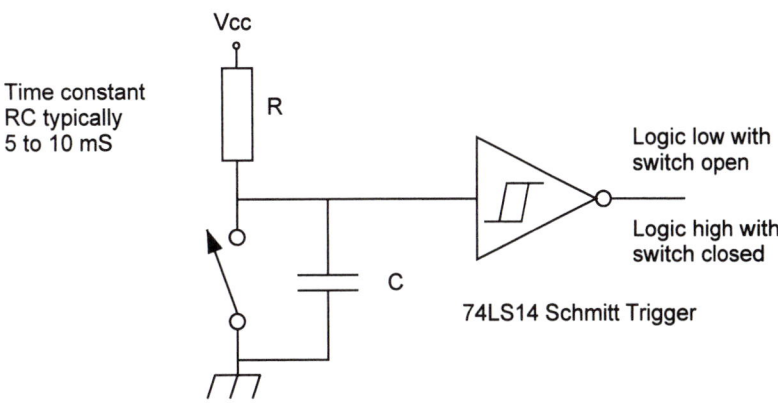

(c) Integrating debouncer with Schmitt trigger.

Figure 7-23 Hardware debouncing methods.

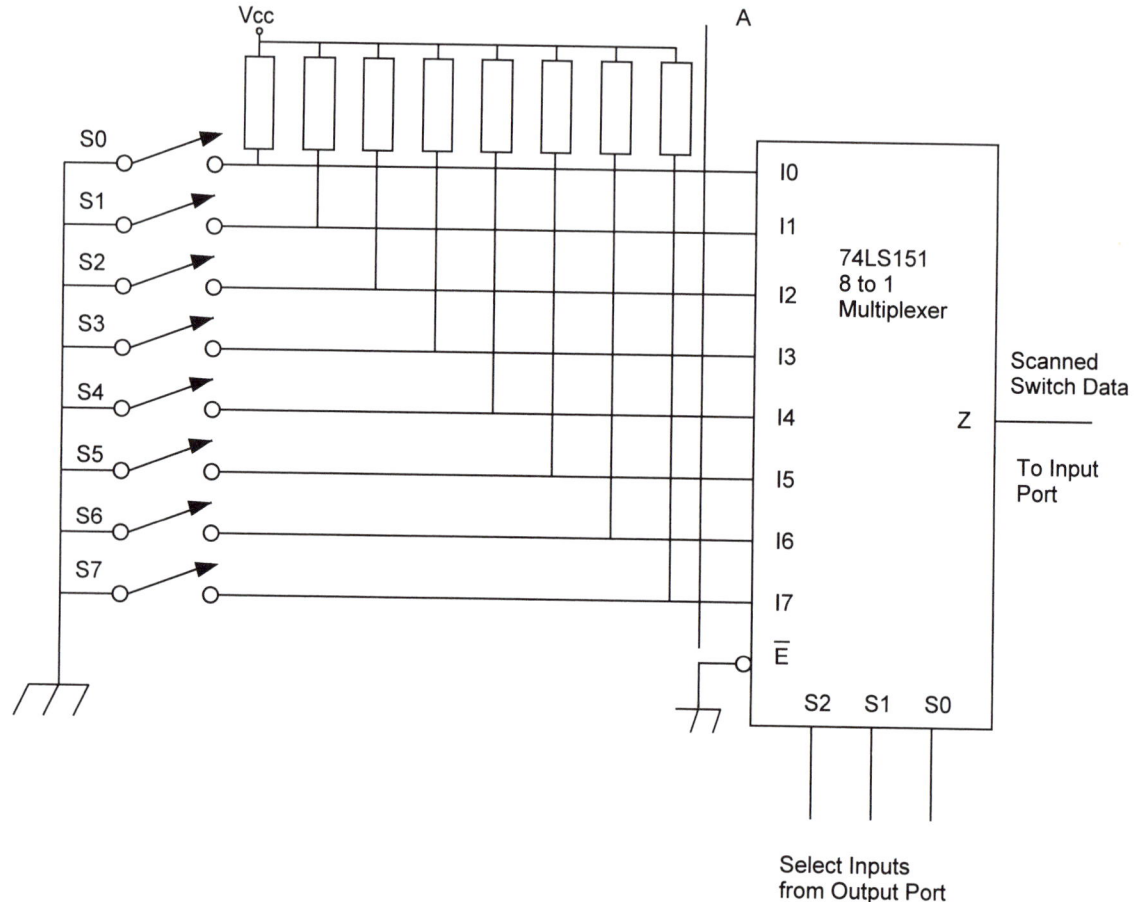

Figure 7-24   Linear array of switches.

n-Key rollover and *n-key lockout* solve the problems of a typist hitting more than one key at once.

one key to another, is called *n-key rollover*. Providing for two-key rollover is commonly done. The keyboard hardware and software store the rapidly depressed keys in a first-in, first-out (FIFO) buffer for later readout. An alternative strategy is *n-key lockout*, where only the first or last of the sequence of keys depressed within some short period is recorded. Keyboard encoder chips incorporating all the scanning, debouncing, diodes, n-key rollover, and interrupt generation are available. Typical chips are the National

EXAMPLE 7-5   For the linear array of switches in Figure 7-24, give a truth table showing which switch is read for each scan code output by the processor.

Solutions:

Scan Code	Switch	Scan Code	Switch
000	S0	100	S4
001	S1	101	S5
010	S2	110	S6
011	S3	111	S7

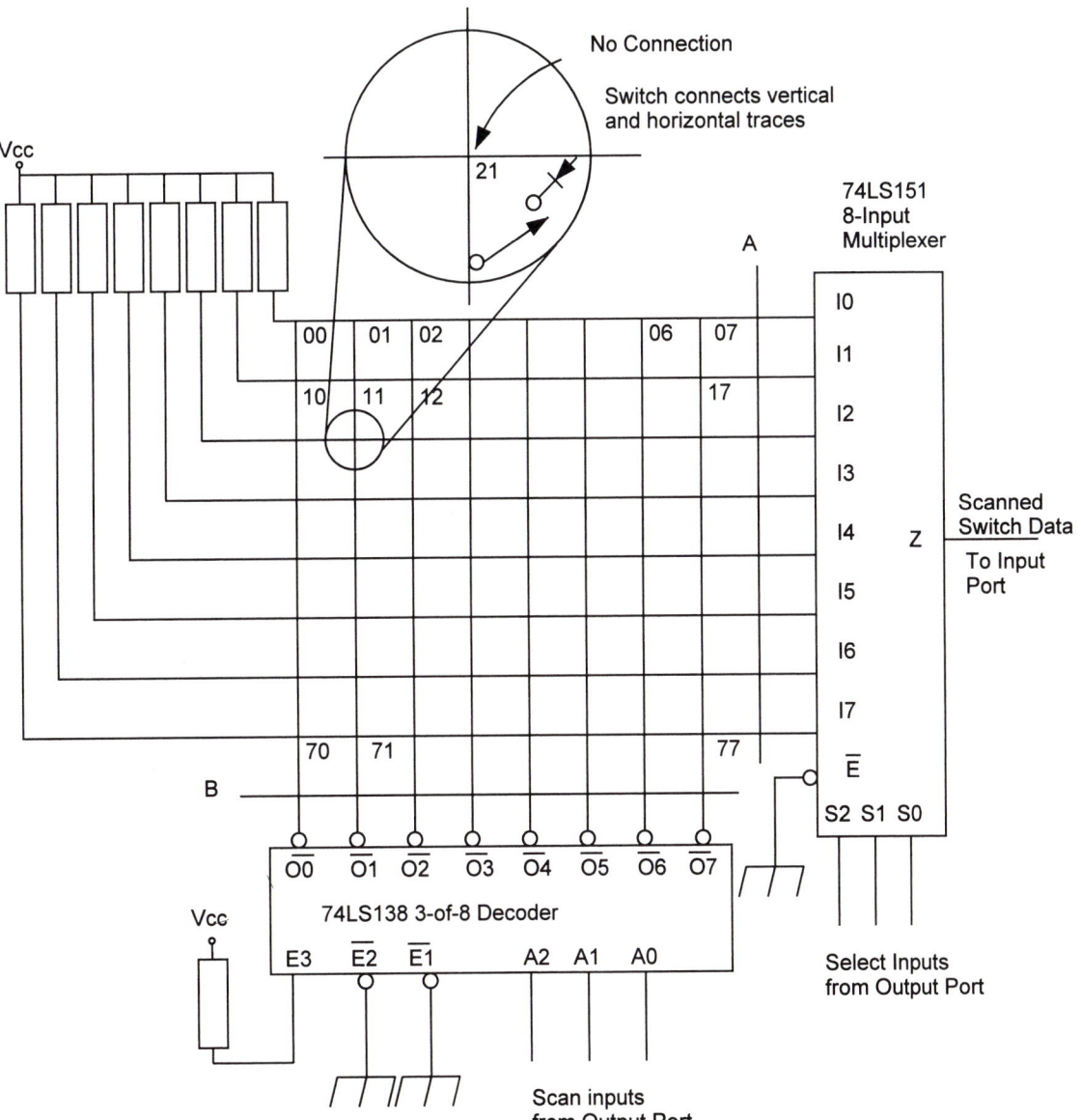

Figure 7-25   Keyboard matrix of switches.

Semiconductor 74C922 and the Intel i8279. Using these chips can eliminate scanning software and hardware and provide a much easier-to-implement keyboard interface.

Simple Display Devices

The most simple display device is a single light-emitting diode (LED). An LED lights when current of 10 to 20 milliamperes is passed in the forward direction. Figure 7–27(a) shows how to interface a single LED.

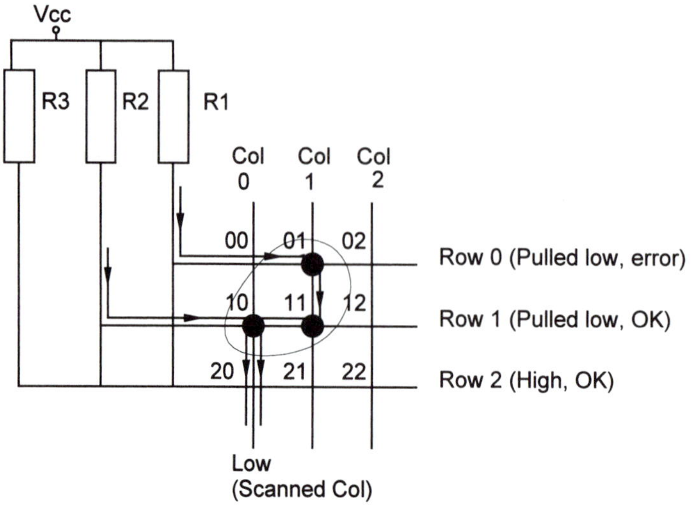

Vcc

R3 R2 R1

Col 0 Col 1 Col 2

00 01 02 — Row 0 (Pulled low, error)

10 11 12 — Row 1 (Pulled low, OK)

20 21 22 — Row 2 (High, OK)

Low
(Scanned Col)

Figure 7–26 Keyboard ghosting.

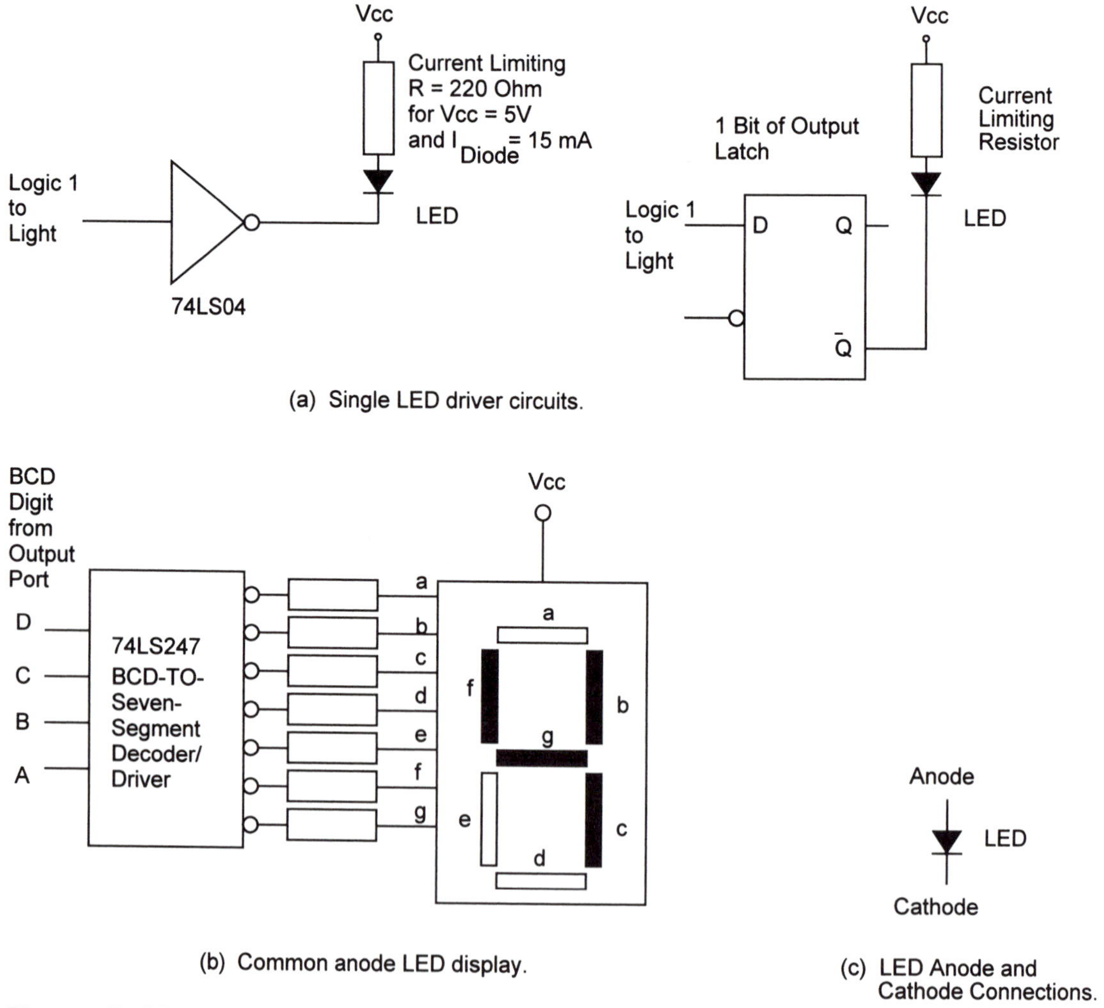

Vcc

Current Limiting
R = 220 Ohm
for Vcc = 5V
and I_{Diode} = 15 mA

Logic 1
to
Light

LED

74LS04

Vcc

1 Bit of Output
Latch

Current
Limiting
Resistor

Logic 1
to
Light

D   Q

Q̄

LED

(a) Single LED driver circuits.

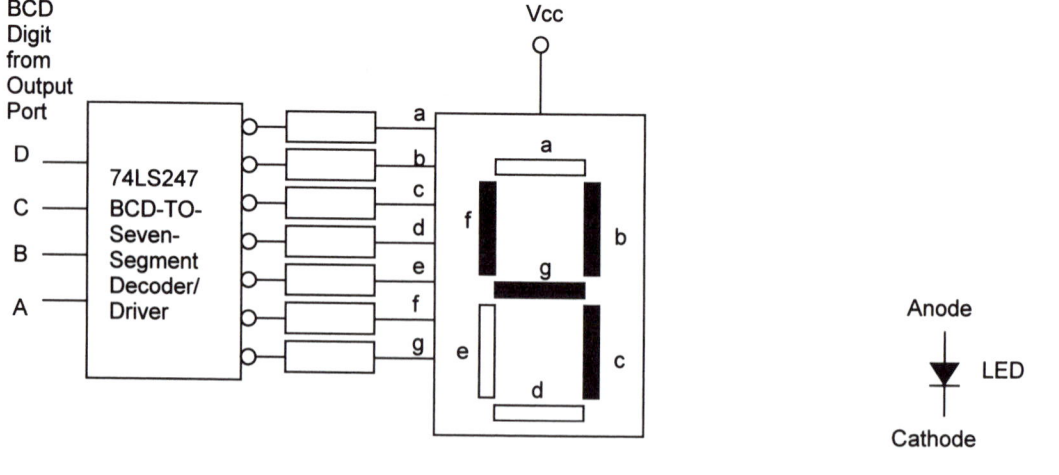

BCD
Digit
from
Output
Port

D

C

B

A

74LS247
BCD-TO-
Seven-
Segment
Decoder/
Driver

a
b
c
d
e
f
g

Vcc

a

f   b

g

e   c

d

(b) Common anode LED display.

Anode

LED

Cathode

(c) LED Anode and
Cathode Connections.

Figure 7–27 Simple LED driver circuits.

A seven-segment LED display shows numeric characters. LED displays come in two varieties, common anode and common cathode. Figure 7–27(b) is a common anode display using a 74LS247 BCD-to-Seven_Segment Decoder/Driver. A BCD number is output by the CPU to the 74LS247, and its active low outputs turn on the appropriate segments to display the number.

Sometimes more than one display is required. Figure 7–28 shows how to multiplex a four-digit display using only one decoder/driver and common cathode LEDs. Each of the four digits is illuminated in turn by a two-bit code at the input of the 74F539 decoder/demultiplexer. This is called a refreshed display, and if each display is turned on at a greater rate than about 20 Hz, our eyes will not detect any flickering.

Multielement, 16-segment, and dot matrix displays can form alphanumeric characters. These are shown in Figure 7–29(a) and (b). The matrix elements can be LED or liquid crystal display

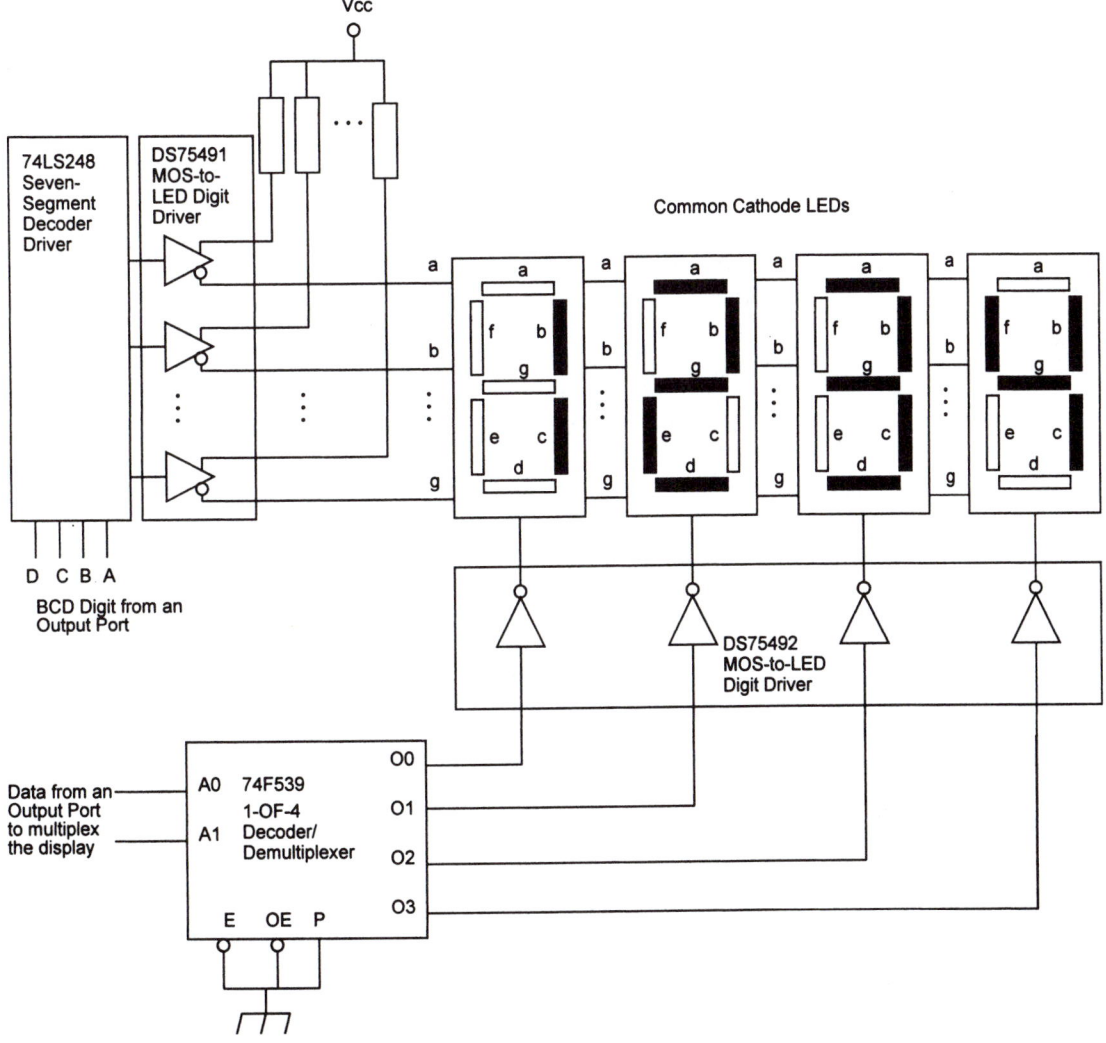

Figure 7–28 Multiplexed LED displays.

(a) 16-segment alphanumeric display.

(b) 7x9 dot matrix display.

Figure 7-29 Multielement displays.

(LCD), with multicharacter LCD displays predominating because their power requirements are much lower than an equivalent LED display.

7.7 Programmable I/O Devices

> A wide variety of *programmable I/O* devices are offered by IC manufacturers.

A turning point in the design of microprocessor systems was the development of programmable I/O devices, introduced by Motorola in 1974. These integrated circuits are dedicated to a particular I/O job, such as parallel or serial I/O, but are programmable to allow some flexibility in use. All have internal registers that are initialized by the program to control the device. The Motorola 6821 Peripheral Interface Adapter, Figure 7–30, is typical of all programmable I/O devices. It is programmable for input and output by writing the appropriate data to the control registers. Many microprocessor manufacturers have a variety of programmable I/O chips. Table 7–5 shows a selection of Intel devices and Table 7–6 those offered by Motorola. Although Intel chips could be used in a Motorola processor-based system, it is usually easier to choose peripheral devices from the same manufacturer as the CPU. Table 7–7 gives a tabulation by function.

7.8 More I/O Ideas

Buffered I/O

The term *I/O buffering* refers both to the temporary storage of data between the I/O device and the CPU (*data buffering*) and to the conversion between different electrical characteristics found in CPUs, data buses, and I/O devices (*electronic buffering*).

> *Data buffering* allows a mismatch in the operating speeds of I/O and the CPU.

Data buffering: Data buffering is the storage of data by the I/O device, either within the I/O interface or memory. An example can be seen in Figure 7–31(a), where the input device latches data into an input latch. The latch "buffers" the data and keeps it until new data are latched by the input device. Buffering of this sort is a form of I/O synchronization where a device puts its data into the latch when it is ready.

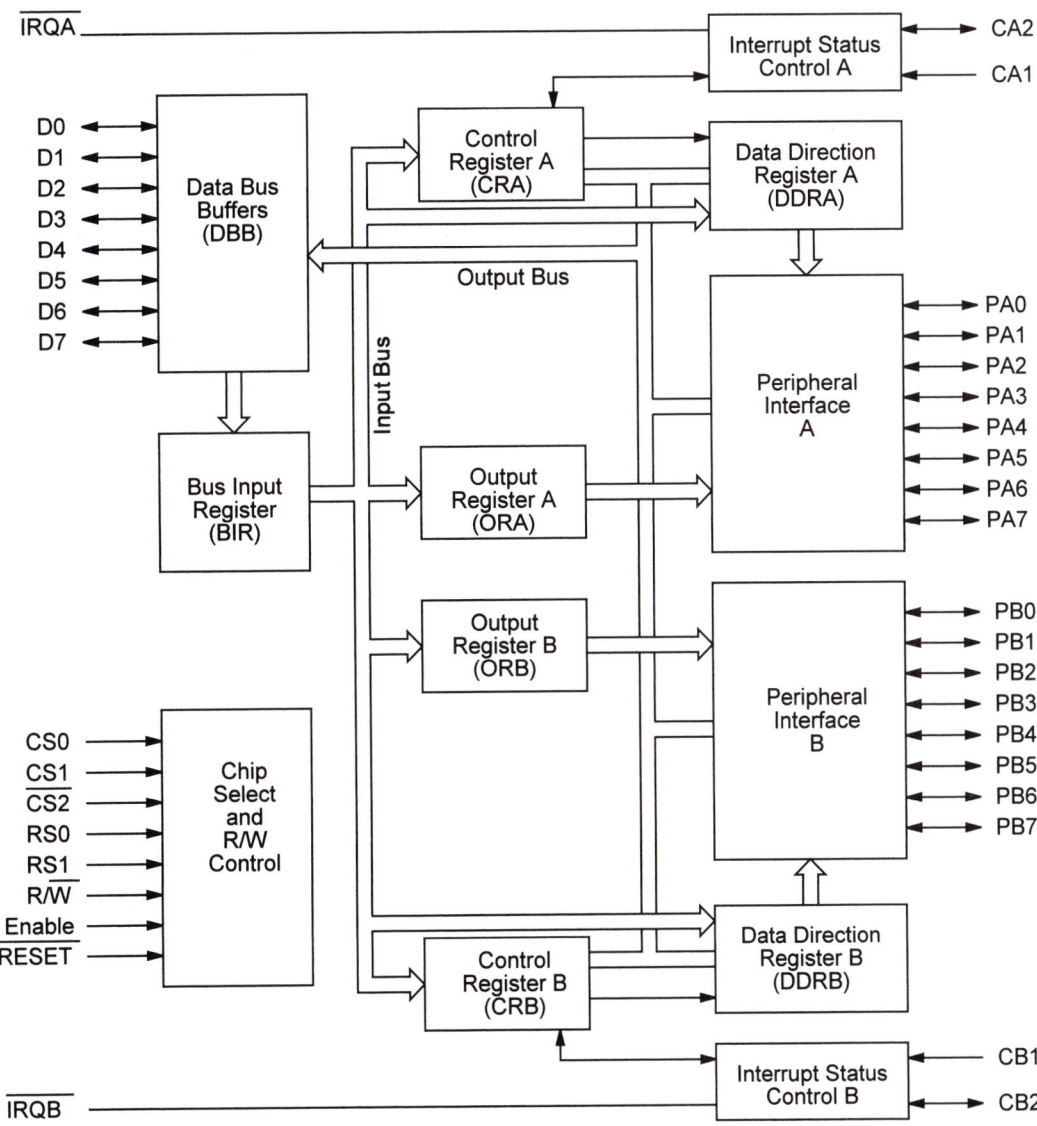

Figure 7-30   Motorola 6821 Peripheral Interface Adapter (reprinted with permission of Motorola

For the simple case presented in Figure 7–31(a), there is no way for the CPU to tell if the data in the latch are new or old. Handshaking signals can be added between the interface and the input device, as shown in Figure 7–31(b). A status register (like that shown in Figure 7–15) is included with two handshaking bits. **DATA_TAKEN** is a signal to the input device that tells it when the CPU has read the data from the latch. **DATA_TAKEN** is reset when the new data are placed into the latch and set when the CPU reads the data. The **NEW_DATA_AVAIL** bit may be read by the CPU. This bit is set when new data are latched and reset when the CPU reads the latch. Thus soft-

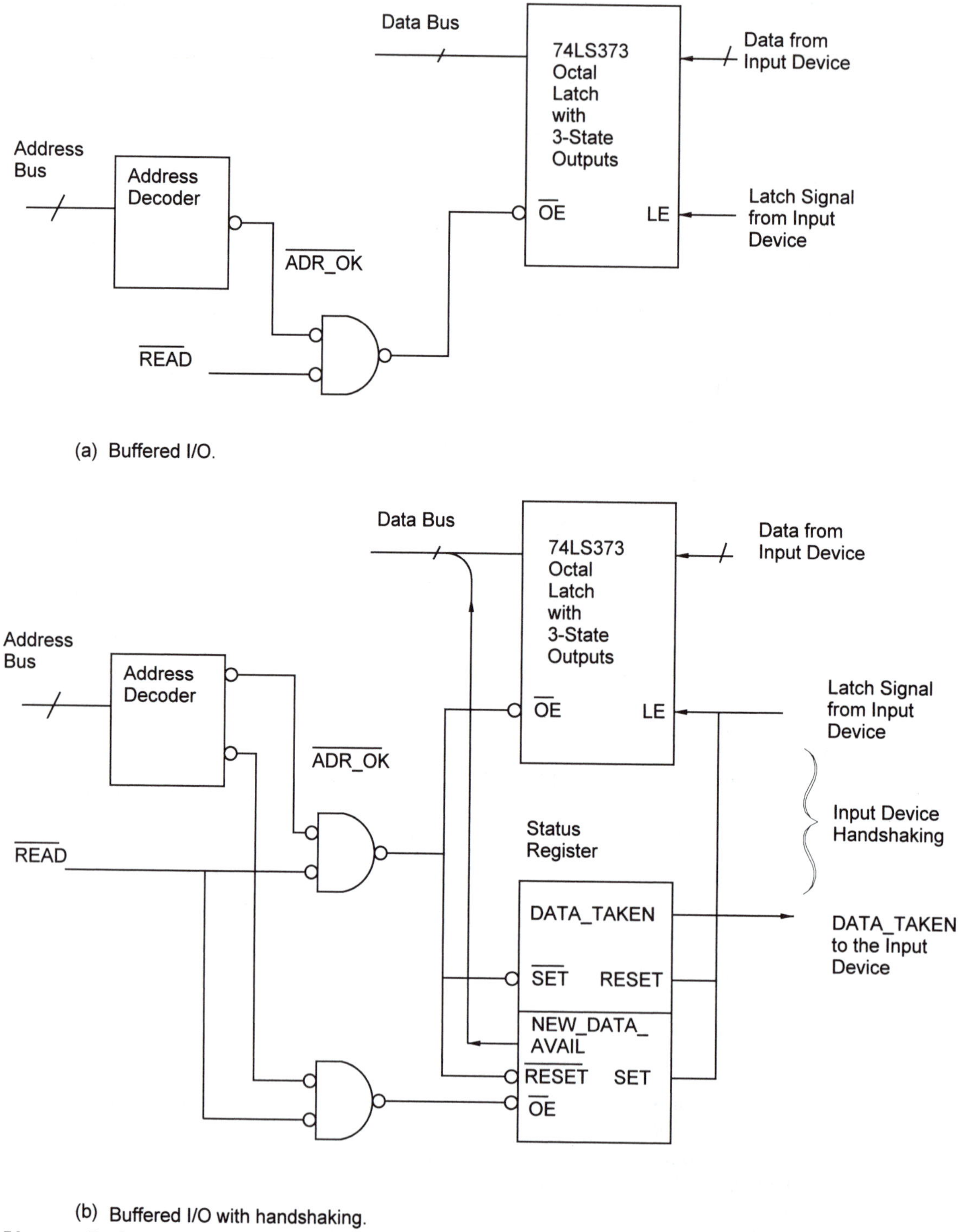

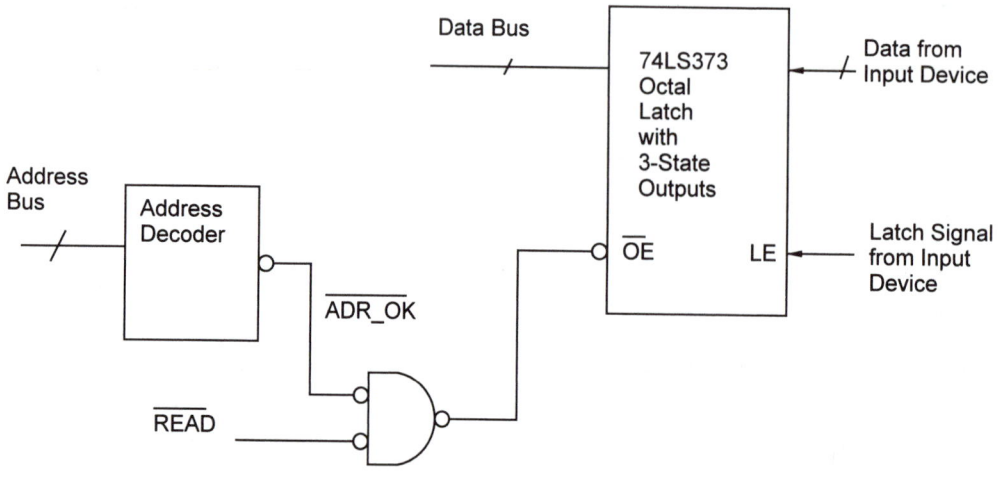

(a) Buffered I/O.

(b) Buffered I/O with handshaking.

Figure 7-31   Single buffered I/O.

TABLE 7-5 Intel programmable I/O devices

i8155	256×8 Static RAM with I/O Ports and Timer
i8207	Advanced Dynamic RAM Controller
i8212	8 Bit I/O Port
i8237	Direct Memory Access Controller
i8251	Serial Communication Interface
i8253	Interval Timer
i8254	Interval Timer
i8255	Parallel Peripheral Interface
i8256	Multifunction Universal Asynchronous Receiver Transmitter
i8257	DMA Controller
i8259	Interrupt Controller
i8271	Floppy Disk Controller
i8272	Single/Double Density Floppy Disk Controller
i8273	HDLC/SDLC Protocol Controller
i8274	Multiprotocol Serial Controller
i8275	CRT Controller
i8276	Small System CRT Controller
i8279	Keyboard/Display Interface
i8282/83	Octal Latch
i8286/87	Octal Transceiver
i8289	Bus Arbiter
i8291	GPIB Talker/Listener
i8292	GPIB Controller
i8294	Data Encryption Unit
i8295	Dot Matrix Printer Controller
i82062	Winchester Disk Controller
i82501	Ethernet Serial Interface
i82586	Local Communications Controller
i82720	Graphics Display Controller

ware can be written to poll this bit and take only new data. Another approach involves the use of interrupts as discussed in Chapter 8.

Double buffering is used in some systems to allow further mismatch between the speeds of the I/O device and the CPU. A double buffered scheme has more than one latch. The input device can put data into one location while the CPU is taking earlier data out of another.

Electronic buffering: Electronic buffering provides voltages and currents appropriate for the devices in use. For example, the logic levels for CMOS and TTL devices are different, and TTL/CMOS and CMOS/TTL buffers provide an electronic translation between the two different levels. The bidirectional bus transceiver shown in Figure 7–18 can source and sink about ten times more current than most CPUs.

7.9 Chapter Summary Points

In this chapter we have discovered how the computer buses work and how to interface I/O devices to the bus. The key elements of the chapter are the following:

- A bus is a parallel, bidirectional information pathway.

- Sources transfer information to a destination over a bus.

- No more than one source can be active.

- Three-state gates allow multiple sources to be on a common bus line.

- An input interface is a set of three-state gates between an information source and a data bus.

- An output interface is a set of latches between the bus and the destination device.

- One of many sources or destinations are chosen by addressing and address decoding.

- The CPU controls the timing of data transfers by generating **READ** and **WRITE** control signals.

TABLE 7-6 Motorola programmable I/O devices

MC1372	Color Television Modulator
MC2670	Display Character and Graphics Generator
MC2671	Programmable Keyboard and Communications Controller
MC2672	Video Timing Controller
MC2673	Video Attributes Controller
MC2674	Advanced Video Display Controller
MC2675	Color/Monochrome Attributes Controller
MC6821	Parallel Peripheral Interface Adapter
MC6822	Parallel Industrial Interface Adapter
MC6828	Priority Interrupt Controller
MC6829	Memory Management Unit
MCM68HC34	Dual Port Memory Unit
MC6835	CRT Controller
MC6839	Floating Point ROM
MC6840	Programmable Timer
MC6843	Floppy Disk Controller
MC6844	Direct Memory Access Controller
MC6845	CRT Controller
MC6846	ROM-I/O Timer
MC6847	Video Display Generator
MC6850	Serial Asynchronous Interface Adapter
MC68HC51	Serial Asynchronous Interface Adapter
MC6852	Synchronous Serial Data Adapter
MC68HC53	Serial Asynchronous Interface Adapter
MC6854	Advanced Data Link Controller
MC6855	Serial Direct Memory Access Processor
MC6859	Data Security Device
MC6860	0-600 BPS Digital Modem
MC6862	2400 BPS Digital Modem
MC68HC68A1	Serial 10-bit A/D Converter
MC68HC68R1,R2	8-bit Serial Static RAM
MC68HC68T1	Real-Time Clock, RAM, and Power Sense/Control
MC6890	8-Bit MPU D/A Converter
MC14499	Serial Interface LED Display
MC68120	Intelligent Peripheral Interface
MC68121	Intelligent Peripheral Interface
MC68230	Parallel Interface/Timer
MC68450	Direct Memory Access Controller
MC68451	Memory Management Unit
MC68488	General Purpose Interface Adapter
MC68681	Dual Asynchronous Receiver/Transmitter (DUART)
MC145000,1	Serial LCD Drivers
MC146818	CMOS Real-Time Clock Plus RAM
MC146823	CMOS Parallel Interface

TABLE 7-7 Programmable I/O devices by function

Function	Intel	Motorola
Parallel interface	i8212, i8155, i8255, i8282, i8283	MC6821, MC6822, MC6846, MC68120, MC68121, MC68230, MC146823
Serial interface	i8251, i8256, i8273, i8274, i82501, i82586	MC6840, MC6850, MC68HC51, MC6852, MC68HC53, MC6854, MC2671, MC68681
Timer	i8155, i8253, i8254	MC6840, MC6846, MC68HC68T1, MC68230, MC146818
Interrupt controller	i8259	MC6828
Disk controllers	i8271, i8272, i82062	MC6843
Display and graphics Controllers	i8275, i8276, i8279, i82720	MC1372, MC2670, MC2672, MC2673, MC2674, MC2675, MC6835, MC6845, MC6847, MC14499, MC145000, MC145001
Keyboard interface	i8279	MC2671
GPIB interface	i8291, i8292	MC68488
Memory Management		MC6829, MC68HC34, MC68451
Memory controller	i8207	
DMA controller	i8257	MC6844, MC6855, MC68450
Bus controller	i8289	
Data encryption	i8294	MC6859
A/D		MC68HC68A1
D/A		MC6890

- I/O addressing may be done with memory-mapped I/O, in which case any memory reference instruction can access I/O, or separate I/O, for which special input and output instructions are included in the instruction set.

- You may choose to decode the entire address bus (full address decoding, which leads to more expensive decoders) or a subset of the address bus (reduced addressing, less expensive but resulting in redundant use of addresses).

- I/O synchronization must often be done to synchronize a fast CPU with a slow I/O device.

- If multiple bus masters require the bus simultaneously, bus arbitration is required.

- Mechanical switches need to be debounced.

- CPU manufacturers have programmable I/O devices that can greatly simplify your system design.

7.10 References and Other Reading

W. S. Stone (1982) provides an excellent discussion of many aspects of interfacing microcomputers and I/O systems, including the transmission line properties of a bus. Fulcher (1989) and Lawrence and Mauch (1987) treat interfacing various specific devices. Peatman (1988) provides a discussion of LCD technology and interfacing. A book with many interfacing examples is by Slater (1989).

Fulcher, J., *An Introduction to Microcomputer Systems Architecture and Interfacing*, Addison-Wesley, Sydney, AU, 1989.
Lawrence, P. D. and K. Mauch, *Real-Time Microcomputer System Design: An Introduction*, McGraw-Hill, New York, NY, 1987.
Peatman, J. B., *Design with Microcontrollers*, McGraw Hill, New York, NY, 1988.
Slater, M., *Microprocessor-Based Design, A Comprehensive Guide to Hardware Design*, Prentice-Hall, Englewood Cliffs, NJ, 1989.
Stone, W. S., *Microcomputer Interfacing*, Addison-Wesley, Reading, MA, 1982.

7.11 Problems

7.1   List parallel I/O devices used with computers you are familiar with, either in the laboratory or a personal computer.

7.2   Describe the advantages of the three-state gate over the open-collector gate when used for multiple sources on a data bus.

7.3   Why are three-state gates used in an input interface?

7.4   The following control signals are associated with a microprocessor:

> **MREQ**—asserted when a memory operation is ongoing.
>
> **IORQ**—asserted when an I/O operation is ongoing.
>
> **WR**—asserted when a write operation is ongoing.
>
> **RD**—asserted when a read operation is ongoing.
>
> **ADROK**—asserted output from an address decoder.

Write the logic equations for: (a) A correctly timed latch signal for an output port. (b) A correctly timed three-state control signal for an input port. (c) A correctly timed signal to select memory for reading or writing.

7.5   In a parallel output operation, how is the synchronization of the data transfer between CPU and a data latch consisting of 8 D-type flip flops accomplished?

7.6   Briefly explain the difference between separate and memory-mapped I/O.

7.7   Discuss the consequences of a CPU designer's decision to implement memory-mapped I/O instead of separate I/O. What does it mean to the CPU designer and what does it mean to you, the system designer using the CPU?

7.8   Which type of I/O addressing, separate I/O or memory-mapped, uses memory reference instructions to access I/O devices?

7.9   Which type of I/O addressing, separate I/O or memory-mapped, requires a control signal called "I/O request" to access I/O devices?

7.10   Design a decoder to produce **BLOCK_SELECT** signals to enable memory and I/O devices to the following specifications:

> 16-bit address bus
> The memory is to be addressed in 8 8K blocks in which:
>   1 8K block is to be used for I/O.
>   1 8K block is to be used for future I/O expansion.

1 8K block is to be used for ROM at high memory addresses.
1 8K block is to be used for future ROM expansion.
1 8K block is to be used for RAM at low memory addresses.
1 8K block is to be used for future RAM expansion.
Show how to use a 74LS138 decoder to generate **BLOCK_SELECT** signals.

7.11 A 74LS138 decoder has the following address bits assigned to its inputs:

Adr	74138 input
A7 =	A2
A6 =	A1
A5 =	A0
A4 =	**E1**
A3 =	**E2**
A2 =	**E3**
A1, A0 =	Don't cares

Assume an eight-bit address and make a table, similar to Table 7–1, showing what addresses each output responds to.

7.12 Using the reduced address decoder shown in Figure 7–13, what decoder output should be chosen for address 257_{16}?

7.13 Compare software polling with hardware handshaking I/O synchronizing.

7.14 What is a multiplexed address bus, and why do CPU designers use them in their designs?

7.15 Discuss the consequences of a CPU designer's decision to implement a multiplexed address bus instead of having the complete address bus at pins on the chip.

7.16 In a multiplexed address bus, the higher-order bits are usually output before the low-order bits. Why is this so?

7.17 Design bus arbitration hardware using a 74LS148 8-Line-to-3-Line Priority Encoder and a 74LS138 1-of-8 Decoder. Assume the bus request and bus grant signals are active low.

7.18 What is switch bounce?

7.19 Discuss the relative merits of software and hardware switch debouncing.

7.20 Design a software scanning algorithm to scan an 8-switch linear array. Assume a 74LS151 8-to-1 Multiplexer is used (see Figure 7–24).

7.21 Design a software scanning algorithm to scan an 8x8 keyboard matrix assuming a 74LS138 1-of-8 decoder and 74LS151 8-to-1 multiplexer are used to interface the keyboard (see Figure 7–25).

7.22 Design an input interface that inputs the binary value of 8 switches. The interface is to also have 8 LEDs that display the last 8-bit value input from the switches. It should not be necessary for the computer to output this value to the LEDs. Assume memory-mapped I/O and that an address decoder exists to give you an **ADR_OK** signal when the computer inputs the switch information.

7.23 Design an input interface for a bank of 16 switches to be interfaced to an 8-bit data bus. Show how each switch is connected to be able to input a 1 or a 0. Assume the CPU has a separate I/O map with an 8-bit I/O address and that the following control signals are available:

$IO/\overline{M}$	1 for I/O, 0 for memory access
WR	1 for writing, 0 for not writing
RD	1 for reading, 0 for not reading

For the sake of simplicity, assume an 8-to-256 decoder with outputs that are asserted high.

Chapter 8

Interrupts and Real-Time Events

OBJECTIVES

This chapter shows how an external or internal important event can interrupt the normal flow of the program. We will discuss the hardware a designer must add to the CPU and how the CPU finds out which of several interrupting devices needs service. When an interrupt occurs, an interrupt service routine is executed. We will discuss how interrupt routines work and give guidelines for writing them.

8.1 Introduction

An interrupt is a way for an *important, asynchronous event* to be recognized and taken care of (*serviced*) by the CPU executing instructions in a normal program. Consider, for example, a computer system controlling an oil refinery. It would have sensors measuring the chemical composition of the product being refined and outputs controlling the process. A typical process control software loop to do this is shown in Figure 8–1. The time taken to go around the loop depends on the complexity of the control algorithms and the speed of the processor. Now consider an important, external, asynchronous event. A fire breaks out in the oil refinery! If the control computer is responsible for activating fire suppression measures, the program should respond immediately and not wait for the software to come around the loop to check on the fire detection sensors. On the other hand, we don't want to write a program that is checking the fire sensors all the time, or even frequently, because it would take time away from the control calculations. This is an ideal application for an interrupt. The interrupt is caused by an external device, the fire sensor, generating a signal called *interrupt request*, or IRQ. The interrupt request is asynchronous; that is, it can happen any time, not necessarily corresponding to any particular time in the instruction execution sequence of the CPU. The IRQ requests the program to take immediate action, called an *interrupt service routine*, or *ISR*. Figure 8–2 shows an interrupt service routine added to the process control software of Figure 8–1. The interrupt service routine is executed whenever the interrupt occurs.

> An *interrupt* is an important asynchronous event that requires immediate attention.

Interrupts also can *synchronize* the operation of the computer with an external process. Consider sending data to a printer. Typically, computers are much faster than printers; so the data output

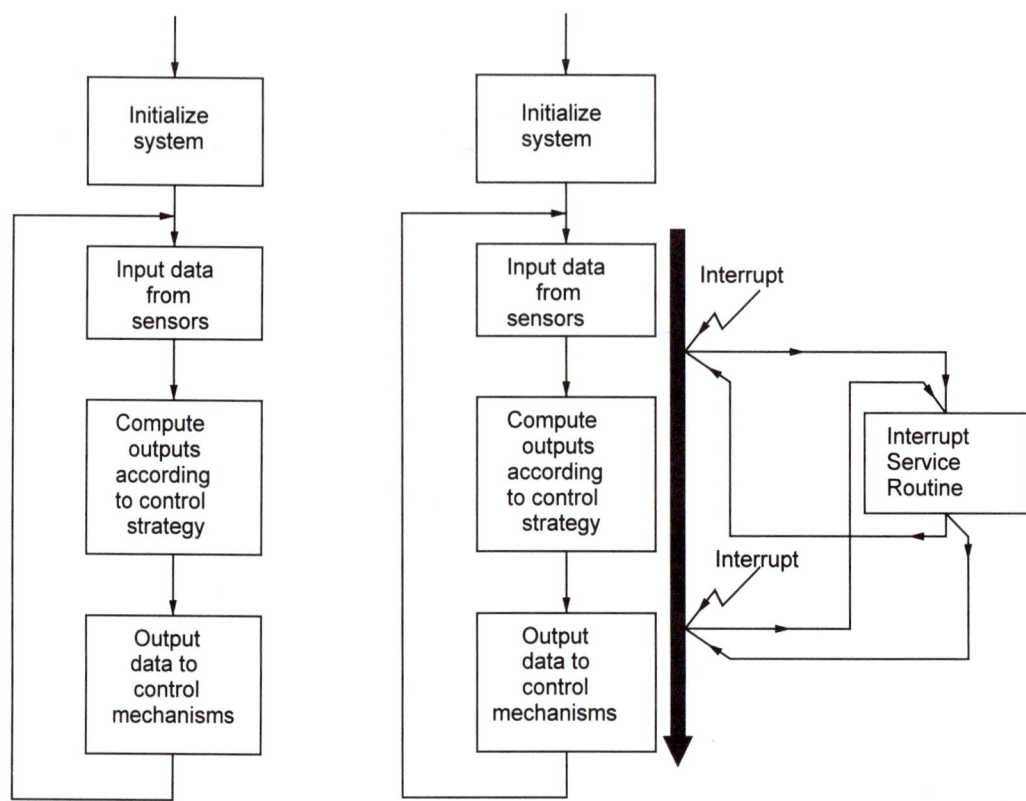

Figure 8-1 Typical process control software.

Figure 8-2 Process control software with interrupts.

must be synchronized to the speed of the printer. In addition to the I/O synchronization techniques such as polling or delay loops discussed in Chapter 7, interrupts may be used. In this case, the printer generates an interrupt to signify that it is ready for the next character. The input of data from a device such as an analog-to-digital (A/D) converter can be synchronized by the A/D generating an interrupt when the conversion is complete.

A term used to describe these systems is *real time.* A real-time system is one that does some process, either at a specific time, say midnight, or at specific intervals, say every 10 milliseconds, or at a time required by some external device or event.

A *real-time system* uses interrupts to control *when* things are done in a program.

In this chapter we look at interrupt hardware and software. Hardware will be designed to decide which of several possible interrupting devices has generated the interrupt. We will also design a solution to the problems that arise when multiple devices simultaneously interrupt the CPU, and we will discuss the interrupt service routine—how to write it and what, and what not, to do.

8.2 Interrupt System Specifications

Let's list the general specifications for an interrupt system. The system is to do the following:

- Allow for asynchronous events to occur and be recognized.

- Wait for the current instruction to finish before taking care of any interrupt.

- Branch to the correct interrupt service routine to service the interrupting device.

- Return to the interrupted program at the point it was interrupted.

- Allow for a variety of interrupting signals, including levels and edges.

- Signal the interrupting device with an acknowledge signal when the interrupt has been recognized.

- Allow the programmer to selectively enable and disable all interrupts.

- Allow the programmer to selectively enable and disable selected interrupts.

- Disable further interrupts while the first is being serviced.

- Deal with multiple sources of interrupts.

- Deal with multiple, simultaneous interrupts.

8.3 Asynchronous Events and Internal Processor Timing

Figure 8–3(a) shows a time line of program execution. The ticks along the line represent the start of each instruction, and instructions in a normal program are executed in sequence. The normal program does not specify *when*, in a real-time sense, an instruction is to be executed, just the *sequence* of instructions. Asynchronous events, the IRQs, can occur any time.

Figure 8–3(b) shows an expanded time line. The discussion of the picoprocessor in Chapter 2 showed that an instruction execution cycle consists of the instruction fetch and instruction execution parts. Further, we know that a sequence controller is controlling the instruction execution cycle. It can be modified to check for an interrupt request before it fetches the next instruction. More states are added to sample the IRQ and generate more control signals, including one to acknowledge the interrupt. This change allows the CPU to finish the current instruction and then to service the interrupt by entering a special interrupt processing sequence; otherwise, it fetches the next instruction.

> The current instruction must be finished before an interrupt request is acted upon.

8.4 Internal CPU Interrupt Hardware

The basic elements of the hardware needed within the CPU to satisfy most of the design requirements are shown in Figure 8–4.

An interrupt request (IRQ) may occur at any time. It may have rising or falling edges or high or low levels. Frequently IRQ is an active-low signal and multiple devices are wire-ORed together. A signal conditioning circuit is included to detect these different types of signals. Because the interrupt can happen at any time, an *interrupt request flip-flop (IRQ-FF)*, is needed to "catch" and "remember" the IRQ signal until the CPU can get around to doing something about it.

> The *interrupt request flip-flop* remembers that an interrupt request has been generated until it is acknowledged.

When IRQ-FF is set, it generates a *pending interrupt* signal that goes toward the sequence con-

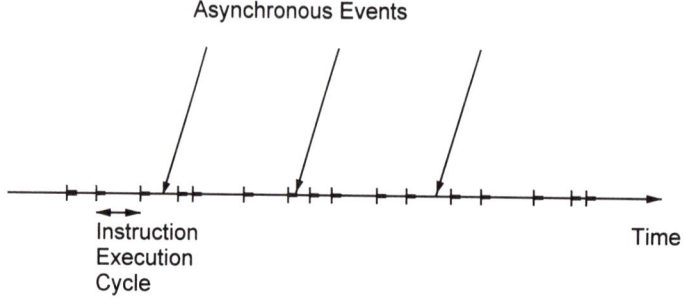

Asynchronous Events

Instruction
Execution
Cycle

Time

(a) Asynchronous events and instruction timing.

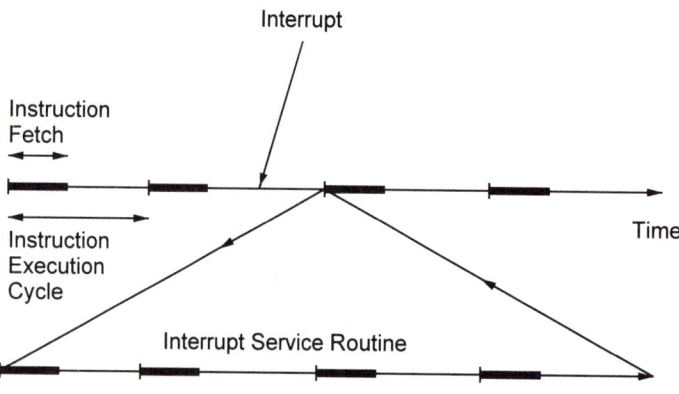

Interrupt

Instruction
Fetch

Instruction
Execution
Cycle

Time

Interrupt Service Routine

(b) Interrupt service routine.

Figure 8-3 Asynchronous events and instruction execution timing.

A *pending interrupt* is an IRQ that has not been acted upon yet.

The *interrupt enable flip-flop* may be set and reset by the programmer and is automatically reset when an interrupt request is acknowledged.

The *return from interrupt* instruction restores the machine state and returns to the interrupt program.

troller. The IRQ-FF is reset when the CPU acknowledges the interrupt has occurred with the *interrupt acknowledge (INTA)* signal.

The programmer has control over the interrupting process by *enabling* and *disabling* interrupts with explicit program instructions. The hardware that allows this is the *interrupt enable flip-flop* (INTE-FF). When the INTE- FF is set, with an enable-interrupt instruction, all interrupts are enabled and the *pending interrupt* is allowed through the AND gate to the sequence controller. The INTE-FF is reset when the CPU asserts INTA acknowledging the interrupt. This prevents further interrupts from coming through the system unless the programmer reenables the INTE-FF. INTE-FF is also reset when the CPU is reset and when a disable-interrupt instruction is executed.

An *interrupt acknowledge* signal is generated by the CPU when the current instruction has finished executing and the CPU has detected the IRQ. This resets the IRQ-FF and INTE-FF and signals the interrupting device that the CPU is ready to execute the interrupt service routine.

At the end of the interrupt service routine, the CPU executes a *return-from-inter-*

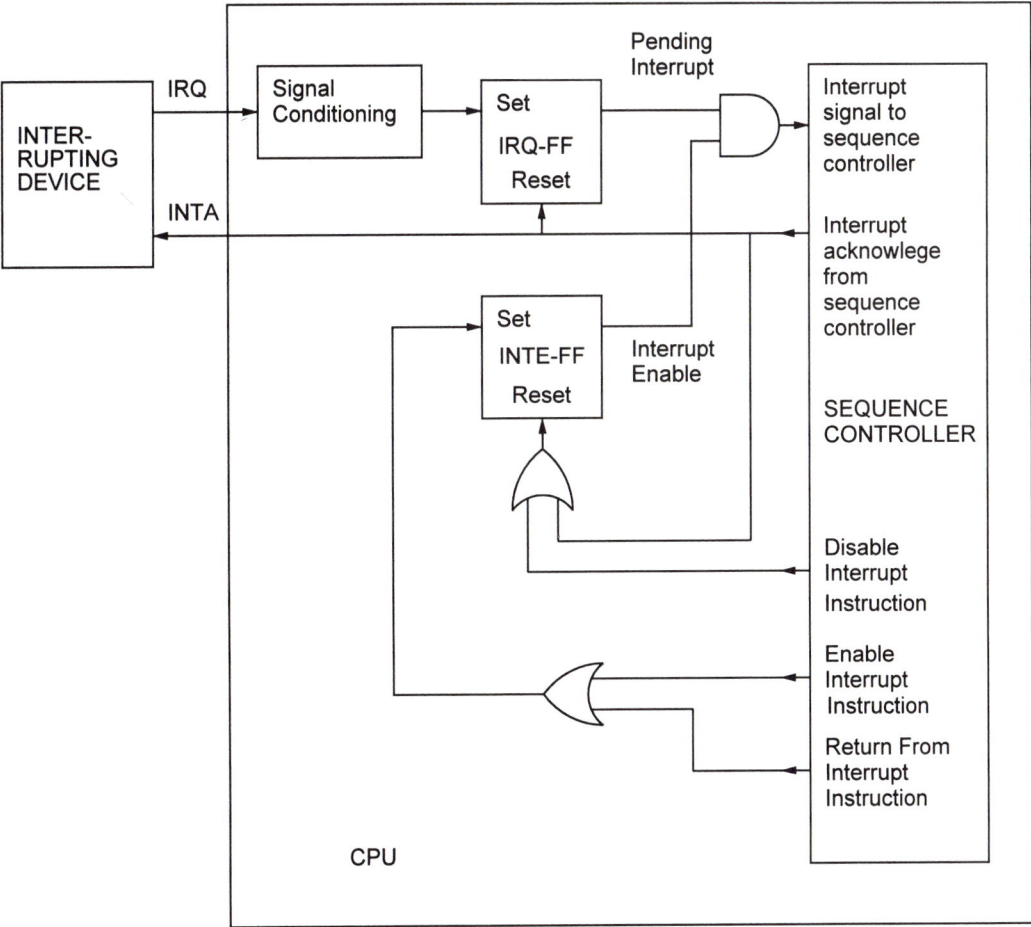

Figure 8−4   Interrupt recognition and acknowledgement hardware.

rupt instruction. Part of this instruction's job is to set the INTE-FF to reenable interrupts. If the IRQ-FF is set during an interrupt service routine, a pending interrupt, if there is one, will be recognized by the sequence controller immediately after the INTE-FF is set. Re-enabling the INTE-FF in an interrupt service routine allows nested interrupts.[1]

8.5 Multiple Sources of Interrupts

The design must deal with multiple devices generating interrupts. Allowing for these requires the system to do the following:

- Determine which of the multiple devices has generated the IRQ to be able to execute the correct interrupt service routine.

---

[1]   Interrupts interrupting interrupts.

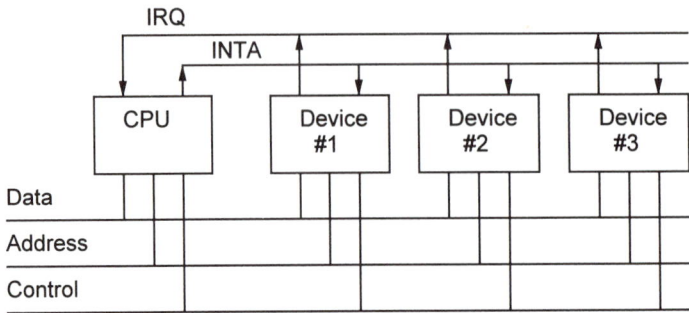

Figure 8-5   Multiple interrupting devices.

- Resolve simultaneous requests for interrupts with a prioritization scheme.

A system with three interrupting devices is shown in Figure 8–5. These I/O devices are interfaced to the CPU with standard input or output interfaces like those designed in Chapter 7. The IRQ signal is generated by each of the interrupt sources and is input to the CPU. This control line must have either three-state drivers or wired-OR, open-collector or open-drain gates with a pull-up resistor. The CPU responds to the IRQ by asserting the interrupt acknowledge (INTA) signal. There are two methods of finding out which of many devices may have generated the interrupt request—polling and vectoring.

> When there are multiple interrupting devices, the CPU must resolve which has generated the interrupt request.

Polled Interrupts

An interrupting device in a polled system is shown in Figure 8–6. The device must have logic to generate the IRQ signal and to set an "I did it" bit in a status register that is read by the CPU. This bit is reset after the register has been read. Polling is a software process where the CPU reads, in turn, each of the potential interrupting device's status registers. When it finds a register with the bit set, the software then knows which device generated the interrupt.

> The interrupting device is found with *software* in a *polled interrupt system.*

To begin the polling process the IRQ must signal the sequence controller to start executing an *interrupt service routine* that first polls the devices and then branches to the appropriate service routine for that device. The CPU uses a *vector* to know where this interrupt service routine is located.[2] The location of a vector is determined by the CPU's designers, and the programmer places the address of the interrupt service routine here. When the IRQ is asserted, the sequence controller fetches the interrupt service routine's address from the vector location and then automatically branches to the routine. We can extend this idea of a vector location containing the address of the interrupt service routine to deal with multiple devices.

---

[2] A vector is something that "points." Thus a vector is the address of the subroutine. Vectors are stored in memory, and indirect addressing is used to transfer to the interrupt service routine.

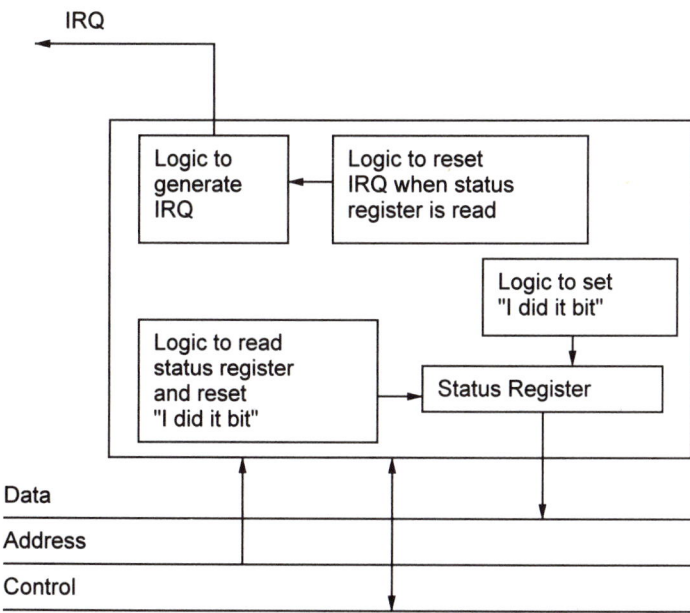

Figure 8-6 Polled interrupt logic.

Vectored Interrupts

The second way to resolve which of several interrupting devices has generated the IRQ is called

> The interrupting device provides a *vector* to identify itself in *vectored interrupts*.

vectored interrupts. A vector is simply an address, and in this case it is the address of the interrupt service routine that must be executed. The CPU and the interrupting devices are connected as shown in Figure 8–5. The CPU's response to the IRQ is to assert the interrupt acknowledge signal, INTA. The interrupting device uses INTA to place information that identifies itself onto the data bus for the CPU to read. This information, loosely called a vector, may be one of several forms. In some processors, an 8-bit code identifies which device has generated the IRQ. In the Intel processors, this code is called a *restart vector*. The CPU reads the 8-bit code, sets the most significant bits to zero, and uses this as the address of the vector. In another version of the design, the interrupting device places the complete address of the interrupt service routine onto the data bus. The sequential logic to do this is more complex in both the sequence controller and in the interrupting device. In any event, a vectored interrupt design requires the interrupting device to identify itself in response to the interrupt acknowledge signal. Figure 8–7 shows the logic required in the interrupting device. The vector information in each device may be hardwired, set by DIP switches, or in registers in programmable interrupting devices.

A second type of vectored interrupt system is one in which the CPU has multiple IRQ input pins, as shown in Figure 8–8. The CPU's designers dedicate specific memory locations for a vector associated with each IRQ line.

An extension of this second type of vectored interrupts is found in modern microcontrollers where many I/O features are integrated within the microcontroller. These have internal sources of interrupts, such as timers, with a vector location associated with each interrupting source.

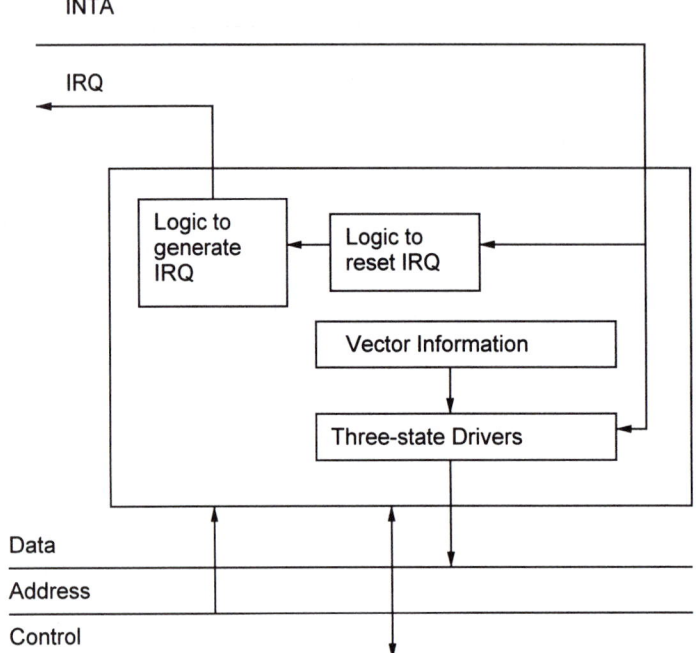

Figure 8-7   Vectored interrupting device hardware.

The vectored interrupt design is more flexible than polling with shorter time delay in getting into the interrupt service routine. Vectored interrupts, however, do require additional hardware for prioritization of simultaneous interrupts.

Multiple Interrupt Masking

In vectored interrupt systems that allow multiple interrupting devices, the programmer must be able individually to enable and disable each. You may want to allow some sensors to generate an interrupt and disallow others. In systems where multiple interrupt request lines are available, such as the CPU shown in Figure 8–8, in modern microcontrollers such as the Motorola M68HC11, and in programmable interrupt controllers like that shown in Figure 8–11, a mask or enable bit is

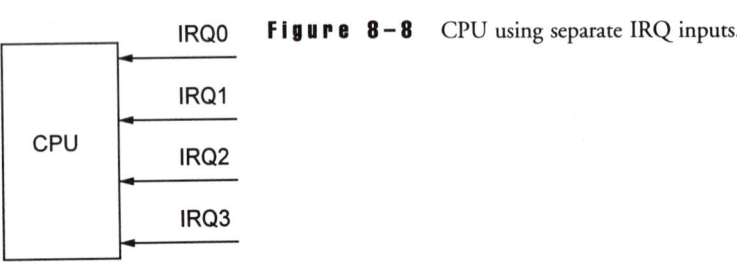

Figure 8-8   CPU using separate IRQ inputs.

associated with each interrupting source. Figure 8–9 illustrates that a 1 in the interrupt enable register will allow the IRQn signal to go on to the interrupt system. Other systems use a *mask* register where a 1 masks (or disables) the interrupt.

8.6 Sequential and Nested Interrupts

Nested interrupts are allowed if the programmer re-enables interrupts in the interrupt service routine.

The system we have designed can resolve many interrupting sources and deal with interrupts that occur sequentially. To recap the design, when an IRQ is generated by the interrupting device, further interrupts will not be recognized by the CPU because the INTE-FF is reset by the INTA signal. This automatically prevents one interrupting another. However, the programmer may allow interrupts to be nested by including the enable interrupt instruction in the interrupt service routine. Depending on the design of the CPU, the INTE-FF may or may not be automatically re-enabled at the end of the current ISR. If it is not, the programmer must re-enable it before returning to the interrupted program or further interrupts will not occur.

8.7 Simultaneous Interrupts—Priorities

Simultaneous interrupts require a prioritization scheme.

We have seen how a system may be designed to resolve which of several interrupting devices has generated an IRQ. This design also allows sequential interrupts to interrupt others if the programmer allows it in the ISR. If two interrupting devices generate an IRQ simultaneously (or at least within one instruction execution cycle), the system must resolve which of the simultaneous requests has the highest priority. There are both software and hardware priority resolution methods.

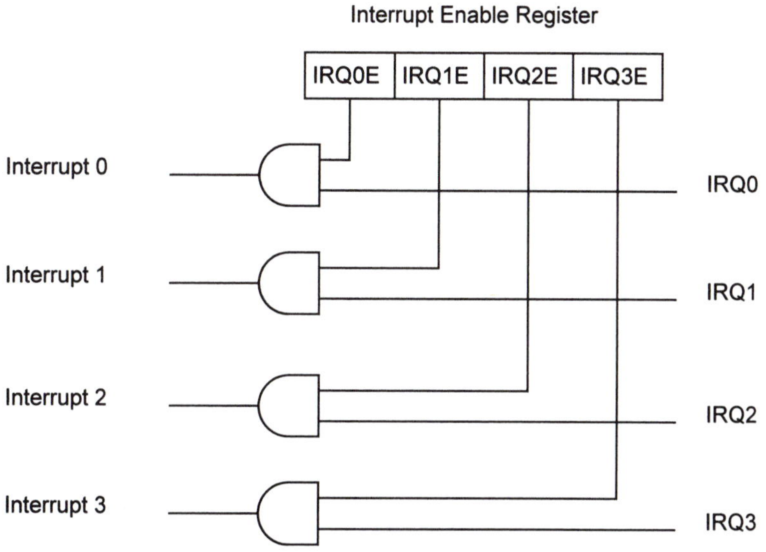

Interrupt Enable Register

| IRQ0E | IRQ1E | IRQ2E | IRQ3E |

Interrupt 0 — IRQ0

Interrupt 1 — IRQ1

Interrupt 2 — IRQ2

Interrupt 3 — IRQ3

Figure 8–9 Interrupt enable register.

Software Priority Resolution

When interrupting devices are polled, the order in which they are polled fixes the priority.

The polled interrupt system described in Section 8.5 to determine which device generated the interrupt may be used for prioritization. One simply writes the polling software to check the highest priority device first. The hardware in the interrupting device must be designed so that a lower priority device continues to assert its IRQ until it receives service.

Hardware Priority Resolution

In systems that use vectored interrupts, hardware prioritization is needed. There are several hardware methods that can be used.

Hardware prioritization must be used in vectored interrupts.

Daisy chain: Figure 8–10 shows a daisy chain configuration. In this scheme, multiple devices may simultaneously assert IRQ. The CPU asserts INTA that is passed down the chain from device to device. The higher-priority devices are the ones that are the closest (electrically) to the CPU. When the INTA signal reaches the device that generated the IRQ, that device responds by putting its vector information on the data bus and not passing along the INTA. Thus lower-priority devices do not receive the INTA, and bus conflicts are avoided. When the interrupt service routine is completed, a subsequent INTA signal may be passed down the chain to the lower-priority device. Logic is required within the daisy chain device to detect the end of the interrupt service routine so the INTA can be passed through to lower-priority devices.

Separate IRQ lines: The CPU with multiple IRQ lines shown in Figure 8–8 can also have a hardware prioritization scheme. In this case, IRQ0 may have higher priority than IRQ1. If simultaneous IRQs occur, the highest-priority one will be serviced.

Hierarchical prioritization: Some systems allow a hierarchy of interrupt priorities. Once an interrupt has occurred, higher-priority interrupts are allowed while lower ones are masked.

Nonmaskable interrupt: The IRQ signals discussed so far may be disabled and enabled, also called masked and unmasked, by the programmer. Most systems have an interrupt line that may not be disabled or masked by the programmer. This is used for very important events, such as a power failure, which must take priority over everything else.

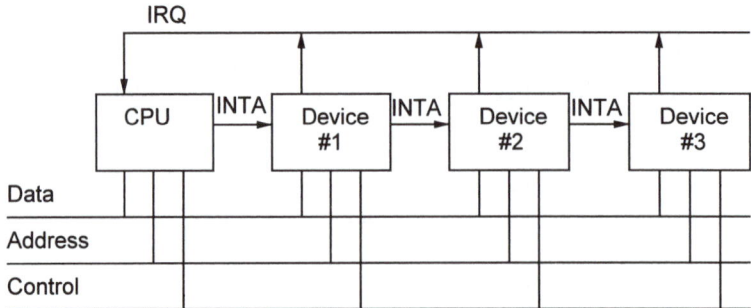

Figure 8-10   Daisy chain interrupts.

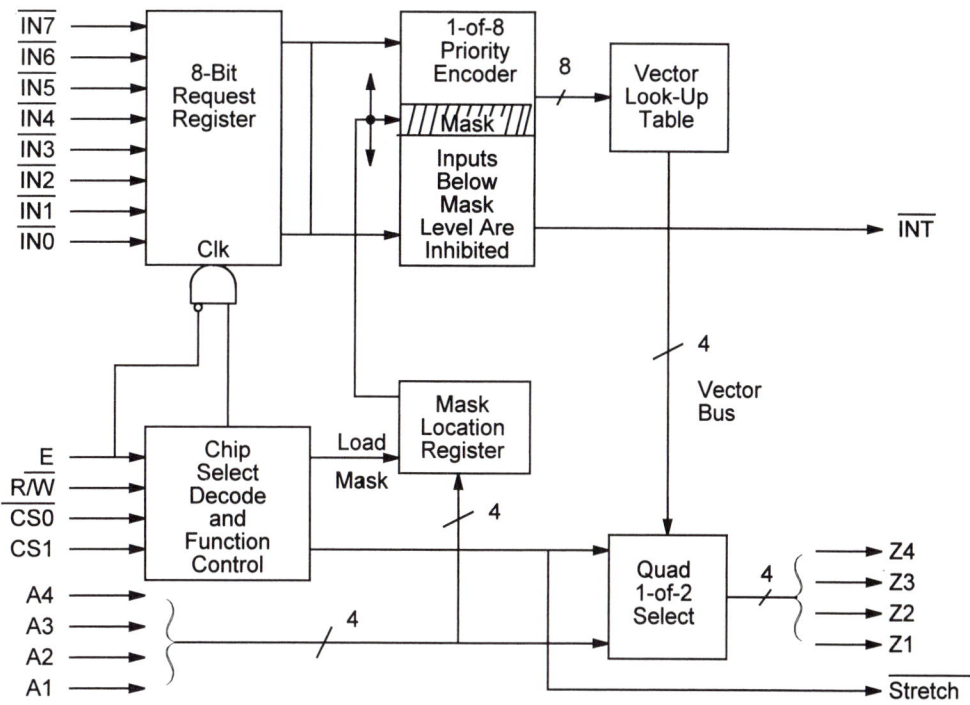

Figure 8-11 Motorola MC6828 Priority Interrupt Controller.

Programmable interrupt controllers: Manufacturers such as Intel and Motorola offer programmable controllers to ease the job of designing the interrupt system. These devices can resolve priorities and can be programmed to generate a vector for several interrupting sources. A typical controller is the Motorola MC6828 Priority Interrupt Controller shown in Figure 8–11.

8.8 Transferring Control to the Interrupt Service Routine

The hardware and software described in the previous sections find the address of the correct interrupt service routine. Before starting to execute the interrupt service routine, the CPU has other tasks to complete. It must, at least, save the return address on the stack. In some processors, all the CPU registers and flags are pushed onto the stack as well. This is called *context saving.*

> *Interrupt latency* is the amount of time taken by the processor to start executing the interrupt service routine.

The delay from the time the IRQ is generated by the interrupting device to the time the ISR starts to execute is called the *interrupt latency.* This is a variable depending on the length of the instruction that must be completed before the IRQ is acknowledged and the amount of data pushed onto the stack. The latency is also affected by whether or not interrupts for the device are enabled. For example, if a higher-priority device is receiving service, the latency for a lower-priority device includes the time taken to finish the first's ISR.

8.9 The Interrupt Service Routine

The hardware in the interrupt system passes control to the appropriate interrupt service routine (ISR) to take care of the situation that caused the interrupt. Using interrupts is an attractive and popular way to make systems quickly respond to events. Using interrupts is not without peril, however. Interrupt-driven routines are often difficult to test and debug. Sometimes when the software is being written the hardware is not available to generate the interrupt. Development systems may not have suitable interrupting capabilities. The debugger in your development system may get in the way of the application's interrupts by using interrupts itself. Nonetheless, interrupts can make many systems simpler and are widely used. To make our job less difficult, here are some pointers for writing interrupt service routines.

> The *interrupt service routine* is the program executed in response to an interrupt request.

Interrupt Service Routine Pointers

Don't modify any registers or flags: The interrupted program will be using the registers and flags, and the ISR must not modify any register or flag. Some, but not all, CPUs push all registers and flags onto the stack before the ISR is entered. If the CPU does not do this automatically, push only the registers needed in the ISR. This will reduce the interrupt latency.

Re-enable or unmask interrupts in the ISR if you need to: The hardware automatically disables further interrupts before transferring to the ISR. If there are higher priority interrupts, you may need to re-enable or unmask them. Some processors automatically re-enable interrupts at the end of the ISR before returning to the interrupted program. If the processor doesn't do this, re-enabling must be done as the last thing in the ISR, if you haven't done so already.

Avoid nested interrupts: Try to avoid interrupt service routines being interrupted.

Restore registers before returning if you need to: Some processors do this automatically; some do not.

Use the proper return instruction: Most CPUs have a different instruction to return from an interrupt service routine than from a subroutine.

Keep the ISR short: Do the minimum amount of processing in an ISR. This is particularly true in a system with multiple interrupting sources and where nesting is not allowed. Keeping the ISR short means that subsequent interrupts are serviced faster.

Interprocess Communication

Frequently, an interrupt service routine and another part of the program must exchange information. For example, an ISR may be incrementing a counter each time a product goes by on an assembly line. Another part of the program may be monitoring this counter to package the product when the counter reaches a certain value. The only interprocess communication technique discussed in Chapter 5 appropriate for interrupt service routines uses global or local data elements, as shown in Figure 8–12. Clearly, except for only the most simple programs, registers cannot be used to pass information back and forth.

We must be concerned about the module coupling problems discussed in Chapter 6. Also, we must be concerned about the timing of the data exchange. In normal program flow, we have some

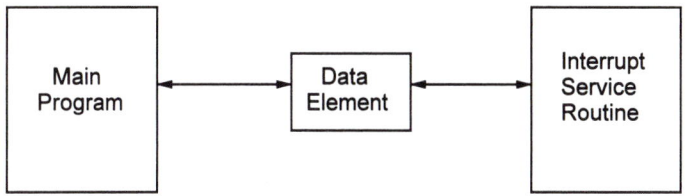

Figure 8-12 Interprocess communications in interrupt service routines.

control over when data are written to data elements. With interrupts, however, the interrupt can occur at any time, and we must ensure that data doesn't get changed while it is being used. Consider the situation in Figure 8–13, where both the main program and the interrupt service routine read, modify, and write the data. There is no problem if the interrupt does not occur while the main program is reading, modifying and writing the data. If it does, the data modification that the ISR produced may be lost. A *critical region* in a program is one in which the interrupted program takes more than one instruction to read, modify, and write data. A solution to this problem is shown in Figure 8–14. The interrupts are disabled in critical regions where there may be interaction between the ISR and the main program.

> A *critical region* in a program should have interrupts disabled before and reenabled after.

8.10 Interrupt Routine Returns

One of the original specifications for the design of the interrupt system was that interrupt service routines are to be treated like subroutines. We have discussed how control is transferred to the ISR, either through polling software or vectors, but we have not considered how a return is made. Transferring to an ISR is just like branching to a normal subroutine, and the system pushes the return address onto the stack in the normal fashion when interrupts occur. Other information may be pushed onto the stack as well, such as the contents of all the registers in the CPU. Different manufacturers have taken different approaches to this. Motorola processors tend to push the registers while Intel processors do not. In each case,

> The return from interrupt instruction is different from a return from a subroutine.

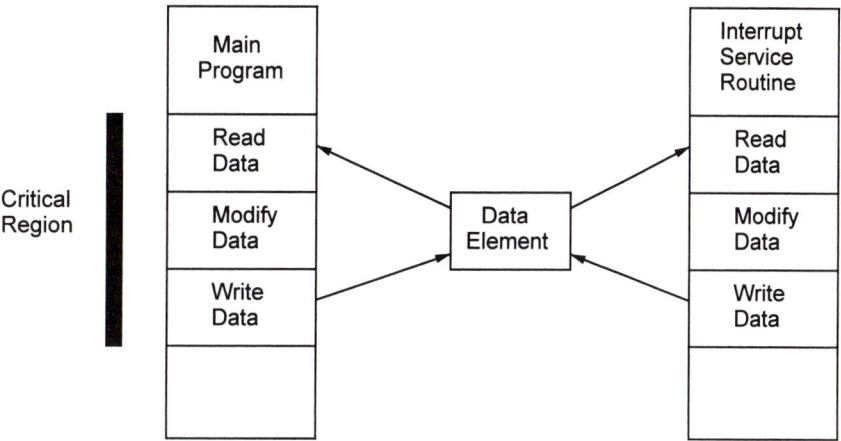

Figure 8-13 Module coupling in interrupt service routine.

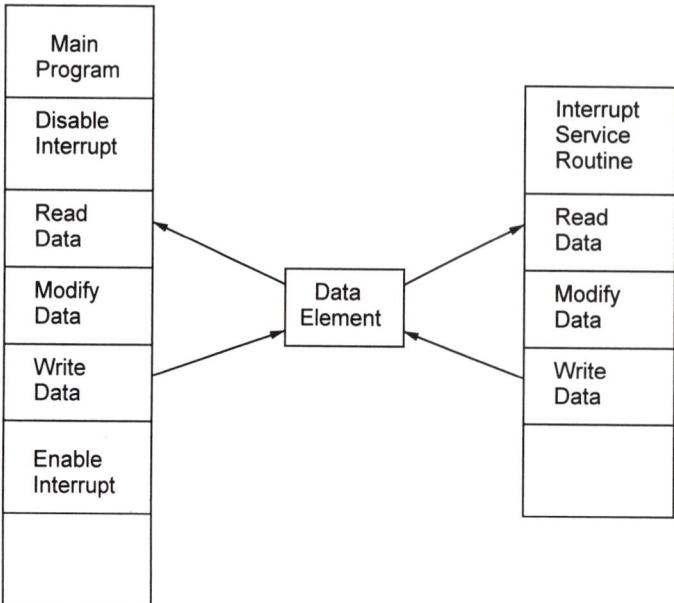

Figure 8-14 Disable interrupts in critical areas of the main code.

however, a *return-from-interrupt* instruction, distinct from the normal subroutine return, is provided for use in the interrupt service routine. This instruction pulls data from the stack and performs other interrupt-related functions that may be necessary.

8.11 Other Interrupt Request Signals

Nonmaskable Interrupts

All processors can disable (mask) normal interrupt requests once they have been enabled (unmasked). Different prioritization schemes to deal with simultaneous, multiple interrupts have been discussed, and we touched briefly on how to allow and disallow nested interrupts.

Nonmaskable interrupts are used for very important events such as a power failure.

In addition to these features that are under the programmer's control, most processors provide an interrupt request signal that is separate from IRQ and is active always once the programmer has enabled it. This is called a *nonmaskable interrupt (NMI)* because once enabled, the programmer cannot disable it.

Nonmaskable interrupts are used in situations where you do not want to miss an event because interrupts are disabled. A common application is called a *power failure interrupt.* If a system must maintain its integrity when the power fails, the onset of power failure can be detected before the power supply voltage goes to zero. There will be a short time to run a small program to save critical data items to, say, battery-powered or nonvolatile RAM. Figure 8.15 shows a typical circuit using a MAX709 Reset Monitor to detect power failure and generate an NMI.

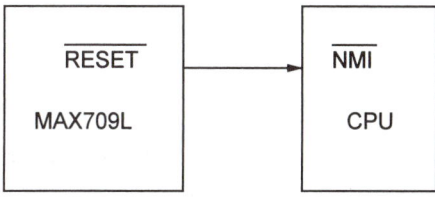

Figure 8-15 Power failure detection and NMI.

Software Interrupt

> The *software interrupt instruction* can be used to test and debug interrupt service routines when the interrupting hardware is not available.

A *software interrupt (SWI)* is a one-byte (or one- instruction-word) instruction that activates interrupt processing without a hardware-generated IRQ. There will be a vector location that contains the address of the routine to be executed in response to this one-byte subroutine call. Software interrupts can be used to simulate a hardware interrupt for testing and debugging when the hardware is not available to generate the IRQ. The SWI is also frequently used for a breakpoint instruction in debugging monitors.

Exceptions

Exceptions are abnormalities that occur during the normal operation of the processor. Examples of exceptions include internal bus errors, attempts to execute illegal instructions, and division by zero. The programmer can provide a service routine for each of these errors (and a vector) and when the CPU hardware detects an error, the interrupt process can be started and the special routine executed.

Reset

Most manufacturers consider the CPU reset to be a type of interrupt. It is a signal asserted on a separate pin, is nonmaskable, and uses a vector (usually) to start the program after reset. It doesn't do other interrupt processes, such as saving the CPU's context, but it does initialize the context to some initial state.

8.12 Conclusion and Chapter Summary Points

The interrupt capabilities of a processor are important and should be considered very early in the evaluation or learning phase. Interrupts can synchronize the operation of the program with real-time events. Interrupts can allow the CPU to continue processing while waiting for I/O devices to become ready for data transfer. Interrupts can also be internally generated when errors or exceptions occur. Most processors also have a software interrupt instruction that is useful for debugging. The important points in this chapter are:

- Interrupts are asynchronous; they may occur at any time.

- Interrupts are disabled when the CPU is reset.

- Interrupts may be controlled, enabled, and disabled, by the programmer.

- Some interrupt systems use polling and some use vectors to resolve which of many devices has generated an interrupt request.

- Simultaneous interrupt priorities may be resolved by software in polling systems and with hardware in vectored systems.

- Systems with multiple interrupting devices have mask or enable bits to control each one individually.

- When the CPU recognizes an interrupt request, it asserts an interrupt acknowledge signal that the external devices may use.

- Before entering the interrupt service routine, the CPU saves the machine context; it always pushes the program counter and, in some processors, the registers onto the stack.

- Interrupts are disabled when the interrupt service routine is entered.

- Interrupt service routines should be kept as simple and short as possible.

- Avoid nested interrupts if possible.

- Use global data elements for interprocess data communications.

- Reenable interrupts before leaving the interrupt service routine, if the CPU does not do it automatically.

- Disable interrupts in the main program in critical areas.

8.13 Further Reading

Byrd, J. S. and Pettus, R. O., *Microcomputer Systems, Architecture and Programming*, Prentice Hall, Englewood Cliffs, NJ, 1993.

Lawrence, P. D., and K. Mauch, *Real-Time Microcomputer System Design: An Introduction*, McGraw-Hill, New York, NY, 1987.

Peatman, J. B., *Design with Microcontrollers*, McGraw Hill, New York, NY, 1988.

8.14 Problems

8.1   List five possible applications for interrupts.

8.2   Describe the actions a CPU takes between the time an interrupt request occurs and when the interrupt service routine is entered.

8.3   Why are further interrupts disabled when the first occurs?

8.4   What is the INTE-FF used for?

8.5   What is a pending interrupt?

8.6   Describe two methods by which a CPU can determine which of several devices has generated an interrupt.

8.7   What are vectored interrupts?

8.8   What are polled interrupts?

8.9   Which type of interrupt, vectored or polled, requires hardware for priority resolution?

8.10 For a processor with 10 interrupting devices, which type of architecture, polled or vectored, provides the fastest transfer of control to the interrupt service routine for a specific interrupt?

8.11 What is an advantage of polled interrupts over vectored interrupts?

8.12 What is an "I did it bit," and how is it used?

8.13 "An interrupt system must allow asynchronous events to interrupt an ongoing process." Give five more hardware and software attributes of an interrupt system.

8.14 What must be done to solve the problem of two devices generating simultaneous interrupts in a system with polled interrupts?

8.15 What must be done to solve the problem of two devices generating simultaneous interrupts in a system with vectored interrupts?

8.16 Design the hardware for an input interrupting device in a polled interrupt system. Assume an 8-bit switch register for data, a one-bit status register for an "I did it bit" and a push-button switch to generate a wired-OR $\overline{\text{IRQ}}$ signal. The status register and switch register are each to occupy an address in the 8-bit I/O address space. Assume separate I/O with control signals $\overline{\text{IOWR}}$ and $\overline{\text{IORD}}$.

8.17 Design the hardware for an input interrupting device in a vectored interrupt system. Assume an 8-bit switch register for data, a push-button switch to generate a wired-OR $\overline{\text{IRQ}}$ signal, and an 8-bit register occupying one I/O address to be used as a programmable 8-bit vector. The switch register is to occupy an address in the 8-bit I/O address space. Assume separate I/O with control signals $\overline{\text{IOWR}}$ and $\overline{\text{IORD}}$..

8.18 Discuss the differences and similarities between a subroutine and an interrupt service routine.

8.19 What is a software interrupt?

8.20 What is a daisy chain?

8.21 Design the logic for a daisy chain interrupt prioritization device. Assume an interrupt acknowledge-in (INTI) signal that is to be passed to the output (INTO) if, and only if, the device is *not* generating an interrupt request.

8.22 Define interrupt latency.

8.23 What does interrupt latency depend upon?

8.24 What is a critical region in a program?

Chapter 9

Computer Memories

OBJECTIVES

This chapter covers the basic principles of memory elements and the design of memory systems. Different types of memory are explained, and the timing of memory read and write operations, and the interaction of memory with the CPU are covered.

9.1 Introduction

There are two types of memory, RAM and ROM, available to the computer system designer. Every computer system has both, and the choice of how much, and the location in the memory map, of each type depends on the computer system being designed. *Random access memory*, or RAM, may be read from and written to. The semiconductor RAM used in systems today is volatile. Anything stored in memory is lost when the power is removed. This has not always been the case in computer memories. Before the rapid advances of semiconductor memory in the mid-1970s, small magnetic cores were used. Core memories could be read and written and retained information when the power was removed. Semiconductor memory technology has replaced core memory because far more storage capacity can be achieved in less space with lower power consumption and lower cost.

> All computers have both *RAM* and *ROM.*

ROM, on the other hand, is *read only memory.* Once it is programmed, either at the integrated circuit factory as part of the manufacturing process, or in the field, for field-programmable devices, it can only be read. ROM is nonvolatile; it retains its information when the power is turned off.

9.2 Computer Types and Memory Maps

We will distinguish between two general types of computers. These are (1) *dedicated-application* systems and (2) *general purpose*, or multiple-application, systems. Both have RAM and ROM. RAM is used for variable information. This can be data used by programs and can also be the programs themselves in general-purpose, multiple-application systems. ROM is used for constant information that must be retained while the power is disconnected. ROM is used for the program in specific application systems and for "boot-up" programs used to get general-purpose systems going in the morning when we turn the power on or when the computer is reset.

You are probably most familiar with general-purpose, multiple-application computers like personal computers. Dedicated-application computers do a single task or set of tasks. Examples of these systems include microcontrollers in vending machines and the computer in an automobile controlling the fuel injection system. These systems are very different from the general-purpose system even though the CPU, memory, and I/O concepts learned in the previous chapters apply equally to both. The amount of RAM and ROM in these systems distinguishes one from another.

> The amount of RAM and ROM depends on the type of system.

The General-Purpose Computer System

A general-purpose system can be seen in Figure 9–1. It has a powerful CPU, copious amounts of RAM for programs, and some ROM for the boot-up code and low-level system I/O drivers. There is a disk system for program and data storage and human-oriented I/O such as a keyboard, monitor screen, and printer.

Many application programs, including word processors, spread sheets, assemblers, compilers, and debuggers run on these systems. All are loaded into the RAM memory from the disk by a *disk operating system*, or *DOS*. There is an additional component of software in ROM that is called *firmware*. This code is the *basic input/output software*, or *BIOS*. It loads the operating system from the disk, called *bootstrapping*, before other programs are executed. The memory map of a general purpose system is shown in Figure 9–2. We see most of the memory is RAM, which is used for the operating system resident code and for application programs.

> General-purpose systems use ROM for the basic I/O software and large amounts of RAM for programs and data.

The Dedicated-Application System

A dedicated-application system, seen in Figure 9–3, is one in which the computer is designed to do some particular job or jobs. Dedicated-application systems differ from general purpose systems in the following ways:

- They are designed to contain the least amount of hardware to accomplish the job at the least cost.

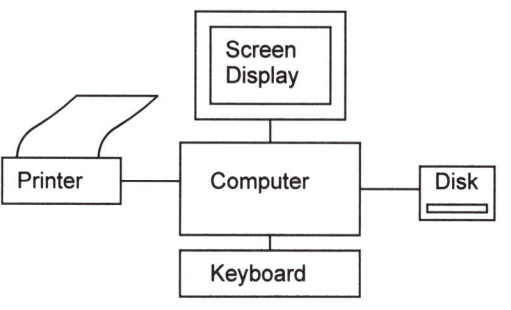

Figure 9–1 General-purpose computer system.

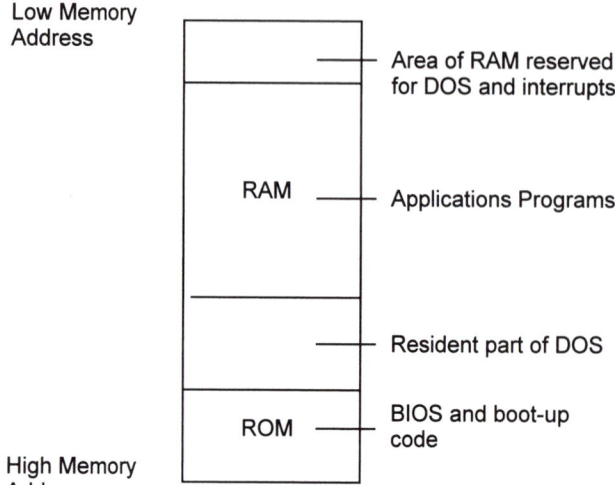

Figure 9–2   General-purpose system memory map.

> A dedicated-application system contains much more ROM for the program and less RAM for data storage than general-purpose computers.

- Unless it is part of the application, there is little or no human- oriented I/O such as displays, keyboards, etc.

- The program is kept in ROM. There is no disk system from which the program can be loaded.

- Only data variables and the stack are kept in RAM.

The memory map for a dedicated system is shown in Figure 9–4. Only enough RAM and ROM to do the job is included in the system. The entire memory map does not have to be filled; if memory isn't needed, it is not included in the system. The system designer gains an additional benefit from this other than just reducing the cost of the memory. Memory addresses that are not used can become "don't cares" and simplify address decoder design.

Figure 9–3   Dedicated-application system.

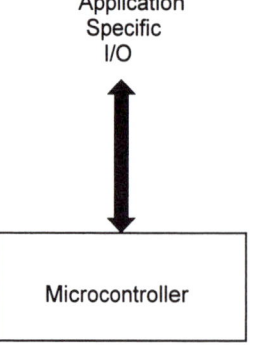

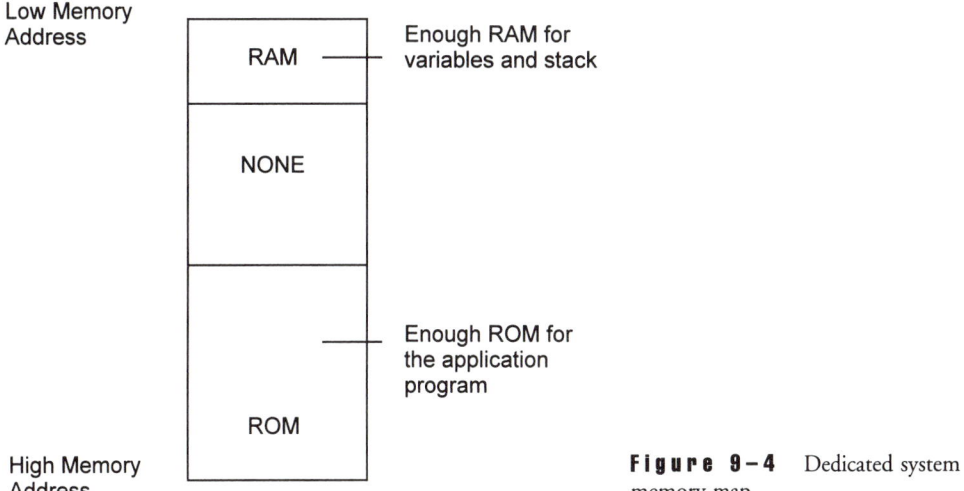

Figure 9–4 Dedicated system memory map.

9.3 Semiconductor RAM

The memories used in computer systems are semiconductor integrated circuits. A random access memory chip consists of an array of memory cells, a decoder for addressing a particular cell, and signals to control the direction of data flow. A $2^N \times 1$-bit memory can be seen in Figure 9–5. The N- bit address selects 1 of 2^N memory cells. The $\overline{CE}$ signal (chip enable, or sometimes $\overline{CS}$, chip select) is derived by decoding the rest of the address bus. $R/\overline{W}$ controls whether the memory cell is being read from or written to. This chip has separate data-in and data-out pins, D_i and D_o, but some memory chips have a single data I/O pin.

We can understand the operation of a memory element by considering Figure 9–5(b). Assume the 1-bit memory cell is a D-type flip-flop (it could be another type of flip-flop or storage cell such as a MOS capacitor). When a bit is to be written into the flip-flop, $\overline{CELL\_ADR\_OK}$, $\overline{CE}$, and $\overline{R/W}$ must be asserted (all low). This will generate a clock signal for the flip-flop and latch the data. To read from the cell, a three-state gate must be enabled.

The design suggested in Figure 9–5(b) is not very practical. For example, if N = 10 for a 1K $\times$ 1 bit memory, a 10-to-1024 decoder to provide the $\overline{CELL\_ADR\_OK}$ signal for all 1024 cells would be expensive. An alternative cell address decoder is shown in Figure 9–6. The 1024-bit array of memory cells is arranged in a 32-bit x 32-bit square array whose elements are addressed by 5-bit, row and column addresses. The row address selects 1 of 32 rows of cells in the array. The column address activates multiplexers and demultiplexers for the data-in and data-out pins. The combination of the row and column addresses selects 1 of 1024 cells in this way.

Memory Cell Types

A *static memory* cell is a flip-flop.

There are two kinds of memory cells, *static memory* and *dynamic memory*. A typical static cell is shown in Figure 9–7. It is a flip-flop and the transistors could be bipolar, as shown, or MOS devices. The bipolar flip-flop operates as follows. Assume the

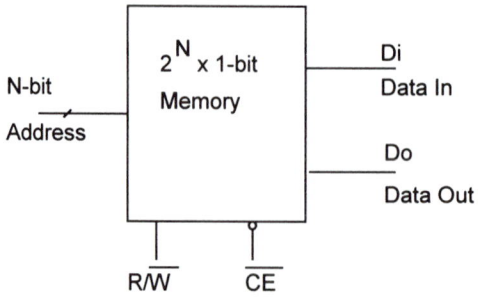

(a) 2^N x 1-bit memory.

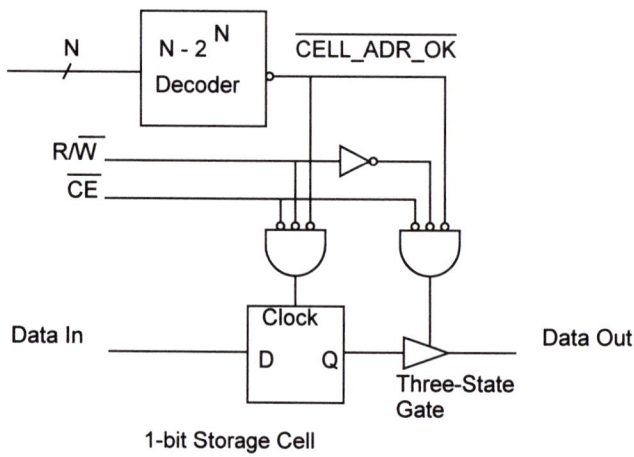

(b) 2^N x 1-bit hardware model.

Figure 9–5 One bit of the $2^N \times 1$ bit memory.

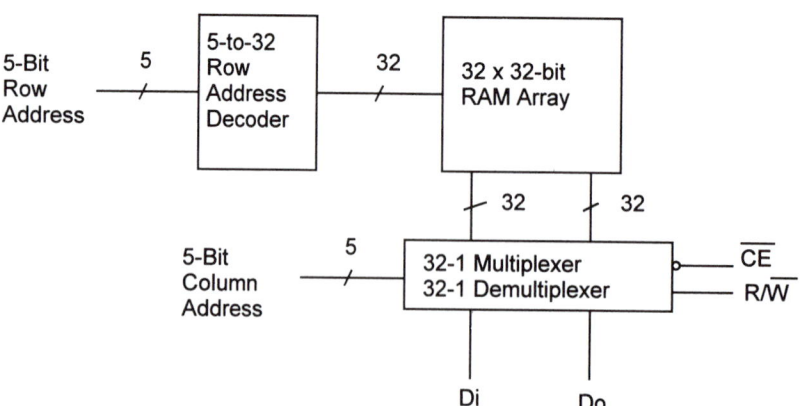

Figure 9–6 32×32 bit RAM array.

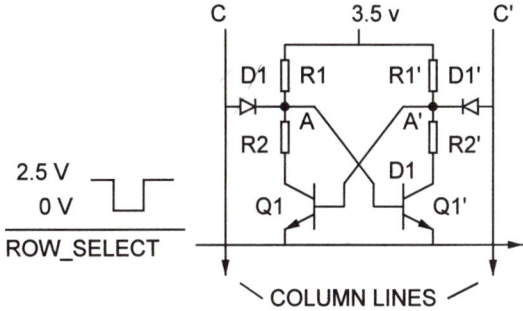

Figure 9-7 Static RAM (SRAM) cell.

ROW_SELECT is high (2.5 volts) and that transistor Q1 is on. Current flows through R1 and R2, which are chosen to make the voltage at point A higher than the column line C. Q1' is off, making the voltage at point A' higher than column line C'. Thus, when the row is not selected, the diodes D1 and D1' isolate the cell from the column lines C and C'. When the cell is read, **ROW_SELECT** is asserted (it now is 0 volts), point A becomes lower than C, and current flows in diode D1 from column line C. This current flow could signify a logic one stored in the cell. A logic zero is stored by turning Q1 off and Q1' on. Now, when **ROW_SELECT** is asserted, the C column line will not have current flow while C' will. Writing into the cell involves asserting the **ROW_SELECT** and driving either C or C' to set Q1 or Q1' depending on whether a zero or one is to be stored.

The static cell in Figure 9–7 consists of resistors, diodes, and transistors. A much simpler memory, and therefore capable of storing more bits per area, is *dynamic memory*. This cell is a capacitor where the absence or presence of charge denotes a stored one or zero. Figure 9–8 shows a typical dynamic memory cell. The MOS capacitor can be written to by activating the row, or word, line to turn the MOS transistor on and charge the capacitor through the column, or bit, line. The cell can be read by turning the transistor on and sensing a voltage on the column.

> A *dynamic* memory cell is a capacitor.

A problem with dynamic memory is that the charge stored on the capacitor leaks away to the substrate. Thus dynamic memory must be refreshed at periodic intervals by activating the **ROW_SELECT** line while holding all column lines at a particular voltage level. All cells in the row can have the capacitor's charge (or lack of charge) refreshed at once.

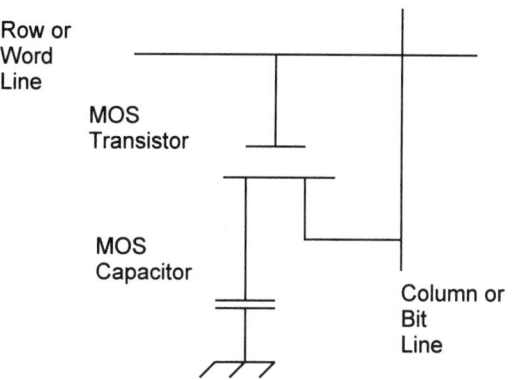

Figure 9-8 Dynamic RAM (DRAM) cell.

Static RAM Chips

Static RAM, *SRAM*, is generally easier to use in a microcontroller application.

Static RAM, or *SRAM*, consists of arrays of flip-flops such as that shown in Figure 9–7. Although SRAM has lower bit density and thus lower storage capability than dynamic RAM, it is simpler to use. SRAM does not need to be refreshed like the dynamic RAM chips.

A typical SRAM chip is the Motorola MCM6064 8K x 8-bit Static RAM shown in Figure 9–9. A selection of available SRAM devices is given in Table 9–1.

Dynamic Memory

A typical dynamic RAM, or *DRAM*, is the 1M × 1-bit Intel 21010, shown in Figure 9–10.

The chip has 10 address bits, separate data-in and data-out pins, a write enable ($\overline{\text{W}}$), and two other control signals. *Row address strobe,* $\overline{\text{RAS}}$, and *column address strobe,* $\overline{\text{CAS}}$, control the multi-

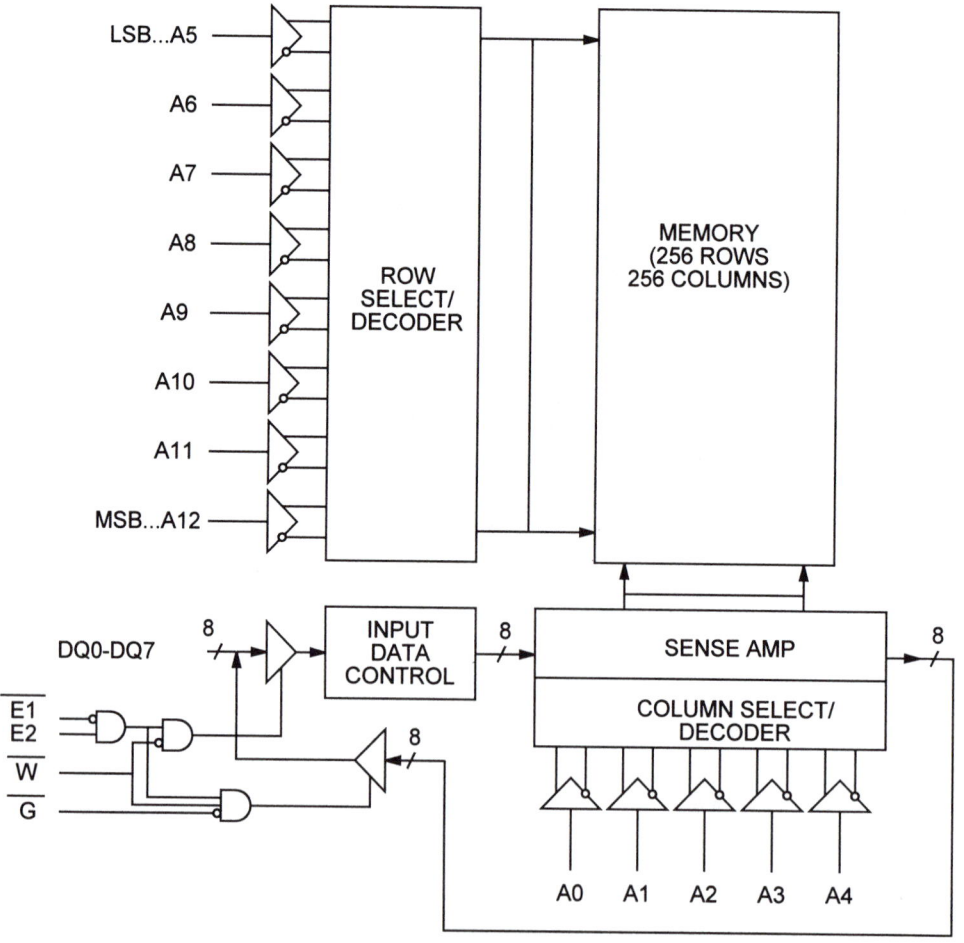

Figure 9–9   Motorola MCM6064 SRAM (reprinted with permission of Motorola Corp.).

TABLE 9-1 SRAM chips

Capacity	Manufacturer
8K × 8-bit	Intel, Motorola
16K × 4-bit	Motorola
32K × 8-bit	Intel, Motorola, Mitsubishi
64K × 1-bit	Motorola
64K × 4-bit	Intel, Motorola
128K × 8-bit	Mitsubishi
1M × 1-bit	Mitsubishi, Motorola, Intel
512K × 8-bit	Motorola

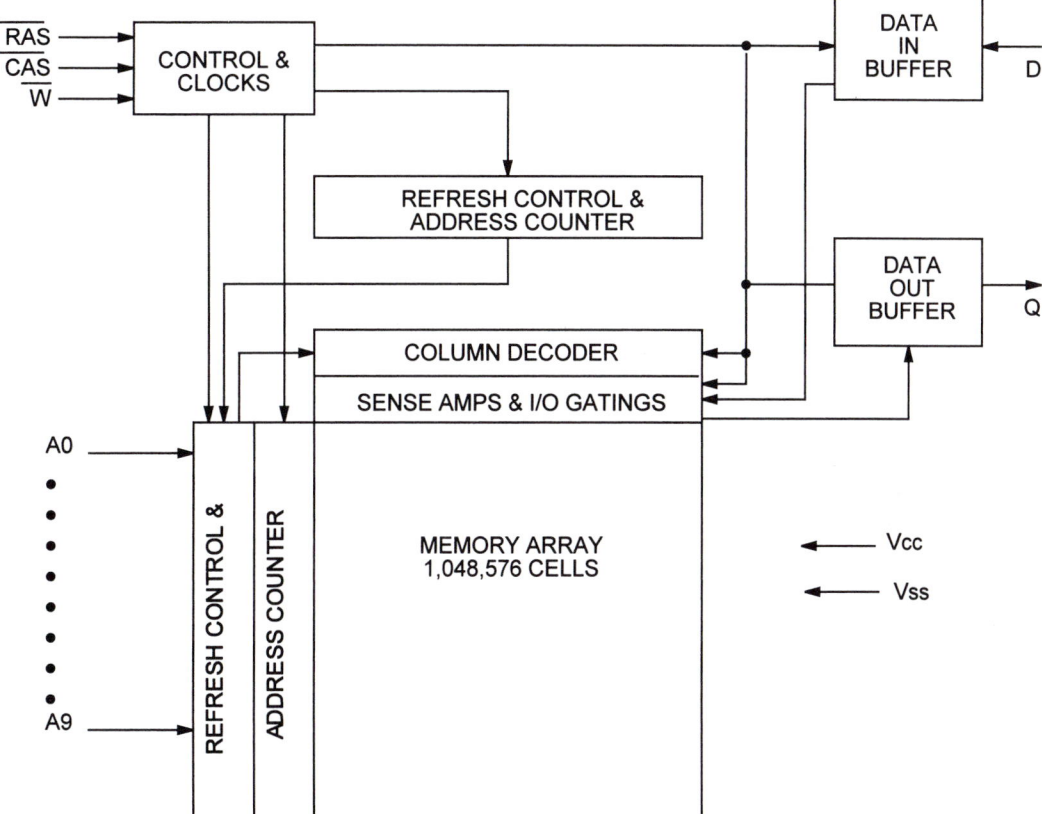

Figure 9-10   Intel 1,048,576 × 1-bit dynamic RAM (reprinted with permission of Intel Corp.).

TABLE 9-2 DRAM chips

Capacity	Manufacturer
256K × 1-bit	TI, Intel, Motorola
256K × 4-bit	TI, Intel, Motorola
1M × 1-bit	TI, Intel, Motorola
1M × 4-bit	Mitsubishi
4M × 1-bit	Intel

TABLE 9–3 Pseudostatic RAM devices

Capacity	Manufacturer
32K × 8-bit	Hitachi
128K × 8-bit	Hitachi

plexing of the two 10-bit address fields that make up the full 20-bit address required for the 1M bits. A selection of typical DRAM devices is given in Table 9–2.

DRAM Refresh

The DRAM memory cell requires a periodic refresh operation.[1] There are several refresh methods.

$\overline{\text{RAS}}$-**only refresh:** This is the most common method of dynamic refresh. The row addresses are strobed by asserting $\overline{\text{RAS}}$ while $\overline{\text{CAS}}$ is held high. The cycle must be repeated for every row address.

$\overline{\text{CAS}}$-**Before-$\overline{\text{RAS}}$ refresh:** $\overline{\text{CAS}}$-before-$\overline{\text{RAS}}$ eliminates the need for external refresh addresses. If $\overline{\text{CAS}}$ is held low a specified time before $\overline{\text{RAS}}$ is asserted, on-chip refresh circuitry automatically furnishes the refresh address. This method takes slightly longer than $\overline{\text{RAS}}$-only refresh.

Hidden refresh: This refresh is done while maintaining the latest valid data at the output and extending $\overline{\text{CAS}}$ and cycling $\overline{\text{RAS}}$.

DRAM memory controllers are available to ease the job of refreshing dynamic RAM chips. These controllers interface the DRAM chips to the system bus and handle all refresh operations automatically.

Pseudostatic RAM

A memory that combines the high storage capacity of dynamic RAM and ease of use of static RAM is *pseudostatic RAM* (Table 9–3). Dynamic storage cells are used and on-chip refresh circuitry is included so the device appears to the user as static RAM. Some care must be taken when using these to avoid a conflict when the system attempts to access the memory while an internal refresh is taking place. There are two strategies that may be included in the design of the chip to solve this problem. First, a separate pin may be included to tell the RAM when it can execute a refresh cycle without conflicting with an external access request. External logic can pulse this input to refresh the chip. In the second approach, a "ready" or "wait" output from the RAM may be used for handshaking in a system where "wait states" can be generated.

> Pseudostatic RAM is dynamic RAM with on-chip refresh circuitry.

---

[1] The refresh timing depends on the manufacturer and the chip. Typically, DRAM needs to be refreshed at intervals of 2 to 4 milliseconds.

9.4 ROM Memory

There are various types of ROM memory chips (Table 9–4). *Mask programmable* ROMs are programmed during the manufacturing stage. To use these, the system designer decides what is to go into the ROM and then specifies the *mask* used by the manufacturer. There is usually a *mask charge* for this service, which may be several thousand dollars, but the individual cost of each chip after that is low, often only pennies each. Thus mask programmed devices are suitable for high-volume applications. Other ROM devices are *field programmable* and may be programmed by the user. These are called *programmable read only memories*, and include *UV-erasable PROMs* (*EPROMs*), *one-time programmable* (*OTP*) *EPROMs*, and fusible-link *PROMs*. EPROMs are electrically programmable and erased by irradiating the chip through a quartz window with ultraviolet (UV) light. An OTP EPROM is an EPROM without the window so that once programmed, it cannot be erased. The term PROM usually denotes a bipolar fusible-link device. Another type of programmable read only memory is the *electrically erasable PROM* (*EEPROM*), which can be programmed and erased while in use.

> The least expensive ROM for large production runs is *mask programmed* at the factory. For system development and small production runs, *field programmable* ROMs are preferred.

The ROM Memory Cell

The ROM memory cell is simply a wire or connection that is either made or not made in the programming process. Figure 9–11 shows the mask programmed ROM cell. The binary information is represented by the presence or absence of the gate on the MOS transistor. Activating the word line puts a one or a zero on the bit line. Other types of ROM memory cells are variations on this theme.

Programmable Read Only Memory

Programmable ROMs fall into two categories—erasable and nonerasable devices—and there are two types of erasable PROMs. These are the *UV-erasable EPROM* and the *electrically-erasable EEPROM* (also called electrically-alterable, *EAPROM*). The first EPROM was the Intel 1702, introduced in 1971. This memory was a 256 × 8-bit chip and could be programmed, erased, and reprogrammed during the development cycle. This greatly speeded up the development process and reduced the cost because the part did not

> The *UV-erasable PROM*, EPROM, made the prototyping of dedicated application systems much easier.

TABLE 9–4 Read only memories

Type	Capacity	Manufacturer
EPROM and OTP	8K × 8-bit to	Various
EPROM	512K × 8-bit	
FLASH	32K × 8-bit to	Intel
	256K × 8-bit	
Fusible-link PROM	32 × 8-bit to	Various
	1024 × 4-bit	

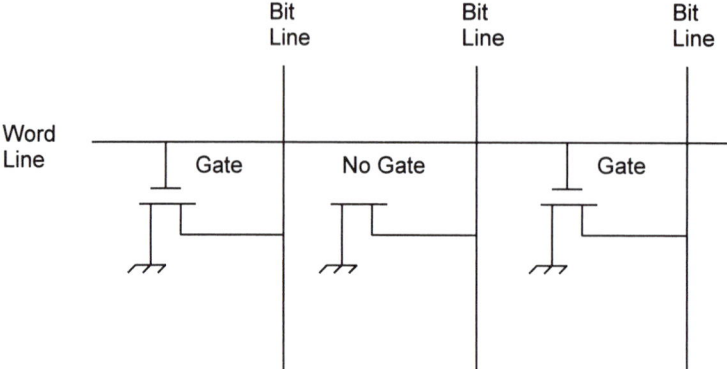

Figure 9-11 ROM cell.

have to be thrown away if the program had to be changed. The cell in an EPROM is a MOS transistor without a connection to the gate. This is called a *floating-gate, avalanche-injection, charge storage device*. A model is shown in Figure 9–12. To program the EPROM, the chip is placed into a *PROM programmer*, and during the programming cycle, the address and data are sent to the chip and the programming voltage is applied. To change the state of the gate, electrons are either injected by an avalanche mechanism into the silicon floating gate or not. Thus, after programming, the channel between the source and the drain either conducts or does not. If the chip needs to be erased, it must be removed from its circuit and placed into a *PROM eraser*. Here it is irradiated with ultraviolet light at a wavelength less than 400 nanometers. This disperses any charge stored in the floating gate back into the substrate and erases the memory. Sunlight and some types of fluorescent lamps contain energy in this wavelength region, and manufacturers caution users that an EPROM can become erased by an exposure of one week in direct sunlight and three years under fluorescent lamps. In applications where this danger exists, an opaque cover should be placed over the quartz window.

Fusible-link ROMs may be programmed once. A bipolar transistor connects the word line to the bit line through the polycrystalline fuse, as shown in Figure 9–13. When programmed, the fuse is blown out.

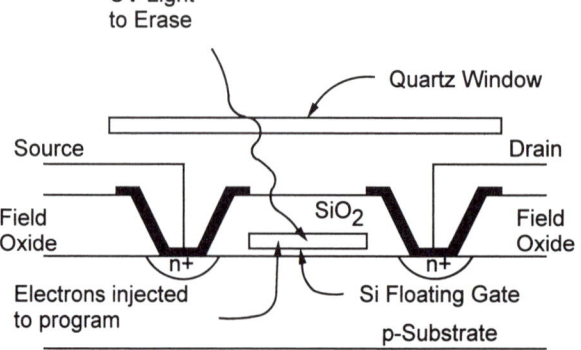

Figure 9-12 EPROM storage cell.

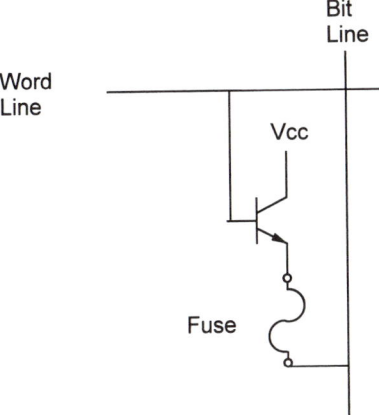

Figure 9-13 Fusible-link ROM.

Nonvolatile RAM—EEPROM, FLASH, and NVRAM

The *EEPROM* (Also *E²PROM* or *EAPROM*), shown in Figure 9–14, is a further development of the EPROM. Note its similarity with Figure 9–12. A second polysilicon gate, called the control gate, is added above the floating gate. A control voltage may be applied to this gate to program and erase the cell by injecting or dispersing electrons in the floating gate.

> *EEPROM* can be erased and reprogrammed without having to be removed from the circuit.

A memory chip that is similar to the EEPROM is called a *FLASH* memory. This technology has been developed by the Intel Corporation and offers more storage per chip than the standard EEPROM. Its drawback is that the entire memory must be erased where single locations can be erased and reprogrammed in the EEPROM devices.

The EEPROM is an attractive memory technology. It can be programmed and erased electrically without removing the chip from the circuit in use. The programming voltages needed to inject the electrons into the floating gate are usually higher than the normal 5 volt supply, and most manufacturers include a *charge pump* to generate the programming voltage. The time required to write is longer than a comparable RAM chip, and there is a maximum number of times it can be programmed (the industry standard as of 1993 is 10,000 program/erase cycles). These devices are ideal for maintaining the system status or for configuration information that does not change very often. You would not want to use an EEPROM where the data must be written often.

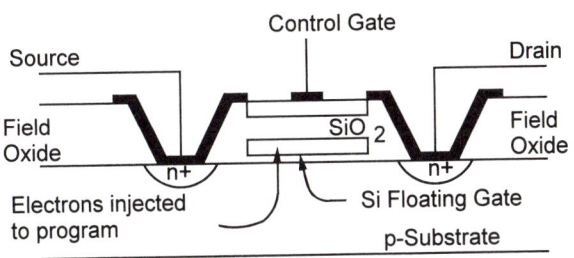

Figure 9-14 Electrically erasable PROM.

TABLE 9–5 Nonvolatile memories

Type	Capacity	Manufacturer
EEPROM	128 × 8-bit to 128K x 8-bit	Various
NVRAM	64 × 4-bit	Xicor
	256 × 4-bit	Xicor
	512 × 8-bit	Xicor and Intel

> NVRAM contains standard RAM cells with EEPROM cells as backup.

Another type of nonvolatile memory is *shadow RAM*, or *nonvolatile RAM, NVRAM*.[2] NVRAM (Table 9–5) is a standard RAM cell and one EEPROM cell for each memory location. The RAM is read and written at full speed, and there is no limit on the number of read/write cycles. When data are to be saved in the EEPROM, say when the system is about to be shut down or a power failure occurs, the EEPROM can be written to save the data.[3]

9.5 Memory Timing Requirements

> The memory system designer must consider the timing requirements of both the CPU and the memory.

There are two components of memory timing that we must understand before designing a memory system. First, remember that the CPU is controlling the information transfer in the system. It generates the control signals, such as **READ/$\overline{\text{WRITE}}$**, and, in the absence of a handshaking signal such as **WAIT** or **READY**, takes data from or puts data on the bus at specific times, as shown in Figure 9–15. The CPU clock controls the overall timing, and although the figures show only one clock cycle, a processor may use more for each read or write cycle.

CPU Read and Write Cycles

The CPU controls all reading and writing of information. Figure 9–15(a) and (b) define the following times for the CPU read and write cycles:

t_{CYC} **Cycle time:** The total time to complete a write or read cycle.

t_{AD} **Address delay:** The delay from the start of the write or read cycle until the address appears on the external address bus. This delay accounts for multiplexing and other CPU-generated delays.

t_{AV} **Address valid:** The time that the address is valid on the external address bus. The CPU takes it away or changes it at the end of the write or read cycle.

The CPU Read Cycle

t_{RED} **Read enable delay:** The delay from the start of the read cycle until the read enable signal is asserted. This is found in CPUs that have separate $\overline{\text{READ}}$ and $\overline{\text{WRITE}}$ control signals.

---

[2] Called *NOVRAM* by Xicor, its original supplier.
[3] This would be an excellent application for a nonmaskable, power-failure interrupt.

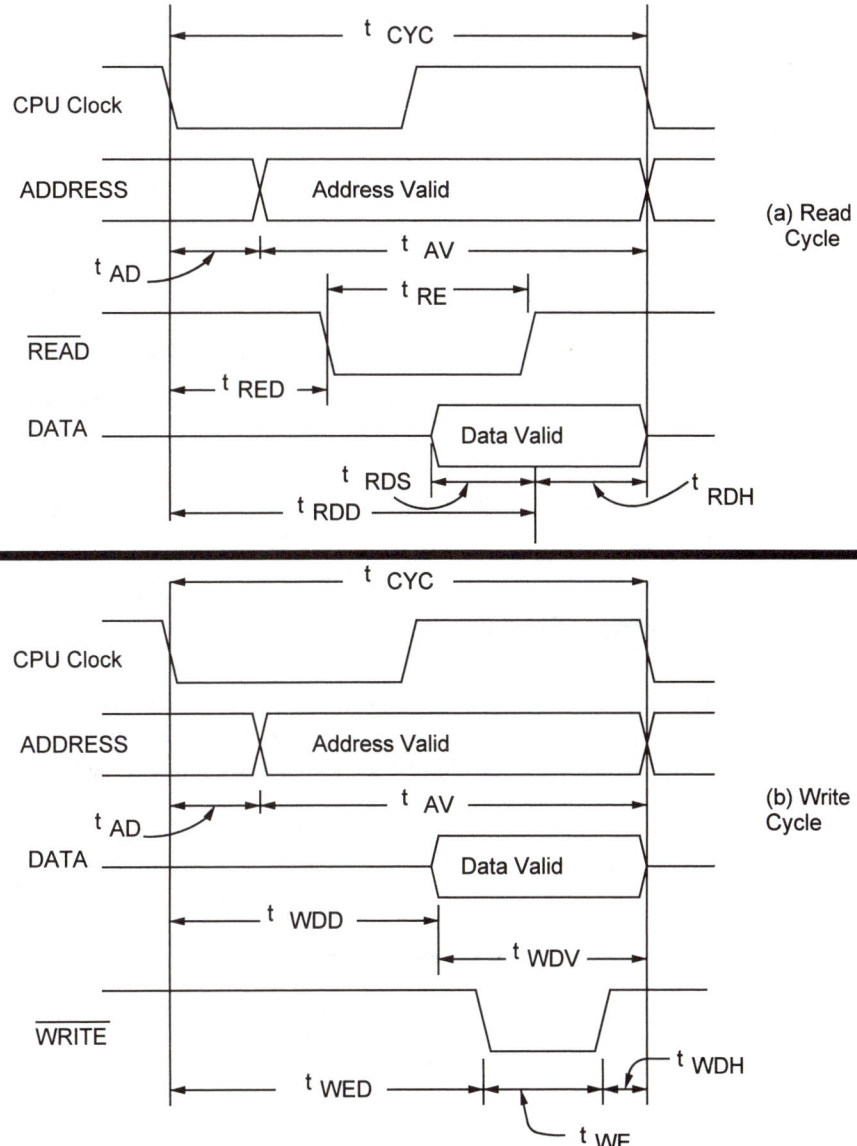

Figure 9-15 Typical CPU read and write cycles.

t_{re} **Read enable pulse length:** The duration of the $\overline{READ}$ signal.

There are three critical times in the read cycle from the point of view of the CPU. The data must be ready to be read t_{RDS} before t_{RDD} and must remain stable t_{RDH} after.

t_{RDD} **Read data delay:** The CPU waits for this time before it reads the data from the data bus.

t$_{RDS}$ **Read data setup:** The time the data must be valid before they are read by the CPU.

t$_{RDH}$ **Read data hold:** The CPU may require the data to be held after it reads them.

The CPU Write Cycle

t$_{WDD}$ **Write data delay:** The CPU waits for this time before it places the data to be written to memory on the data bus.

t$_{WDV}$ **Write data valid:** The time the CPU keeps the data on the data bus.

t$_{WED}$ **Write enable delay:** The CPU waits for this time before it asserts the write enable signal.

t$_{WE}$ **Write enable pulse length:** The duration of the $\overline{\text{WRITE}}$ signal.

t$_{WDH}$ **Write data hold:** The time the CPU holds the data on the data bus after deasserting the write enable signal.

Wait states, as discussed in Chapter 7, can be added to extend these times.

Table 9–6 shows typical time durations for these signals in a Motorola MC68HC11A8 using a 2 MHz clock.

Memory Read and Write Cycles

We now look at the memory system timing from the point of view of the memory. It is easiest to start the discussion with the timing of a static memory chip and then look briefly at a dynamic RAM chip timing. Figure 9–16(a) shows typical read cycle timing diagrams for static RAM and defines the following basic times:

TABLE 9–6 Timing specifications for Motorola MC68HC11A8

Symbol	Parameter	MC68HC11A8 2 MHz Clock (ns)
t$_{CYC}$	Cycle time	500
t$_{AD}$	Address delay	123
t$_{AV}$	Address valid	379
t$_{RED}$	Read enable delay[4]	247
t$_{RE}$	Read enable pulse length	222
t$_{WDD}$	Write data delay	375
t$_{WDV}$	Write data valid	147
t$_{RDD}$	Read data delay	469
t$_{RDS}$	Read data setup	30
t$_{RDH}$	Read data hold	30
t$_{WED}$	Write enable delay	133
t$_{WE}$	Write enable pulse length	389
t$_{WDH}$	Write data hold	0

---

[4] In the Motorola system, a read enable may be generated by ANDing the system E-clock and $\overline{\text{R/W}}$.

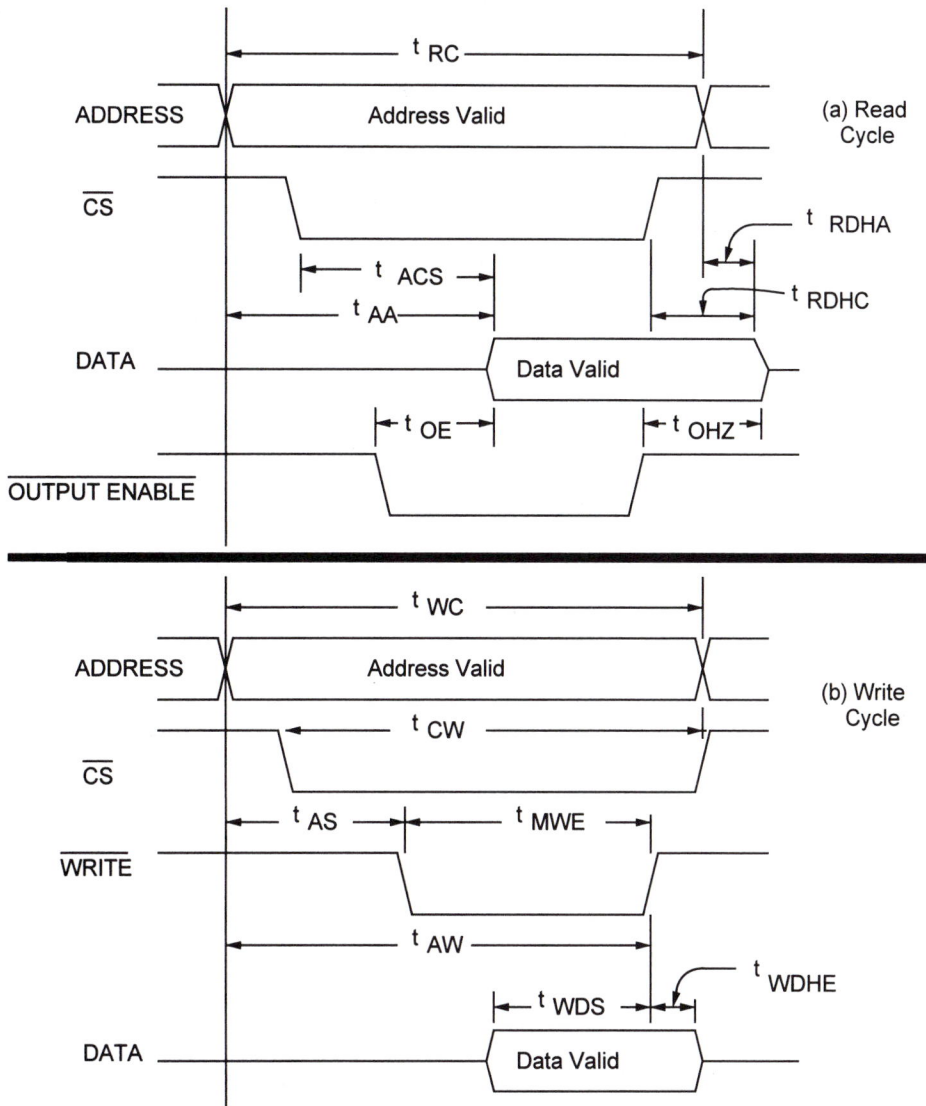

Figure 9-16 Typical memory read and write cycles.

The Memory Read Cycle

t_{RC} **Read cycle:** This is the total time for the read cycle.

t_{ACS} **Chip select access:** The maximum time required by the memory for the $\overline{CS}$ to be asserted before the data are available.

t_{AA} **Address access:** This is the maximum time required by the memory for the address to be present before the data are available.

t_{RDHA} **Read data hold after address:** The time the memory may hold the data at the output after the address is changed.

t_{RDHC} **Read data hold after chip select:** The minimum time the chip will hold the data after being de-selected.

t_{OE} **Output enable access:** On chips that have an output enable, this parameter gives the maximum time for the chip to respond with the data.

t_{OHZ} **Output enable to output high Z:** On chips that have an output enable, this parameter specifies the time the data will remain valid before going into three-state (high impedance).

There are two times for reading data that are important to memory system designers. The read cycle time, t_{RC}, is the minimum time that the addresses must be stable (unchanging) at the chip. The address access time, t_{AA}, is the maximum time required by the memory before the data are available. Although most manufacturers draw the timing diagrams showing t_{RC} and t_{AA} looking different, they are usually the same.

The Memory Write Cycle

The memory write cycle timing diagram is shown in Figure 9–16(b), and we can define the following times:

t_{WC} **Write cycle:** This is the minimum total time required by the memory to complete a write cycle. This may or may not be the same as the read cycle time t_{RC}.

t_{CW} **Chip selection to end of write:** The minimum time the $\overline{CS}$ signal must be asserted.

t_{AS} **Address setup:** The minimum time the address must be valid before the $\overline{WRITE}$ signal is asserted.

t_{MWE} **Write enable:** The minimum time $\overline{WRITE}$ must be asserted.

t_{AW} **Address valid to end of write:** The minimum time the address must be valid.

t_{WDS} **Write data setup:** The minimum time the data must be valid before the end of write enable.

t_{MWDHE} **Write data hold after enable:** The minimum time the data must be valid after the $\overline{WRITE}$ signal is de-asserted.

Again, there is a minimum time, the write cycle time, t_{WC}, that the address must be present and stable at the chip. For some memories, the chip select signal must go low at least t_{CW} (chip selection to end of write) nanoseconds before the time the CPU takes the data away. In other memories, this is not an important parameter. The write enable signal, $\overline{WRITE}$, may be asserted t_{AS} (address setup time) after the addresses are valid. The data being written into the memory must be valid at least t_{WDS} (write data setup) nanoseconds and must be held for the data hold time, t_{MWDHE}, after the $\overline{WRITE}$ goes high. Table 9–7 shows the timing for the Motorola MCM6064 8K × 8-bit SRAM chip.

The timing diagrams for an Intel 21010 1M × 1-bit DRAM is shown in Figure 9–17. The additional control signals, $\overline{RAS}$ and $\overline{CAS}$, must be asserted in sequence to multiplex the 20-bit address into the 10 address lines.

The diagrams presented in this section may not look exactly like those found in data books because manufacturers' diagrams may include other timing signals and may not directly provide the times given in this section. However, the times given above can always be derived from the data

TABLE 9-7 Motorola MCM6064-12 timing

Symbol	MCM6064-12 Parameter	(ns) Min	Max
Read cycle			
t_{RC}	Read cycle time	120	
t_{ACS}	Chip select access Time		120
t_{AA}	Address access time		120
t_{RDHA}		10	
t_{RDHC}	Read data hold	10	
t_{OE}	Output enable access time		40
t_{OHZ}	Output enable to output high Z		40
Write Cycle			
t_{WC}	Write cycle time	120	
t_{CW}	Chip selection to end of write	NA	
t_{AS}	Address setup time	0	
t_{MWE}	Write enable width	60	
t_{AW}	Address valid to end of write	85	
t_{WDS}	Write data setup	50	
t_{WDHE}	Write data hold time	0	

sheets and can be used to determine if any critical timing requirements exist. Section 9.6 shows how to take into account all timing requirements and other system propagation delays to match memory with the CPU.

9.6 Putting It All Together

Now that we understand how the memory chips work, and particularly what their timing requirements and the CPU's timing requirements are, let us look at the interface between memory and the CPU. Figure 9–18 shows a CPU with a multiplexed address bus and static memory. In a system with buffers and other logic, there is a gap between the time when signals are generated by the CPU and when they arrive at the memory. The memory design must account for these additional time delays. For example, in Figure 9–18, the address delay, t_{AD}, is the delay from the start of the memory cycle to the time the address latch enable, ALE, strobes the address into the latch. The actual time the memory receives the address will be delayed by the propagation time of the latch, t_{PL}, and address bus buffers, t_{PADR}. Similarly, the time at which the $\overline{CS}$ signal is asserted will be delayed by the propagation time of the address decoder t_{PDEC}. In some systems, there may be bidirectional data bus buffers between the memory and the data bus. This causes a delay between the output of the data from the memory and when the data arrive at the CPU.

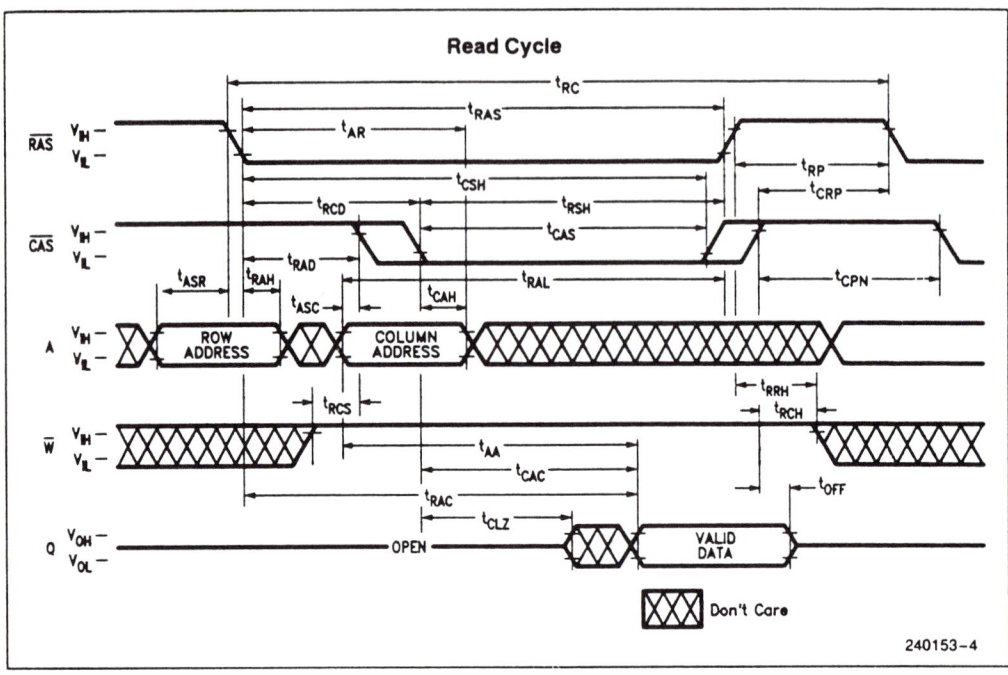

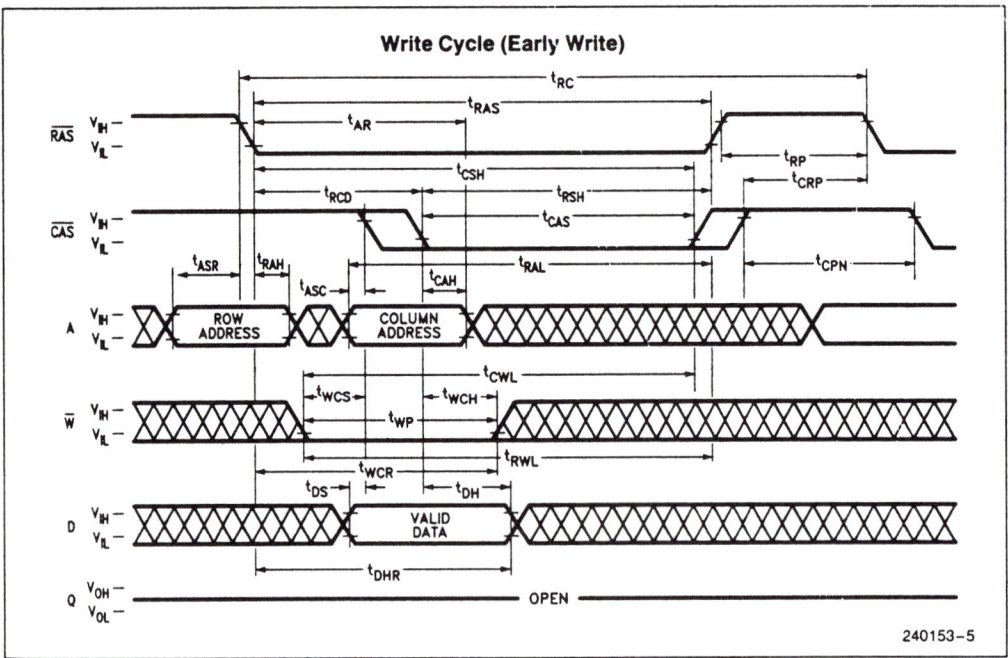

Figure 9-17 Intel 21010 dynamic RAM read and write cycle timing (reprinted with permission of Intel Corp.).

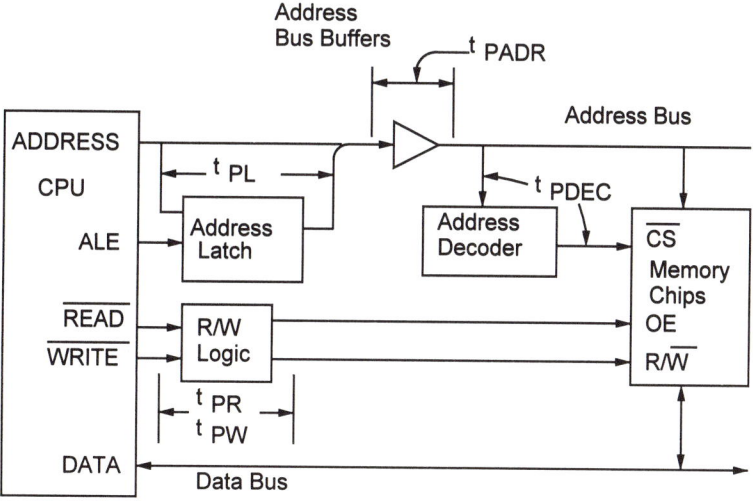

Figure 9–18 CPU–memory interface.

Let's define the following propagation delays for the memory interface in Figure 9–18:

t_{PL}: Propagation time for the address latch.

t_{PADR}: Address buffer propagation time.

t_{PDEC}: Address decoder propagation time.

t_{PW}: Logic propagation time for a write control signal.

t_{PR}: Logic propagation time for a read control signal.

The actual propagation times in any system will depend on the design of the memory interface. For example, a system may not have address buffers or there might not be a multiplexed bus. In any event, the CPU and memory times defined in Section 9.5 can be found from the CPU and the memory data sheets. With these in hand, and with the design of the memory interface and its propagation delays known, we can use the following procedure to see if the memory and CPU timing requirements match.

First consider the memory read operation. The CPU outputs the address, asserts the $\overline{\text{READ}}$ control signal, and reads the information on the data bus at the time given by t_{RDD}. Figure 9–19 shows the alignment of the timing of the CPU and the memory for a read cycle. You can see how the various buffers and decoders delay the signals getting to the memory and the data getting back to the CPU. The memory must respond with the data t_{RDS} ns before the CPU reads it and it must hold the data t_{RDH} ns after the data have been read. To satisfy these constraints, the following equations are derived. All of the criteria must be met. If any fail, the memory chip's timing makes it unsuitable for use.

Equation (9.1) shows that the time the address is available from the CPU must be greater than the minimum time the memory needs it.

$$t_{RC} \leq t_{AV} \tag{9.1}$$

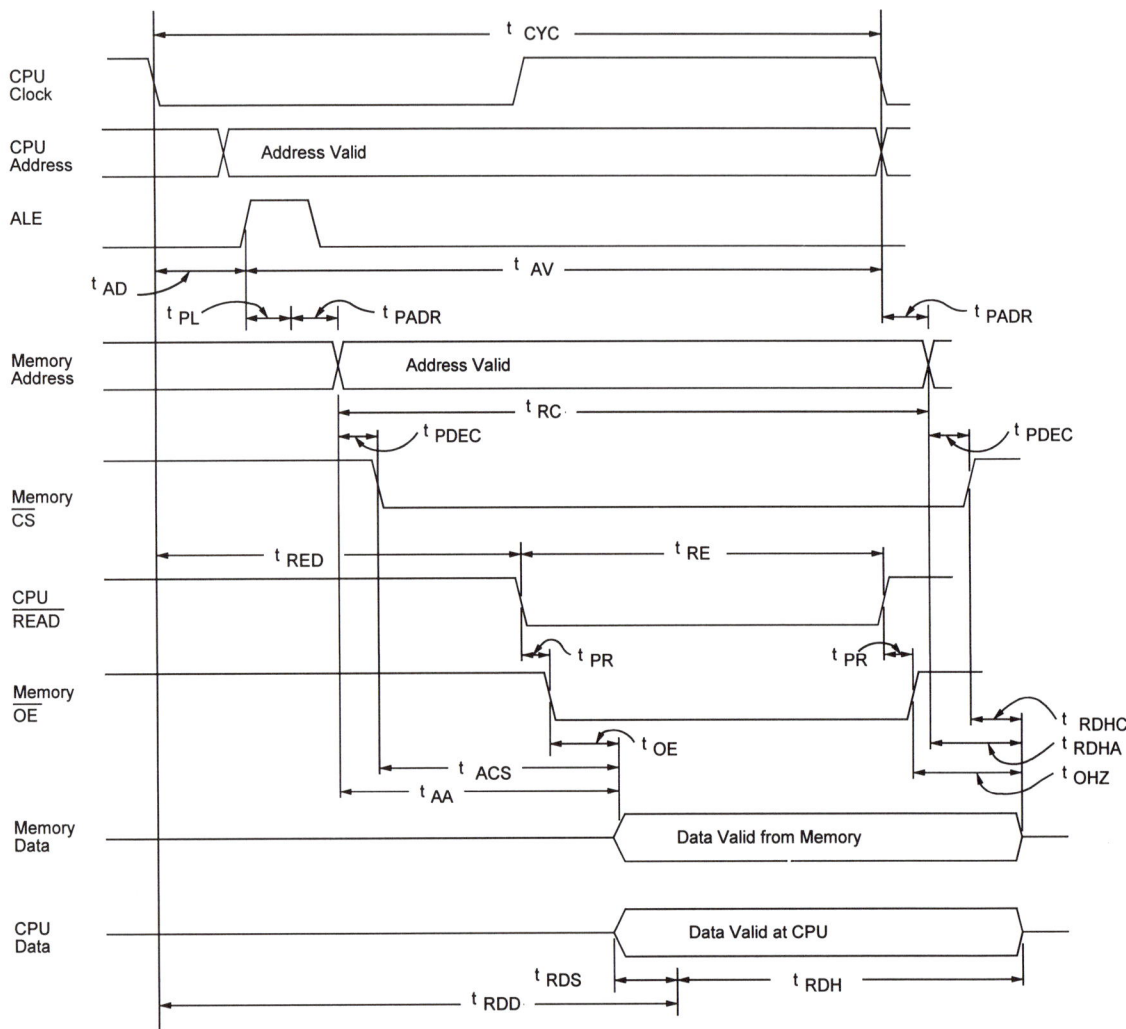

Figure 9-19 CPU reading data from memory.

Equation (9.2) ensures that the address is at the chip long enough (t_{AA}) to satisfy the data setup time.

$$t_{AD} + t_{PL} + t_{PADR} + t_{AA} \leq t_{RDD} - t_{RDS}$$
$$t_{AA} \leq t_{RDD} - t_{RDS}[-\ ]t_{AD} - t_{PL} - t_{PADR} \quad \textbf{(9.2)}$$

Equation (9.3) must be satisfied to ensure that the chip select signal is present long enough (t_{ACS}) to meet the data setup time.

$$t_{AD} + t_{PL} + t_{PADR} + t_{PDEC} + t_{ACS} \leq t_{RDD} - t_{RDS}$$
$$t_{ACS} \leq t_{RDD} - t_{RDS} - t_{AD} - t_{PL} - t_{PADR} - t_{PDEC} \quad \textbf{(9.3)}$$

Equation (9.4) ensures that the output enable signal occurs soon enough (t_{OE}) to meet the setup time.

$$t_{RED} + t_{PR} + t_{OE} \leq t_{RDD} - t_{RDS}$$
$$t_{OE} \leq t_{RDD} - t_{RDS} - t_{RED} - t_{PR} \tag{9.4}$$

Equation (9.5) is to establish that the data are held long enough (t_{RDH}) after the address is removed.

$$t_{RDD} + t_{RDH} \leq t_{RDHA} + t_{PADR} + t_{AV} + t_{PL} + t_{AD}$$
$$t_{RDHA} \geq t_{RDD} + t_{RDH} - t_{PADR} - t_{AV} - t_{PL} - t_{AD} \tag{9.5}$$

Equation (9.6) shows that the read data are held long enough (t_{RDHC}) after the chip select is removed.

$$t_{RDD} + t_{RDH} \leq t_{RDHC} + t_{PDEC} + t_{AV} + t_{PADR} + t_{PL} + t_{AD}$$
$$t_{RDHC} \geq t_{RDD} + t_{RDH} - t_{PDEC} - t_{AV} - t_{PADR} - t_{PL} - t_{AD} \tag{9.6}$$

Finally, Eq. (9.7) ensures that the data are held long enough (t_{OHZ}) after the output enable signal is deasserted.

$$t_{RDD} + t_{RDH} \leq t_{OHZ} + t_{PR} + t_{RE} + t_{RED}$$
$$t_{OHZ} \geq t_{RDD} + t_{RDH} - t_{PR} - t_{RE} - t_{RED} \tag{9.7}$$

Figure 9–20 shows the details of a CPU writing to memory. The timing equations that must be satisfied are given in Eqs. (9.8)–(9.12).

The basic write cycle time must be satisfied by the length of time the CPU maintains the address on the address bus. This is given in Eq. (9.8)

$$t_{WC} \leq t_{AV} \tag{9.8}$$

Equation (9.9) ensures that the address is on long enough (t_{AS}) before the write enable pulse.

$$t_{AD} + t_{PL} + t_{PADR} + t_{AS} \leq t_{PW} + t_{WED}$$
$$t_{AS} \leq t_{PW} + t_{WED} - t_{AD} - t_{PL} - t_{PADR} \tag{9.9}$$

Equation (9.10) must be satisfied to ensure the address is valid long enough (t_{AW}) before the end of the write enable pulse.

$$t_{AD} + t_{PL} + t_{PADR} + t_{AW} \leq t_{PW} + t_{WE} + t_{WED}$$
$$t_{AW} \leq t_{PW} + t_{WE} + t_{WED} - t_{AD} - t_{PL} - t_{PADR} \tag{9.10}$$

The write data setup time (t_{WDS}) is satisfied if Eq. (9.11) is satisfied.

$$t_{WDD} + t_{WDS} \leq t_{PW} + t_{WE} + t_{WED}$$
$$t_{WDS} \leq t_{PW} + t_{WE} + t_{WED} - t_{WDD} \tag{9.11}$$

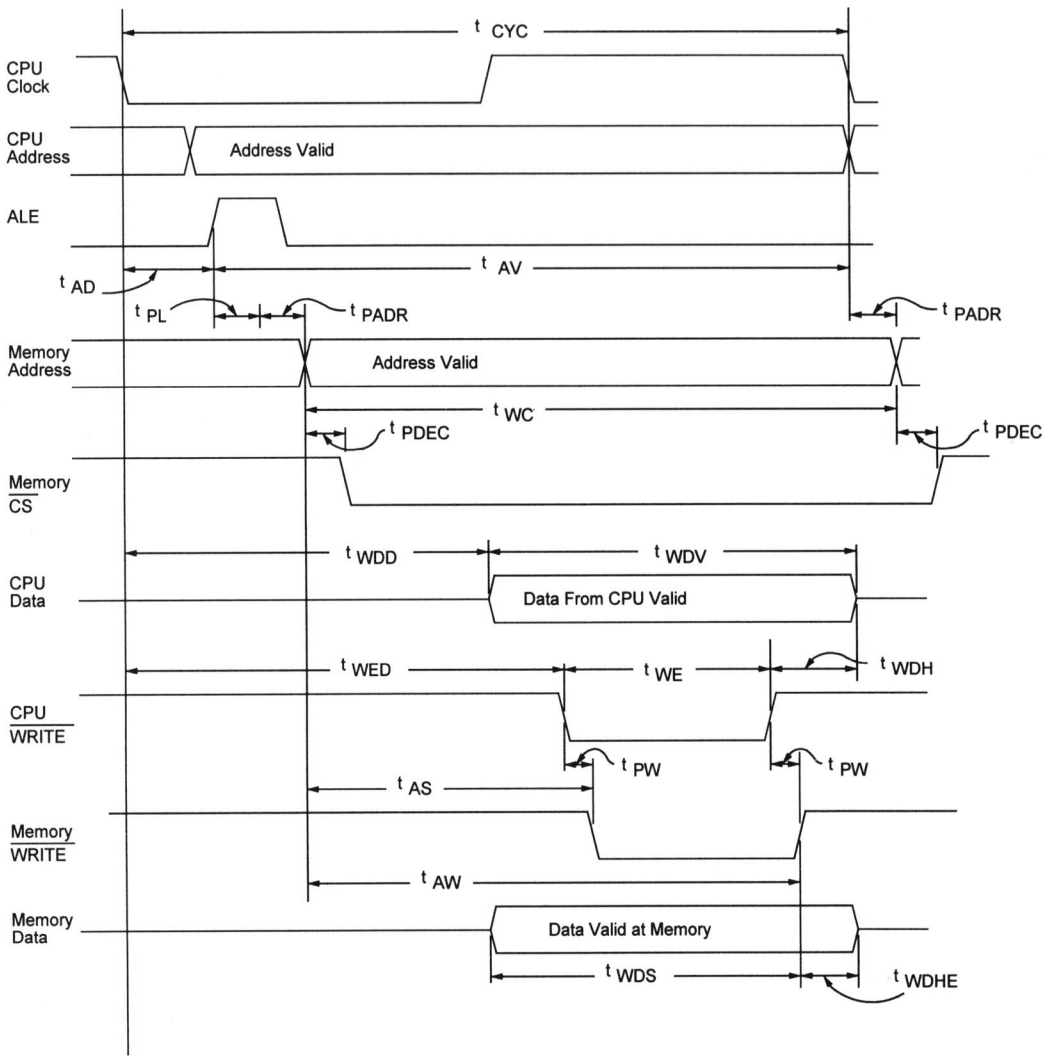

Figure 9-20 CPU writing data to memory.

Finally, the data hold time (t_{WDHE}) is specified by Eq. (9.12).

$$t_{WDD} + t_{WDV} \geq t_{WED} + t_{WE} + t_{PW} + t_{WDHE}$$
$$t_{WDHE} \leq t_{WDD} + t_{WDV} - t_{WED} - t_{WE} - t_{PW}$$

(9.12)

9.7 Conclusion and Chapter Summary Points

- RAM can be read from and written to and is normally volatile.

- EEPROM and NVRAM are nonvolatile RAM types.

EXAMPLE 9–1 **Using the information for a Motorola MC68HC11A8 given in Table 9–6 and the MCM 6064-12, 8K x 8-bit SRAM given in Table 9–7, check to see if the 6064-12 can be used in a system with the MC68HC11A8. Assume the propagation delays are: $t_{PADR} = 0$ (no address buffer), $t_{PR} = 10$ ns, $t_{PW} = 0$, $t_{PL} = 10$ ns, and $t_{PDEC} = 20$ ns.**

Solution:

Read cycle analysis

1. $t_{RC} \leq t_{AV}$:
   $120 \leq 379$ (OK)
2. $t_{AA} \leq t_{RDD} - t_{RDS} - t_{AD} - t_{PL} - t_{PADR}$
   $120 \leq 469 - 30 - 123 - 10 - 0 = 306$ (OK)
3. $t_{ACS} \leq t_{RDD} - t_{RDS} - t_{AD} - t_{PL} - t_{PADR} - t_{PDEC}$
   $120 \leq 469 - 30 - 123 - 10 - 0 - 20 = 286$ (OK)
4. $t_{OE} \leq t_{RDD} - t_{RDS} - t_{RED} - t_{PR}$
   $40 \leq 469 - 30 - 247 - 10 = 182$ (OK)
5. $t_{RDHA} \geq t_{RDD} + t_{RDH} - t_{PADR} - t_{AV} - t_{PL} - t_{AD}$
   $10 \geq 469 + 30 - 0 - 379 - 10 - 123 = -13$ (OK)
6. $t_{RDHC} \geq t_{RDD} + t_{RDH} - t_{PDEC} - t_{AV} - t_{PADR} - t_{PL} - t_{AD}$
   $10 \geq 469 + 30 - 20 - 379 - 0 - 10 - 123 = -33$ (OK)
7. $t_{OHZ} \geq t_{RDD} + t_{RDH} - t_{PR} - t_{RE} - t_{RED}$
   $40 \geq 469 + 30 - 10 - 222 - 247 = 20$ (OK)

Write cycle analysis

1. $t_{WC} \leq t_{AV}$:
   $120 \leq 379$ (OK)
2. $t_{AS} \leq t_{PW} + t_{WED} - t_{AD} - t_{PL} - t_{PADR}$
   $0 \leq 0 + 133 - 123 - 10 = 0$ (OK)
3. $t_{AW} \leq t_{PW} + t_{WE} + t_{WED} - t_{AD} - t_{PL} - t_{PADR}$
   $85 \leq 0 + 389 + 133 - 123 - 10 - 0 = 389$ (OK)
4. $t_{WDS} \leq t_{PW} + t_{WE} + t_{WED} - t_{WDD}$
   $50 \leq 0 + 389 + 133 - 375 = 147$ (OK)
5. $t_{WDHE} \leq t_{WDD} + t_{WDV} - t_{WED} - t_{WE} - t_{PW}$

   $0 \leq 375 + 147 - 133 - 389 - 0 = 0$ (OK)

We conclude that this memory will be satisfactory.

- ROM can be only read from, once it has been programmed.

- ROM programmed in the manufacturing process is called mask programmed ROM.

- Field programmable ROMs include EPROMs and bipolar fusible link PROMS.

- EPROMs without the quartz window for erasing are called one time programmable ROMS.

- Dynamic RAM (DRAM) requires refreshing. Static RAM (SRAM) does not.

- DRAM generally contains more bits/chip than SRAM.

- SRAM is easier to design into a system.

- There are a number of decisions to be made when designing memory systems including the following:

  Choosing the amount of RAM and ROM to be used.

  Choosing the addresses in the memory map for each type.

  Choosing the memory chips with timing requirements which match the CPU's timing.

  Matching the timing requirements for memory/CPU involves a detailed analysis of the hardware to be used in the memory interface. Close study of manufacturer's data sheets is required.

9.8 Further Reading

Byrd, J.S., and Pettus, R. O., *Microcomputer Systems, Architecture and Programming*, Prentice Hall, Englewood Cliffs, NJ, 1993.

Lawrence, P.D., and K. Mauch, *Real-Time Microcomputer System Design: An Introduction*, McGraw-Hill, New York, NY, 1987.

Peatman, J. B., *Design with Microcontrollers*, McGraw Hill, New York, NY, 1988.

Slater, M., *Microprocessor-Based Design: A Comprehensive Guide to Hardware Design*, Prentice Hall, Englewood Cliffs, NJ, 1989.

Most manufacturers offer applications notes and data sheets for their memory products. These are invaluable references when starting to do a memory design for any system.

9.9 Problems

9.1   Briefly explain the following terms: chip select; Memory map.

9.2   A microcomputer is to be used in a dedicated controller application. Its memory map is

0000H	ROM
1FFFH	
2000H	None
7FFFH	
8000H	RAM
0FFFFH	

Where must the code and constant data be located? Where must the variable data buffers be located?

9.3   Design an 8K × 8-bit memory block using the 8K × 1-bit memory chip

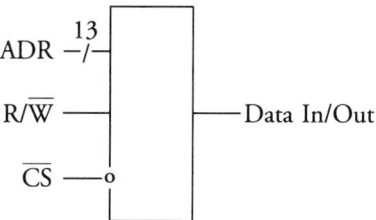

where ADR are the 13 address bits, $R/\overline{W}$ is 1 for reading, 0 for writing, and $\overline{CS}$ is 0 to select the chip when reading or writing and to enable the Data Out when reading. Assume the CPU generates a 16-bit address and the $R/\overline{W}$ control signal. Design the address decoding so that the memory responds to the 8K address block $E000 to $FFFF.

9.4   When comparing dynamic and static memory, which has the largest cell size?

9.5   Which memory type, dynamic or static, requires refreshing?

9.6   A CPU reads from the data bus 150 ns after supplying the address to the address bus. Which memory access time specification would be best to use for RAM memory in this system? (a) 10 ns; (b) 110 ns; (c) 150 ns; (d) 200 ns.

9.7   A 16-megabyte memory is to be designed using 1Meg x 1-bit chips. How many RAM chips will be required? How many address lines will be used on each chip? How many address line are required for the entire memory?

9.8   Memory is to be interfaced to a CPU as shown in Figure 9–18. Assume that the memory $\overline{OE}$ is the $\overline{READ}$ signal delayed by one t_{PR}. The following times are known for the memory read cycle (all times are in nanoseconds):

CPU times	Memory times	Propagation times
t_{CYC} = 500	t_{RC} = 100	t_{PADR} = 10
t_{AD} = 100	t_{AA} = 100	t_{PDEC} = 10
t_{AV} = 400	t_{ACS} = 50	t_{PR} = 10
t_{RED} = 250	t_{OE} = 10	
t_{RE} = 200	t_{RDHA} = 10	
t_{RDD} = 375	t_{RDHC} = 10	
t_{RDS} = 50	t_{OHZ} = 10	
t_{RDH} = 50		

(a) Using graph paper with 10 ns/div resolution, draw the complete read cycle similar to that shown in Figure 9–19 showing the actual times for all signal transitions. Show when the CPU reads the data and show the actual data setup and hold times. (b) Using the seven equations for read cycle timing, evaluate whether or not this memory will respond with the data fast enough for the CPU. (c) Your boss says that there are some memory chips that are cheaper to buy but with $t_{RC}=t_{AA}=200$ ns. All other memory times are the same. Will these work in the system? Justify your answer. Would memory with read cycle time of 250 ns work?

9.9   Repeat Problem 9.8 except do the write timing analysis. In addition to the times given in Problem 9.8, the following times are known:

CPU times	Memory times	Propagation times
$t_{WDD} = 250$	$t_{WC} = 100$	$t_{PW} = 10$
$t_{WDV} = 200$	$t_{AW} = 70$	
$t_{WED} = 300$	$t_{WDS} = 50$	
$t_{WE} = 100$	$t_{WDHE} = 5$	
$t_{WDH} = 50$	$t_{AS} = 10$	

Chapter 10

Serial Input/Output

OBJECTIVES

In this chapter we dispel the mysteries and myths of the serial interface. Nearly everybody who has connected a serial device to a computer has had trouble of some kind. We will see that interfacing serial devices is not difficult when we understand the basics of serial data transmission and how to use the handshaking signals defined for the RS-232-C interface.

10.1 Introduction

Chapter 7 discussed parallel I/O interfaces to input and output data. A disadvantage of parallel I/O is that a wire for each bit is needed, and when the source and destination are more than a few feet apart a parallel cable can be bulky and expensive. In addition, long runs of parallel wires can act as a transmission line that is susceptible to reflections and induced noise. Serial I/O techniques can offer a solution to these problems. Data to be transferred are sent one bit at a time, using fewer wires. By defining appropriate standards for the logic levels, we can reduce the effects of long transmission lines and combat noise problems.

10.2 The Components of an Asynchronous Serial Communication System

Figure 10–1 shows a serial communication system. There is a parallel I/O interface that transfers data from the source to the *transmit data buffer* and from the *received data buffer* to the destination. When the transmitter is to send data, data are written, in parallel, into the transmit data buffer. These data are transferred to the *parallel in/serial out shift register* and T_{clock} shifts the data out to the receiver. At the receiver, R_{clock} shifts it into the *serial in/parallel out shift register*. After all data bits have been shifted, they are transferred to a *received data buffer,* where they can be read by an input operation at the destination. Figure 10–2 shows a transmitter and receiver packaged together in a single integrated circuit. This device is called a *uni-*

> A *UART* is a parallel-serial and serial-parallel data converter.

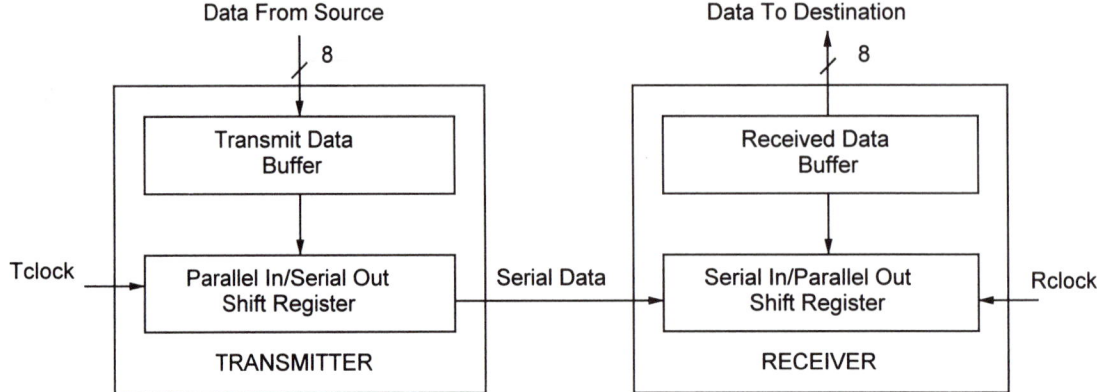

Figure 10-1 Serial communication system.

versal asynchronous receiver/transmitter, or *UART,* and is the basis for most serial communication hardware. Besides the data bus and clock signals shown in Figure 10–2, there are other signals for handshaking and control. We discuss the need for these in the next sections and give a complete description of a programmable UART in Section 10.6.

The design of the serial communication interface using a UART must consider the following questions:

- How are the data to be coded?

- If the data are sent in serial, which bit is sent first?

- How is the receiver synchronized with the transmitter?

- What is the data rate?

- How are the electrical signals for logic values defined?

- How does the system provide for handshaking?

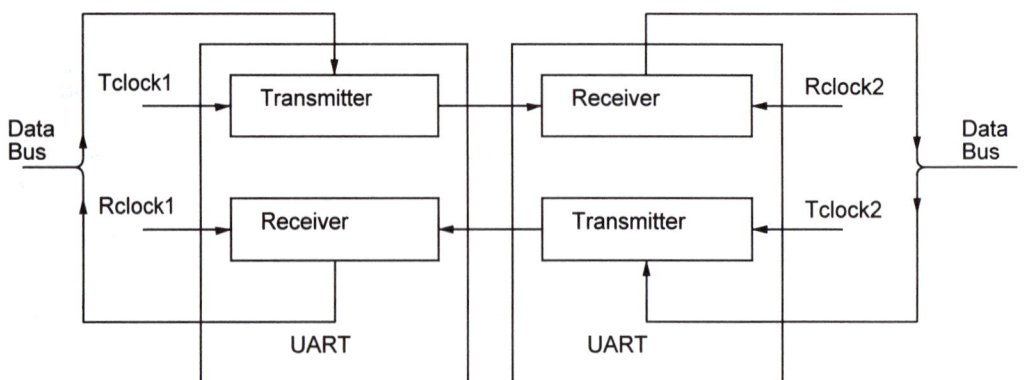

Figure 10-2 Universal asynchronous receiver/transmitter.

Data Coding and Transmission

Any binary code that both ends agree upon can be used. Serial data transfer is frequently used to send data between a terminal and a computer. Here, the information is the key pressed on the keyboard or the character displayed on the screen. There are several codes used for alphanumeric information, but the most common in microcomputer work is the *American Standard Code for Information Interchange*, or *ASCII*. The ASCII code, shown in Section 10.7, uses seven bits to encode 96 printable characters and 32 control characters.

> Any data code can be used for serial data transfer.

We have two choices for the order of data transmission. The designers of the UARTs have chosen to send the least significant bit first. Sending characters in this way is called *asynchronous* serial communication because the characters can be sent at any time and not synchronized with any process in either the sending or receiving unit. For example, characters typed on a keyboard are sent when you type them. The designers of UARTs provided a way to synchronize the receiver shift register with the transmitter shift register to cope with the asynchronous transmissions. The data bits are encapsulated between two other bits known as the *start bit* and *stop bit*. Figure 10–3 shows the format of the data and shows several terms used in serial data communications.

> Serial data bits are synchronized at the receiver by first sending a *start bit*, then the data, and then a *stop bit*.

Mark and space: The logic one and zero levels are called *mark* and *space*. When the transmitter is not sending anything, it holds the line at the mark level, i.e., logic one. This is also called the *idle* level.

Start bit: When the transmitter has data to send, it first changes the line from the mark to the space level for one bit time. This synchronizes the receiver with the transmitter. When the receiver detects the start bit, it knows to start clocking in the serial data bits.

Data bits: Almost any number of data bits can be sent between the start and stop bits, depending on the length of the transmit and receive shift registers. Typically, between five and eight are used.

Parity bit: When ASCII data are being sent, only seven bits are needed to encode the character. Most UARTs allow up to eight (and sometimes nine) bits to be sent between the start and stop bits, and so a parity bit may be included. The parity bit is added to the data to make the total number of ones odd (odd parity) or even (even parity). The parity bit may be used to detect errors in the data.

Stop bit: The stop bit is added at the end of the data bits. This gives at least one-bit time between successive characters. Some systems require more than one stop bit.

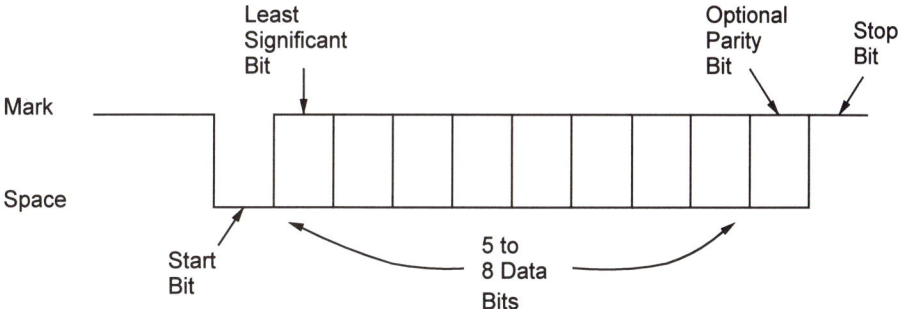

Figure 10–3 Serial character transmission.

TABLE 10–1 Data rates used in serial communication
Standard Data Rates - Baud
110, 150, 300, 600, 900, 1200, 2400, 4800, 9600, 14,400, 19,200, 38,400, 57,800

Data Transmission Rate

The rate at which bits are sent is often called the *baud rate*. This is a misused term because a *baud* is a unit of signaling speed and signifies the number of times a second the state of the line is changed. It is the reciprocal of the length of the shortest element in the code and is given in bits per second. Baud is a contraction of the surname of an early pioneer in serial data communications, J. M. E. Baudot.[1] The data rate can be any value and standard data rates are shown in Table 10–1.

> The *baud rate* is the number of bits per second.

10.3 Standards for the Serial I/O Interface

Several standards have been developed to define the interface between two UARTs in a serial communication system. Interface standards are necessary to allow different manufacturers' equipment to be interconnected and must define the following elements:

- Handshaking signals.

- Direction of signal flow.

- Types of communication devices.

- Connectors and interface mechanical considerations.

- Electrical signal levels.

The EIA[2] RS-232-C standard is used in most serial interfaces. However, where the signals must be transmitted farther than 50 feet or at greater than 20 Kbits/second, another electrical interface standard such as RS-422, RS-423, or RS-485 should be chosen. For each of these, handshaking, direction of signal flow, and the types of communications devices are based on the RS-232-C standard.

---

[1] J. M. E. Baudot (1845–1903) invented a five-bit code for sending data in a telegraph system. It was adopted by the French telegraph system in 1877 and became one of the standards used for international telegraph communication.

[2] The Electronic Industries Association is an organization that publishes engineering standards to serve the public interest by eliminating misunderstandings between manufacturers and purchasers. EIA standards can be purchased from:

EIA Engineering Department
Standards Sales
2001 I Street, N.W.
Washington, DC 20006
(200) 457-4966

Handshaking Signals

Serial data transfer requires handshaking signals for synchronization and control of the transmitter and receiver. All signals in the RS-232-C interface other than the transmitted and received data are for handshaking. To understand these, we must first look at types of communication systems and at modems.

Communication System Types

There are three ways that data can be sent in serial communication systems, as shown in Figure 10–4.

Simplex system: A *simplex* system, Figure 10–4(a), is one in which data are sent in one direction only, say, to a serial printer. If the computer doesn't send data faster than the printer can accept it, no handshaking signals are required. Two signal wires are needed for this system.

A full-duplex system: A *full-duplex* (*FDX*) system is shown in Figure 10–4(b). Here data are to flow in both directions, say, between a terminal and a computer. This is called a four-wire system, although two signal wires and a common ground are sufficient.

A half-duplex system: A *half-duplex* (*HDX*) system, Figure 10–4(c), is one in which data are transferred in two directions with only one pair of signal wires. Additional hardware and handshaking signals must be added to an HDX system.

Most serial I/O is *full duplex.*

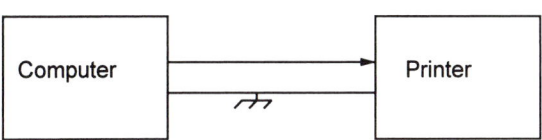

(a) Simplex communications.

Figure 10–4 Simplex, half-duplex, and duplex communication systems.

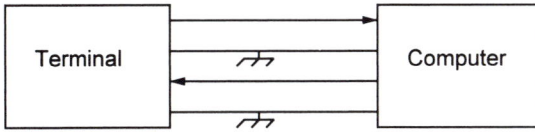

(b) Full-duplex communications (FDX)

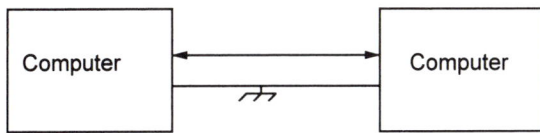

(c) Half-duplex communications (HDX)

Half-Duplex Handshaking Signals

Figure 10–5 shows a half-duplex system with additional interface circuitry and the handshaking signals defined for the RS-232-C interface standard. The interface blocks have a three-fold responsibility. First, they give a full-duplex channel between themselves and the terminal or computer. Second, they decide whether they or their opposite interface is sending or receiving data. Third, they use and control the *request to send* (*RTS*) and *clear to send* (*CTS*) handshaking signals. The RTS signal is asserted by the terminal or computer when data are to be sent. When the interface finds that the other system is not sending data, it asserts the CTS signal. The sending station must wait until it is clear to send before transmitting.

> A *half-duplex* system needs handshaking signals.

Half-duplex systems are not often used these days, although the RTS/CTS handshaking signals have been retained to control the flow of data. For example, in the simplex channel shown in Figure 10–4, the printer could control a CTS signal to signify when it was ready to accept new data. Data *flow control* is discussed more fully in Section 10.8.

Data Terminal Equipment and Data Communication Equipment

The blocks labeled "Interface" in Figure 10–5 are, in practice, modems, and the two-wire half-duplex line is a telephone line. Modems are called *data communications equipment* (*DCE*), and the terminals or computers to which they are attached are called *data terminal equipment* (*DTE*). The direction of signal flow for data and handshaking signals is defined for each in Section 10.4. First, let us discuss how the handshaking signals are used.

Modems

To understand the rest of the signals in the RS-232-C interface, we must see how modems work. Figure 10–5 shows a terminal connected to a computer through two interfaces that we will now call *modems*.

> A *modem* modulates and demodulates tones for telephone line transmission.

A modem is a *modulator/demodulator*. It converts logic levels into tones to be sent over a telephone line. This is the modulation process. At the other end of the line a demodulator converts the tones back to logic levels. In a half-duplex system, as shown in Figure 10–5, a single set of tones is defined, one tone for mark and one for space.

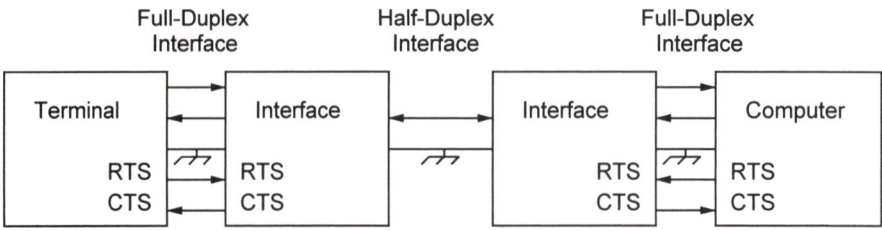

Figure 10–5   Half-duplex system with handshaking.

TABLE 10–2 Originate and answer modem tone definitions for Bell 212A

Originate modem	Direction	Answer modem
Modulator tones		Demodulator
1070 Hz—Space	→	
1270 Hz—Mark		
Demodulator		Modulator tones
	←	2025 Hz—Space
		2225 Hz—Mark

Half-duplex modems are no longer used because modems have been developed to allow full-duplex data transmission over a telephone line. A full- duplex system has two kinds of modems, called *originate* and *answer* modems, and two sets of tones. The tones defined for a Bell 212A™ 1200 baud modem are shown in Table 10–2.

Modem Handshaking Signals

The rest of the handshaking signals in the RS-232-C standard are for modem control and hand-shaking. See Figure 10–6.

> Modem handshaking signals are defined in the RS-232-C standard.

Ring indicator (RI): The telephone company transmits a special tone that rings the phone. The modem can detect this and assert the *RI* signal. The terminal or computer can use RI to start some special process such as notifying the user that the other end is calling or to answer the telephone in an answer modem.

Data set ready (DSR): This signal tells the DTE that the modem (also called a *data set*) has established a connection over the telephone line to the far end.

Data terminal ready (DTR): This signal comes from the DTE and informs the modem that it is ready to operate. This is usually just an indication that the power is turned on in the terminal but could be controlled by a computer. An intelligent answer modem can use it to answer a call automatically only when the computer or terminal is ready.

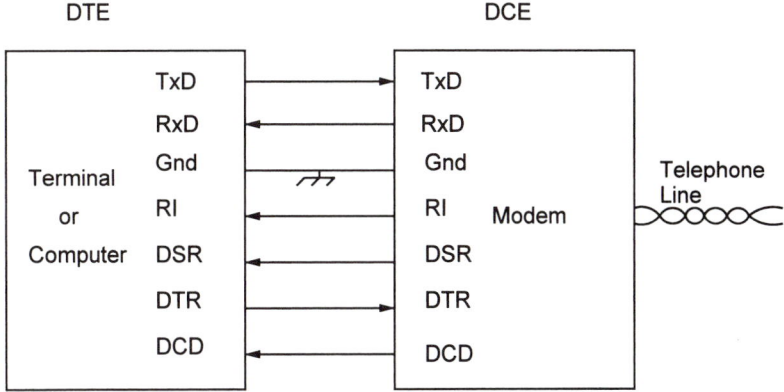

Figure 10–6 Modem handshaking signals.

TABLE 10-3 RS-232-C signal definitions

DE9	DB25	Signal	Purpose
	1	PG	*Protective ground:* This is usually the shield in a shielded cable. It is designed to be connected to the equipment frame and may be connected to external grounds.
3	2	TxD	*Transmitted data:* Sourced by DTE and received by DCE. Data terminal equipment cannot send unless RTS, CTS, DSR, and DTR are asserted.
2	3	RxD	*Received data:* Received by the DTE, sourced by DCE.
7	4	RTS	*Request to send:* Sourced by DTE, received by DCE. RTS is asserted by the DTE when it wants to send data. The DCE responds by asserting CTS.
8	5	CTS	*Clear to send:* Sourced by DCE, received by DTE. CTS must be asserted before the DTE can transmit data.
6	6	DSR	*Data set ready:* Sourced by DCE, received by DTE. Indicates that the DCE has made a connection on the telephone line and is ready to receive data from the terminal. The DTE must see this asserted before it can transmit data.
5	7	SG	*Signal ground:* Ground reference for the signal is separate from pin 1, protective ground.
1	8	DCD	*Data carrier detect:* Sourced by DCE, received by DTE. Indicates that a DCE has detected the carrier on the telephone line. Originally it was used in half-duplex systems but can be used in full-duplex systems, too.
4	20	DTR	*Data terminal ready:* Sourced by DTE, received by DCE. Indicates the DTE is ready for sending or receiving.
9	22	RI	*Ring indicator:* Sourced by DCE, received by DTE. Indicates that a ringing signal is detected.

Data carrier detect (DCD): The DCD signal is asserted when the carrier, or tone defined for a mark, is being generated by the modem on the other end. DCD was used originally in half-duplex systems such as that shown in Figure 10–5. When one end wanted to transmit, it first asserted the RTS line. The modem then checked the DCD bit. If it found it asserted, it knew the other end was sending. When DCD was deasserted, CTS was asserted, allowing transmission from the requesting terminal.

The complete RS-232-C standard defines all signals and signal directions for DTE and DCE devices. There are three schemes for labeling the signals including mnemonic acronyms, alphabetic circuit codes, and CCITT (International Telegraph and Telephone Consultative Committee) numeric codes. The most descriptive and most frequently used are the signal acronyms shown in Table 10–3. Also shown are the RS-232-C standard pin numbers for the DB25 connector and the pins that have been defined for the DE9 connector used on IBM personal computers and compatibles. The signals shown are the main ones used in serial interfaces. The RS-232-C standard also defines another set of signals that are used for secondary data transmission. These are very rarely used.

10.4 RS-232-C Interconnections

A null modem cable is used to connect two DTE computers together.

When two serial ports are connected, the data rate, the number of data bits, whether parity is used, the type of parity, and the number of stop bits must be set properly and identically on each UART. You must also have the proper cables. There are three kinds of cables from which to choose, depending on the type of devices to be interconnected. These are the full DTE–DCE cable shown in Figure 10–7, a DTE–DTE *null modem* cable shown in Figure 10–8, and a minimal DTE–DCE cable that works in many applications shown in Figure 10–9. A minimal null modem cable for DTE–DTE connections may be constructed as shown in Figure 10–10.

A problem that many users have when first encountering the RS- 232-C interface is in reconciling the *direction* of data flow with the *signal name*. Look at the directions shown for the signals on the DTE device in Figure 10–7. Notice that pin 2, transmit data (TxD), is a data output. On the other side, TxD for a DCE device is an input! Unfortunately, many manufacturers do not provide enough details in their documentation for us to know if a signal is an input or output. You cannot tell by the name alone. You must also know if it is a DTE or DCE device. To provide the proper cable you may have to resort to inspecting the schematic diagram or measuring voltages to find out which pin is an output.

10.5 Standard Electrical Signal Levels

Figure 10–3 shows two logic levels, mark and space, and various standards have been used to define these.

20-milliamp current loop: An older standard used in the days of mechanical teleprinters and teletypes is the 20-milliamp current loop. Here, 20 mA of current signifies a mark and zero current a space.

TTL logic levels: A system may define mark and space with standard TTL voltages and currents. Normally this is not done where the data must be transmitted over any significant distance because TTL gates do not have enough noise margin for noisy environments.

RS-232-C Standard

The signal levels for RS-232-C mark and space are shown in Table 10–4. Notice that the signal level for a mark is low.

RS-232-C signal levels have been defined to give a large noise margin.

The RS-232-C interface driver and receiver pair is shown in Figure 10–11. The driver and receiver are *single-ended* because the signal line is referenced to the ground. The driver and receiver convert TTL logic levels to the RS-232-C levels that provide much greater noise margin. RS-232-C drivers can be used effectively if the distance doesn't exceed 50 feet and the data rate is not higher than 20 Kbits/second. As the line distances get longer or the data rate higher, another signaling standard should be chosen.

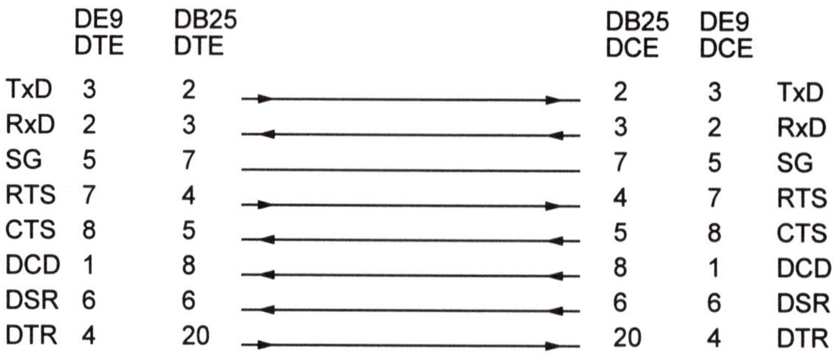

	DE9 DTE	DB25 DTE		DB25 DCE	DE9 DCE	
TxD	3	2	→	2	3	TxD
RxD	2	3	←	3	2	RxD
SG	5	7	—	7	5	SG
RTS	7	4	→	4	7	RTS
CTS	8	5	←	5	8	CTS
DCD	1	8	←	8	1	DCD
DSR	6	6	←	6	6	DSR
DTR	4	20	→	20	4	DTR

Figure 10-7   Full DTE–DCE cable.

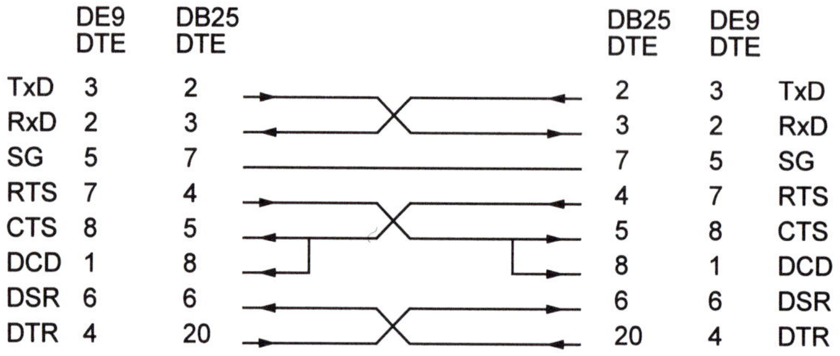

	DE9 DTE	DB25 DTE		DB25 DTE	DE9 DTE	
TxD	3	2	✕	2	3	TxD
RxD	2	3		3	2	RxD
SG	5	7	—	7	5	SG
RTS	7	4	✕	4	7	RTS
CTS	8	5		5	8	CTS
DCD	1	8		8	1	DCD
DSR	6	6		6	6	DSR
DTR	4	20	✕	20	4	DTR

Figure 10-8   DTE–DTE null modem cable.

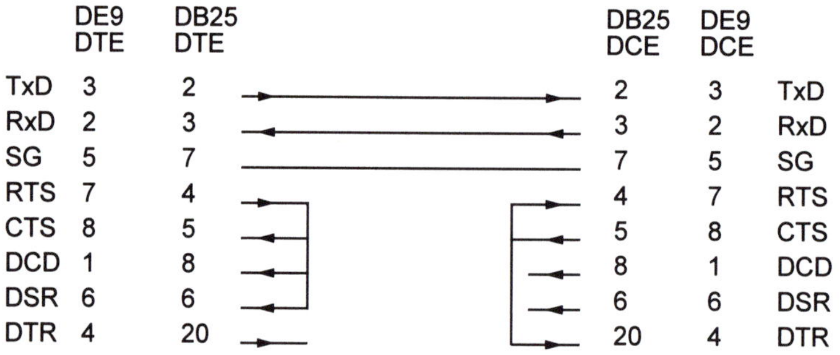

	DE9 DTE	DB25 DTE		DB25 DCE	DE9 DCE	
TxD	3	2	→	2	3	TxD
RxD	2	3	←	3	2	RxD
SG	5	7	—	7	5	SG
RTS	7	4		4	7	RTS
CTS	8	5		5	8	CTS
DCD	1	8		8	1	DCD
DSR	6	6		6	6	DSR
DTR	4	20		20	4	DTR

Figure 10-9   Minimal three-wire cable.

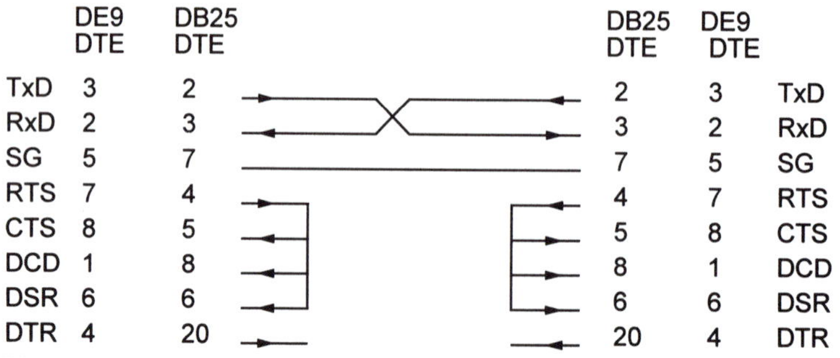

	DE9 DTE	DB25 DTE		DB25 DTE	DE9 DTE	
TxD	3	2	✕	2	3	TxD
RxD	2	3		3	2	RxD
SG	5	7	—	7	5	SG
RTS	7	4		4	7	RTS
CTS	8	5		5	8	CTS
DCD	1	8		8	1	DCD
DSR	6	6		6	6	DSR
DTR	4	20		20	4	DTR

Figure 10-10   Minimal null modem cable.

TABLE 10-4 RS-232-C logic levels	
Mark	−25 to −3 volts
Space	+25 to +3 volts

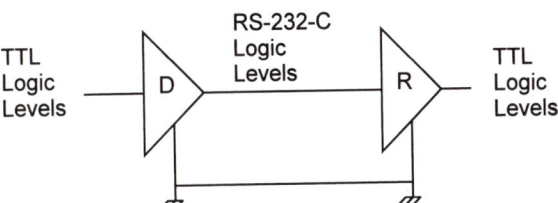

Figure 10-11   RS-232-C interface.

RS-423 Standard

The RS-423 interface can transmit at higher data rates and over longer distances than RS-232-C.

The RS-423 interface is shown in Figure 10–12. It, too, is a single-ended system, but the drivers are especially matched and tuned to one another to allow the longer distances and higher data rates shown in Table 10–5. RS-423 also allows a driver to broadcast data to 10 receivers. The electrical specifications for RS-423 signaling are given in Table 10–8.

RS-422 Standard

The RS-422 standard uses matched differential line drivers and receivers for higher performance.

A problem experienced with the single-ended drivers and receivers of RS- 232-C and RS-423 is that for long line lengths, noise and ground shifts can cause errors in the received data. Noise and ground shifts appear as common-mode signals; that is, they affect each line equally. The RS-422 line drivers and receivers operate with differential

Figure 10-12   RS-423 interface.

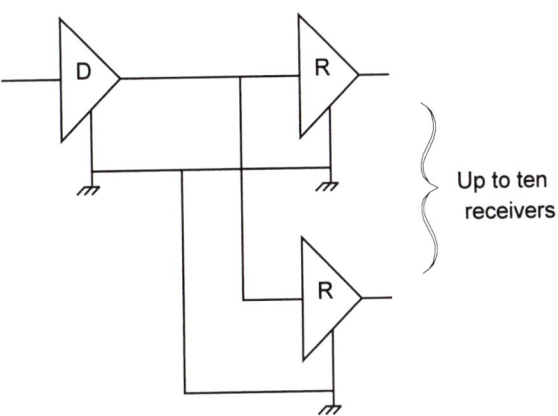

TABLE 10–5 RS-423 line length and data rate

Line length (ft)	Data rate
30	100 Kbits/s
300	10 Kbits/s
4000	1 Kbits/s

amplifiers, as shown in Figure 10–13. These drivers eliminate much of the common-mode noise experienced with long transmission lines. Their source and load impedances match twisted-pair transmission lines,[3] and the line lengths and data rates that can be achieved are shown in Table 10–6. The electrical specifications are given in Table 10–8.

RS-485 Standard

The RS-485 standard allows a bus architecture with multiple sources and receivers.

The RS-485 standard is similar to RS-422 in that it uses differential line drivers and receivers. However, as shown in Figure 10–14, the standard provides for multiple drivers and receivers in a bussed environment. Up to 32 driver/receiver pairs can be used together. Tables 10–7 and 10–8 give the RS- 485 specifications.

Serial Interface Electrical Specifications

Table 10–8 provides a summary of the electrical specifications for these four interface standards. RS-232-C is the most commonly used standard for connecting computers to serial devices such as printers and modems. Most computers are equipped with an RS-232-C "COM" port. Choose one of the other three standards when the data rate is higher than 20 Kbits/s or the distance is greater than 50 feet.

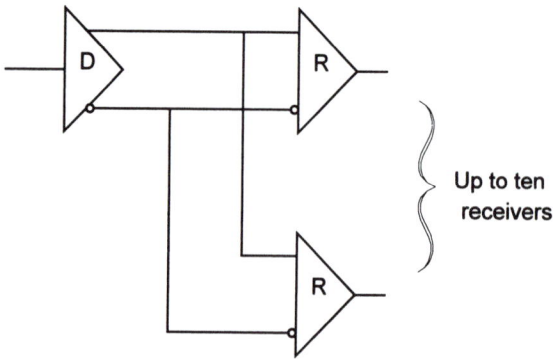

Figure 10–13   RS-422 interface.

Up to ten receivers

---

[3] Approximately 100 Ω.

TABLE 10-6 RS-422 line length and data rate

Line Length (ft)	Data rate
40	10 Mbits/s
400	1 Mbits/s
4000	100 Kbits/s

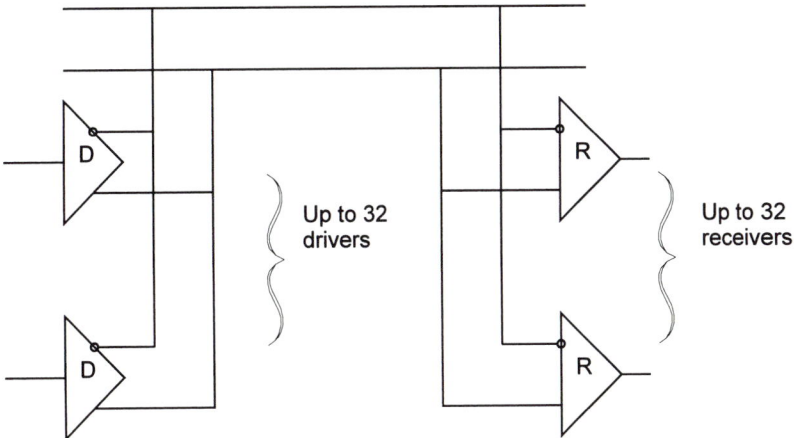

Figure 10-14 RS-485 interface.

TABLE 10-7 RS-485 line length and data rate

Line length (ft)	Data rate
40	10 Mbits/s
400	1 Mbits/s
4000	100 Kbits/s

TABLE 10-8 Summary of RS-232-C, RS-423, RS-422, and RS-485 standards

Specification	RS-232-C	RS-423	RS-422	RS-485
Receiver input voltage	±3 to ±15	±200 mV to ±12 V	±200 mV to ±7 V	±200 mV to −7 to +12 V
Driver output signal	±5 to ±15 V	±3.6 to ±6 V	±2 to ±5 V	±1.5 to ±5 V
Maximum data rate	20 Kb/s	100 Kb/s	10 Mb/s	10 Mb/s
Maximum cable length	50 feet	4000 feet	4000 feet	4000 feet
Driver source impedance	3–7 KΩ	450 Ω min	100 Ω	54 Ω
Receiver input resistance	3 KΩ	4 KΩ minimum	4 KΩ minimum	12 KΩ minimum
Mode	Single-ended	Single-ended	Differential	Differential
Number of drivers and receivers allowed on one line	1 Driver / 1 Receiver	1 Driver / 10 Receivers	1 Driver / 10 Receivers	32 Drivers / 32 Receivers

10.6 The UART

The key building block of a serial communication system is the universal asynchronous receiver/transmitter, or UART. The function of the UART is to change serial data to parallel on input and parallel data to serial for output, as shown in Figure 10–1. UARTs also provide other functions such as the handshaking signals needed for the RS-232-C interface. A typical programmable UART is the Motorola MC6850 Asynchronous Communications Interface Adapter, *ACIA*, whose block diagram is shown in Figure 10–15. Let's inspect the signals on the chip and see how to interface it to a system. Then we will look at control and status bits in the internal registers.

> Programmable UARTs are used in microcomputer systems for serial I/O.

The *transmit* and *receive clocks* shift the data in and out. These clock frequencies are usually 16 or 64 times the data rate to allow the UART to test for the data in the middle of the bit time. For example, if a 16X clock is chosen, the UART waits for eight clock periods after detecting the high-to-low transition at the beginning of the start bit and then 16 periods after that to test for each data bit.

A parallel I/O interface connects the UART to the CPU. The rest of the control signals on the *chip select and read/write control* block are used for this interface. The *enable* signal in Motorola systems is connected to the CPU's *E-clock* and *read/write* to the **R/W̄** CPU control signal. Three chip

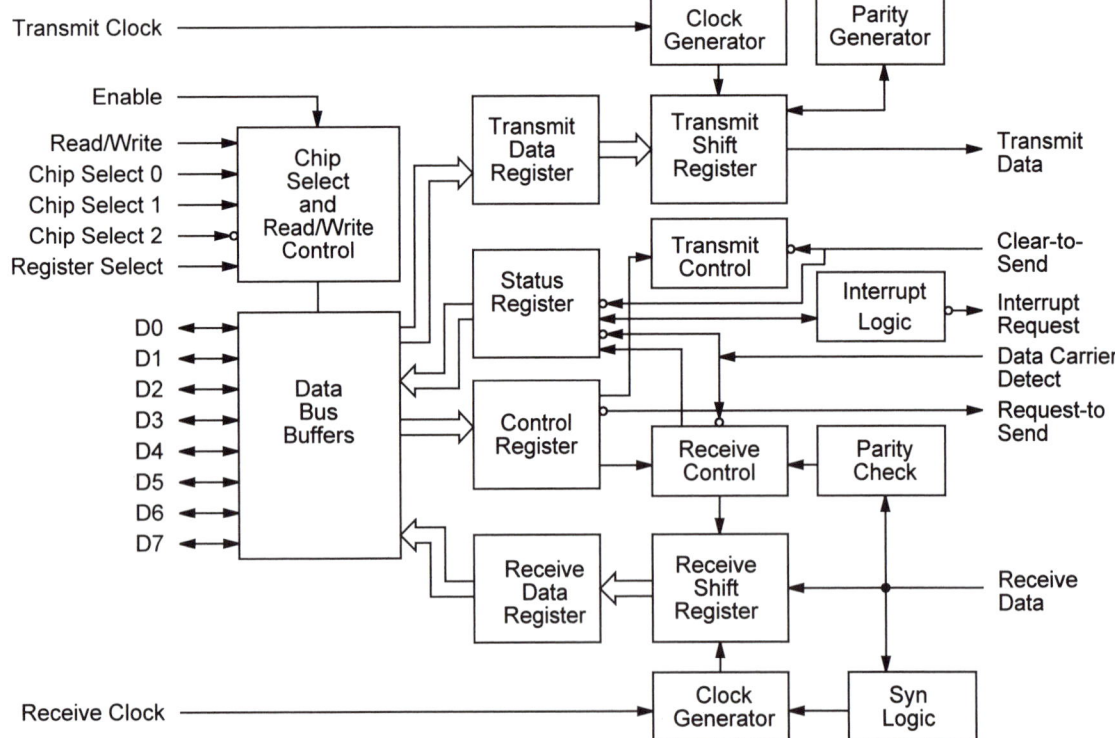

Figure 10–15   Motorola MC6850 asynchronous communications interface adapter (reprinted with permission of Motorola Corp.).

TABLE 10-9 ACIA registers

R/W	Register select	Register selected
0	0	Control register
0	1	Transmit data register
1	0	Status register
1	1	Receive data register

selects, *Chip Select 0*, *Chip Select 1*, and *Chip Select 2* help decode the UART's I/O address. The ACIA contains four registers, including *received* and *transmitted data* registers, a *control* register, and a *status* register. These registers are selected by *register select* and **R/W̄**, as shown in Table 10–9. An *interrupt request* signal may interrupt the CPU under conditions enabled by setting bits in the control register. An eight-bit data bus completes the parallel I/O interface to the CPU.

The serial interface is on the right of the block diagram in Figure 10–15. All signals are the same as those defined for a DTE RS-232-C interface except that the handshaking signals are active low.

The UART's four internal registers are for data, control, and status information. The UART must be initialized by the software writing bits into the control register. A status register is used by the software to check on the status of the port.

UART Control Register

The control register must be initialized by the program.

Figure 10–16 shows the control and status register bits in the ACIA. *CR1* and *CR0* are *counter divider select* bits. They divide the transmit and receive clocks by a factor of 1, 16, or 64. *CR4*, *CR3*, and *CR2* are *word select* bits that select the number of data bits, the type of parity, and the number of stop bits. *CR7*, *CR6*, and *CR5* control the receiver and transmitter interrupting capabilities and allow the software to control the request to send signal.

UART Status Register

The status register shows the status of the data transfer and error conditions.

The status register contains error bits and status bits. These may either generate interrupts or be polled by the software. *Received data register full* is set when data are transferred from the serial input register to the received data register and is reset when the CPU reads the data. This bit can be polled to see if new data have arrived since the last data were read. *Transmit data register empty* is set when data are transferred from the transmit data register to the serial output register. RS-232-C modem handshaking bits *data carrier detect* and *clear to send* can be found in the bit-2 and bit-3. Bit-7 is the *interrupt request* bit and simply shows the state of the hardware interrupt request. The rest of the bits in the status register indicate that various errors may have occurred.

UART Error Conditions

A *framing error* occurs when the UART detects an invalid stop bit. This usually means that the data rates on both ends are different. A *receiver overrun* occurs when data are transferred from the

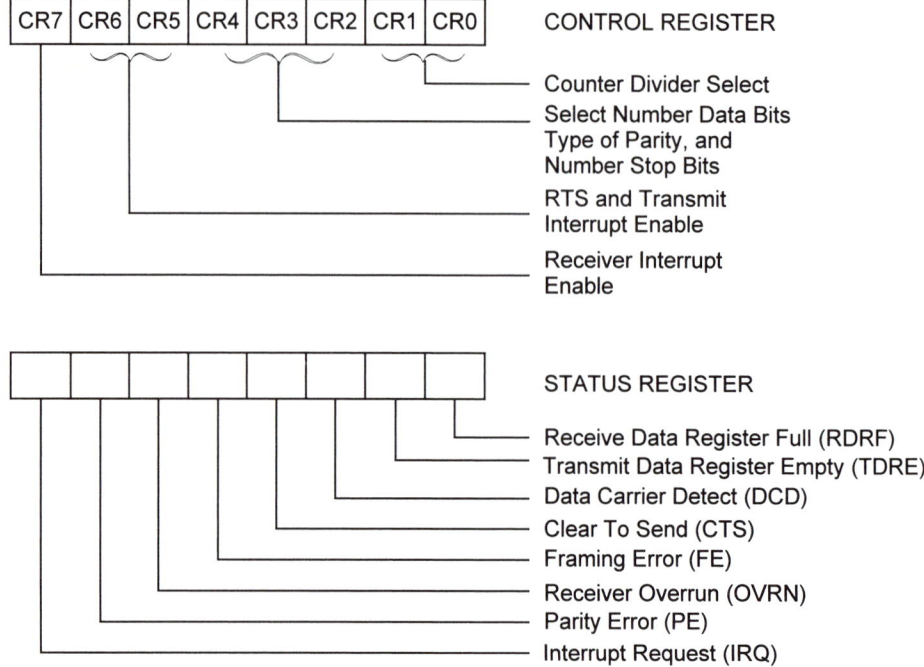

Figure 10-16 ACIA control and status registers.

serial input register to the received data register before the CPU has read the last data. When this bit is set, the software is not reading the incoming data fast enough, and data have been lost. The *parity error* bit is set when parity is enabled and a character is received with incorrect parity.

10.7 ASCII Data and Control Codes

When data are being sent between a terminal device (a keyboard and a display) and a computer, the *American Standard Code for Information Interchange, ASCII,* is the most commonly used code. The ASCII code uses seven bits to encode 96 printable and 32 *control* characters, as shown in Table 10–10. The printable characters are shown in the rightmost six columns in Table 10–10 with the codes $20–$7E. The control codes, columns 0 and 1, are used by serial devices to provide some control of what is being transferred. For example, the CR code ($0D) is sent to cause the printing terminal or display to perform a carriage return. The definitions for the other control codes are given in detail in Appendix A.

Control codes are often used by software to provide special functions. For example, in some systems you can stop and start the output to a terminal by typing the DC3 ($13) and DC1 ($11), respectively. The control key on the keyboard of your terminal or PC allows you to send control codes. When the control key is pressed and held while another, printable character is typed, the effect is to map columns 4 and 5 (and 6 and 7) into columns 0 and 1. For example, to send the DC3 character, one would press and

> A *control code* may be sent by holding down the terminal's control key while typing another printable key.

TABLE 10–10 ASCII codes for alphanumeric characters (7-bit code)

LS digit	MS digit							
	0	**1**	**2**	**3**	**4**	**5**	**6**	**7**
0	NUL	DLE	SP	0	@	P	`	p
1	SOH	DC1	!	1	A	Q	a	q
2	STX	DC2	"	2	B	R	b	r
3	ETX	DC3	#	3	C	S	c	s
4	EOT	DC4	$	4	D	T	d	t
5	ENQ	NAK	%	5	E	U	e	u
6	ACK	SYN	&	6	F	V	f	v
7	BEL	ETB	'	7	G	W	g	w
8	BS	CAN	(	8	H	X	h	x
9	HT	EM	)	9	I	Y	i	y
A	LF	SUB	*	:	J	Z	j	z
B	VT	ESC	+	;	K	[	k	{
C	FF	FS	,	<	L	\	l		
D	CR	GS	–	=	M	]	m	}
E	SO	RS	.	>	N	^	n	~
F	SI	US	/	?	O	_	o	DEL

hold the control key and type either S or s. This control-key/printable-key combination is known as control-S.

10.8 Flow Control

Flow control refers to a higher level of handshaking needed to control the software transferring data via serial ports. For example, when transferring data from one computer to another, the receiving computer may not be able to deal with the incoming data fast enough, and data may be lost. If this happens, it must send a message to the other computer to stop sending data until it is ready to receive some more. There are two ways to achieve flow control.

EXAMPLE 10–1   **Show what happens to the binary code words that are sent if the control key is held while the following printable keys are pressed. Give the defined control code for each.**

Q, q, G, J

Solution:

The control key maps characters in columns 4 and 6 to column 0 and 5 and 7 to 1. Therefore, the following binary codes result:

Character	Character code		Control code		Control code
Q	$51	01010001	$11	00010001	DC1
q	$71	01110001	$11	00010001	DC1
G	$47	01000111	$07	00000111	BEL
J	$4A	01001010	$0A	00001010	LF

Hardware flow control: The request to send (RTS) and clear to send (CTS) handshaking signals are used in hardware flow control. The sending and receiving computers must control and sense these bits in the communication software. Most programmable UARTs such as the MC6850 described above give the user this capability.

Software flow control: Software flow control is called the *XON/XOFF* protocol. The XOFF character (ASCII DC3, $14, Ctrl-S) is sent by the receiving station to turn the transmission off. The XON character (ASCII DC1, $11, Ctrl-Q) turns it on again. The communication software must detect these characters being sent.

10.9 Debugging and Trouble Shooting

The serial interface has caused problems for many computer users. The major problems stem from a lack of documentation about what hardware has been implemented and in not setting up the UART data transmission parameters correctly. The following procedure is suggested to help solve your serial interfacing problems.

Choose the Correct Cable

The cable to be used depends on the types of interfaces to be interconnected. You must find out if the devices are DTE or DCE. If the documentation does not show this, disconnect all cables and check for a negative voltage at pin DB25-2 or DE9-3. If a negative voltage exists when no characters are being sent, the interface is a DTE; otherwise, it is a DCE. When one device is a DTE and the other DCE, a DTE-DCE cable is required. If both are DTE or both DCE (unlikely), a null modem cable is required.

The number of wires in the cable depends on the handshaking and flow control used in the system. Hardware handshaking and flow control require a full DTE-DCE or null modem cable as shown in Figure 10–7 or Figure 10–8. If software flow control or no flow control is used, a minimal cable such as Figure 10–9 or Figure 10–10 can be used.

Choose the Correct Communication Parameters

After connecting the two interfaces with the correct cable, make sure that the software at each end is using the same parameters. The data rate (baud rate), number of data bits, type of parity, and the number of stop bits must be specified. In some communication systems, the type of flow control can be chosen.

10.10 Chapter Summary Points

- A UART is a universal asynchronous receiver/transmitter. It sends and receives serial data.

- The two logic states in serial communication are called mark and space.

- The data sent starts with a start bit and ends with a stop bit.

- The start bit synchronizes the receiver with the transmitted data.

- The ASCII code is most often used for serial I/O when the data are alphanumeric characters.

- Any data rate may be used, but there are standard ones used for character I/O.

- Handshaking signals are defined for the RS-232-C interface.

- A simplex communication system sends data in one direction.

- A half-duplex system can send data in two directions but only one way at a time.

- A full-duplex system can send data in two directions at once.

- Data terminal equipment (DTE) and data communication equipment (DCE) are defined in the RS-232-C standard.

- Modems modulate and demodulate tones for telephone line communication.

- A null modem cable can connect two DTE devices.

- Control codes may be sent from a terminal by holding down the control key while typing another printable key.

10.11 Problems

10.1   What are the parallel data buffers in a UART?

10.2   In Figure 10–2, what design limitations would you place on T_{clock1}, T_{clock2}, R_{clock1}, and R_{clock2}?

10.3   Why are the transmit and receive clocks usually a factor of 16 or 64 times the data rate?

10.4   Briefly explain the following terms: framing error; parity error; DCE; DTE; UART.

10.5   To initiate a serial data transfer a UART first: (a) sends the least significant bit; (b) sends the start bit; (c) sends the stop bit; (d) sends the parity bit (e) none of these.

10.6   Which data bit is sent first from a UART?

10.7   Draw the waveform seen on the serial data out line when a UART sends the ASCII character "L" using seven bits of data plus odd parity.

10.8   How does a UART initiate a serial data transfer?

10.9   How does the receiver in a UART maintain its synchronization with the transmitter in asynchronous operation?

10.10   How many bits/second (baud) is a serial port sending when the character rate is 120 characters/second? Assume ASCII characters with even parity.

10.11   If the data rate is 9600 baud, what is the rate ASCII characters can be sent assuming 7 data bits and 1 parity bit?

10.12   Draw a diagram of a UART including the receiver, transmitter, and other associated signals required to make it operate.

10.13   A UART sends the following data. What is the binary value of the data?

10.14   What parity is being used in the UART shown in Problem 10.13?

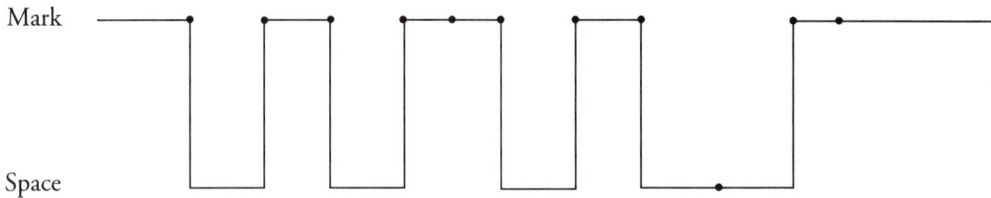

10.15   Assuming the ASCII code is being used for the data in Problem 10.13, what is the character being sent?

10.16   Why is the RS232 voltage specification for mark and space logic levels used for serial communications instead of TTL voltage levels?

10.17   What are the two types of communication devices defined by the RS-232- C interface standard?

10.18   Draw a cable used to connect DTE to DCE RS232 serial devices. Show pins 2, 3, 4, 5, 6, 7, 8, 20 with signal names and signal direction flows.

10.19   Draw a cable used to connect DTE to DTE RS232 serial devices. Show pins 2, 3, 4, 5, 6, 7, 8, 20 with signal names and signal direction flows.

10.20   What is the cable called that connects a DTE to DTE?

10.21   How does a modem signify that it has detected the opposing modem's tone for a mark?

10.22   How does a modem signify that it has detected an incoming call?

10.23   How does a modem signify that it has established a connection with the modem at the other end?

10.24   How does a modem know that the power on the computer or terminal has been turned on?

10.25   What electrical signalling standard should be chosen for the following serial data links?

Data rate	Distance
20 Kbit/s	<50'
20 Kbit/s	100'
100 Kbit/s	4000'

10.26   What electrical signalling standard should be used for a system of serial I/O devices on a bus?

Chapter 11

Analog Input and Output

OBJECTIVES

In this chapter we consider the world of analog signals. Computers must read analog information and act upon it in many applications. This requires an analog-to-digital converter. In other situations, an analog output signal may be required; this calls for a digital-to-analog converter. In this chapter we will discuss both devices and learn how to specify the correct one for the job to be done.

11.1 Introduction

Analog input and output converters allow us to process continuous signals as functions of time. There are many reasons to do this. One of the many advantages digital signal processing has over analog is that once the analog signal is converted to digital values, it is generally free from noise. Audiophiles recognize this feature when playing their CDs. The music is recorded digitally and is converted to an analog signal for playback. The digital signal is not corrupted by dust and dirt like LP records or audio tape. Another reason for converting to the digital domain is that once signals are digitized, they can be manipulated by the computer, often to produce effects that are unachievable using analog signal processing. In medical imaging, computer-aided tomography (CAT) scans are produced by manipulating digital images. Today, we are seeing a great migration away from analog delivery of information. Digital television and digital telephone services are now readily available. With the increased availability of broadband networks, such as optical fibers, even more digital data will be at our fingertips.

Digitizing signals does have drawbacks. The analog signal can never be exactly represented or reconstructed. There will always be some error, but good system design can minimize these errors. A digitized signal, when transmitted over a communication channel, requires a greater bandwidth than the original channel. For example, a normal analog voice telephone circuit channel requires about 4 kHz bandwidth. The equivalent digital channel is 64 Kb/s. The extra bandwidth is justified by being able to enhance the signal and to repeat it over long distances without degradation, and by opening the communication channel to other digital services such as data transfer between computers.

In this chapter we will learn about analog-to-digital (A/D) and digital-to-analog (D/A) conversion. We will learn how to specify a converter for a particular application and how a variety of A/Ds and D/As work.

11.2 Data Acquisition and Conversion

A *data acquisition system* to input analog data is shown in Figure 11–1. This receives analog information from physical processes and uses *transducers* to convert these processes to electrical signals, either voltages or currents. Following the transducer is a block labeled *signal conditioning* to provide the following functions:

Isolation and buffering: The input to the A/D may need to be protected from dangerous voltages such as static discharges or reversed polarity voltages.

Amplification: Rarely does the transducer produce the voltage or current needed by the A/D. The amplifier is designed so that the full-scale signal from the analog input results in a full-scale signal to the A/D.

Bandwidth limiting: The signal conditioning provides a low-pass filter to limit the range of frequencies that can be digitized. To understand why this is so, we will consider the sampling theorem and learn about aliasing in Section 11.3.

In applications where several analog inputs must be digitized, an *analog multiplexer* follows the signal conditioning. This computer-controlled switch, shown in Figure 11–2, allows multiple analog inputs, each with its own signal conditioning for different transducers. The multiplexer channel is selected by the CPU generating an address on the multiplexer select lines.

The *sample-and-hold* circuit is a critical element in the system. It is here because the analog-to-digital converter, next in the chain, requires a small, but significant, amount of time to convert the analog signal to its digital code. This is called the *conversion time*, and if the analog signal changes during this time, errors may be introduced. The sample-and-hold reduces these errors by quickly sampling the signal and holding it steady while the A/D converts it.

The A/D converts the sampled signal to digital values. We discuss the *A/D converter*, its speci-

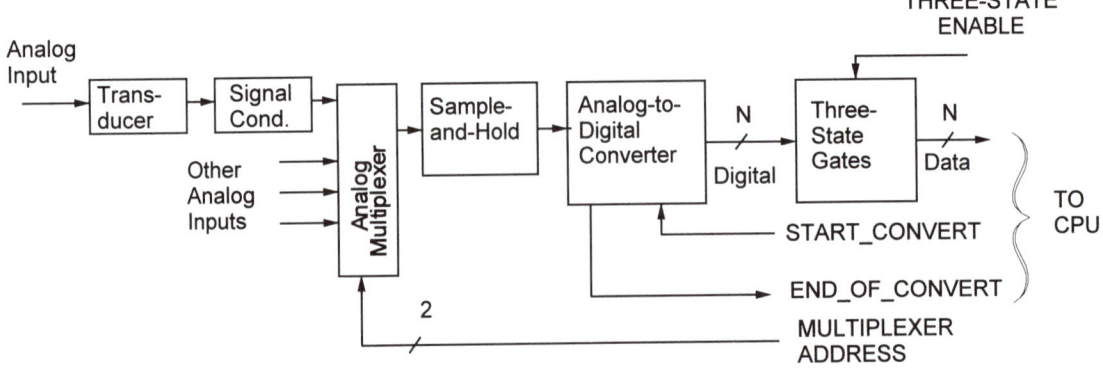

F i g u r e 1 1 – 1   Data acquisition system.

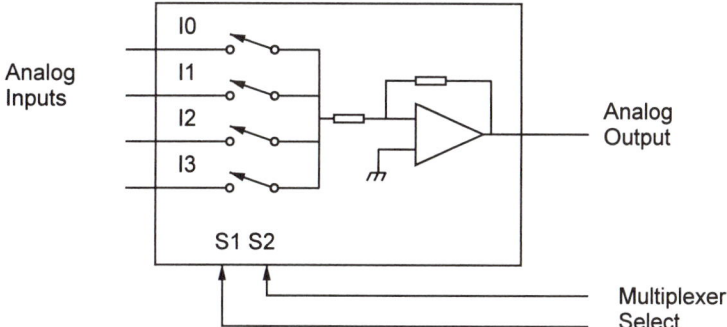

Figure 11–2　Analog signal multiplexer.

fications, errors, and types of A/Ds in the following sections. However, let us first consider the implications of sampling an analog waveform.

11.3 Shannon's Sampling Theorem and Aliasing

Claude Shannon showed that when a signal, $f(t) = X \sin 2\pi f_{sig}t$, is to be sampled (digitized), the *minimum sampling frequency must be twice the signal frequency.*[1] Consider the waveform in Figure 11–3 whose frequency is f_{sig}. When the sampling frequency, f_{sample}, is twice f_{sig}, the waveform is sampled at points A and B. The problem we now pose, and the problem that digital signal processors must solve when *reconstructing* a waveform from sampled data, is this. Given the two samples A and B as shown in Figure 11–4, find a sinusoidal waveform to fit. You are allowed to adjust the frequency, the amplitude, and the phase, and you may assume that when the samples were taken the sampling criteria were satisfied. That is, there are no frequencies higher than one-half f_{sample}. By observing that the two samples are equal in magnitude and opposite in sign, we can convince ourselves that the frequency we are trying to reconstruct is $f_{sample}/2$. By adjusting the amplitude and the phase we can find the

> The frequency at which signals are sampled must be at least two times the highest frequency in the signal.

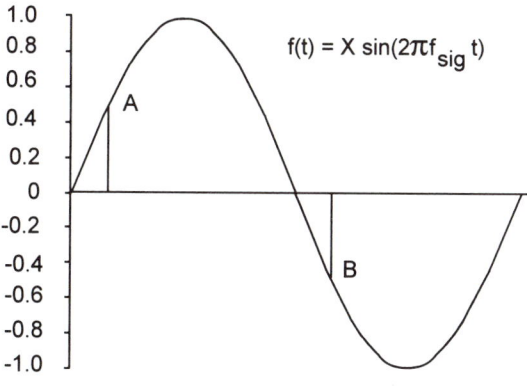

$f(t) = X \sin(2\pi f_{sig} t)$

Figure 11–3　Sinusoidal waveform sampled at twice the signal frequency.

[1]　C. E. Shannon, "A Mathematical Theory of Communication." *Bell System Tech. J.* 27, 1948, pp. 379–423.

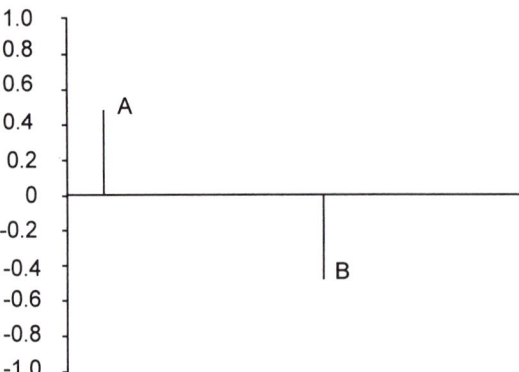

Figure 11-4 Sampled waveform.

correct solution $f(t) = X \sin 2\pi(f_{sample}/2)t) = X \sin(2\pi f_{sig}t)$. If there are more than two samples per period, the reconstruction is easier. We conclude that when signals are digitized according to Shannon's sampling theorem, the input signal can be reconstructed from the digital values.

Now consider the following scenario. The waveform shown in Figure 11–5 is sampled at sampling frequency f_{sample}. This signal, $g(t) = Y \sin(2\pi g_{sig}t)$, is a little higher frequency than $f(t)$ and the sampling does not meet the Shannon criterion. The waveform is said to be *undersampled*. The digital values are again A and B, equal in magnitude, opposite in sign. Our digital signal processor now has a dilemma. Working only from the digital values, the digital signal processor *must assume* that the sampling criterion has been met and so $f(t)$ is reconstructed, not $f(t)$. This is an example of *aliasing*. The second signal, $g(t)$, is higher frequency than $f_{sample}/2$. Undersampling a waveform makes it appear as if it were a *lower frequency*. The signal $g(t)$ is an *alias* for $f(t)$, and this causes an error in the signal reconstruction. For all A/D converters, the sampling frequency must be at least twice the highest frequency in the signal to avoid aliasing. The signal conditioning stage in Figure 11–1 must contain a filter to pass only low frequencies and attenuate frequencies above one-half the sampling frequency. This is called an *antialiasing* filter, and the maximum frequency that one can sample without aliasing, $f_{sample}/2$, is called the *Nyquist* frequency.

> Signals that are *undersampled* cause *aliasing*.

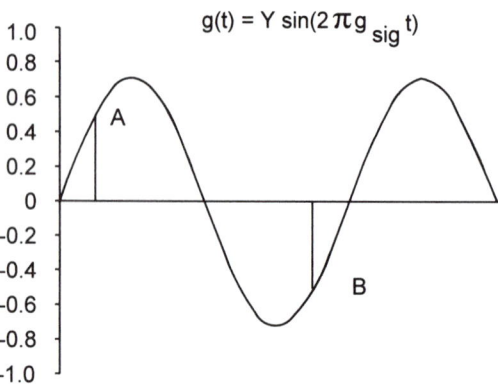

$g(t) = Y \sin(2\pi g_{sig} t)$

Figure 11-5 Undersampled waveform.

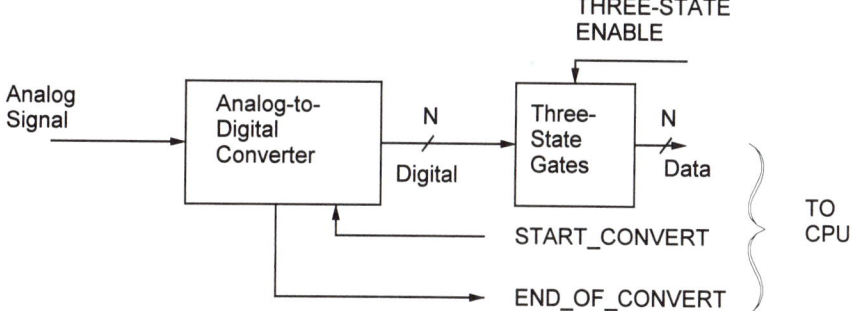

Figure 11–6   Analog-to-digital converter system.

11.4 Analog-to-Digital Conversion

The *analog-to-digital converter* part of this system is shown in Figure 11–6. On the right, a parallel input interface to the CPU is seen. This interface is the same as those designed in Chapter 7 with a data bus and an address decoder to assert the **THREE_STATE ENABLE** when the CPU is to read the converted data. Two additional control signals are needed. **START_CONVERT** is asserted by the CPU to begin the A/D conversion. This can be done with an output port bit or an address decoder. **END_OF_CONVERT** informs the CPU when the conversion is complete. This could be read as a status register bit in a polled I/O system or could generate an interrupt.

> The A/D is interfaced to the rest of the system with a standard parallel input port.

A/D Converter Types

> There are a number of analog-to-digital converter types. The one chosen depends on the application and on the performance required.

Successive approximation A/D: Perhaps the most widely used A/D is the *successive approximation A/D* shown in Figure 11–7. Each bit in the successive approximation register is tested, starting at the most significant and working toward the least significant. As each bit is set, the output of the D/A converter is compared with the input. If the D/A output is lower than the input signal, the bit remains set and the next bit is tried. Bits that make the D/A output higher than the analog input are reset. N bit-times are required to set and test each bit in the successive approximation register.

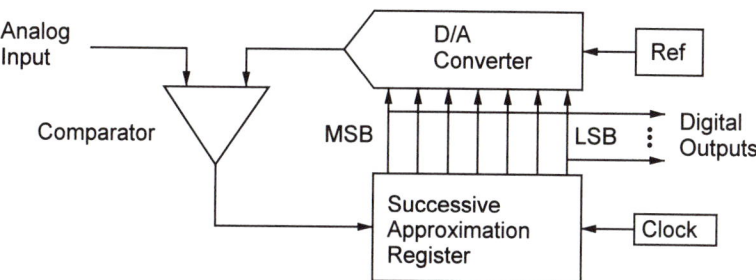

Figure 11–7   Successive approximation A/D.

Tracking A/D converter: The *tracking A/D converter* is shown in Figure 11–8. This close cousin of the successive approximation converter has an up/down counter controlled by the comparator. If the input signal is higher or lower than the output of the D/A converter, the counter counts up or down, respectively. This converter may quickly converge to the correct digital value when the signal is not changing rapidly. If large, rapid, input changes are seen, the counter may have to count through its full range before reaching the final value.

Dual-slope A/D converter: An interesting and useful converter is the *dual-slope* or *integrating A/D converter*, shown in Figure 11–9. The converter integrates the input signal for a fixed time, T_1, with higher input signals integrating to higher values. During the second period, T_2, the switch is changed to the minus reference voltage and the integrator discharges to zero at a constant rate. The time it takes to discharge, T_2, gives the digital value.

> A *dual-slope A/D* can have very high rejection of periodic noise.

The dual-slope integrating A/D is remarkably efficient at recovering signals from periodic noise. A common problem in many applications is 60 Hz noise from power lines. By making T_1 equal to the period of the interference (1/60th second), the positive half-cycle of interference is canceled by the negative half-cycle.

Parallel A/D converter: A parallel, or *flash*, A/D converter is shown in Figure 11–10. It is an array of 2^N-1 comparators and produces an output code in the propagation time of the comparators and the output decoder. Thus it is very fast, but also more costly in comparison to other designs.

Two-stage parallel A/D converter: This converter, shown in Figure 11–11, has nearly the performance of the parallel converter but without the complexity of 2^N-1 comparators. This design is also called a *subranging* or *multistep* converter. The input signal is converted in two pieces. First, a coarse estimate is found by the first parallel A/D. This digital value is sent to the D/A and the summer, where it is subtracted from original signal. The difference is converted by the second parallel converter and the result combined with the first A/D to give the digitized value. These converters offer high resolution and high-speed conversion for applications like video signal processing.

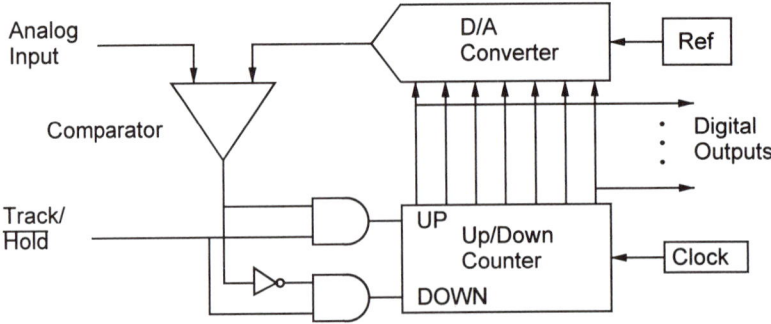

Figure 11–8   Tracking A/D converter.

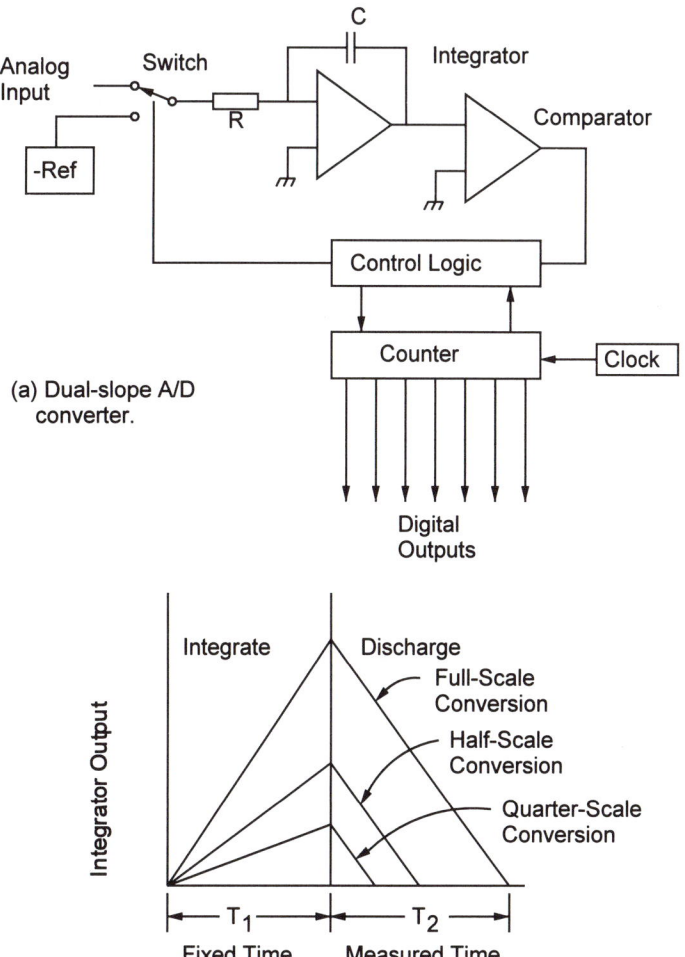

(a) Dual-slope A/D converter.

(b) Integrator output for dual-slope A/D.

Figure 11-9 Dual-slope A/D converter.

A/D Converter Specifications

Conversion time: The conversion time is the time required to complete a conversion of the input signal. It establishes the upper signal frequency limit that can be sampled without aliasing.

$$f_{MAX} = \frac{1}{2 * conversion\ time}$$ **(11.1)**

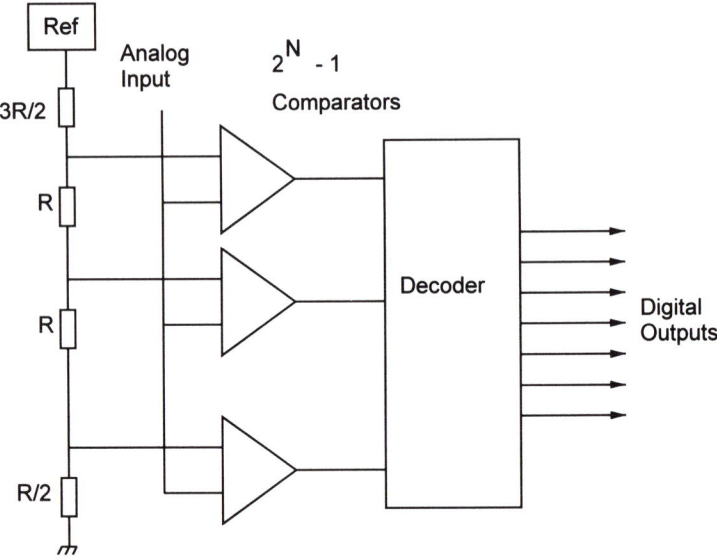

Figure 11−10   Parallel or flash A/D converter.

Resolution: The number of bits in the converter gives the resolution and thus the smallest analog input signal for which the converter will produce a digital code. It may be given in terms of the full-scale input signal:

$$Resolution = \frac{full\text{-}scale\ signal}{2^n}$$

(11.2)

Often the resolution is just given as the number of bits, n, or stated as one part in 2^n. Sometimes the resolution is given as a percent of maximum.

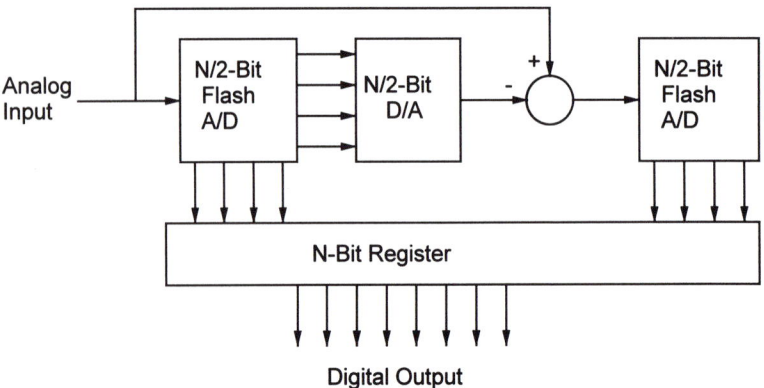

Figure 11−11   Two-stage parallel A/D converter.

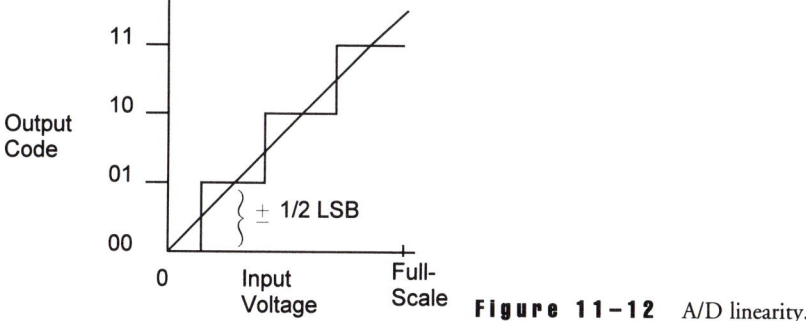

Figure 11-12   A/D linearity.

Accuracy: Accuracy is often confused with resolution. Resolution relates the smallest signal (or noise) to the full- scale value. Accuracy relates the smallest signal to the measured signal. Accuracy is given as a percent and describes how close the measurement is to the actual value.

$$\textit{The signal is accurate to within } \frac{V_{RESOLUTION}}{V_{SIGNAL}} \times 100\% \qquad \textbf{(11.3)}$$

Linearity: Linearity is the deviation in output codes from a straight line drawn through zero and full-scale. The best that can be achieved is $\pm^{1}/_{2}$ of the least significant bit ($\pm^{1}/_{2}$LSB), as shown in Figure 11–12.

Missing codes: The transfer function for a converter with a missing code is shown in Figure 11–13. A missing code could be caused by an internal error, especially by the D/A converter in a successive approximation converter.

Aperture time: This is the time that the A/D converter is "looking" at the input signal. It is usually equal to the conversion time. We will see in the next section how any change in the input signal during this time may cause an error in the output code.

Figure 11-13   A/D missing codes.

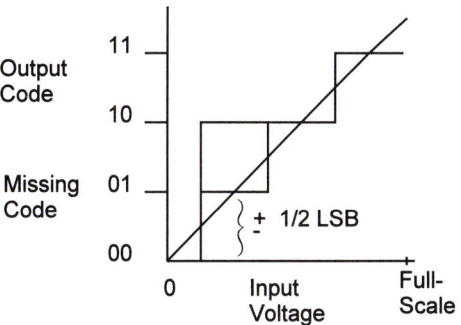

EXAMPLE 11–1   An A/D converter has a conversion time of 100 μs. What is the maximum frequency that can be converted without aliasing?

Solution:

The maximum sampling frequency is the reciprocal of the conversion time = 10 kHz. The maximum signal frequency that can be converted is 5 kHz.

EXAMPLE 11–2   An 8-bit A/D converter is to digitize a five-volt, full-scale signal. What is the resolution?

Solution:

The resolution is 5/256 = 19.5 mV. Another way of stating the resolution is 1 part in 256 or 0.4% of full-scale value.

EXAMPLE 11–3   An 8-bit A/D converter digitizes a five- volt, full-scale signal. What is the accuracy with which the A/D can digitize the following signals.

50 mV, 1 V, 2.5 V, 4.9 V

Solution:

The resolution is 5 V/256 = 19.5 mV. The measurement will be accurate to within the following:

50 mV	(19.5 mV/50 mV) = 39%
1 V	(19.5 mV)/(1 V) = 1.9%
2.5 V	(19.5 mV)/(2.5 V) = 0.8%
4.9 V	(19.5 mV)/(4.9 V) = 0.4%

A/D Errors

> The minimum *quantization error* is $\pm^1/_2$ LSB.

The fundamental error in A/D conversion is called the *quantization error*. This is due to the resolution of the converter and can be no less than $\pm^1/_2$LSB. Quantization levels are illustrated in Figure 11–12, where the output code changes at discrete levels and is at best within $\pm^1/_2$ of the A/D resolution of the true value.

There are three sources of errors in A/D conversion: *noise, aliasing,* and *aperture time.* We would like these to be less than the basic quantization error.

Noise: All signals have noise, as shown in Figure 11–14. We would like the peak-to-peak noise to be less than $\pm^1/_2$ LSB. This means we must either choose the converter resolution appropriately or reduce the signal noise.

Aliasing: The errors due to aliasing are difficult to quantify. They depend on the relative amplitude of the signals at frequencies below and above the Nyquist frequency. The system design should include a low-pass filter to attenuate frequencies above the Nyquist frequency.

Signal + Noise

$\}$ + 1/2 LSB

Figure 11-14 Analog signal plus noise.

Aperture time: A significant error in a digitizing system is due to signal variation during the aperture time. This error is shown in Figure 11–15, where the signal is changing when the aperture is open. A good design will attempt to have the uncertainty, ΔV, be less than one least significant bit. A design equation for the aperture time, t_{AP}, in terms of the maximum signal frequency, f_{MAX}, and the number of bits in the A/D converter is given in Eq. (11.4). The aperture time needed to reduce the error to $\pm^1/_2$ LSB is surprisingly short, as shown in Example 11.4.

> The *aperture time* for even a modest frequency is surprisingly short.

$$t_{AP} = \frac{1}{2\pi f_{MAX} 2^n} \qquad \textbf{(11.4)}$$

Sample-and-Hold

In many A/D converters, the aperture time is the same as the conversion time. The A/D is "looking" at the signal while it is converting it. In Example 11–4 the conversion time for a 1 kHz signal is 0.5 ms while the aperture time is 0.62 μs. The aperture time is the more restrictive specification but it would be much more expensive to buy a converter with a conversion time of 0.62 μs just to satisfy the aperture time requirements. A circuit called a *sample-and-hold* (*S/H*), shown in Figure 11–16, was included in the design shown in Figure 11–1. This can achieve the short aperture time while allowing a less expensive converter to satisfy the conversion time.

> The *sample-and-hold* achieves the very short aperture time usually needed.

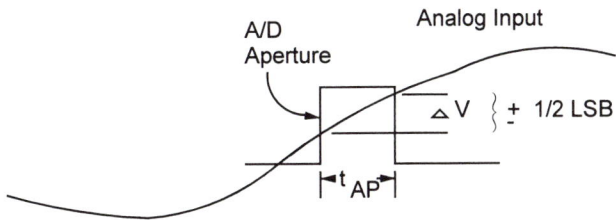

A/D Aperture

Analog Input

ΔV $\}$ + 1/2 LSB

t_{AP}

Figure 11-15 Aperture time error.

EXAMPLE 11–4 A 1 kHz sinusoidal signal is to be digitized to eight bits. Find the maximum conversion time that can be used and still avoid aliasing and the aperture time so that the aperture error is $< \pm^1/_2$ **LSB**.

Solution:

There must be at least two samples per period; so the maximum conversion time is 0.5 ms. The aperture time is given by Eq. (11.4) and is

$$t_{AP} = 1/[(2\pi)(10^3)(256)] = 0.62 \ \mu s$$

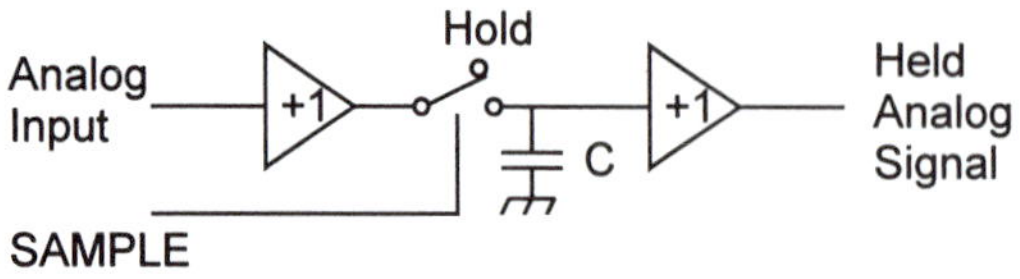

Figure 11-16   Sample-and-hold circuit.

The sample-and-hold is a high-quality capacitor and a high-speed semiconductor switch. The **SAMPLE** command closes the switch for a very short time, and the capacitor charges or discharges to the input voltage. When the switch is opened, the voltage is held for the A/D during its conversion time.

Choosing an A/D Converter

The designer must choose the number of bits, or resolution, and the speed, or conversion time, of the converter. The type of digital code output from the converter may be chosen. The aperture time must be calculated and a decision made to include a sample-and-hold and an antialiasing filter in the system.

Choosing the A/D resolution: There are two ways to find the resolution needed in the A/D. The first is to find the dynamic range of the input signal and to choose the number of bits based on this. The *dynamic range* of any signal is defined as:

$$Dynamic\ range = \frac{V_{MAX}}{V_{NOISE}} \tag{11.5}$$

V_{MAX} is the maximum input signal, and V_{NOISE} is the noise. We would like the noise to be within $\pm^1/_2$ LSB as shown in Figure 11–14, and for this to be true, the number of bits is

$$N \geq \log_2 \frac{V_{MAX}}{V_{NOISE}} \tag{11.6}$$

This is the best one can do unless signal processing, such as averaging, can reduce the noise.

Another way to choose the number of bits is based on the resolution required in the signal. Here, V_{MIN} is the required resolution, and it determines the number of bits as shown in Eq. (11.7). See Example 11–5.

$$N \geq \log_2 \frac{V_{MAX}}{V_{MIN}} \tag{11.7}$$

Choosing the A/D conversion time: The A/D conversion time is chosen by considering potential signal aliasing. The highest-frequency component in the signal must be sampled at least twice in a period. A design equation for conversion time is given as:

$$A/D\ conversion\ time \leq \frac{1}{2\ f_{MAX}} \tag{11.8}$$

EXAMPLE 11–5   A transducer is to be used to find the temperature over a range of zero to 100°C. We are required to read and display the temperature to a resolution of ±1°C. The transducer produces a voltage from 0 to 5 volts over this temperature range with 5 millivolts of noise. Specify the number of bits in the A/D converter (a) based on the dynamic range and (b) based on the required resolution.

Solution:

(a)   The dynamic range is (5 V)/(0.005 V) = 1000. Thus a 10- bit A/D converter is required if the noise is to be $\pm^1/_2$ LSB.

(b)   The required resolution is 100°C/1°C = 100. A 7-bit converter will meet these specifications. (Normally an 8-bit converter would be chosen in a microprocessor-based system. The least significant bit can be thrown away or used for signal processing.)

TABLE 11–1   8-bit binary codes for unipolar A/D

Percent of full-scale	+10 V full-scale	Unsigned binary	One's-complement binary
0	0.00	00000000	11111111
0 + 1 LSB	+0.039	00000001	11111110
25%	+2.5	01000000	10111111
50%	+5.0	10000000	01111111
75%	+7.5	11000000	00111111
Full-scale 1 − LSB	+9.961	11111111	00000000

Choosing the output code: The output code may be chosen when the A/D is specified. Different codes are available, depending on the input signal. For unipolar devices, unsigned-binary or complement-binary codes are available as shown in Table 11–1.

A bipolar-input A/D must encode negative and positive signals. Table 11–2 shows a variety of coding schemes.

Choosing a sample-and-hold: The specification for the aperture time is given in Eq. (11.4). Almost any variable signal will require a sample-and-hold, although there are *sampling A/D converters* that have the sample-and-hold built in.

TABLE 11–2   8-bit codes for bipolar A/D

Percent full-scale	±5 V full-scale	Two's-complement	Signed-magnitude	Offset binary
−(Full-scale)	−5.00	10000000	None	00000000
−(Full-scale) + 1 LSB	−4.96	10000001	111111111	00000001
−75%	−3.75	10100000	11100000	00100000
−50%	−2.50	11000000	11000000	01000000
−25%	−1.25	11100000	10100000	01100000
−1 LSB	−0.04	11111111	10000001	01111111
0		00000000	10000000 and 00000000	10000000
+1 LSB	+0.04	00000001	00000001	10000001
+25%	+1.25	00100000	00100000	10100000
+50%	+2.50	01000000	01000000	11000000
+75%	+3.75	01100000	01100000	11100000
Full-Scale - 1 LSB	+4.96	01111111	01111111	11111111

EXAMPLE 11–6   **Find the maximum conversion time for an A/D converter to digitize the following signals:**

1 kHz sinusoid, 1 Hz sinusoid, 1 MHz sinusoid, a video signal with a bandwidth limited to 5 MHz

Solution:

1 kHz—500 μs; 1 Hz—500 ms; 1 MHz—500 ns; 5 MHz video signal—100 ns.

EXAMPLE 11–7   **For each of the signals in Example 11–6, give the required aperture time for an 8-bit A/D converter.**

Solution:

1 kHz—0.62 μs; 1 Hz—0.62 ms; 1 MHz—0.62 ns; 5 MHz video—0.12 ns.

EXAMPLE 11–8   **Specify the A/D converter maximum conversion time, number of bits, cutoff frequency for the antialiasing filter, and the aperture time to digitize the following signal:**

$\pm$5 volts peak-to-peak, 5 mV peak-to-peak noise, f_{MAX} = 3 kHz

Solution:

The dynamic range is (10 V/5 mV) = 2000. Therefore, $N \geq \log_2 2000 \geq 10.9$ and the number of bits N = 11. The maximum conversion time to prevent aliasing is 1/(2 $\times$ 3000) = 170 μs. The antialiasing filter should have a cutoff frequency of 3 kHz. The aperture time of the sample-and-hold is 1/2 $\times$ π $\times$ 3000 $\times$ 2^{11}) = 26 ns.

Choosing the antialiasing filter: The cutoff frequency (-3 dB point) should be set to either the maximum frequency expected in the signal or to one-half the sampling frequency, whichever is the lower. The order of the filter, which specifies the attentuation in dB/decade, depends on the nature of the input signal and how much energy is above the Nyquist frequency.

11.5 Digital-to-Analog Conversion

The *digital-to-analog converter* is shown in Figure 11–17. A parallel output interface connects the D/A to the CPU. The latches may be part of the D/A or the output interface as we designed in Chapter 7. The analog output signal from the D/A is quantized as shown in Figure 11–18.

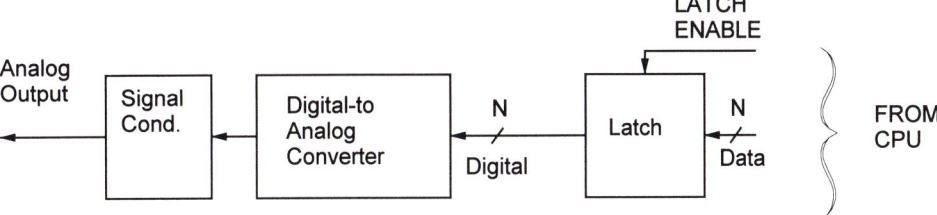

Figure 11–17   Digital-to-analog converter.

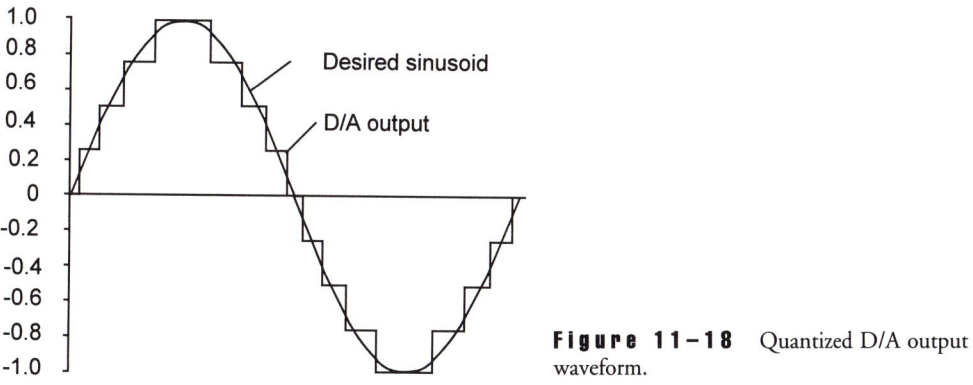

Figure 11–18   Quantized D/A output waveform.

A signal conditioning block may be used as a filter to smooth the quantized nature of the output. The signal conditioning block also provides isolation, buffering, and voltage amplification if needed.

D/A Converter Types

The most basic circuit is the *binary-weighted register D/A* shown in Figure 11–19(a). As the switches for the bits are closed, a weighted current is supplied to the summing junction of the amplifier. For high-resolution D/A converters, the binary-weighted type must have a wide range of resistors. This can lead to temperature stability and switching problems.

R-2R Ladder D/A: Figure 11–19(b) shows another popular design. Here, a wide range of resistor values is not required; however, single-pole double-throw switches are. As the switches are changed from the grounded to the reference position, a binary-weighted current is supplied to the summing junction.

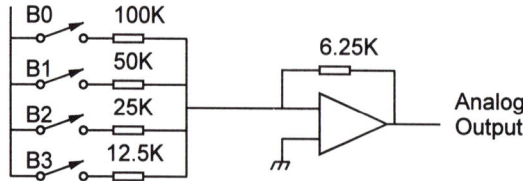

(a) Binary weighted D/A.

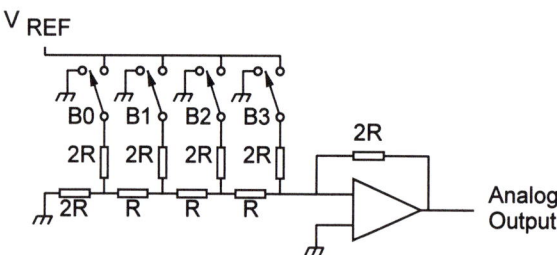

(b) R/2R ladder network D/A.

Figure 11–19 D/A converters.

Multiplying D/A: The R-2R ladder D/A can be used as a *multiplying D/A* by using the reference voltage as an input. The reference voltage can vary over the maximum voltage range of the amplifier and is multiplied by the digital code.

D/A Converter Specifications

Resolution and linearity: The *resolution* is determined by the number of bits and is given as the output voltage corresponding to the smallest digital step, i.e., 1 LSB. The *linearity* shows how closely the output voltage follows a straight line drawn through zero and full-scale.

Settling time: This is the time taken for the output voltage to settle to within a specified error band, usually $\pm 1/2$ LSB. Settling time is shown in Figure 11–20.

Glitches: High-speed D/A converters have glitches as well as settling time problems. A glitch is caused by asymmetrical switching in the D/A switches. If a switch changes from a one to zero faster than from a zero to a one, a glitch may occur. Consider changing the output code of an 8-bit D/A

Figure 11–20 D/A settling time.

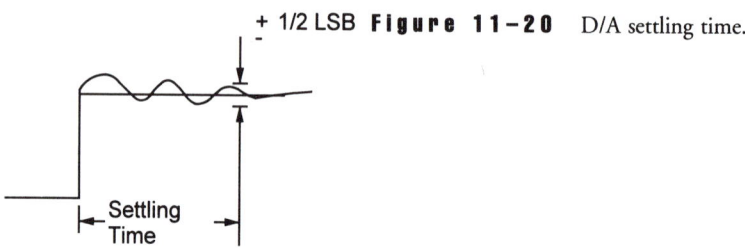

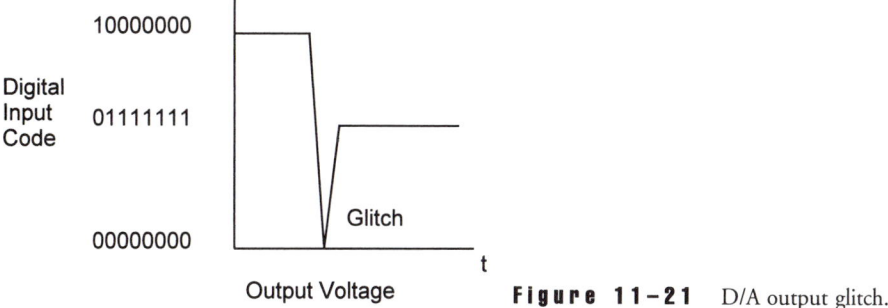

Figure 11–21   D/A output glitch.

from 10000000 to 011111111. These codes are adjacent, and we would expect the output to go from one-half full-scale to one resolution value less than that. However, if the switches can switch faster from a one to a zero, the output code will go through a transitory state sequence 10000000 to 00000000 to 01111111. This results in a short but sometimes noticeable glitch in the output signal. See Figure 11–21. Glitches are especially noticeable in video displays.

D/A converter glitches can be eliminated by following the D/A with a sample-and-hold as shown in Figure 11–22. The S/H is strobed to sample the data after the glitch has occurred and after the D/A settling time.

11.6 Other Analog I/O Methods

Before closing this analog I/O chapter, let's look at some nontraditional ways to achieve analog input and output.

Voltage-to-frequency converters: A *voltage-to-frequency converter* (*V-F*) or *voltage-controlled oscillator* (*VCO*) produces an output frequency proportional to the input voltage. A typical device is shown in Figure 11–23. The counter is set to zero at the start of the conversion cycle and read by

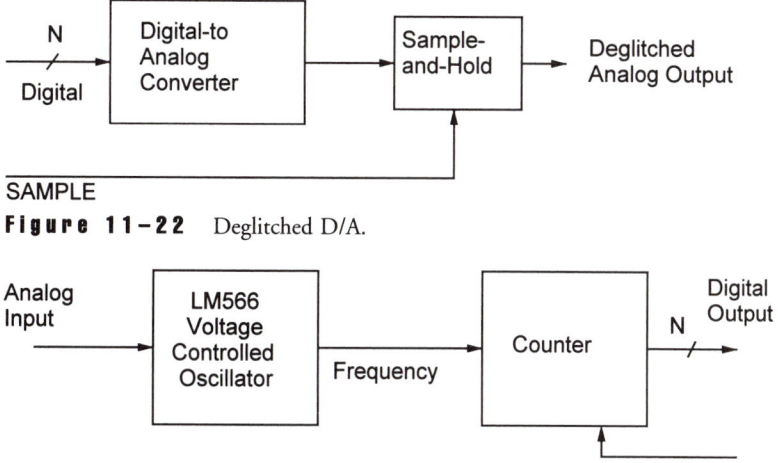

Figure 11–22   Deglitched D/A.

Figure 11–23   Voltage-to-frequency converter.

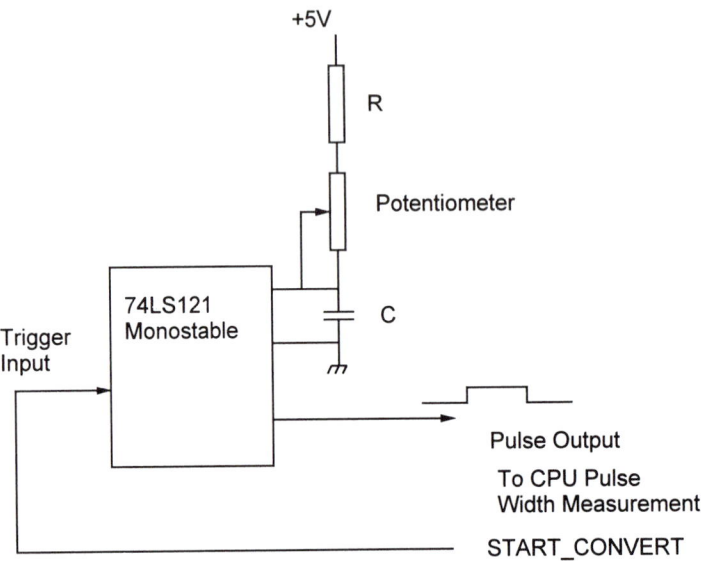

Figure 11–24   Pulse-width modulation for analog input.

the CPU a predetermined time later. The number in the counter gives the digital value, but the CPU must accurately wait for the prescribed amount of time. This technique is good for slowly varying signals or where an average value over a time is required.

Pulse-width-modulated analog input: In some cases, the position of a potentiometer may be the desired information. For example, a user may vary a control parameter by turning a knob on the front panel. If the potentiometer is not needed for another purpose, it can control the width of an output pulse of a monostable multivibrator. Figure 11–24 shows this circuit. The width of the output pulse must be measured by the CPU. This is conveniently done with a microcontroller such as the M68HC11.

Pulse-width-modulated analog output: Figure 11–25 shows a pulse wavetrain. The pulse width is t and the period is T. When the pulse train is low-pass filtered with a cutoff frequency of less than 1/T Hz, the output voltage is At/T.

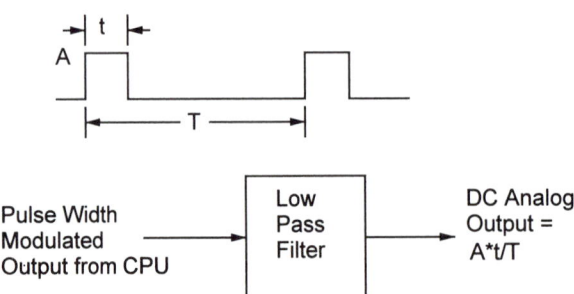

Figure 11–25   Pulse-width modulation for analog output.

11.7 Chapter Summary Points

- A data acquisition system consists of transducers, signal conditioning, an analog multiplexer, a sample-and-hold, an analog-to-digital converter, and a parallel input interface to the CPU.

- Transducers convert physical processes to electrical signals.

- Signal condition provides isolation and buffering, low-pass filtering, and amplification.

- Shannon's theorem specifies the maximum frequency that can be sampled for a given sampling frequency.

- The maximum frequency that can be sampled is called the Nyquist frequency and is equal to one-half the sampling frequency.

- An undersampled waveform can cause aliasing.

- Aliasing causes errors in the digitized values.

- The successive approximation A/D is probably the most common.

- The tracking A/D can quickly respond to small changes in the input but requires more time for large changes.

- A dual-slope integrating A/D should be used where there is periodic noise, such as 60 Hz line noise.

- Parallel and two-stage parallel A/D converters have the shortest conversion time and are used for high-speed applications.

- An A/D conversion frequency must be twice the maximum signal frequency.

- The resolution of an A/D is determined by the number of bits.

- The aperture time is the most restrictive specification, and a sample-and-hold is generally used to meet it.

- Digital-to-analog converters have a settling time specification. This is the time taken for the output to settle within $\pm^1/_2$ LSB of the final value.

- High-speed D/A converters may have glitches in the output caused by asymmetrical switching.

11.8 Further Reading

Kurtz, R. L., *Interfacing Techniques in Digital Design with Emphasis on Microprocessors*, John Wiley & Sons, New York, NY, 1988.

Lawrence, P. D., and K. Mauch, *Real-Time Microcomputer System Design: An Introduction*, McGraw-Hill, New York, NY, 1987.

Zuch, E. L., Ed., *Data Acquisition and Conversion Handbook, A Technical Guide to A/D and D/A Converters and Their Applications*, Datel Intersil, Mansfield, MA, 1979.

11.9 Problems

11.1   Briefly explain the following terms: aperture time; conversion time; aliasing; Nyquist frequency.

11.2   A 10 volt (maximum) signal is to be digitized to a resolution of at most 0.01 volts. How many bits are needed in an A/D converter to do this?

11.3   What is Shannon's sampling criterion?

11.4   How does a successive-approximation A/D converter work?

11.5   How does a dual-slope A/D converter work?

11.6   How does a flash converter work?

11.7   The A/D converter conversion time is 100 μs. What is the maximum frequency that can be digitized without aliasing occurring?

11.8   An A/D converter is required to digitize a 1 kHz sinusoidal waveform. What is the maximum allowable conversion time for the A/D? Assume a sample-and-hold circuit is being used to give the correct aperture time.

11.9   An A/D is to digitize a 10 volt full-scale signal to a resolution of 1 part in 1024. (a) How many bits are required? (b)When a 9 volt signal is being digitized, what is the accuracy of the measurement? What is the accuracy when a 1 volt signal is digitized?

11.10   A transducer is to be used to find the temperature over a range of -100 to $100°C$. We are required to read and display the temperature to a resolution of $\pm1°C$. The transducer produces a voltage from -5 to $+5$ volts over this temperature range with 5 millivolts of noise. Specify the number of bits in the A/D converter (a) based on the dynamic range and (b) based on the required resolution.

11.11   Specify for an A/D converter (1) maximum conversion time, (2) number of bits, (3) cutoff frequency for the antialiasing filter, and (4) the aperture time to digitize each of the following signals: (a) ±5 volts peak-to-peak, 5 mV peak-to- peak noise, $f_{MAX} = 3$ kHz; (b) 0 to 10 volts peak, 5 mV peak-to-peak noise, $f_{MAX} = 100$ kHz; (c) ±1 volt peak-to-peak, 5 mV peak-to-peak noise, $f_{MAX} = 1$ kHz; (d) 1 volt peak RS-170 video signal with a maximum bandwidth of 5 MHz with a required resolution of 1 part in 256.

11.12   An A/D converter is to be specified for the following measurement:

The signal is DC (it will not vary during the conversion time); the signal range is 0 to 10 volts; there is 1 mV of noise; when a 1 volt signal is being measured, the measurement is to be within $\pm0.5\%$ of the true value.

How many bits are required, and how would you specify the conversion time and aperture time?

Binary Codes

A.1 Binary Codes Review

Coding is a two-part process consisting of encoding and decoding. Encoding represents the information with a code. Decoding converts the code back to the information. Whenever a binary code is chosen, we consider the following:

The type of information to be encoded: Is the information numerical? Are there negative and positive numbers? Are there fractional or just integer numbers? If the information is not numerical, is there a standard code to be used?

The number of bits needed to represent the information: The number of bits needed depends on the amount of information to be encoded.

$$\text{Number of bits} \geq \log_2 \text{(number of information elements)} \tag{1}$$

Binary Codes for Numerical Information

There are several codes that represent numbers. The five that are most important to users of microcomputers are (1) unsigned-binary, (2) signed/magnitude, (3) one's-complement, (4) two's-complement, and (5) binary coded decimal.

EXAMPLE A–1   A binary code is needed to identify each of the 83 members of a class. How many bits are required?

Solution:

$N \geq \log_2$ (number codes)
$\log_2 83 = 6.375$; therefore, $N = 7$

How much larger can the class grow before another bit is needed?

Solution:
$2^7 = 128$. The class can grow by 45 students.

EXAMPLE A–2   What are the weights of each of the bits p - w in an unsigned-binary code word pqrst.uvw?

Solution:

Code:	p	q	r	s	t	.	u	v	w
Weights:	2^4	2^3	2^2	2^1	2^0		2^{-1}	2^{-2}	2^{-3}

Unsigned-binary Code

The *unsigned-binary code*, also called the *natural-binary code*, is a positive weighted code where each bit in the code word has a weight (or value) according to its position. Each digit is assigned a position starting from the right (at the binary point) with zero, increasing to the left, and decreasing to the right. The weight of each position is the base raised to the power of the digit position.

Unsigned-binary codes are used for positive numerical information.

The unsigned-binary code uses all positive weights and represents only positive information. The number of bits, and therefore the number of codes, determines how much information can be encoded. In an r-bit code word the number of codes is

$$Number\ of\ codes = 2^r \tag{2}$$

The range of numerical information that can be represented in a code word with p-integer and q-fractional bits is

$$Range = 0\ to\ 2^p - 2^{-q} \tag{3}$$

The resolution is the value of the least significant bit. In this case

$$Resolution = 2^{-q} \tag{4}$$

Signed/magnitude, one's-complement, two's-complement, and offset-binary codes are used for positive and negative numbers.

The unsigned-binary code can represent only positive information. There are several other codes used for negative information including signed/magnitude, radix-1-complement, radix-complement, and offset binary or excess-n codes. The three most commonly used in the microcomputer world are the signed/magnitude, radix-1-complement (one's-complement), and radix-complement (two's-complement) codes.

EXAMPLE A–3   How many codes are there, what is the range of numbers that can be represented, and what is the resolution of an unsigned-binary code word pqrst.uvw?

Solution:

Number of codes = 2^8 = 256
Range = zero to $2^5 - 2^{-3}$ = zero to 31.875
Resolution = 2^{-3} = 0.125

EXAMPLE A–4   Signed/magnitude binary code examples.

0 1 0 1 1 · 1 1 = +11.75
1 1 0 1 1 · 1 1 = −11.75

The leftmost bit is the sign bit, and the magnitude is encoded with a 6-bit, straight-binary code.

Signed/Magnitude Binary Code

The *signed/magnitude binary code* is similar to our decimal number system. The decimal code word for plus ten is written +10 or just 10. Minus ten is encoded −10. Two additional symbols, + and −, are added to the front of the digits used for the magnitude. These symbols double the number of code words, as needed to represent both the positive and negative worlds. Notice that there are two codes for zero. By convention the code for minus zero is never used.

In the binary system, an additional bit to encode the sign is added to the binary digits encoding the magnitude. A zero is positive and one negative. Example A–4 shows a seven-bit binary code with one bit used as a sign and six bits to encode the magnitude.

The range of information that can be represented with p-integer bits (including the sign bit) plus q-fractional bits is

$$-(2^{p-1} - 2^{-q}) \text{ to } + (2^{p-1} - 2^{-q}) \tag{5}$$

For Example A–4, the range is −15.75 to +15.75. Again, there is a code for plus and minus zero.

One's-Complement Code

The definition of the *radix-1* or *one's-complement* of a number X is

$$One's\ complement = 2^p - X - 2^{-q} \tag{6}$$

where p is the number of integer bits and q the number of fractional bits.

Example A–6 shows the one's-complement code for ±11.75. The leftmost bit is an *indicator* (called the *sign bit*) for the sign of the number with 0 representing positive and 1 negative. The

---

EXAMPLE A–5   How many codes are there, what is the range of numbers that can be represented, and what is the resolution of a signed/magnitude binary code word pqrst.uvw, where p is the sign bit?

Solution:

Number of codes = 2^8 = 256 (but two are used for zero)
Range = $-(2^4 - 2^{-3})$ to $(2^4 - 2^{-3})$ = −15.875 to 15.875
Resolution = 2^{-3} = 0.125

EXAMPLE A–6   One's-complement binary code examples.

0 1 0 1 1 · 1 1 = +11.75
1 0 1 0 0 · 0 0 = −11.75

EXAMPLE A–7   Find the 1's complement code for −6.25 assuming a code of the form pqrst.uvw.

Solution:

+6.25 = 00110.010
−6.25 = 11001.101

EXAMPLE A–8   What are the weights of each of the bits p - w in a two's-complement binary code word pqrst.uvw?

Solution:

Code:	p	q	r	s	t	·	u	v	w
Weights:	-2^4	2^3	2^2	2^1	2^0		2^{-1}	2^{-2}	2^{-3}

---

range and resolution of the one's-complement code are the same as the signed/magnitude code, and, again, there are two codes for zero.

Two's-Complement Code

> Two's-complement is the code used for negative numbers in microcomputer systems.

In the binary number system, the radix-complement is the *two's-complement* binary code. The definition of the p-integer bit, two's-complement of number X is

$$\text{Two's complement} = 2^p - X. \tag{7}$$

This is a *negatively* weighted code because the most significant bit has a negative weight, as shown in Eqs. (8) and (9).

$$1011.011 = 1x(-2^3) + 0x2^2 + 1x2^1 + 1x2^0 + 0x2^{-1} + 1x2^{-2} + 1x2^{-3} \tag{8}$$

If the weights are added in decimal,

$$1011.011 = -8 + 2 + 1 + 0.25 + 0.125 = -4.625_{10} \tag{9}$$

There is only one code for zero in the two's-complement scheme. The extra code represents the most negative number. We can see this by looking at the range of the two's-complement binary code. For a number with p-integer and q-fractional bits, the range is

EXAMPLE A–9 How many codes are there, what is the range of numbers that can be represented, and what is the resolution of a two's complement binary code word pqrst.uvw?

Solution:

Number of codes $= 2^8 = 256$
Range $= -(2^4)$ to $(2^4 - 2^{-3}) = -16.000$ to 15.875
Resolution $= 2^{-3} = 0.125$

$$Range = -(2^{p-1}) \ to \ +(2^{p-1} - 2^{-q}). \tag{10}$$

For the example in Eq. (9), the range is -8.00 to $+7.875$. The resolution is $2^{-q} = 0.125$.

The Sign of the Number

In all three codes shown above, the most significant bit gives the sign of the number, although the sign-bit for signed/magnitude code could be placed anywhere in the code word. In two's-complement codes the sign-bit carries a negative weight.

Finding the Code for the Negative

In decimal, when we want the code for the negative of a number, we "take the negative of it" by simply changing the sign. For a signed/magnitude binary code, the same is true. The sign bit is *complemented*. The procedure is more complex when the numbers are represented by a two's-complement code. We find the code for the negative by *taking the two's-complement*. This is analogous to "taking the negative" of a signed/magnitude code. There are two ways to find the two's-complement of any number. The first can be derived by comparing Eqs. (6) and (7).

$$Two's\text{-}complement \ code = one's\text{-}complement \ code + 2^{-q} \tag{11}$$

This procedure is shown in Example A–10, where the one's-complement is formed (complement every bit) and then 1 is added to the least significant bit.

To use the second method, start at the least significant bit and, moving toward the most significant, copy the bits until the first "one" has been copied. Then complement all the remaining bits.

EXAMPLE A–10 Taking the two's-complement.

$3.25 =$	0	0	1	1	·	0	1	0	0
1's complement $=$	1	1	0	0	·	1	0	1	1
Add 2^{-4}	0	0	0	0	·	0	0	0	1
$-3.25 =$	1	1	0	0	·	1	1	0	0

EXAMPLE A–11   Taking the two's-complement by the second method.

```
  3.25 =    | 0  0  1  1  ·  0 | 1  0  0
            | Complement       | Don't Complement
 −3.25 =    | 1  1  0  0  ·  1 | 1  0  0
```

Two's-Complement Arithmetic

The beauty of using the two's-complement code for signed numbers is that the hardware to do addition and subtraction is the same as the hardware for unsigned-binary coded arithmetic. Further, one can easily subtract two numbers by adding the two's-complement of the subtrahend to the minuend. This is shown in Example A–13 for a six-bit two's-complement code.

Binary Coded Decimal

A four-bit, unsigned-binary code is sometimes used to encode the ten decimal digits 0–9. This is called *natural binary coded decimal* and is used so frequently that it is usually just called *binary coded decimal* or *BCD*. Table A–1 shows the natural BCD code.

Hexadecimal Codes

The hexadecimal, or base 16, number system is a shorthand for strings of binary digits. Like the BCD code, the 16 hexadecimal digits, 0–9, A–F, are encoded using an unsigned-binary code. The hexadecimal digits and their binary codes are shown in Table A–1.

You Have to Know the Code

If you are given a binary number and asked what it means, you can't answer unless you know what code is being used. Table A–1 shows the different information that is decoded from a four-bit code word using the different codes covered in this section.

Binary Codes for Non-Numerical Information

Sometimes encoded (or decoded) information isn't a number. A common example is the alphanumeric information sent from a keyboard to a computer or from a computer to a display. Codes used for this application are called unweighted codes because, unlike the numerical codes, there

---

EXAMPLE A–12   Find the 2's-complement code for −6.25 assuming a code of the form pqrst.uvw.

Solution:

+6.25 = 00110.010
−6.25 = 11001.110

EXAMPLE A–13   Subtraction by the addition of the two's-complement.

Subtraction

+5	0	0	0	1	0	1
−3	−0	0	0	0	1	1
+2	0	0	0	0	1	0

Subtraction by addition
of the two's complement

+ 5	0	0	0	1	0	1
+(−3)	1	1	1	1	0	1
+ 2	0	0	0	0	1	0

EXAMPLE A–14   Using an 8-bit, 2's-complement code (5 integer and 3 fractional bits) compute 8.75–10.5.

Solution:

8.75 =	0	1	0	0	0 ·	1	1	0	(Two's-complement for 8.75)
10.5 =	0	1	0	1	0 ·	1	0	0	(Two's-complement for 10.5)
−10.5 =	1	0	1	0	1 ·	1	0	0	(Two's-complement for −10.5)

Therefore

8.75 =	0	1	0	0	0 ·	1	1	0
+(−10.5) =	1	0	1	0	1 ·	1	0	0
	1	1	1	1	0 ·	0	1	0

The result is negative. To find the magnitude of the result, take the two's-complement.
$$0 \quad 0 \quad 0 \quad 0 \quad 1 \cdot 1 \quad 1 \quad 0 = 1.75$$
and so the answer is −1.75

TABLE A–1   Four-bit binary code comparison

Code word	Straight binary	One's compl.	Two's compl.	Signed/ magnitude	BCD	Hex
0000	0	0	0	0	0	0
0001	1	1	1	1	1	1
0010	2	2	2	2	2	2
0011	3	3	3	3	3	3
0100	4	4	4	4	4	4
0101	5	5	5	5	5	5
0110	6	6	6	6	6	6
0111	7	7	7	7	7	7
1000	8	−7	−8	−0	8	8
1001	9	−6	−7	−1	9	9
1010	10	−5	−6	−2	Not used	A
1011	11	−4	−5	−3	Not used	B
1100	12	−3	−4	−4	Not used	C
1101	13	−2	−3	−5	Not used	D
1110	14	−1	−2	−6	Not used	E
1111	15	−0	−1	−7	Not used	F
Range	0 → 15	−7 → +7	−8 → +7	−7 → +7	0 → +9	0 → 15

EXAMPLE A–15   **Using an 8-bit packed BCD code, give the code for the decimal numbers 23, 45, 99.**

Solution:

A packed BCD code has the 4 bits for each decimal digit in one-half of each byte. The most significant nibble has the most significant digit's code.
23 =   0 0 1 0 0 0 1 1,   45 = 0 1 0 0 0 1 0 1,
99 =   1 0 0 1 1 0 0 1

EXAMPLE A–16   **What is the largest decimal number that can be encoded with an 8-bit packed BCD code, and what is its unsigned-binary equivalent?**

Solution:

The largest number is 99, and its packed BCD code is 10011001. The straight-binary equivalent is 1100011.

EXAMPLE A–17   **Find the hexadecimal code for the 16-bit binary word 1010001101011111.**

Solution:

Break the string of binary digits into groups of four, starting from the rightmost bit. Then use the hexadecimal digit for each group of four.
1010   0011   0101   1111 =
  A   3   5   F

isn't a weight associated with a digit position. To find out what a code means, you must look it up in a table. The ASCII codes for alphanumeric information are shown in Table A–2.

The two leftmost columns (MS digit = 0 and 1) are control codes that have been define for serial data communications.

NUL	Null	All zeros character.
SOH	Start of header	Used at the beginning of a sequence of characters, which constitutes a machine-readable address of routing information. The header is terminated by the STX character.
STX	Start of text	A character that precedes a sequence of characters to be treated as an entity. STX may be used to terminate a sequence of characters started by SOH.
ETX	End of text	Character used to terminate a sequence of characters started with STX.
EOT	End of transmission	Indicates the conclusion of a transmission.

TABLE A-2 ASCII 7-bit codes for alphanumeric characters

LS digit	MS digit							
	0	1	2	3	4	5	6	7
0	NUL	DLE	SP	0	@	P	'	p
1	SOH	DC1	!	1	A	Q	a	q
2	STX	DC2	"	2	B	R	b	r
3	ETX	DC3	#	3	C	S	c	s
4	EOT	DC4	$	4	D	T	d	t
5	ENQ	NAK	%	5	E	U	e	u
6	ACK	SYN	&	6	F	V	f	v
7	BEL	ETB	'	7	G	W	g	w
8	BS	CAN	(	8	H	X	h	x
9	HT	EM	)	9	I	Y	i	y
A	LF	SUB	*	:	J	Z	j	z
B	VT	ESC	+	;	K	[	k	{
C	FF	FS	,	<	L	\	l		
D	CR	GS	-	=	M	]	m	}
E	SO	RS	.	>	N	^	n	~
F	SI	US	/	?	O	_	o	DEL

ENQ	Enquiry	Used as a request for a response from a remote station.
ACK	Acknowledge	Character transmitted by a receiver as an affirmative response to the sending station.
BEL	Bell	Character used to control an alarm or attention device.
BS	Backspace	Controls the movement of the printing mechanism back one space.
HT	Horizontal tab	Controls the movement of the printing mechanism to the next predefined tab position.
LF	Line feed	Moves the printing mechanism to the next line. In some systems this may be interpreted as a "new line" (NL) where the print mechanism moves to the beginning of the next line.
VT	Vertical tab	Controls the movement of the printing mechanism to the next predefined printing line position.
FF	Form feed	Moves the printing mechanism to the start of the next page.
CR	Carriage return	Moves the printing mechanism to the start of the line.
SO	Shift out	Indicates that the code combinations following are outside the character set of the standard ASCII table until a Shift In character is received.
SI	Shift in	Indicates that the code characters following are to be interpreted according to the standard ASCII table.

DLE	Data link escape	Changes the meaning of a limited number of following characters. DLE is usually terminated by a Shift In character.
DC1, DC2, DC3, DC4	Device controls	These characters are used to control ancillary devices associated with data processing.
NAK	Negative acknowledge	Transmitted by a receiver as a negative response to the sender.
SYN	Synchronous idle	Character used by a synchronous transmission system in the absence of any other characters to maintain synchronism between the transmitter and receiver.
ETB	End of transmission block	Used to indicate the end of a block of data.
CAN	Cancel	Indicates that the data with which it is sent are in error or are to be disregarded.
EM	End of medium	Sent with data to represent the physical end of the medium.
SUB	Substitute	A character that may be substituted for a character that is invalid or in error.
ESC	Escape	A control character intended to provide code extension. It is usually a prefix affecting the interpretation of a limited number of contiguously following characters.
FS	File separator	These information separators may be used within data.
GS	Group separator	
RS	Record separator	
US	Unit separator	

A.2 Problems

A.1 Encode your name using the ASCII code.

A.2 Decode the ASCII message 44 65 73 69 67 6E 69 6E 67 20 77 69 74 68 20 6D 69 63 72 6F 70 72 6F 63 65 73 73 6F 72 73 20 69 73 20 46 55 4E 21.

A.3 Prove that two's-complement overflow cannot occur when two numbers with different signs are added.

A.4 Give the decimal value of the following binary code words assuming (i) unsigned-binary, (ii) two's-complement, and (iii) one's-complement codes: (a) 10101010; (b)01010101; (c) 11001100; (d) 00110011; (e) 10000000; (f) 01111111.

A.5 Find the two's-complement binary code for the following decimal numbers: (a) 26; (b) -26; (c) 32.125; (d) -32.125.

A.6 Find the decimal equivalent of the following two's-complement numbers: (a) 0101101.1; (b) 1010010.1; (c) 1000; (d) 1010.1101.

A.7 A 6-bit, two's-complement code is to be used for integer numbers. What is the range of information, the resolution, and how many codes are there?

A.8   Find the binary code words for the following hexadecimal numbers. (a) AE; (b) 62FB; (c) 0A22; (d) ABCE.

A.9   Find the hexadecimal code words for the following binary code words: (a) 01011010; (b) 11110101; (c) 110101; (d) 101.

A.10   What kind of code is used to encode the operation part of an instruction—unsigned-binary, two's-complement, or unweighted?

A.11   Suppose the hardware required to add two's-complement numbers was different from that to add unsigned-binary numbers. What changes would have to be made to the design of the picoprocessor in Chapter 2 to accommodate this?

Solutions to Selected Problems

Solutions to Chapter 2 Problems

2.1   If all move instructions are coded in one byte with source and destination operands as shown in Table 2–7, how many move instructions can be defined?

Sixteen, including the MOV A,A, MOV B,B instructions.

2.3   What is the purpose of the instruction decoder?

To decode the instructions which come from memory and to provide information to the sequence controller.

2.5   Explain why computers have *ready* or *wait* control lines.

The ready control signal allows the speedy microprocessor to be synchronized with slower I/O, such as a human setting data on switches.

2.7   The hardware designers propose adding four more general purpose registers. What impact does this have on the design of the move instruction and the sequence controller?

Four more general-purpose registers means that the move instruction must use three bits to encode each of the source and destination registers. Thus the operand field occupies six bits and encroaches upon the operation code field. There are a couple of solutions to this problem. One is to simply use another byte to encode the source and destination operands. The other is to reorganize the operation codes so that a two bit code could designate all move instructions, leaving six bits for the operands.

2.9   Design the hardware required to implement the HALT instruction described in Section 2.6.

One method to halt the processor is to stop the clock. This doesn't work with all processors but it will with some. Use an S-R flip-flop that is set by the main RESET signal and an AND gate to gate the clock to the sequence controller. When the sequence controller decodes the HALT instruction, it generates a control signal to reset the S-R flip-flop, thereby halting further clock signals.

2.11   Describe the instruction execution cycle for the MOV instruction.

The program counter points to the instruction to be executed; this address is applied to the memory; the op code from this address is transferred to the instruction decoder; the sequence controller generates timed control signals required to transfer data from the source to the destination register; the program counter is incremented to the next instruction to be executed.

2.13   Discuss the changes that must be made to the sequence controller of Figure 2–14 to add a direct address memory reference instruction. This is a three-byte instruction with the first byte the op code, and the second two bytes the address of the data location in memory.

A direct memory address instruction is three bytes—op code, high address, low address. The sequence controller must decode the op code and then generate control signals to:

Increment the program counter and get the first byte of the address from memory.

Increment the program counter and get the second byte of the address from memory.

Transfer the memory address of the data to the Memory Address Register.

Transfer the data to or from memory and the source or destination register.

Increment the program counter to point to the next instruction.

Solutions to Chapter 3 Problems

3.1   Do the following 8-bit binary additions and for each case give the expected result in the Carry, Zero, Sign, and Overflow flags.

(a)   10100011
     + 00111011
       11011110
     CZSV=0010

(b)   11111111
     + 00000001
       00000000
     CZSV=1100

(c)   01110001
     + 01000000
       10110001
     CZSV=0011

(d)   10100010
     + 10000000
       00100010
     CZSV=1001

(e)   01111111
     + 10000000
       11111111
     CZSV=0010

(f)   10101010
     + 01010101
       11111111
     CZSV=0010

3.3   For Problem 3.1, assume the binary numbers are in two's-complement binary code. Show the equivalent decimal arithmetic operations and indicate if overflow has occurred.

(a) $-93 + 59 = -34$
No overflow

(b) $-1 + 1 = 0$
No overflow

(c) $113 + 64 = -79$
Overflow

(d) $-94 - 128 = 24$
Overflow

(e) $127 - 128 = -1$
No overflow

F. $-86 + 85 = -1$
No overflow

3.5   What is the meaning of the sign bit = 1 when unsigned-binary coded numbers are added? It means that the most significant bit of the result is 1.

3.7   What is the meaning of the carry bit = 1 when unsigned-binary coded numbers are added? An overflow has occurred.

3.9   What is the meaning of the zero bit = 1 when unsigned-binary coded numbers are added? The result is zero.

3.11   What is the meaning of the overflow bit = 1 when unsigned-binary coded numbers are added? The overflow bit has no meaning in unsigned-binary arithmetic.

Solutions to Chapter 4 Problems

4.1   Name five ways to address an operand.

register; indexed; memory indirect; register indirect; direct; immediate; relative;

4.3   What kind of addressing mode is used to transfer data from one register to another?

Register addressing.

4.5   What addressing mode is best to use to access several sequential elements in a data array—immediate, direct, indexed, or register?

Indexed.

4.7   To increase the memory address space in a computer system, one must

(c) increase the number of address lines.

4.9   A register indirect address instruction

(b) has the address of the operand in a register.

4.11   A colleague suggests adding a register to implement register indirect addressing in your CPU described in Problem 4.10. How many bits should the register have to be able to address the full range of addresses? 20.

Solutions to Chapter 5 Problems

5.1   Discuss the advantages of using a relocatable assembler versus an absolute assembler.

The main advantage of the relocatable assembler is that it allows software to be developed in modules and later linked together to form the executable code.

5.3   Describe the operation of a two-pass assembler.

The two-pass assembler first reads the source code looking for definitions and labels. It makes a table of these and then on the second pass it is able to supply the information where it is needed. This allows what is called "forward referencing" where a value may be used before it is defined.

5.5   What is a macro-assembler?

A macro-assembler is one in which a programmer can define a "macro" that consists of several assembly language statements. The macro can then be used in the program instead of repeating the sequence of statements.

5.7   What is a native assembler?

An assembler that executes on the same computer it is producing code for.

5.9   Define what is meant by assembly-time, link-time, load-time, and run-time.

Assembly-time:	The time that the assembler is run. Constants are evaluated and some addresses may be resolved at this time.
Link-time:	The time the separate modules are combined together.
Load-time:	The time the code is loaded into the memory of the computer. In some systems where the code is relocatable (such as in personal computers) the final addresses resolution is done at this time.
Run-time:	The time the program runs. Variable data values are evaluated at run-time.

5.11   What is a breakpoint?

A set of conditions, such as a program address, that when true cause the program to stop executing and to transfer control to a debugging program.

5.13   What is the difference between a trace and a breakpoint?

Setting breakpoints in the program allows the program to run at full speed until it hits the breakpoint. The trace runs the program more slowly, but you can see the program flow and watch the variables at each step.

5.15   Why must the stack pointer be initialized as one of the first things done in a program?

If the stack pointer is not initialized to point to RAM memory, it may be pointing to ROM or even an area where there is no memory. If this happens, the program most likely would not return from a subroutine.

Solutions to Chapter 6 Problems

6.1   List five principles of top-down design.

Understand the problem completely; design in levels; ensure correctness at each level; postpone details; successively refine your design; design without using a programming language

6.3   Write the pseudocode and draw the flow chart symbol to represent the decision **IF A** is **TRUE, THEN B ELSE C.**

```
IF A
    THEN
```

```
        BEGIN B
          . . .
        END B
      ELSE
        BEGIN C
          . . .
        END C
      ENDIF A
```
See Figure 6–6.

6.5   Write the pseudocode and draw the flow chart symbol to represent the repetition
WHILE A is TRUE, DO B.

```
    WHILE A
      BEGIN B
        . . .
      END B
    ENDWHILE A
```
See Figure 6–8.

6.7   Write a design using structured flow charts or pseudocode to implement the following
problem description:

Prompt for and input a character from a user at the keyboard.

If the character is alphabetic and is upper case, change it to lower case and output it
to the screen.

If the character is alphabetic and is lower case, change it to upper case and output it
to the screen.

If the character is numeric, output it with no change.

If it is any other character, beep the bell.

Repeat this process until an ESC character is typed by the user.

```
DO
  OUTPUT a prompt
  INPUT a character
  IF the character is alphabetic
  THEN
    IF the character is upper case
      THEN
        Change the character to lower case
      ELSE
        Change the character to upper case
    ENDIF its upper case
    OUTPUT the character to the screen
  ELSE
```

```
   IF the character is numeric
      THEN
         OUTPUT the character to the screen
      ELSE
         OUTPUT a bell to the screen
   ENDIF its numeric
 ENDIF its alphabetic
ENDO
WHILE The character is not an ESC
```

6.9   Show how to implement the following problem statement in software for a microprocessor controller using the pseudocode algorithmic method.

In many cars the seat belt alarm buzzer is also used to warn against leaving the key in the ignition or leaving the lights on. The following statement describes how such a system might operate.

The alarm is to sound if the key is in the ignition when the door is open and the motor is not running, or if the lights are on when the key is not in the ignition, or if the driver belt is not fastened when the motor is running, or if the passenger seat is occupied and the passenger belt is not fastened when the motor is running.

```
IF the key is in the ignition
   THEN
      IF motor is not running
         THEN
            IF the door is open
               THEN
                  SOUND the alarm
            ENDIF the door is open
         ELSE (the motor is running)
            IF driver's belt is not fastened
               THEN
                  SOUND the alarm
            ENDIF the driver's belt not fastened
            IF passenger seat occupied
               THEN
                  IF passenger belt not fastened
                     THEN
                        SOUND the alarm
                  ENDIF passenger belt not fastened
            ENDIF passenger seat occupied
      ENDIF the motor is not running
   ELSE (the key is not in the ignition)
      IF the lights are on
         THEN
            SOUND the alarm
```

```
       ENDIF the lights are on
     ENDIF the key is in the ignition
```

6.11   Give a design using structured pseudocode to accomplish the following:

A user is to input a character to select one of three processes. Valid characters are A, B, C, and Q. A, B, and C select processes A, B, or C, respectively. Process A requires a byte of information to be input from an A/D converter, converted to a decimal value in the range of 0 to 5, and displayed on the screen. Processes B and C are not defined at this stage. Prompts and error messages are to be displayed. You do not have to give details of the decimal conversion required in process A.

```
DO
  PROMPT for an input
  GET the input
  IF the input is A
    THEN
       GET A/D value
       CONVERT to decimal
       PRINT the result
    ELSE
       IF the input is B
         THEN PROCESS B
         ELSE
           IF the input is C
             THEN PROCESS C
             ELSE
               IF the input is NOT Q
                 THEN OUTPUT error message
               ENDIF the input is NOT Q
           ENDIF the input is C
       ENDIF the input is B
  ENDIF the input is A
ENDO
WHILE the input is not Q
EXIT
```

Solutions to Chapter 7 Problems

7.1   List parallel I/O devices used with computers you are familiar with, either the laboratory or a personal computer.

printers (could be serial I/O though), LEDs, switches

7.3   Why are three-state gates used in an input interface?

When a three-state gate is disabled, it presents a high impedance to the bus. This allows multiple sources to be connected to the bus.

7.5   In a parallel output operation, how is the synchronization of the data transfer between CPU and a data latch consisting of 8 D-type flip-flops accomplished?

7.7   Discuss the consequences of a CPU designer's decision to implement memory-mapped I/O instead of separate I/O. What does it mean to the CPU designer and what does it mean to you, the system designer using the CPU?

To the CPU designer, memory-mapped I/O results in a simpler design for the sequence controller. Separate I/O instructions do not need to be provided because any memory reference instruction can access I/O. The system designer using the CPU, memory-mapped I/O means the address decoders needed for each I/O device must decode the full address bus instead of a smaller address generally used in separate I/O. Less memory will be available for program and data use.

7.9   Which type of I/O addressing, separate I/O or memory-mapped, requires a control signal called "I/O request" to access I/O devices? Separate I/O.

7.11   A 74LS138 decoder has the following address bits assigned to its inputs:

Adr	74138 input
A7 =	A2
A6 =	A1
A5 =	A0
A4 =	$\overline{E1}$
A3 =	$\overline{E2}$
A2 =	E3
A1, A0 =	Don't cares

Assume an eight-bit address and make a table, similar to Table 7–1, showing what addresses each output responds to.

	Address bits		
	A7 A6 A5 A4	A3 A2 A1 A0	
	Decoder inputs		
Decoder output	A2 A1 A0 $\overline{E1}$	$\overline{E2}$ E3	Addresses
$\overline{00}$	0 0 0 0	0 1 X X	$04 – $07
$\overline{01}$	0 0 1 0	0 1 X X	$24 – $27
$\overline{02}$	0 1 0 0	0 1 X X	$44 – $47
$\overline{03}$	0 1 1 0	0 1 X X	$64 – $67
$\overline{04}$	1 0 0 0	0 1 X X	$84 – 87
$\overline{05}$	1 0 1 0	0 1 X X	$A4 – $A7
$\overline{06}$	1 1 0 0	0 1 X X	$C4 – $C7
$\overline{07}$	1 1 1 0	0 1 X X	$E4 – $E7

7.13   Compare software polling with hardware handshaking I/O synchronizing.

Software polling requires that software check a status bit to find out if the I/O device is ready. This means extra software must be written; however, the software could be doing other things while it is waiting for the I/O to become ready. In a hardware handshaking scheme, extra hardware is needed in the CPU and I/O device to control the handshaking signals. Software is not needed because when the device is not ready, it causes the CPU to enter a wait state until it is ready. This is potentially faster than polling I/O.

7.15   Discuss the consequences of a CPU designer's decision to implement a multiplexed address bus instead of having the complete address bus at pins on the chip.

The CPU designer saves on the number of pins required to output the address information. These pins can then be eliminated or used for other functions. However, an additional control signal must be provided to signify when an external latch must capture the address. Thus the sequence controller is more complex. This decision also delays the time that the ADR_OK* control signal is asserted, which may influence the design of the I/O and memory.

7.17   Design bus arbitration hardware using a 74LS148 8-Line-to-3-Line Priority Encoder and a 74LS138 1-of-8 Decoder. Assume the bus request and bus grant signals are active low.

7.19   Discuss the relative merits of software and hardware switch debouncing.

Software methods reduce the amount of hardware needed in a system. This is an advantage for minimal part-count designs. When hardware is used, the software designer does not have to worry about the switch bounce problem.

7.21   Design a software scanning algorithm to scan an 8x8 keyboard matrix assuming a 74LS138 1-of-8 decoder and 74LS151 8-to-1 multiplexer are used to interface the keyboard (see Figure 7–25).

7.23   Design an input interface for a bank of 16 switches to be interfaced to an 8-bit data bus. Show how each switch is connected to be able to input a 1 or a 0. Assume the CPU has a separate I/O map with an 8-bit I/O address and that the following control signals are available:

$IO/\overline{M}$	1 for I/O, 0 for memory access
WR	1 for writing, 0 for not writing
RD	1 for reading, 0 for not reading

For the sake of simplicity, assume an 8-to-256 decoder with outputs that are asserted high.

Solutions to Chapter 8 Problems

8.1   List five possible applications for interrupts.

Fire sensors; counting; analog conversion completed; timing; generating waveforms.

8.3   Why are further interrupts disabled when the first occurs?

So that the programmer has some control over the interrupt processes. Further interrupts can be enabled by the programmer if desired.

8.5   What is a pending interrupt?

        An interrupt request that has not been acted upon.

8.7   What are vectored interrupts?

        Interrupts that use a vector or hardware-generated address to determine which of several devices has generated the interrupt request.

8.9   Which type of interrupt, vectored or polled, requires hardware for priority resolution? Vectored.

8.11   What is an advantage of polled interrupts over vectored interrupts?

        Polled interrupts may be software prioritized without external prioritization hardware.

8.13   "An interrupt system must allow asynchronous events to interrupt an ongoing process." Give five more hardware and software attributes of an interrupt system.

        Must return to the program instruction following the one that was interrupted; interrupts must be disabled when the interrupt service routine is entered; the programmer must have control over whether or not interrupts are enabled or disabled; the CPU must provide an interrupt acknowledge signal; the system must be able to determine which of many devices has generated an interrupt; simultaneous interrupts must be able to be resolved; interrupts must be re-enabled when leaving the interrupt service routine; the status of all registers must be preserved.

8.15   What must be done to solve the problem of two devices generating simultaneous interrupts in a system with vectored interrupts?

        External hardware must be used to determine the priority.

8.17   Design the hardware for an input interrupting device in a vectored interrupt system. Assume an 8-bit switch register for data, a push button switch to generate a wired-OR $\overline{\text{IRQ}}$ signal, and an 8-bit register occupying one I/O address to be used as a programmable 8-bit vector. The switch register is to occupy an address in the 8-bit I/O address space. Assume separate I/O with control signals $\overline{\text{IOWR}}$ and $\overline{\text{IORD}}$.

8.19   What is a software interrupt?

        An instruction that can simulate an interrupt without hardware generating an interrupt request.

8.21   Design the logic for a daisy chain interrupt prioritization device. Assume an interrupt acknowledge-in (INTI) signal that is to be passed to the output (INTO) if, and only if, the device is *not* generating an interrupt request.

8.23   What does interrupt latency depend upon?

        The length of the current instruction; the amount of data to be pushed onto the stack; whether or not the processor is all ready in an interrupt service routine with interrupts disabled.

Solutions to Chapter 9 Problems

9.1   Briefly explain the following terms:

Chip select: A chip select is asserted to select the memory chip when the correct address is on the address bus.

Memory map: A memory map is a diagram that shows what type of memory and its use for all the addresses.

9.5   Which memory types, dynamic or static, requires refreshing? Dynamic memory.

9.7   A 16-megabyte memory is to be designed using 1Meg × 1-bit chips.

How many RAM chips will be required? 128.

How many address lines will be used on each chip? 20.

How many address line are required for the entire memory? 24.

9.9   Repeat Problem 9.8 except do the write timing analysis. In addition to the times given in Problem 9.8, the following times are known:

CPU times	Memory Times	Propagation Times
$t_{WDD} = 250$	$t_{WC} = 100$	$t_{PW} = 10$
$t_{WDV} = 200$	$t_{AW} = 70$	
$t_{WED} = 300$	$t_{WDS} = 50$	
$t_{WE} = 100$	$t_{WDHE} = 5$	
$t_{WDH} = 50$	$t_{AS} = 10$	

(b) The write cycle analysis (Fig. S1–1) equations are:

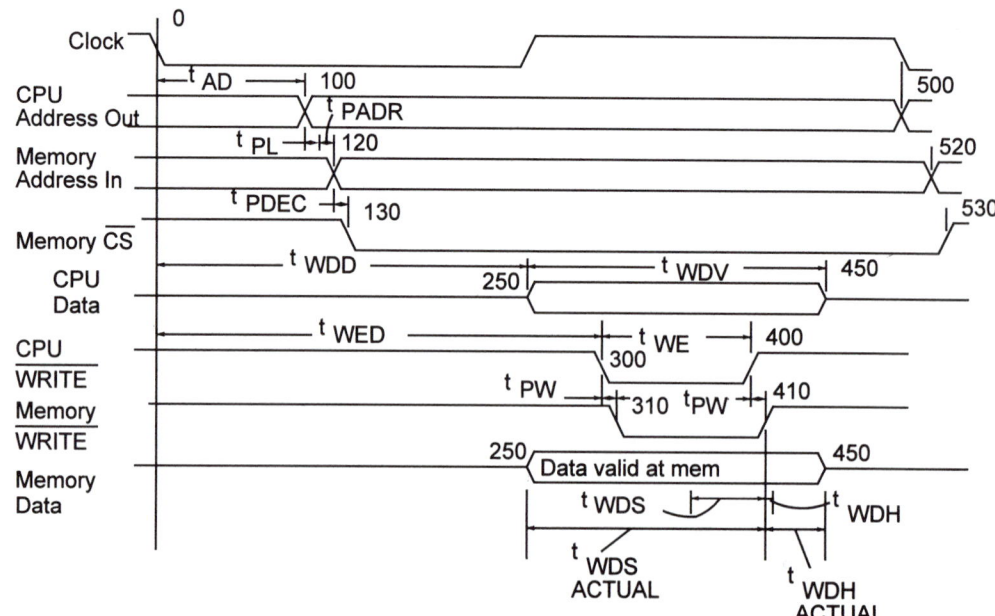

Check that the write cycle is shorter than the address valid time.

$t_{WC} \leq t_{AV} : 100 \leq 400$ (OK)

Check that the address is on long enough before the write enable pulse.

$t_{AS} \leq t_{PW} + t_{WED} - t_{AD} - t_{PL} - t_{PADR}$

$10 \leq 10 + 300 - 100 - 10 - 10 = 190$ (OK)

Check that the address is valid long enough before the end of the write enable pulse.

$t_{AW} \leq t_{PW} + t_{WE} + t_{WED} - t_{AD} - t_{PL} - t_{PADR}$

$70 \leq 10 + 100 + 300 - 100 - 10 - 10 = 290$ (OK)

Check that the write data setup time is satisfied.

$t_{WDS} \leq t_{PW} + t_{WE} + t_{WED} - t_{WDD}$

$50 \leq 10 + 100 + 300 - 250 = 160$ (OK)

Check that the data hold time is satisfied.

$t_{WDHE} \leq t_{WDD} + t_{WDV} - t_{WED} - t_{WE} - t_{PW}$

$5 \leq 250 + 200 - 300 - 100 - 10 = 40$ (OK)

The memory satisfies write cycle timing considerations.

(c) Memories with $t_{WC} = 200$ and 250 ns will be suitable for writing. However, as shown in Problem 9.8, the read cycle fails for 250 ns memory.

Solutions to Chapter 10 Problems

10.1   What are the parallel data buffers in a UART?

      Transmit data buffer, receive data buffer

10.3   Why are the transmit and receive clocks usually a factor of 16 or 64 times the data rate?

      This allows the receiver to find the middle of the bit time and to find the logic value. This eliminates problems with any clock jitter or inaccuracies.

10.5   To initiate a serial data transfer a UART first

      (b) sends the start bit.

10.7   Draw the waveform seen on the serial data out line when a UART sends the ASCII character "L" using seven bits of data plus odd parity.

10.9   How does the receiver in a UART maintain its synchronization with the transmitter in asynchronous operation?

The receiver detects the start bit and by knowing the baud rate and by maintaining an accurate clock, synchronization is maintained.

10.11   If the data rate is 9600 baud, what is the rate ASCII characters can be sent assuming 7 data bits and 1 parity bit? 960 characters/second.

10.13   A UART sends the following data. What is the binary value of the data?

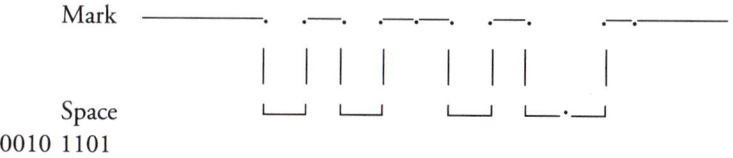

Mark

Space

0010 1101

10.15   Assuming the ASCII code is being used for the data in Problem 10.13, what character is being sent?

The minus sign −.

10.17   What are the two types of communication devices defined by the RS-232-C interface standard?

Data Terminal Equipment (DTE), Data Communication Equipment (DCE)

10.19   Draw a cable used to connect DTE to DTE RS232 serial devices. Show pins 2, 3, 4, 5, 6, 7, 8, 20 with signal names and signal direction flows.

```
DTE                    DTE
TXD 2  ->-\ /-<-  2 TXD Cross over 2 to 3
RxD 3  -<-/ \->-  3 RXD
RTS 4  ->-\ /-<-  4 RTS Cross over 4 to 5
CTS 5  -<-/ \-<-  5 CTS
DCD 6  -<- ->-    6 DCD Leave open
GND 7  ─────────  7 GND
DSR 8  -<-\ /->-  8 DSR Cross over 8 to 20
DTR 20 ->-/ \-<-  20 DTR
```

10.21   How does a modem signify that it has detected the opposing modem's tone for a mark?

It asserts the DCD signal.

10.23   How does a modem signify that it has established a connection with the modem at the other end?

It asserts the DSR signal.

10.25   What electrical signalling standard should be chosen for the following serial data links?

Data Rate	Distance	Standard
20 Kbit/s	<50'	RS-232-C
20 Kbit/s	100'	RS-423
100 Kbit/s	4000'	RS-422 or RS-485

Solutions to Chapter 11 Problems

11.1   Briefly explain the following terms:

Aperture time   The time the A/D or sample-and-hold is "looking" at the analog input signal.

Conversion time   The time between START_CONVERT and END_OF_CONVERT.

Aliasing   An effect caused by frequencies in the digitized signal that are greater than twice the sampling frequency.

Nyquist frequency   The maximum frequency that can be in the input signal without aliasing.

11.3   What is Shannon's sampling criterion?

For a signal to be reconstructed, it must be sampled at twice its maximum frequency.

11.5   How does a dual-slope A/D converter work?

It integrates the input signal for a fixed time. At the end of this time, it discharges the integrated value at a fixed rate and measures the time taken to reach zero. This time is then related to the digital value.

11.7   The A/D converter conversion time is 100 Ês. What is the maximum frequency that can be digitized without aliasing occurring? 5 kHz.

11.9   An A/D is to digitize a 10 volt full-scale signal to a resolution of 1 part in 1024.

(a) How many bits are required? 10 bits

(b) When a 9 volt signal is being digitized, what is the accuracy of the measurement?

The resolution is 10 V/1024 = 9.8 mV. The accuracy at 9 volts is within (9.8 mV/9 V)=0.1%.

What is the accuracy when a 1 volt signal is digitized?

(9.8 mV/1 V) = 0.9%

11.11   Specify for an A/D converter (1) maximum conversion time, (2) number of bits, (3) cutoff frequency for the antialising filter, and (4) the aperture time to digitize each of the following signal:

(a) ±5 volts peak-to-peak, 5 mV peak-to-peak noise, f_{MAX} = 3 kHz.

The dynamic range is (10 V/5 mV) = 2000. Therefore, n ≥ $\log_2$ 2000 ≥ 10.9 and the number of bits n = 11. The maximum conversion time to prevent aliasing is (1/2*3000) = 170 μs. The antialiasing filter should have a cutoff frequency of 3 kHz. The aperture time of the sample-and-hold is $1/(2*_{,,}*3000*2^{11})$ = 26 ns.

(b)   0 to 10 volts peak, 5 mV peak-to-peak noise, f_{MAX} = 100 kHz.

Dynamic range = 2000, number of bits = 11. Maximum conversion time = 10 μs. Antialiasing filter cutoff = 100 kHz. Aperture time = 0.77 ns.

(c)   ±1 volt peak-to-peak, 5 mV peak-to-peak noise, f_{MAX} = 1 kHz.

Dynamic range = 400, number of bits = 9. Maximum conversion time = 500 μs. Filter cutoff = 1 kHz. Aperture time = 0.31 μs.

(d)   1 volt peak RS-170 video signal with maximum bandwidth of 5 MHz with a required resolution of 1 part in 256.

Resolution 1 part in 256, number of bits = 8. Maximum converstion time = 100 ns. Filter cutoff = 5 MHz. Aperture time = 0.12 ns.

Solutions to Appendix A Problems

A.3   The range of an n-bit two's-complement number is from -2^{n-1} to $+ (2^{n-1}-1)$, zero is a positive number. Overflow is a number greater than $(2^{n-1}-1)$ or less than -2^{n-1}. The most positive number than can be formed by adding a negative to a positive is $-1 + (2^{n-1}-1) = 2^{n-1}-2$, no overflow. The most negative number that can be formed by adding numbers of opposite signs are $-2^{n-1} + 0 = -2^{n-1}$. No overflow.

A.5   Find the two's-complement binary code for the following decimal numbers.

(a) 011010;   (b) 100110;   (c) 0100000.001;   (d) 1011111.111

A.7   Range: -32 to $+ 31$ Resolution: $2^0 = 1$ Number of Codes: 64.

A.9   Find the hexadecimal code words for the following binary code words.

(a) 5A;   (b) F5;   (c) 35;   (d) 5.

A.11   Suppose the hardware required to add two's-complement numbers was different from that to add unsigned-binary numbers. What changes would have to be made to the design of the picoprocessor in Chapter 2 to accommodate this?

Index